Grassroots Garveyism

THE JOHN HOPE FRANKLIN
SERIES IN AFRICAN AMERICAN
HISTORY AND CULTURE
Waldo E. Martin Jr. & Patricia Sullivan,
editors

Grassroots Garveyism

Garveyism

THE UNIVERSAL NEGRO
IMPROVEMENT ASSOCIATION
IN THE RURAL SOUTH,
1920–1927

MARY G. ROLINSON

The University of North Carolina Press

Chapel Hill

© 2007 The University of North Carolina Press
All rights reserved
Manufactured in the United States of America
Set in Scala and The Serif types
by Keystone Typesetting, Inc.

The paper in this book meets the guidelines for permanence
and durability of the Committee on Production Guidelines for
Book Longevity of the Council on Library Resources.

Library of Congress Cataloging-in-Publication Data
Rolinson, Mary G.
Grassroots Garveyism: the Universal Negro Improvement
Association in the rural South, 1920–1927 / Mary G. Rolinson.
p. cm. — (The John Hope Franklin series in African American
history and culture)
Includes bibliographical references and index.
ISBN-13: 978-0-8078-3092-5 (cloth: alk. paper)
ISBN-13: 978-0-8078-5795-3 (pbk.: alk. paper)
1. Universal Negro Improvement Association—History.
2. Garvey, Marcus, 1887–1940—Influence. 3. Black
nationalism—Southern States—History—20th century.
4. African American political activists—Southern States—
History—20th century. 5. African Americans—Southern States—
Politics and government—20th century. 6. African Americans—
Race identity—Southern States—History—20th century.
7. Southern States—Politics and government—1865–1950.
8. Southern States—Race relations—History—20th century.
9. Southern States—Rural conditions. I. Title.
E185.61.R745 2007
305.896′073—dc22   2006030921

cloth 11 10 09 08 07 5 4 3 2 1
paper 11 10 09 08 07 5 4 3 2 1

For Frank

Contents

Illustrations and Maps

Acknowledgments

After more years than I care to emphasize, I am delighted to finally have the opportunity to thank the people who have helped me in so many ways to make this book possible. I met my husband, Frank, in 1988, about the same time I began researching the Garvey movement in the South. His love, patience, and understanding have been my motivation and inspiration on this long journey. The arrival of our boys has made life more meaningful and joyful and has given me insight into the southern Garveyites' determination to be respected, especially for their children's sake. I especially want to thank my parents for their positive influence and steadfast love.

Over the years, substantial assistance was provided by the Schomburg Center for Research in Black Culture, especially by manuscript curator Diana Lachatanere, who helped me find the division card files in the Universal Negro Improvement Association Records collection. The reference librarians and interlibrary loan specialists at Georgia State University and the University of Georgia have always been efficient and helpful in numerous ways. Thanks to the employees of the National Archives II in College Park, Maryland, especially Clarence Lyons, who assisted me by making available the critically important records of the Department of Justice and the U.S. Pardon Attorney. A very special thanks to the archivist, whose name I did not write down, who quickly understood the need to reorganize and more carefully preserve the Garvey records at Archives II, which were in disarray. I spent a number of years at the Federal Archives at East Point, Georgia, searching through the 1920 population schedules. So many kind and interesting elders doing family research offered encouragement for my project and anecdotes describing the rural South in the 1920s. The 1930 census became available in the late stages of my research, and now that all census records are digitized and searchable through Ancestry.com and other databases, I must thank the wonders of technology for making this type of research so much easier. It is also important to mention here that only through the work of Robert A. Hill, editor, and the many researchers and assistant editors of *The Marcus Garvey and Universal Negro Improvement Association Papers* over the past twenty years is a broader understanding of this very complex subject possible. All present and future Garvey scholars owe them a tremendous debt.

I appreciate the many archival professionals and institutions for their dutiful protection of many priceless historical documents. The Library of Congress manuscript collections were always available and well organized. I owe a very special thanks to the Special Collections Department of the Woodruff Library, Emory University, especially to Linda Matthews and Randall Burkett, for their willingness to make their extensive African American collections available to me. Randall, along with Garvey scholars like Robert A. Hill, Tony Martin, Judith Stein, and Emory Tolbert, have encouraged me to pursue research on the southern wing of the Garvey movement. Their foundational scholarship on the topic and their varied suggestions have been invaluable to me.

I would like to thank the dedicated professors who first guided me on this project in its embryonic stages at the University of Georgia. Numan V. Bartley, who I deeply regret did not live to see this book published, was my master's thesis adviser, and he helped me realize the broader potential of the subject I had chosen to explore. Robert Pratt and William McFeely also read the thesis and gave me early critical appraisals. John C. Inscoe convinced me to expand the research and push the limits of extant sources beyond the *Garvey Papers* and *Negro World*.

Many of my life experiences have helped me formulate the questions I have tried to address in historical context in this book. There is no substitute for the opportunities that I have had as a public high school teacher in a rural county, an employee of the Georgia General Assembly, and a frequent visitor to the rural South. I especially want to acknowledge the contributions of many people I have known during these experiences for sharing their ideas with me. In particular, I want to thank the many rural people of Georgia, Mississippi, and Arkansas who shared their remembrances of Garveyism and the 1920s with me. Mr. David Carter of Toledo, Ohio, shared information about his grandfather Jonas Odom, who was a key Garvey supporter in rural Baker County, Georgia. Mrs. Fannie Kaigler, originally from Berrien County, Georgia, and Mr. Milburn Crowe, the late historian of Mound Bayou, Mississippi, were very helpful and interested people who did not live to see the finished product of this research. I also appreciate the assistance of Mr. Starlin Hymonds of Holly Grove, Arkansas, who offered to drive around with me for hours to find some of the rural churches and towns in the Delta, many of which are now well hidden or nonexistent. Several white residents of the rural areas I studied provided interesting and essential insight into their home counties. They are Mr. Lamar Whittle, formerly of Sylvester, Georgia; Mrs. Ann Odom Bush of Newton, Georgia, and her sister Ms. Lou Odom Curles, of Atlanta, Georgia; Mrs. Carrie Davidson of Marvell, Arkansas; and Mr. Lee McCarty of Merigold, Mississippi.

My greatest debt of gratitude goes to my mentors and colleagues at Georgia State University. I had three dedicated advisers who shared their varied expertise with me while serving as my teachers and as members of my dissertation committee. John Michael Matthews, who was extremely generous with his time and judicious in his critiques, helped me formulate the structure of this work early on and kept me searching for more evidence. Jacqueline Rouse gave me the confidence I needed at times to challenge conventional wisdom on controversial topics while encouraging me to find ways in which Garveyism was part of the modern civil rights movement and not something separate. She and Glenn T. Eskew pushed me hard to look for links with earlier southern black thought and later convinced me to keep working toward an important new interpretation of southern African American history. Cliff Kuhn, Gary Fink, James Heitzman, Wendy Venet, and Diane Willen all encouraged and supported my research in important ways.

Among the scholars who have read and commented on recent versions of this book are many whose work I have long admired. Steven Hahn read the manuscript for the University of North Carolina Press and made very helpful recommendations. His recent book also has provided some critical nineteenth-century background for the southern grassroots foundation of the Garvey movement. Two other unidentified readers for the press pushed me on critical issues, and the clarification they sought hopefully has made this book clearer and more thoughtful. Pete Daniel also read the manuscript and made some substantial suggestions for revision that have enhanced the overall work in significant ways. Jeff Norrell and Melissa Walker took time from their own books-in-progress to read the manuscript and make key suggestions. In the end, however, any errors in documentation or interpretation are solely my own.

Other friends, family, and colleagues who I would like to thank for their various contributions and assistance are Alice Gambrell, Rachel Levin, Sara Weigle, Susan Hunsinger, Ilene Zeff, Ann Wilks, Peggy Galis, Stewart J. Brown, Jahi Issa, Jonathan Bryant, Mark Schultz, Jennifer Lund Smith, John McBrayer, Rich Howe, Jane Holloway, Robin Taylor, Carolyn Overton Morton,

Christine Lutz, Larry Youngs, Robert Woodrum, Montgomery Wolf, Zanetta Trahan, Prentiss McGhee, Ada Perry, Linda Rochelle Lane, Leroy Davis, Susan McGrath, Susan Ashmore, Janet Hudson, Fitzhugh Brundage, Stephen G. N. Tuck, Henry Gambrell, Luck Davidson, Jeannie Whayne, and Kenneth C. Barnes.

Grassroots Garveyism

Introduction

Rediscovering Southern Garveyism

The stubborn fact remains that a man of a disadvantaged group, by his almost unsupported strength and personal magnetism, has founded so large a power in the English-speaking world as to add to the current vocabulary of that language a new word, "Garveyism."
—William Pickens, The Nation, 28 December 1921

Garveyism did not disappear after Marcus Garvey's deportation from the United States in 1927. Although it now goes by different names, Garveyism's meanings remain essential to popular black nationalism and fundamental to many other strands of contemporary black thought. Garvey, a Jamaican of African ancestry, spread this ideology during World War I while promoting the Universal Negro Improvement Association (UNIA) as a worldwide race uplift organization for millions of people in the African diaspora. The founder's voracious reading and shrewd observation of successful black leaders of his time informed his potent synthesis of ideas and strategies. Ultimately, through talented organizers and the wide circulation of his *Negro World* newspaper, Garvey connected with thousands of laboring blacks around the world, most significantly in the United States.[1]

Marcus Garvey was born in 1887 in St. Ann's Bay, a town on the north shore of the British West Indian colony of Jamaica. His aloof father was a bricklayer and an avid reader, and his doting, deeply religious mother came from a family of peasant farmers.[2] In 1914, at the age of twenty-seven, Garvey founded the UNIA and African Communities League in Jamaica. After traveling to the United States, he reincorporated the organization in New York in July 1918. The UNIA reached its pinnacle of membership and influence in 1921 and 1922 with over a thousand divisions in the United States, Canada, the West Indies, South America, Africa, Europe, and Australia. By 1927, when its leader was only forty-one years old, the organization had become fragmented, and Garvey had been deported to Jamaica. Although short-lived and meteoric, the Garvey movement is widely recognized as the first global expression of popular black nationalism. Its endurance in black thought and influence on subsequent protest movements deserves greater recognition and explanation.

The historical record associates the American wing of the UNIA primarily with northern, urban, working-class blacks. What has remained obscured, though it is in many ways more significant, is that this organization's program enjoyed broad popularity in the South because it also embodied the practical and spiritual aspirations of rural farmers. Garvey recognized this fact, proclaiming that "the South [is] the character-making center of Negroes. The South [has] given more character to the Negro than any other section of the world. It [has] made more real Negro men and women than [have] been made anywhere else, but, paradoxically, it [is] the part of the world where Negroes [have] suffered most within the pale of civilization."[3]

Garvey envisioned black people in all parts of the world attaining economic independence from the control of whites. In his view, self-determination and self-sufficiency could be achieved only through organization along race lines and successful economic competition against other races. In the summer of 1919 he created the Black Star Line (creatively named to mirror the world-renowned White Star Line, builder of the *Titanic*), a fleet of steamships that blacks would own through stock purchase and run without the assistance of whites. This venture promised to test assumptions about the fitness of the Negro race at the highest echelon of capitalism while providing a race-conscious investment opportunity.[4]

The UNIA also emphasized political organization, encouraging black people from all corners of the African diaspora, especially those in America, the Caribbean, and Africa, to join forces, with their allegiance going first to their race. UNIA men could join the organization's African Legions, while its women could serve with the Black Cross Nurses. Instead of promoting political rights within the various nations in which blacks lived, Garvey's organization provided a provisional government, army, divisions (the UNIA's suggestive paramilitary nomenclature for local branches), and auxiliaries for a nation of dispersed Africans around the globe. Garvey's position in the organization was president general, and his title was Provisional President of Africa.

The UNIA founder placed primary emphasis on the development of race consciousness because he saw blacks identifying with nations and organizations that did not recognize or value their loyalty and sacrifice. This problem was especially apparent in the post–World War I era, when black veterans were denied citizenship rights and some were even abused and murdered on their return from service in Europe. Through speeches and literature, Garvey forcefully dispelled prevailing myths of black inferiority and promoted racial pride. As part of his plan to restore the dignity of the millions of people of African ancestry who formed oppressed segments of society almost everywhere they lived, Garvey promoted racial purity and separatism, arguing that people of mixed race were more prone to confused identities.[5] Although many mixed-race African Americans joined the movement, there was a clear emphasis on moving the race toward a more "purely African" composition. Garvey's rhetoric suggested that if a black person chose a white partner, he or she was demonstrating a sort of self-hatred.

The most challenging of the UNIA's goals necessitated a clash with the imperialist powers of Europe, particularly Britain and France, which controlled the lion's share of Africa. A continuous struggle for the political independence of the African continent, in Garvey's view the rightful homeland of all people of African descent, remained central to the UNIA program for black uplift. Ultimately, the organization hoped to develop an African nation, to expel European imperialists, and to compete with the white-ruled nations then at the forefront of modern capitalist enterprise. He called this "African redemption," a term that had a crucial (but *not* coincidental) semantic relationship to the goals of two generations of African American Christian missionaries in Africa.

Very little of Garvey's ideology was original, and much of it derived from a masterful intertwining of the most important strands of black thought from the nineteenth century. Those who caught fire with the movement often described themselves as awakening from a prolonged slumber. From Garvey they were not learning new ways of thinking but were being reminded of things they already knew and believed. The UNIA's greatest importance was in how Garvey formed an organization and gave a comprehensive strategy for racial uplift to the masses; he accomplished this remarkable feat primarily through his *Negro World* newspaper, through the ministers of urban and rural communities, and through his own charismatic leadership.

The broad and visionary nature of Garvey's program for racial self-determination has provided many paths for exploration by scholars of the Garvey movement. The cult of personality surrounding the UNIA leader himself has attracted a large share of the scholarly attention. But what remains is the question of Garvey's legacy and the importance of the UNIA and its ideals to African American history. This much-needed examination of UNIA supporters in the rural, southern United States provides not only a clearer picture of who the American Garveyites were but also a deeper understanding of the evolution of Garveyism and of African American thought in general during a period of dramatic demographic, economic, and social transformation.

Close to 80 percent of the UNIA's total of 1,176 divisions were in the United States. By 1926, the UNIA had 423 divisions in the eleven former Confederate states and almost 500 in the rest of the United States.[6] Its astonishingly rapid spread and remarkable number of adherents during the 1920s only hint at the UNIA's powerful influence. The sheer numbers and varied locations of its members in all parts of the United States, the Caribbean, Africa, and elsewhere demonstrate the geographic diversity of Garveyites.[7] But remarkably, in keeping with its goal to be a *universal* Negro improvement association, there was wide agreement on the basic elements of the complex and multifaceted ideology known as "Garveyism" found in the UNIA program, ritual, philosophy, and propaganda. Just as Garvey and the organizers of the UNIA did, historical interpretations of the worldwide effort must recognize practical reasons for differences in the local and even regional application of the movement's policies. At the same time, we should remember that most African Americans in the Garvey movement, just like most black Americans of the 1920s, whether urban or rural, northern or southern, were rural southerners by birth. In coming to terms with the rural, southern origins of most black Americans, Garvey settled into a course of action that made sense to many of them in the context of their formative experiences with whites of social subordination, economic dependence, and repeated political betrayal.

Millions of black people in the South and elsewhere joined the UNIA and endorsed Garvey because his was a movement of ideas and of adjusting attitudes, which addressed the fact that seemingly insurmountable problems required visionary solutions. The popularity of the movement grew out of the universality of its philosophy for racial improvement in the long term. Garvey's organizational genius was recognizing that he must appeal to the ideals and instincts of men and women only one or two generations removed from slavery. Some of these people had migrated to cities, but most of them remained in the rural Deep South. He came to understand the typical, not the exceptional, black American experience and molded his philosophy to have maximum resonance.[8] When Amy Jacques Garvey, the leader's wife, tried unsuccessfully to edit his copy for essays in the UNIA's *Negro World* newspaper, he replied, "I am writing for the masses . . . people who have not been accustomed to serious writing matter. I must hammer in what I want to impress on their minds."[9] This study of the southern, rural Garveyites enables us to imagine the attraction of Garvey's fiercely nationalist philosophy, while it enriches our understanding of how UNIA supporters constructed a framework for coping with racial problems and developed a sense of racial pride.

A continual problem for historians, beyond that of regional and local variations in the Garvey movement, has been that Garvey's program and the UNIA's personnel expanded and shifted constantly, and his rhetoric was modified over time, as he came to grips with his enormous popularity and numerous critics. After spreading relatively unchecked for almost three years in the United States, by 1921 the UNIA faced both mounting criticism by African American race leaders and pursuit by the suspicious and hostile United States government. Most Garvey scholars agree that this new set of conditions pushed Garvey into a more defensive posture. The leader's open hostility toward respected leaders of the black intelligentsia has caused scholars often to dismiss Garvey and only occasionally to defend him. Was he the incendiary radical he seemed to be in his 1919 Harlem speeches or the allegedly reactionary race purist he became in 1921, a change that culminated in his notorious summit with the acting imperial wizard of the Ku Klux Klan on 25 June 1922? This central historiographical debate lies between two extreme views: whether Garvey sincerely wanted to challenge all conventions of the racial and class structure of the United States, leading his followers toward some sort of race war, or whether he was so unscrupulously opportunistic that he became a conservative accommodator of white racial purists, segregationists, disfranchisers, and lynchers. An important consideration in solving this puzzle is recognizing that many early Garveyites were West Indians, whereas later on the dominant, loyal group was native-born Americans.

Historian Winston James provides a compelling study of the critical influence of West Indian radicals on African American activism in this period. He powerfully outlines the pervasive presence of assertive West Indian immigrants in the forefront of outspoken journalism and radical organizations for black improvement, especially in New York. West Indian leaders had a powerful appeal among native-born black Americans and, as James convincingly argues, spurred blacks into more militant protest.[10] Garvey fits within this paradigm, but unlike that of most other West Indians, his rhetoric cooled noticeably over time. In 1930 Garvey wrote a series of autobiographical sketches for the *Pittsburgh Courier* in which he provided an explanation for his most controversial public statement, spoken to a packed house at Madison Square Garden during the UNIA's 1920 convention: "I declared at the height of my exuberance that 'Four hundred million Negroes were sharpening their swords for the next world war.' Among all the things I said these words were taken out and cabled to every capital in Europe and throughout the world. The next morning every first class newspaper proclaimed me as the new leader of the Negro race and featured the unfortunate words that I used. Words which have been making trouble for me ever since 1920."[11] There remains no scholarly consensus about the UNIA leader's sincerity and intentions. Did he mean what he said at the Garden? Did he never seriously consider violence as a strategy but simply got carried away in the heat of the moment? Was he forced by necessity to change his rhetoric while never changing his plans? Or, to hold on to power or to save himself did he change his rhetoric, tactics, and plans?

It is abundantly clear, whatever his intentions, that the extreme aspects of Garvey's "conservative turn" hurt his popularity with the black intelligentsia and perhaps West Indian immigrants but not with southern-born supporters. As Garvey became familiar with the American racial landscape, he shifted his rhetoric, alienating some West Indians without losing the respect of mostly circumspect southern blacks with different formative experiences and different conceptions of what was possible vis-à-vis white society. In the 1920s West Indian–born black people did not inhabit the cotton belt areas of southwest Georgia, the Arkansas Delta, and the Yazoo-Mississippi Delta, the specific regions of the rural South under examination here.[12] Yet as time progressed, these and a few other sections of the South held by far the greatest concentrations of UNIA divisions in the United States.

In the UNIA's first two years it enjoyed phenomenal success, as thousands joined the local divisions in New York, Boston, Pittsburgh, Philadelphia, and Washington, D.C.[13] Not coincidentally, New York and Boston were the two most popular destinations in the United States for black British West Indians.[14] Garvey's growing popularity took his newspaper and organization into the South, first to coastal Virginia and Florida and soon to other busy southern cities and towns. Friendship and kinship networks spread the word of the UNIA and Garvey's mystique to the original homes and farms of migrants to the northern and southern cities. The UNIA's expansion into rural areas took place primarily in the U.S. South, where by 1922, over 400 UNIA divisions had sprung up.[15]

The West Indian immigrant population who comprised a significant portion of the UNIA membership in New York and southern Florida did not exist significantly, if at all, in rural, southern, interior communities. In the southern Black Belt cleavages among West Indian leaders and American leaders or between West Indian and American black members did not create conflict. By contrast, philosophical differences between black Americans and West Indians, who tended to be more militant or radical, stymied the organization and aroused the suspicion of local whites in communities in coastal Florida, New York, and even New Orleans.[16] Southern rural Garveyites in the interior communities examined here exhibited solidarity. Their communities were tightly knit, discreet, and void of immigrant blacks. The Garveyites in urban areas were dockworkers, manual laborers, miners, industrial workers, and seamen with wage jobs and varied levels of skill, external organization, sources of information, community networks, choices, and mobility. But most had the same agricultural roots as Garveyites in the South, who were isolated, living in black-majority communities, and financially tied down. To these people, the *Negro World* and the UNIA, an accessible international organization, were profoundly important.

In this study two important questions are how Garveyism remained so popular despite its controversial tactical and rhetorical adjustments and how it became a catalyst to movements that followed the UNIA's heyday. Robert A. Hill, editor of the UNIA and Garvey papers, has written a seminal essay identifying the initial radical nature of Garvey's rhetoric up to July 1921. Whereas Garvey's earlier speeches emphasized political empowerment and resistance, his later ones turned toward racial separatism and compromise.[17] Interestingly enough, most southern rural Garveyites joined the movement during the so-called radical phase, and yet the UNIA leader's continued and even increased popularity with the southern masses through the movement's later years indicated a remarkable loyalty, which did not survive as strongly in other regions of the United States.[18] Garvey's changing rhetoric and his financial and legal problems made less of a negative impact in the rural South. Followers there focused on supporting their new leader and preserving the UNIA program in order to improve conditions, and they adapted to his changing circumstances and rhetoric without wavering in support.

Although intuitively we might expect southern rural supporters to object quickly to any efforts to negotiate with or tolerate racist segregationists, they seemingly objected less to Garvey's new strategies than did urban elite blacks. Garvey's curious associations with white supremacists and their causes suggest that he may have made these surprising changes in refining an actively southern-focused strategy—in a deliberate attempt to unite the largest demographic segment of African American people.[19] The stable and loyal base provided by southern UNIA supporters partially explains the logic of Garvey's increasing emphasis on organizing in the region.

The United States's investigation of the "alien agitator" eventually led to a lengthy prosecution of the UNIA leader, and Garvey went to prison for mail fraud. In 1927 President Calvin Coolidge commuted Garvey's sentence, and U.S. immigration authorities ordered his deportation to Jamaica. Garvey's movement suffered gravely from these circumstances, and his larger plans for focusing on the South never came to fruition. Yet the UNIA's presence throughout the South for almost a decade did have important consequences for black thought and protest strategy in the region.

Repudiated by emerging black leaders, Garvey faded from popular memory after his deportation. Nevertheless, many African American supporters cherished the most useful and meaningful tenets of his philosophy, incorporating them into their beliefs and values. Many early recorders of the movement dismissed Garvey as a charlatan and the UNIA as a curiosity. Nevertheless, the National Association for the Advancement of Colored People (NAACP) and other race organizations adopted some of his principles while simultaneously obscuring and invalidating his former leadership. Former Garveyites looked to the NAACP and other new organizations to create leverage for racial advancement and self-determination.

Historiography

Although there are reams of books and articles on Garvey and Garveyism, southern Garveyism has never been documented or interpreted. A major reason for this gap is that the data sources are scattered and incomplete. In addition, the local, state, and national newspapers of the 1920s either completely ignored the UNIA or were exasperatingly biased against Garvey. But for me the nagging fact remained that thousands of black southerners joined the UNIA and sympathized with Garvey, and the movement was being imperfectly understood. A historical recovery project was in order, and empiricism naturally came first. Over the years of my research, which began in 1988, it has become more and more obvious why no historian had ever attempted the task of reconstructing southern Garveyism.

The 1920 census population schedules became available in 1992, finally making it possible to determine that rural southern Garveyites were mostly married, literate, Black Belt tenant farmers and sharecroppers with wives and daughters in their households. Yet with this discovery another problem emerged: the members of this demographic group have rarely been taken seriously as thinkers and agents of their own destiny. There is very little in the historical literature to aid in our understanding of the thought of black, landless farmers in the 1920s. Part of this is a holdover from W. E. B. Du Bois's concept of a "talented tenth"—those African Americans who were allegedly most qualified for leadership and for setting an appropriate agenda for African American protest in the early twentieth century. In addition, in the discourse of racial and identity politics, more attention focuses on historical subjects whose ideology supports current theory. Since the subjects of the emerging data archive on southern Garveyism clearly embraced race as an organizing principle, the findings of this project enter a contentious academic arena. Nevertheless, I hope all can appreciate that this study enriches our understanding of the complexity and diversity of African American intellectual history.

While I hope this study will contribute to an understanding of where Garveyism fits within the larger theoretical framework of the African diaspora, this is not the task at hand.[20] Instead, I have used empirical data to locate and identify flourishing UNIA divisions and their members and to imagine and suggest the practicalities and motivations behind their ideology and actions. After years of mining the fragmentary sources on the southern UNIA and critically examining evidence on host communities where the Black Belt and cotton agriculture overlapped, I offer not only empirical data on southern Garveyites and the UNIA but also an evidence-driven discussion of how southern, rural blacks have been ignored as intellectuals; why Garveyite women in rural areas may have accepted dubious "protection" from black men; why some black activists in the South could appear to be separatist, "capitalist" Garveyites and "color-blind" communists or socialists at the same time; and why the violent, vigilante tactics of the Ku Klux Klan were sometimes adopted and emulated by the Klan's own victims. At the same time, I place Garveyism squarely within the African American protest tradition, even though it may at first seem illogical to do so with a movement that favored racial separatism and black nationalism over political and social integration; racial nationalism over citizenship; self-defense (and in extreme cases even vigilantism) over nonviolence; and, perhaps to some extent, even patriarchy over feminism.

Most Garvey scholarship focuses not on Garveyites but on the UNIA leader and his personal and political struggles. The earliest scholarly study of Marcus Garvey and the UNIA, Edmund David Cronon's *Black Moses* (1955), provides a helpful narrative of the leader's life while portraying Garvey as deeply flawed and his movement as utopian. This interpretation suffers from the limited availability of primary research material at this early period. Although Cronon enjoyed the assistance of Garvey's widow, Amy Jacques Garvey, he did not benefit from later documentary discoveries and compilations.[21] In 1970 a Harlem antinarcotics organization called the Community Thing recovered files of the UNIA headquarters from an abandoned building on Lenox Avenue. These documents form the basis for the UNIA Records of the Central Division (New York), 1918–59, held by the Schomburg Center for Research in Black Culture at the New York Public Library. These papers include much data from the parent body, the UNIA's central administration. Not on microfilm but held as part of this collection is the key to any study of UNIA divisions and their members. It is a card file of each division listing the location, charter number, officers, and fragmentary data for divisions active between 1926 and 1928.

Another crucial source that Cronon lacked was most issues of the UNIA organ, the *Negro World*, published from 1918 to 1933. Most issues from after

February 1921 and a few from before that date are now widely available. The empirical data in the *Negro World* includes letters to the editor from specific people and places, lists of financial contributors with amounts and addresses, and reports from individual divisions and regional organizers. The opinions of UNIA convention delegates from the South are repeated verbatim in numerous issues, as are the exact texts of Marcus Garvey's weekly addresses. Cronon studied Garveyism too early to benefit from these sources; thus, the smaller, more scattered southern rural divisions are not acknowledged in his work.

In 1963 Amy Jacques Garvey published a personal account of her husband's life and activities in a book that is filled with revealing anecdotes and that notes the loyalty of southern UNIA divisions. Naturally, in the interest of promoting a positive image for her long-deceased husband, she lacked objectivity and focused more on Garvey the man than on the Garveyites he inspired.[22] In 1971 Theodore Vincent offered a useful study of Garveyism's link to subsequent black separatist movements. Although utterly convincing, in key portions of the text where the South might come into play documentation is sparse, making it difficult to substantiate connections. The author covered many aspects of the movement and acknowledged its diverse membership, but he did not examine individual Garveyites or local divisions. Yet Vincent's work was the first to suggest the breadth of Garvey's appeal among blacks in the 1920s and separatism's endurance in contemporary black thought.[23]

In his 1974 collection of essays on the movement, John Henrik Clarke placed Garvey in historical context in the various parts of the black world in which Garveyism flourished. For example, Clarke made the connection between Garvey's economic and emigrationist policies and those of Booker T. Washington and Bishop Henry McNeal Turner. Clarke's essays are mostly suggestive and impressionistic, but they provide insightful bases for further research. Extending and documenting Clarke's earlier suggestions of the ideological precursors to the UNIA become critical here in proving how well prepared the southern soil was for cultivating Garveyism.[24]

In 1976 Tony Martin published the most thoroughly researched narrative of Garvey and the UNIA to date and emphasized for the first time the broad appeal of the movement in the South. The appendix of this important book lists, from the parent body card files, the locations of the hundreds of UNIA divisions from the 1926–28 fragments. Martin's work covered important and decisive issues that Garvey confronted in dealing with the U.S. government and his rivals but did not deal with the members or the activities of local UNIA divisions.[25]

In 1983 the first volume of editor Robert A. Hill's splendid multivolume series of *The Marcus Garvey and Universal Negro Improvement Association Papers* appeared. The first seven of the eleven volumes center on the movement in the United States and shed much additional light on the southern wing of the UNIA. These papers represent a "comprehensive survey of all the presently available historical manuscripts and records" of the Garvey movement and provide data that enable us to interpret the movement objectively and through a variety of documentary evidence, ameliorating a problem that has marred much of the previous work on the UNIA and Garvey.[26]

Two critical sources for UNIA research are precariously biased. In the propaganda organ of the UNIA, the *Negro World*, one finds nothing negative or unflattering about Garvey except hints provided by articles in which the UNIA or its leader is vigorously defended against criticism. Garvey's own *Philosophy and Opinions*, edited and published in 1923 by his wife while they lobbied strenuously for clemency for his mail fraud conviction, contains much conciliatory language and little of the more radical rhetoric found in Garvey's earlier speeches. Sources contemporary to Garvey's time all must be utilized carefully. Several white newspapers in the Northeast and a few southern ones found space to report on the Garvey movement, but only to ridicule the UNIA leader's ambition to create a black-ruled nation or to colonize Liberia or his alleged intimation that "God is Black." Several papers poked fun at the UNIA's pretentious titles, as *Time* magazine mocked "the Ladies of the Royal Court of Ethiopia."[27] The black and white press both regularly reported Garvey's most embarrassing problems and scandals. And much of the worst suspicion and most demeaning derision came from the passionately anti-Garvey black press, especially after the Black Star Line's finances came into question in 1921 and after Garvey met with leaders of the Klan in 1922. When A. Philip Randolph, a prominent black socialist and leader of the "Garvey Must Go" campaign, received a threatening note and a human hand in his mail, the *Savannah Tribune* blamed the UNIA president.[28] Historians' use of the anti-Garvey black press, usually such an effective foil for the distortions of white-authored sources on questions of race, has led to persistent and pervasive interpretive bias. More recently, Marcus Garvey's iconic status among contemporary youth, reggae artists, filmmakers, and other forces in popular culture has celebrated his image and legacy uncritically.

While most of the previously mentioned studies of Garveyism focus on the political and organizational activities of the UNIA's leader, some have examined other aspects of the movement. Randall K. Burkett has concentrated on the spiritual aspects of Garveyism and the involvement of black clergy in promoting the UNIA. In a study that is fundamental to understanding the nature of southern Garveyism, although it does not address the region specifically, Burkett argues that Garvey fashioned the UNIA into a black civil religion. He focuses on how the UNIA leader adopted, under the advisement of prominent Negro clergymen, rituals and activities that gave Garveyism spiritual resonance. Burkett brings to our attention the wide participation of local ministers and the ways in which black churches became centers of divisional activities. The history of the organization in the rural South, especially, conforms to the argument offered in this essential work.[29]

Another prominent study of Garvey sees economic forces in modern society as catalysts for the UNIA's programs of economic independence, especially the incorporation and stock sales of the Black Star Line. Judith Stein focuses heavily on the context of industrialization and radical politicization, and she sees the popularity of the UNIA as part of the emergence of a black petite bourgeoisie primarily interested in economic opportunity in the modern capitalist context. Although she entitles one of her chapters "The UNIA Goes South: Marcus Garvey and the Ku Klux Klan," we learn little about the UNIA divisions or members in the South, and more about Stein's objection to Garvey's association with the Klan as a strategy for organizing in the region after the demise of the Black Star Line.[30]

The only book-length study of American Garveyites at the local level is Emory Tolbert's *The Universal Negro Improvement Association and Black Los Angeles: Ideology and Community in the American Garvey Movement*. In this 1980 publication we finally see a community study that traces the movement and its members in a single geographic location. Tolbert's work demonstrates the diversity of members at the local level and the variation in goals from one division to the next.[31] He is the first scholar to make explicit the fact that UNIA members outside the South were southern people. Most black migrants to Los Angeles came overwhelmingly from the South, especially from Texas and Arkansas. Tolbert develops a composite of the Los Angeles UNIA members as conservative, religious, family men who were not necessarily committed to nonviolence.[32] Tolbert pointed the historiography of Garvey and Garveyism toward the study of the Garveyite. This shift was essential to the present study of Garveyites in rural divisions in particular areas of the South.

Toward a New Interpretation

Because most existing scholarship leaves the impression that the UNIA was a purely urban phenomenon, most textbooks and popular sources mischaracterize the UNIA in the same way. No historian has addressed the sizable southern wing, even though several Garvey scholars recognized long ago that the UNIA had a wide following in the southern United States during the 1920s. On closer inspection it became clear that the vast majority of UNIA divisions below the Mason-Dixon Line were located in communities of fewer than 2,500 people, places that are rural by definition, according to the U.S. Census Bureau. This popular misconception is not surprising given that little has been documented of the individuals and communities that organized hundreds of divisions in eleven southern states. We are more aware of the existence of Garveyites outside of the South who lived in American cities, many of whom were recent arrivals from the West Indies or the South.[33] Moreover, those who have studied Garvey's newspaper carefully are aware of laboring blacks who joined the UNIA divisions of the urban South by the thousands, most notably in Norfolk and Newport News, Virginia, Charleston, South Carolina, Winston-Salem, North Carolina, and New Orleans.[34] Most striking in the 1926–28 division listings, however, is the obvious popular appeal of Garvey's calls for race pride, racial separatism, and Negro nationalism in hundreds of rural, agricultural communities in the Deep South, particularly in cotton-dominated counties. A closer look at this segment of Garveyites offers not only a glimpse into the elusive intellectual history of rural southern farmers but also a fuller understanding of the dynamics and nature of Garveyism.

Research in African American history and culture has increased exponentially in the last thirty years, largely because of interest in the ideological and activist roots of the modern civil rights movement. As we trace these origins back, decade by decade, historians have discovered the interaction of complex forces within black society and the impact of historical sea changes such as the two world wars and the New Deal.[35] Yet most of what we have learned in terms of black thought relates to the activities and contributions of urban, middle-class people who left more records, lived in more densely populated communities, and had more time and energy to devote to racial uplift. We have tended to attribute to the black intellectual elite a disproportionately large voice for articulating the dreams, aspirations, and attitudes of all African Americans. For black, southern, and rural people, daily survival occupied most of their energy and resources, and this study is an attempt to reconstruct their experiences. Its premise is that however busy and burdened this group was, however few records they left behind, and however far their ideology may have deviated from the liberal integrationist framework, these African Americans had strong impulses to determine and improve their own futures and found ways to do so through organization and independent thought.[36] Southern, rural Garveyism is a noteworthy example of an understudied ideology of African Americans in the 1920s. Many aspects of it are familiar in the more recent development of black organization and protest in the South, yet they have not previously been attributed to the UNIA's influence.

Numerous studies involving black Americans in the 1920s focus on the Great Migration, urbanization, and the Harlem Renaissance.[37] Existing works on the UNIA parallel this urban, northern focus. Jack Temple Kirby and Stewart E. Tolnay have documented the "extinction of the black farmer" after centuries of the predominance of agriculture as a way of life for African Americans.[38] Furthermore, as "urban culture" becomes a euphemism for "black culture," we are becoming increasingly forgetful that as late as the 1920s, the majority of African Americans remained in the South as rural, agricultural people. As black people's conditions improved, often in urban settings, it became easier for historians to trace their activities and hear their voices.

In 1920 9 million of the 10 million African Americans in the United States lived in the South. Five million, or half of all blacks, lived in rural areas; and 36 percent worked in agriculture, by far the most common occupation for African Americans.[39] The UNIA members and sympathizers who came from this southern agricultural plurality of the African American population represent a significant strain of black thought that has been sparsely documented. In addition to the vast majority of those who stayed in the South, blacks who migrated from rural to urban areas before 1920 brought rural memories and perspectives to American cities for at least a generation. Samples of their perspectives merit thorough investigation and documentation.

Historians illuminating rural, southern black life in the 1920s have addressed the essentials of economic, political, and social life. Sharecropping, tenant farming, and the crop lien shaped the economic circumstances of most southern, rural African Americans. The reality of disfranchisement, peonage, and lynching, particularly in rural areas, is commonly known.[40] The social history of rural blacks in the 1920s has focused almost exclusively on educational and church-centered activities. We know too little about the aspirations and ideals of black, southern, and rural men and women who mostly struggled in poverty during the 1920s.[41] How did they perceive their prospects in American society, in the future, and as a class, race, or nation? Steven Hahn's recent study of black organization in the South prior to the Great Migration has provided essential background for seeing black self-determination and politics as having developed outside of traditional party and government forums. He suggests that Garveyism found a natural home in the rural South because it extended organizing and community-building processes that had roots as far back as the antebellum slave societies.[42] Although *Grassroots Gar-*

veyism provides an overview of Garveyism in the entire South, urban and rural, state by state, the discussion progresses toward a focus on the rural American Garveyite whose dependence within the southern system of cotton agriculture, relative isolation from multiple sources of outside information, and life in a predominantly black community shaped his or her worldview.

Although word of mouth has always been an important force in the dissemination of news and ideas, print media were the dominant sources of information for the literate urban dweller in the United States in the 1920s. For the rural poor, however, itinerant ministers, church circulars, mail from relatives who had migrated North, or newspaper subscriptions to a white newspaper or perhaps the black-oriented *Chicago Defender* or Garvey's Harlem-based *Negro World* might have provided the only sources of outside information even though one lived in a densely populated "rural" area.[43] The sometimes newly acquired literacy combined with limited reading material was of course a double-edged sword in the rural South. The fewer the sources, the more powerful each one became. No group recognized this fact as well as the white landowners who controlled the counties in which they owned their land and hoped to control their labor. The post offices in these places monitored incoming return addresses and magazine and newspaper subscriptions and made their objections to radical or incendiary literature known. How, despite some restrictions, and the extent to which Garvey's message of economic and social separatism, redemption of Africa, and race pride reached literate rural people and the impression it made are interpreted in this study.

As Garvey reconciled his fiercely racial ideology with his ambition to organize the largest African American populations, the South's realities played a role in the tone and dissemination of his philosophy. For the most part, however, he remained fairly consistent in his ideals while adjusting rhetoric and program emphases to the contemporary racial and political context. One must understand the events and challenges confronting Garvey to make sense of his speeches and writings and to understand them as a complete and coherent ideology.

Recognizing the shifting context makes it possible to extrapolate the essential philosophical elements that attracted such large numbers of southern supporters to the UNIA. The *Negro World*, the propaganda organ of Garvey and the UNIA, provided a week-to-week record of the issues and news confronting the black diaspora. How Garvey, the managing editor, and the paper's other editors, like Hubert Harrison, William H. Ferris, and T. Thomas Fortune, chose to organize the information and how they calibrated Garvey's rhetoric in his front-page addresses indicated the changing emphases of the movement and its ideology over time as observed by a majority of readers in the South who had little personal access to the leader or his organizers. Tracing the evolution of Garveyism by reading through this weekly paper in sequence offers us an opportunity to view the ideology as it was seen by relatively isolated southern readers in rural areas.

The Tenets of Garveyism

From the available copies of the *Negro World* that coincide with the years in this study, specifically 1920–27, a number of the most important and most consistently held tenets of Garveyism emerge. First and foremost, Garveyism stressed the supreme necessity for race consciousness among people of African heritage. Garvey repeated often that blacks living under Jim Crow had inadvertently achieved an awareness, togetherness, and racial identity because of white domination.[44] Second, and as an extension of this foremost belief, the UNIA leader wanted "Negroes," as he insisted on calling people of African ancestry, to understand how organization along racial lines instead of class lines could provide strength and leverage for blacks within class-conscious organizations and across lines of nationality. This Negro nationalism envisioned by Garvey included the need for economic and social independence. In particular, Garveyites were encouraged to engage in occupations that precluded dependence on whites. In social affairs the UNIA leader stressed the importance of blacks' maintaining racial purity in order to prevent complete amalgamation and also as a way of warning white men to cease their exploitation of black women. In order to preserve the dignity of the Negro race, Garvey advocated self-defense instead of submission.

Garvey understood the modern importance of having a literary history. He saw the way in which imperialist nations had used written histories to justify their supposed superiority over peoples without documented traditions and historical achievements. In the absence of a literary history, colonizers and white supremacists had distorted the African past and obscured achievements of blacks in the diaspora. Thus, he set out to create an awareness of and epistemological base for a glorious African history dating back to ancient Egyptian civilization.[45] This psychological component served to galvanize people of African ancestry and provided the basis for another important facet of Garveyism: a rejection of pervasive ideas of inherent black inferiority.

Widely accepted contemporary literature asserted the white man's duty to civilize Africans and other members of the "darker races," while popular fiction portrayed southern blacks as beastly and uncivilized.[46] Although he did not reject the notion that certain Africans required "civilization and spiritual redemption," Garvey saw this as the exclusive duty of enlightened, modern-ized blacks. This responsibility, he argued, stemmed from a need for all races to recognize Africa as blacks' natural and rightful home. The implications of this aspect of Garveyism were especially contradictory. While partial, voluntary repatriation of dispersed blacks to Africa became an integral goal of the UNIA program, and while struggles for African independence from European impe-rialism were encouraged, promotion of the spiritual redemption of Africa implied that the Western world and its Judeo-Christian traditions were indeed culturally superior.[47] Garvey, his organizers, and many followers constantly repeated the goal of African "redemption" in speeches and letters. This term easily described two very different agendas, especially as interpreted by south-erners. In one sense, just as the southern white Redeemers had reclaimed southern politics after Reconstruction, the UNIA hoped to lead redeemers in Africa who would force out Britain, France, and the various other European colonizers. A politically independent Africa could lead and advocate for people of African ancestry spread all over the globe. An equally meaningful and probably more current and familiar concept to the Baptist and African Meth-odist Episcopal congregants of the South was the spiritual redemption at-tained by those saved from sin by accepting Christ. As long as the definition of African redemption remained vague, it could represent both meanings. Thus, race pride, solidarity, nationalism, independence, self-defense, and redemp-tion formed the essence of the ideology for southern Garveyites. Many of these sacred elements that propelled the Garvey movement remained at the center of the African American protest tradition and formed the foundation for dra-matic social change in the twentieth century.

The scope of Garvey's and the UNIA's influence is impossible to quantify precisely. Although we know that the UNIA paper enjoyed a wide circulation of 25,000 in 1920 and as much as 75,000 in 1921, detailed subscription records for the *Negro World* could have also illuminated the demographics of its base readership.[48] The fact remains, however, that keen observers of social move-ments who lived during the UNIA's heyday provide some of the most interest-ing evidence of the popularity of Garveyism. Chandler Owen, a leading black socialist organizer of the 1920s and Garvey's most vociferous critic, remarked in frustration that no other black social movement could prosper as long as Garvey's popularity continued. Charles S. Johnson, the assiduous black so-ciologist, measured Garveyite sentiment in his study of black youth in the southern Black Belt and concluded that "the one outstanding example of articulated racial ideology affecting southern Negroes was the Garvey Back-to-Africa Movement. . . . An incidental but significant feature of this movement

[is] the attempt to impute new and attractive meanings to blackness to rid Negro psychology in general of the unfortunate emotional connotations of blackness." Benjamin E. Mays, southern educator and mentor to a generation of civil rights activists, including Martin Luther King Jr., remarked at length on the powerful influence of Garvey's black pride message: "No matter how illusory his dreams, and regardless of what certain Negro critics thought of him, Garvey had the qualities of leadership to stir the 'black masses.' He had charisma, he was eloquent, he was black. No other black leader, in my time, had attracted the masses as did Garvey. He did for Negroes what no other leader before him had done and what no black leader would do again until the 1960's: He made them proud of their heritage, proud of being black."[49]

In order to measure further the appeal of the movement, Garvey scholars must work with the fragments of evidence available. Some of this data appears in the form of membership records from the twilight years of the American Garvey movement, 1926 through 1928; much is taken from the weekly *Negro World*'s "News and Views of UNIA Divisions"; much of it comes from government records, including petitions for Garvey's release from federal prison;[50] and the rest emerges from various other correspondence and indirect data. Interview opportunities with Garveyites and their children are becoming increasingly scarce with the passage of time.

Despite protests by females from urban UNIA divisions that the UNIA did not provide opportunities for women to lead and make policy, it is evident that rural, agricultural women played a significant role in sustaining the small, local divisions in the rural South.[51] Conditions in this setting offered more opportunities for women to take an active role as organizers and micromobilizers than the urban divisions did.[52] Issues pertaining to black women, especially their sexual exploitation, weighed heavily on black men and women in the rural South. The UNIA's position in favor of race purity bore directly on this issue and gained strong support among rural Garveyites. A discussion of this element of Garveyism in chapter 5 offers an opportunity to measure resistance to black patriarchy in a rural setting within this early nationalist organization.

Why did Garvey alienate black elites, including many West Indian intellectuals who supported him early on, and perhaps some of the grassroots support he had in cities? What promise did Garvey and the UNIA see in organizing southern farmers? Some suggested the UNIA cynically used financial contributions from vulnerable and easily influenced country folk. Yet, perhaps Garvey recognized there was a large black constituency that black urban intellectuals had lost touch with or abandoned. His desire for mass leadership required him to adopt the agenda and strategies of the people he ultimately chose. In this line of interpretation, it is useful to view the 1920s in the South as an ideological battleground between the central administrations of the UNIA and NAACP, which chose mutually damaging strategies. During this decade, Garveyism spread unchecked in the South, while the NAACP lost ground and stagnated in the same region. In 1920, under its first black executive secretary, James Weldon Johnson, the NAACP also adopted a southern focus; yet it failed to maintain many branches it had formed in most areas below the Mason-Dixon Line from 1917 to 1920 due to a merciless backlash that lasted until the late 1930s. During the crucial 1920s, both organizations recognized the absolute necessity of gaining support from southern constituents, who formed the largest pool of African Americans, in order to gain legitimacy as their spokesmen. This ideological crossroads and the integrationist triumph eventually determined the future of American race relations.

Organization of the Book

The first chapter of this book describes the most important strains of black thought in the South in the century prior to the Garvey movement and how these ideologies prepared the way for the UNIA to be readily accepted by black people in the South. Chapter 2 examines the UNIA's early experiences in Virginia, Florida, and North Carolina, which taught the leadership to choose organizers carefully and to deal with local authorities pragmatically.

Chapter 3 provides an overview of the UNIA structure in the South on a state-by-state basis. It documents the geographical and chronological spread of UNIA divisions by tracing the publicized activities of important southern divisions, as well as the steps of national, regional, and local organizers in the southern region.[53] These patterns are important to understanding precisely when and how the UNIA spread and the dynamics of organization in rural areas. Also discussed in chapter 3 is how the *Negro World* formed the essential link between Garvey and the southern UNIA divisions. The paper's contents reveal significant information about the attitudes and motivations of southern Garveyites. With skilled southern-born newspapermen and writers working on Garvey's behalf, the *Negro World* printed news articles, letters, and editorials appropriate to the aims of the UNIA. In addressing topics important to southern blacks, the *Negro World* artfully emphasized issues that demonstrated black power. The predominance of black laborers in southern agriculture and their importance to its prosperity received marked attention. The *Negro World* enjoyed reporting on the labor crisis in southern agriculture because it implied black economic potency. At the same time, the paper frequently included items on lynching and the Ku Klux Klan, two subjects that dramatized black powerlessness and the intransigence of white racism. Garvey and his editorial staff accurately gauged the interests and the sentiments of their southern readers, as the UNIA's popularity in the South indicated.

Chapters 4 and 5 focus on the communities and racial ideology of the three sections of the rural South that are the focus of this study. As my focus narrowed from the South, to the rural South, to the Black Belt, to cotton-dominated areas, obvious areas of interest were counties or subregions in which the highest concentration of UNIA divisions appeared. Southwest Georgia, the Arkansas Delta, and the Yazoo-Mississippi Delta were all cotton-dominated, rural areas with a high proportion of black population and UNIA divisions. All three areas hosted recognized episodes in black or biracial organization in the decades after the UNIA's demise and also had histories with strong connections to influential figures and movements that had paved the way for Garveyism in the 1920s. I intentionally eliminated urban and coastal sections of the South and the sugar-dominated river parishes of Louisiana in order to concentrate on agricultural workers in cotton-dominated counties. North Carolina's UNIA divisions were predominantly urban, and those in rural areas were widely dispersed rather than densely concentrated in farming communities. The UNIA flourished in cotton counties in the Black Belt in very dense concentrations in Bolivar and Tallahatchie Counties in Mississippi, Worth and Mitchell Counties in Georgia, and Phillips and Monroe Counties in Arkansas; these became very specific case studies in the focus areas.

Louisiana blacks, particularly in the river parishes in southern Louisiana, universally embraced the UNIA. In fact, Louisiana had the largest number of UNIA divisions in a single state, with eighty. But there were very important differences between UNIA organization in Louisiana and other southern states. Two very dynamic state organizers who were based in New Orleans had a continuous presence there. S. V. Robertson founded the New Orleans division, organized in southeast Louisiana, and then was sent briefly to organize in Georgia in 1922. During 1922, Thomas W. Anderson, a second-generation Louisiana longshoreman, became the new and equally energetic state organizer for Louisiana. In 1923 Robertson took the movement further north along the river. UNIA locals in outlying parishes felt reverberations from scandals that rocked the New Orleans division. This large unit's membership was quite diverse, unlike other Deep South divisions. In addition, Garvey visited the Crescent City several times, and his presence had an enormous impact. Louisiana hosted larger numbers of West Indian–born black slaves in 1850, more than any other state, slave or free, so there was a marked West Indian heritage there.[54] Another unique feature in Louisiana's organization was the

Black Star Line, which was more of an inspiration to those working directly along the lower Mississippi River, one of the world's busiest maritime commercial centers.

With the exception of the divisions in Natchitoches Parish in northwest Louisiana, where cotton tenancy was the rule for Garveyites, the parts of the state where Garveyism flourished were more industrialized and more cosmopolitan. Many of the UNIA's division leaders worked in sugar and oil plants and in the lumber and shipping industries along the Mississippi River.[55] There were social and cultural influences in the region that made it significantly different from the areas under examination in the southern cotton belt. The lower Mississippi was originally French and predominantly Catholic. Interracial relations were more fluid, but there were more pronounced caste distinctions among Negroes, mulattoes, and other mixed-race people. Sugarcane cultivation created different patterns of association and organization than did cotton; thus labor and schedules were dictated by the brutally labor-intensive crop.[56] All of these cultural factors make Louisiana a rich case study in Garveyism but create a unique set of variables.[57]

Areas of earnest civil rights activity by the Student Nonviolent Coordinating Committee (SNCC) among rural people in the 1960s directed this study toward southwest Georgia and the Yazoo-Mississippi Delta.[58] The dense concentration of rural divisions around Albany, Georgia, and the all-black town of Mound Bayou, Mississippi, intrigued me as I began mapping the movement. In eastern Arkansas the seemingly contradictory phenomena of the Phillips County massacre of rural African Americans precipitated by formation of a black farmers' union in 1919, followed by the existence of a biracial organization, the Southern Tenant Farmers Union, in the 1930s, made the decade in between particularly intriguing.[59] The thorough concentration of UNIA divisions in this area in the 1920s suggested powerful possibilities for an explanation of what happened between these two events.

After selecting three sections of the South that bore much similarity and had interesting possibilities, I developed a composite of the rural, southern Garveyite through a cross-reference of divisional and census records. Chapter 4 describes the characteristics and circumstances of these UNIA supporters. The 1920 and 1930 censuses contain much pertinent information on the composition of individuals' households, their employment, their financial status, their color (black or mulatto), and their ages, state or national nativity, and literacy. Similarities in their situations provided a basis for understanding their priorities and motivations for supporting the UNIA. A comparison of UNIA households in 1920 and again in 1930 indicated in various cases stability, upward economic mobility or stagnation, urban or northward migration, and in many cases, presumably the death of former Garvey supporters.

Chapter 5 interprets the UNIA's appeal to rural southern members based on primary data pulled from numerous sources that described local conditions. Hundreds of letters and petitions to the Department of Justice and the Office of the Pardon Attorney of the United States revealed the devotion to Garveyism of UNIA members all over the rural South. These documents, combined with monthly divisional reports reprinted in the *Negro World* and letters and editorials from UNIA supporters, aided in identifying the most dynamic divisions and members and their perspectives. Local newspapers, local histories, and in a few cases firsthand recollections of local UNIA activities provided information on host communities. It is impossible to know how a continuation of the mass-based Garvey movement might have changed the dynamics of southern race relations.

Chapter 6 attempts to place the organization's legacy in the development of black activism at later stages. For example, Georgia and the Delta regions illustrated the striking contrast between UNIA and NAACP success. The almost exclusively rural character of Garveyism in Georgia is notable and may well be linked to the NAACP's popularity in urban areas of the state. Georgia exemplified a more established region of southern agriculture with an entrenched system of race relations. In addition, the strength of the UNIA in southwest Georgia reminds us that the Albany movement harnessed the laboring class in the area around Dougherty County in the 1960s for civil rights protest. The Yazoo-Mississippi Delta, so rich in its own civil rights and race history, contrasts with rural Georgia because of its newer character and its postbellum development of commercial plantation agriculture and distinctive racial dynamics. This region had the largest concentration of UNIA organization in the South.

The Great Depression seems to have disrupted growing black solidarity in some ways and opened up opportunities for more class-based organization. On the one hand, New Deal liberalism of the early 1930s may have provided enough hope for biracial cooperation to blacks in urban settings to weaken the separatist and pan-African tendencies espoused by Garvey.[60] Some of Franklin Roosevelt's make-work programs and relief schemes benefited African Americans in a time of dire need. But on the other hand, tenant farmers, many of whom were evicted from the land as a result of the Agricultural Adjustment Administration's programs to take cotton land out of cultivation, felt even more alienated from the white-dominated American body politic. By the mid-1930s, many urban and rural blacks supported the NAACP or at least sought its help. Some joined communist organizations like the Share Cropper's Union in Alabama or socialist-influenced ones like the Southern Tenant Farmers Union in Arkansas.[61] Recent studies of the post–World War II civil rights movement indicate that working-class, rural people joined the citizenship struggle and played a key role in its success.[62]

Although invisible in the historical literature, many rural southern African Americans through the 1930s, 1940s, and 1950s persisted in the separatist mindset represented later by the Black Power movement and the Nation of · Islam. Despite the significant yet limited legal successes of the civil rights struggle, black nationalism continues to flourish in multiple forms and permutations. Many civil rights activists had already moved fully into a Pan-Africanist orientation by the mid-1960s. This strain of black thought's long and unbroken existence in the South gained its earliest articulation, widest exposure, and broadest support during the height of the Garvey movement.[63] Although the legacy of racial consciousness and pride that the UNIA inspired cannot be adequately measured, it played a larger role than is currently acknowledged in solidifying the psychological strength and endurance of generations of black southerners in their struggles for dignity, fair treatment, and self-determination.

1 Antecedents

He spoke from his soul . . . and ah, Garvey spoke the words that you thought you was speaking yourself. . . . They were in your thoughts, in your mind, in your brains, but still you did not speak them the way Garvey spoke them. And it . . . ah, it was in one accord. It was just like, ah, everybody had one mind. —Virginia Collins, Louisiana Garveyite, 2001

Many of Marcus Garvey's inspiring words and ideas sounded familiar to his followers because they were not necessarily new.[1] Many of the most important themes of Garvey's speeches, both spoken and transcribed weekly in the *Negro World*, echoed the voices of generations of black clergymen, journalists, and other influential black leaders of the American South. So much of what appealed to American Garveyites, whether they were born in the rural South or remained there, came straight out of the collective memory of generations past. From the intermittent African American colonization of Liberia, to the emigrationism, racial pride, and self-defense espoused by African Methodist Episcopal (AME) bishop Henry McNeal Turner, to the efforts to uplift and redeem African societies by African American missionaries from the rural South, to the self-reliance and economic nationalism of Booker T. Washington, Garvey's program blended preexisting strategies familiar to rural southerners, while adding elements that appropriately addressed the postwar setting of the 1920s.

African American leaders struggled with issues of legitimacy. Who did southern blacks consider their leaders in this modern era? Who articulated their agenda, and how did their lives and issues overlap with those of African American migrants to urban areas? Certainly ministers, journalists, and even national figures like Booker Washington and Bishop Turner confronted problems in diverse ways. Garvey successfully appropriated and transformed popular tactics and rhetoric that spoke to rural people's issues: survival, spirituality, coping strategy, pragmatism, strength, and preparation for protest, organization, and community formation and reconstitution.

In the North and in southern cities, alternative approaches to black advancement had begun to take shape, most of which tailored protest to the urban setting and addressed issues confronted by urbanites. The Great Migration, which began the eventual shift of millions of African Americans to cities, had begun, but in the early 1920s southern blacks remained predominantly rural and agricultural. Many held on to previous models for race advancement but recognized their limitations. The UNIA leadership walked a fine line between embracing what was useful from previous efforts and defining ways in which some old practices were obsolete.

The adjustments Garvey wanted to make in strategy required black pride and dignity in interactions with whites and a modern, nationalistic approach to community building and economic development. At Carnegie Hall in August 1919, Garvey, then viewed by Harlem's black leaders as a radical West Indian upstart, went so far as to say, "The white man of the world has been accustomed to deal with the Uncle Tom cringing Negro. Up to 1918, he knew no other Negro than the Negro represented through Booker T. Washington. Today he will find that a new Negro is on the stage."[2]

Another attempt at distinguishing the UNIA program came in an early *Negro World* editorial entitled, "Honorable Marcus Garvey and Our Fossilized Missionaries." In this column J. Arthur Davis, a black American organizer who became the early Miami UNIA division president, stressed the uniqueness of Garvey's plans while comparing their purposes to those of Henry McNeal Turner and other black missionaries to Africa: "Like Bishop Turner, [Garvey] dreams of a Negro flag in Africa. Like our missionaries, he claims that if Africa is to be saved, it must be saved by black men. But he would save it wholesale, while our missionaries have been trying to save it by the retail. For fifty years they have been raising money to that end." Implying that missionaries had "sold out" Africa in the face of European imperialism, Davis argued that Garvey and the UNIA were more sincere. He posited that the creation of a steamship line and the development of commerce were the logical routes to African redemption. It was not enough to transplant black American farmers to Liberia. The industrial development that could make this imagined black nation competitive in the modern world, Davis asserted in the *Negro World*, was essential to the new program.[3]

Although never an advocate of emigration, during his years as a student at Hampton Institute Booker T. Washington had considered, with many others, becoming a missionary to Africa, a continent that had interested him since childhood. Providence, he believed, took him instead to Alabama to found Tuskegee Institute. In 1900, however, he found a concrete way to form a connection with the vast continent across the Atlantic. The German Colonial Society requested the assistance of experts in cotton cultivation, and nine Tuskegee men answered Washington's call to take their farming expertise to Africa. All the volunteers were from the South, the sons of Alabama slaves.[4]

The first four went to Togoland, and later others went to Sudan, South Africa, Congo Free State, and Liberia.[5] Several of these men reported their impressions to Washington, and in 1910 he took his interest a step further: he began to solicit participation in an international conference "[t]o bring together not only students of colonial and racial questions, but more particularly those who either as missionaries, teachers or government officials, are actually engaged in any way in practical and constructive work, which seeks to build up Africa by educating and improving the character and conditions of the native peoples . . . to get from the people on the ground a clearer and more definite notion of the actual problems involved in the redemption of the African peoples."[6] The 1912 international conference at Tuskegee anticipated Garvey's bolder yet similar meetings by eight years and mirrored the Pan-African conference organized by Henry Sylvester Williams of Trinidad in 1900, as well as later meetings associated with W. E. B. Du Bois.[7]

Despite Washington's complicity in assisting colonialists more than Africans themselves, in Garvey's *Philosophy and Opinions*, published in 1923, we find a more forgiving and approving attitude toward the strategies of "Booker T. Washington's Program." While acknowledging the benefits of the Tuskegee idea of industrial training, the UNIA leader argued that the "New Negro" sought also political and military leadership. The political leadership he referred to, of course, would be attained not in the countries of the African diaspora, not as subordinates to whites in a colonial system, but in an independent Africa.[8]

During the golden years of the UNIA, only Haiti, Ethiopia, and Liberia were black-ruled nations. However, Haiti had been under U.S. occupation since 1915, Liberia was propped up by extensive loans from American creditors, and Ethiopia was the last remaining African kingdom not yet under European rule. This mountainous section of eastern Africa was coveted and eventually invaded in 1935 by the Italians, who got a late start in the European imperial land grab.[9] Undeterred by the power of his imperial rivals, Garvey accepted leadership of a provisional, imagined nation of the "Negro People of the World."[10] The bulk of this constituency lived either in parts of Africa and the West Indies dominated by Europe or as second-class U.S. citizens.

Garvey's position on the black man's natural right to and attachment to Africa echoed an earlier proponent of Negro nationalism. A native of the Virgin Islands, Edward Wilmot Blyden, the loudest African voice on the international scene in the 1880s, spoke all over the United States to promote emigration to his adopted home country, Liberia. In 1882 he lectured in the Deep South at institutions of higher learning. He stressed the need for American blacks to come to Liberia and strengthen the black nation with their contributions and skills. He had much earlier asked the *Christian Recorder*, the national AME organ founded in 1852, to solicit half a million American Negroes for Africa. Hollis Lynch, Blyden's biographer, has estimated that Blyden's speech in Washington, D.C., the institutional home to the American Colonization Society (for which he and Henry McNeal Turner served as agents), contained his most important utterances from his U.S. speaking tour. Blyden "predicted that as the Negro masses [became] educated they would grow impatient with their circumscribed lives, and must then feel 'an irrepressible desire to return to the Fatherland.' "[11]

Africa burned not just in the minds of Washington and Garvey, neither of whom ever reached its shores, but also in the imaginations of black farmers in the South. Some of their community elders, born around 1820, had been born in Africa and sold as slaves illegally after the importation ban of 1808. The census of 1920 reported 243 African-born people of color living in the United States, the lowest number of native Africans alive in the United States since the seventeenth century. About a quarter of these were very elderly southern black people who had once been slaves. The others were apparently children born to African American missionaries while serving in Africa.[12] Recorders of the history of Mitchell County in southwest Georgia, later a center of UNIA activity in the Deep South, noted the remarkable longevity of a number of local blacks who had been born in Africa and who lived well past their one-hundredth year. Africa-born former slave Paul Frazier died in 1902 at 110 years old. John Brimberry, who died in 1911 at 131 years of age, identified himself as an "Arbo" kinsman.[13] In 1920 four Yazoo-Mississippi Delta blacks had been born in Africa well before the Civil War, and in Arkansas ten black people recorded Africa as their place of birth. One colored Pulaski County schoolteacher, twenty-eight-year-old Diane McNeil, was Liberian and had Africa-born parents. Although few in number, these direct contacts to Africa reinforced the connection African Americans felt to their heritage. Moreover, oral traditions kept Africa alive in the imaginations of black families all over the United States through the generations. Few had the detail and drama of Alex Haley's *Roots*, a saga of his family's multigenerational odyssey from freedom in the Gambia to freedom in America. None, like Haley's, became a best-selling book and in 1977 the most widely viewed television production in history. But stories of the wisdom of ancestors or remembrances of a former life of freedom had psychological power, especially among people with few literary options.

After the deaths of Turner and Washington, both in 1915, black people in the American South felt a void. This predominantly rural group, located on farms in the Black Belt, missed the national leadership that these great men had represented. Urban leaders like Du Bois and Atlanta Baptist College's (now Morehouse) John Hope offered solutions that seemed more applicable to the middle class or at least to the urban context. Garvey, with the help of his organizers, recognized this drastic need and rare opportunity in the rural South. Over several years Garvey's plans evolved, he used his powerful newspaper to promote his ideas, and he adopted previous leaders' models. By 1922 he had carved out his niche as the recognized leader of the Negro race in the rural South and elsewhere.

A clear link exists between Garvey's philosophies and those of Blyden and Turner. It is certain that Garvey read their writings extensively, although he credited much more ideological influence to the better-known and more recent Washington. Moreover, this continuity of thought extended to the literate members of black, southern communities, especially to those who were pastors. It should not surprise us that Garvey gathered support in areas where Bishop Henry McNeal Turner, the African missionary movement, and the long-lived African colonization movement had a following. The missionary, sacred, and emigrationist components of Garveyism grew out of the powerful influence of evangelical Christianity among nineteenth-century African Americans. These links are most clearly defined in the rural South where these factors had their greatest impact and endurance.

Bishop Turner's long leadership career and enormous influence among rural blacks began as an AME pastor and chaplain for the Union army. He spent his years immediately after the Civil War as the architect of the strong AME church network in Georgia. He traveled constantly, lived and worked in Atlanta and Macon, served in the Georgia legislature, and eventually settled in Savannah in 1872. In 1876 he became the director of AME publications, including the *Christian Recorder,* which made him a national spokesman for the largest black organization in the country. In that year U.S. troops withdrew from the South, and the gains of Reconstruction for blacks began their steady decline. Turner became an outspoken champion of black farmers trapped by debt peonage.[14]

In 1880 the General Conference of the AME church assigned Turner to the Eighth District, which included Arkansas, Mississippi, and the Indian Territory (Oklahoma). Turner spoke at churches and organized new ones all over these states, emphasizing race pride and encouraging the spread of the AME church. A Mississippi audience member noted, "We did not know that our race owned so many great men, but after hearing all the splendid things he said, we went directly home and washed our faces and resolved that we would nevermore try to be white."[15]

Turner's advocacy of black emigration to Africa made him a controversial figure, though sources admit that his views accurately mirrored the sentimental impulses of "the masses" in the South, especially in rural Arkansas.[16] Turner's biographer Stephen Ward Angell calls the bishop's mission to the South, which was mostly responsible for AME membership growth from 20,000 in 1858 to 452,725 in 1896, his most important achievement. Angell paraphrases the remarks of one of Turner's fellow bishops, Reverdy Ransom, on Turner's remarkable accomplishments in the South: "it was impossible that the world would ever witness someone like Turner again, because what he did—transforming an impoverished, scattered people into a disciplined organization wielding great collective power—only needed to be done once. Succeeding generations of African-American ministers and politicians faced the different task of refining the organization that Turner established."[17] This refinement, undertaken by Garvey in the post–World War I era, was adapted to twentieth-century conditions, borrowed heavily from Turner's persuasive and provocative ideology, and appealed to an identical constituency.

During the Civil War, Turner first developed an interest in a black homeland where assimilation of the races would not be necessary.[18] The *Christian Recorder*, of which he later became editorial adviser and publisher, provided a forum for Turner's opinions through the years of his service as an AME pastor and bishop. It circulated widely all over the United States and even further as the church organized internationally in the West Indies, South America, and South Africa. In 1917 it was celebrating its sixty-fifth anniversary as the longest continuous race paper in existence and reported a subscription list of 100,000 readers.[19] Church leaders would read these papers aloud during services or summarize their contents, extending the reach of the issues and editorials well beyond subscribers, as they would later do with Garvey's addresses in the *Negro World*.[20]

In 1893 the monthly *Voice of Missions* began circulating among the AME pastors of the South. For eight years, Turner used this paper as his mouthpiece, placing particular emphasis on his emigrationist ideas and on the need for evangelization in Africa. He publicized trips he made to Liberia, Sierra Leone, and other parts of western and southern Africa and reported a growing white presence there. He pleaded that Africa be reserved for Africans. Turner also used the *Voice of Missions* to respond harshly to his critics in the northern black press, calling them "mushroom pimps" and "coons" who made things harder for southern blacks.[21]

So much of Turner's rhetorical style, especially his tendency toward ad hominem attacks on his ideological foes, as well as his ideas and strategies, resembled those of Garvey that it is hard to imagine that Garvey did not directly benefit from the bishop's influence. Garvey scholar Rupert Lewis has explored Garvey's deep admiration for an associate of Turner's named Joseph Robert Love. Love became a well-known reformer in Jamaica and the publisher of the *Jamaica Advocate* between 1895 and 1905. Before that time, Love had served as head of an AME mission at Savannah, Georgia, and as deacon of the Georgia diocese. Turner, who resided in Savannah during the same period, undoubtedly knew Love well, and it is interesting that both black radicals published race-conscious papers during the same decade spanning the nineteenth and twentieth centuries. Both men's journals emphasized themes of racial pride and self-sufficiency.[22] These themes had importance to future Garveyites because of their link as a foundation for community advancement among black people.

Garvey reported having read Love's publication while living in Jamaica, and we know that Love energetically promoted land reform as a way to elevate the landless Jamaican peasants. These black people, like their southern share-cropper counterparts, were voteless, landless, and yoked to the plantation system. Amy Jacques Garvey's recollections, written well after her husband's death, recalled Love as an important influence on the Jamaican leader as a young man, indicating that the Garveys must have discussed Love with some regularity throughout their life together.[23]

For the purposes of this study, the importance of the direct threads of thought among Turner, Love, and Garvey is most significant in the overlap of their followers. All three men reached thousands through their respective newspapers, and Turner's influence through the AME publications permeated the South first. Between 1876 and 1880 Turner spread his literary influence to every AME district convention in the nation and gained a wide popularity among young AME pastors in the South.[24] In the 1920s Garvey's *Negro World* would gain similar influence among southern clergymen, from both the AME and Baptist denominations, who would in turn spread Garveyism to their flocks.

Prominent in Turner's ideas for solving racial conflict was emigration of black Americans to Africa. Before the Civil War he preached a sermon on "The Redemption of Africa," which encouraged the conversion of Africans to Christianity by African American missionary colonists. This plan was more than missionary work, however; it was an opportunity that both he and later Garvey recognized to reconstitute black communities—part of what we now call black nationalism. As an early black member of the Georgia legislature, Turner "stated his belief that Africa was the ultimate home for blacks." He believed that although southern black farmers "love[d] the South better than gold or precious gems," they also needed land that America could not provide. Around 1880, the state conferences of the AME church in Georgia and South Carolina approved a resolution in support of emigration, citing biblical precedents.[25]

The idea of African Americans' emigrating to Africa predated Turner's remarks by at least fifty years. Paul Cuffe, a black sea captain, transported thirty-eight willing black Americans to Sierra Leone in 1816. A year later the white-dominated American Colonization Society (ACS) emerged with an elaboration of this act and a fanciful solution to the "undesirable" caste system developing with the emergence of a large free black population. The slaveholding South joined the debate of how to deal with the ever-increasing numbers of free blacks in their midst. The ACS proposed to establish a Christian colony in Africa to which free blacks and voluntarily emancipated slaves could go to begin productive lives unburdened by racial prejudice. If successful, ACS proponents argued, the repatriation process could alleviate the tension inherent in the United States's racial caste system of whites, free blacks, and slaves.[26]

Antebellum ACS champions included an eclectic mix of northerners, southerners, slaveholders, and clergymen who were uniformly educated and influential in their communities. Their plan was not popular with leading northern blacks and white abolitionists like William Lloyd Garrison, the influential journalist who in 1832 called the society a "creature without heart, brains, . . . eyeless, unnatural, hypocritical, relentless, unjust."[27] Most free blacks whose opinions are documented, North and South, did not want to emigrate. The idea was most popular with slaves who had no other chance for freedom. Through the slaves who became aware of the ACS, the idea of a "return to the Fatherland" took hold.

The society's plan represented a compromise among white Americans in an increasingly polarized and volatile political context. For the organization's first three years, beginning in 1817, a vague possibility existed that these diverse interests could work together. But in 1820 debates over the extension of slavery into the Louisiana Territory increased white southern defensiveness, which in turn created handicaps for the ACS's cooperative approach. The *Georgia Journal* argued that slaveholders "should not be discussing manumission in any form in the presence of slaves lest they become restless at the prospect of liberty."[28] From 1820 until 1838, however, a small number of prominent white southerners from Georgia, Alabama, and Mississippi showed support for the Liberian solution, even in the face of pervasive hostility from their peers. The growth and demise of the colonization movement in the Deep South clearly reflected major trends occurring in the late antebellum period, including the demographic shifts that created larger ratios of slaves to whites in the Deep South and the rising sectional tension over slavery. The financial deterioration of the organization's parent body and waning political support forced the ACS to give up its custodianship of Liberia in 1847, making Liberia an independent republic and the ACS strictly an emigration agency.

We should not, however, overlook the importance of the continuous existence of the ACS from 1817 into the 1890s and the consistent circulation of the society's *African Repository*, a journal that outlined and favorably reviewed the ongoing emigration to and development of Liberia. Reports of missionaries and of those black Americans who did immigrate to Liberia ignited a slow burning but steady interest in the minds of discontented and alienated blacks all over the South.

Throughout its antebellum career, the ACS drew a large proportion of its support from states in the upper South, where the free black population was greatest. But after the Compromise of 1820 defensive slaveholders came to associate colonization with abolitionism, and positive publicity for the ACS was suppressed during the late antebellum period.[29] The southern states rejected colonization and adopted strict manumission restrictions as a reaction to the growing free black class; however, through various means several thousand voluntarily emancipated slaves and free blacks managed to relocate to Liberia before 1860—1,200 from Georgia alone—keeping this dream of repatriation alive in the imaginations of other black Americans.[30] Ardor for emigration to Africa waned somewhat as black expectations rose during the Civil War and Reconstruction but rekindled during the political and economic backlash of white southern Redeemers.

Rising black expectations were short-lived in the southwest Georgia town of Camilla in Mitchell County, later to become a UNIA stronghold. In 1868, in one of the worst riots in Reconstruction history, white Democrats violently suppressed the local Republican voters, who favored a black candidate for congressman from the Second District. Nine freedmen were murdered and many more injured in Mitchell and neighboring Baker County.[31]

In an increasingly tense and violent atmosphere, predominantly poor black farmers from the South showed their broad, renewed interest in Africa and emigration in the early 1870s in a large body of correspondence to the feeble and underfunded ACS.[32] Turner and Blyden, a longtime resident of Liberia, traveled and spoke all over the United States as agents for the society, but some black leaders flatly rejected the idea of black Americans colonizing Liberia and heaped scorn on Turner for his position. In contrast, the literally thousands of letters of inquiry to the ACS indicate an enormous interest in emigration among black farmers in precisely the areas in which Garveyism flourished two to three decades later. For example, Reverend Levi Kilgo of Mitchell County, Georgia, wrote that conditions were so bad in 1898 that he was ready to take as many as possible to "our Fatherland Liberia." Eight Baptist farmers from Howell, Arkansas, later the seat of a UNIA division, similarly sent applications for settlement in Liberia.[33]

A large portion of these letters came in January after cotton had been picked and brought in for the year and discontent ran high over unfair settlements and debt. In most cases the handwriting and grammar were rudimentary, but evidently people were reading the *African Repository* and seeking more information about the specifics of qualifying as colonists and paying for transportation. Many explained how hard they worked and were willing to work. As Garvey would assert to all Negroes in the near future, J. J. Jackson of Lowndes County, Georgia, expressed it: "I feel that Africa is my home." Theodore Steele, a black teacher in Monroe County, Arkansas, sent an eloquent letter to the ACS secretary, William Coppinger, describing "the very uncomfortable situation we colored people are in at the present. . . . There seems not to be any power of resistance. . . . We are entirely dependent on the landlord. . . . Many of us have emigrated from older southern states to this country; but without gaining any advantage whatever." Attached to Steele's plea for assistance was an application for twenty farmers, two ministers, and himself, each of whom was prepared to pay ten to twenty dollars toward his passage to Liberia.[34]

Two other ministers in Monroe County, Arkansas, promoted and led emigration efforts through the ACS. Reverend G. W. Lowe of Holly Grove had his flock ready to go after the harvest of 1892, but they were disappointed when their schedule did not correspond to the required schedule of the ACS. Bishop Turner appointed A. L. Ridgel of the St. Paul AME Church of Brinkley to the AME Mission of Liberia. Ridgel raised money for his passage in his community with a donation form entitled, "Off to Africa." In language familiar in Garvey's rhetoric, Ridgel sought contributions, "hoping that your love for the redemption of our 'Father Land' " would support the carrying of "the blessed word to the heathen, who are now blinded by ignorance and superstition."[35] Two years later, in 1894, Ridgel wrote to the *Christian Recorder*, reporting the wonderful prospects he had encountered in the "master continent," Africa.[36]

Farmers in the Yazoo-Mississippi Delta sustained a strong interest in Liberia into the 1890s as well. Sarah Nicholson of Greenville wanted to be an agent for the ACS and assured Coppinger that many in her area would emigrate if they had applications and a contact. A. E. Ellis of Friar's Point in Coahoma County inquired about assistance with passage fees and hoped the ACS would "consider our case we are in a hard country [sic] to live. And if possible we want to go to Liberia."[37]

A man named E. J. Rozzell is a remarkable link between the nineteenth-century African colonization program of the ACS and Garvey's UNIA. In January 1893 he and his five children and several families from Riverside, Arkansas, had fled to New Orleans after enraged whites learned of their plans to immigrate to Liberia. He ended up getting only as far as Brunswick, Georgia, where three decades later he was an important organizer for the UNIA. Rozzell is remembered in Brunswick as a native of Arkansas who brought in strike-breakers for longshoremen and for having organized and led Mount Olive Church for over fifty years. He never made it to Liberia under ACS auspices, but he remained a community leader deeply interested in black community organization.[38]

Because farmers in the South became the keenest potential group seeking information and funding for emigration, it follows that Turner's influence with this group remained strong long after younger race spokesmen had repudiated his views. Edwin Redkey has argued that even in later phases of emigration, which coincided with the internal migration north, southern farmers showed a greater affinity for Liberia because their primary economic goal was not northern wages but African land.[39]

How much Garvey had studied the specifics of Turner's emigrationism and the African colonization movement in the United States is difficult to discern, but further study of Turner's views on other subjects suggests more than a coincidental relationship between the two men's ideologies. In 1883 Bishop Turner conducted an editorial debate with Frederick Douglass and northern AME bishop Benjamin Tanner in the *Christian Recorder*. Devising plans and strategies that are identical to several of Garvey's in the later period, Turner emphasized that racial prejudice occurred in all regions of the United States, not just the South. He argued that only a strong and independent African nation ruled by blacks could achieve self-respect for the race. And although Africa was the birthright and "fatherland" of all blacks, in practical terms wholesale emigration of African Americans was undesirable.[40] At other times, in a less contentious atmosphere, Turner framed the complete repatriation of the race as a sacred calling: "There is no more doubt in my mind that we have ultimately to return to Africa than there is of the existence of God. . . . Four millions of us in this country are at school, learning the doctrines of

Christianity and the elements of civil government. And as soon as we are educated sufficiently to assume control of our vast ancestral domain, we will hear the voice of a mysterious Providence, saying 'Return to the land of your fathers.' "[41]

As early as 1866, Turner had given speeches condemning white men for exploiting black women and corrupting their morals while also suggesting that he personally believed blacks and whites should marry within their own races.[42] His solution to lynching in 1897 required blacks to arm their homes for protection and self-defense, an idea Garveyites from the South would echo twenty-three years later. As the bishop wrote in the *Voice of Missions* editorial column, "We advise [the black man] to keep [his guns] loaded and prepared for immediate use, and when his domicile is invaded by bloody lynchers or any mob day or night, Sabbath or work day, turn loose your missiles of death and blow the fiendish wretches into a thousand giblets."[43]

Despite their philosophical similarities, notable differences beyond the separate times in which they flourished divided the two leaders. Turner showed more conciliation toward whites early in his career, whereas Garvey, increasingly under pressure from the U.S. government because of his notoriety as an alien agitator, showed his conciliation later.[44] In prison Garvey developed amicable relationships with Theodore Bilbo, Mississippi's U.S. senator, and Virginia's Earnest Sevier Cox, leader of the White America Society, the most virulent and powerful white supremacists of the age. Garvey also received a visit in prison from John Powell, leader of the Anglo-Saxon Clubs of America, and arranged for him to speak in UNIA's Liberty Hall in 1925.[45]

Turner served the Union army, the Georgia legislature, and the AME church very effectively. Garvey, the Jamaican publisher and race organizer, was neither an American nor a ranking politician or clergyman. This discrepancy mattered little to their shared constituency, which included numerous southern rural blacks who focused squarely on the meaning of race uplift programs to their own situations rather than on their leaders' personal difficulties with critics and opponents. Both men earned the designation "Black Moses" for what many conceived as their divine authority and mission.[46]

Turner by no means held a monopoly on interest in or action on behalf of African redemption before 1915. Supporters of the African mission movement of 1880–1915, which originated in the South, showed a strong commitment to the African homeland. Previous black Baptists in America had developed a theology that encouraged the uplift of African societies through missionary work. Their efforts went beyond conversion of individuals to the Christian faith and came to include christianizing and westernizing traditional African societies. Their contribution to social uplift would take the form of the spiritual and material redemption of Africa. The black Baptists of the National Baptist Convention and the Lott Carey Foreign Mission Convention, despite their organizational conflicts, held African redemption as their most vital common goal.[47]

The UNIA's early publications repeated these objectives. The first UNIA and African Communities League circular emanating from Jamaica in 1914 listed two of its ten general objectives as follows: "To assist in civilizing the backwards tribes of Africa, and To promote a conscientious Christian worship among the native tribes of Africa."[48] The UNIA constitution, written after the organization's incorporation in New York, included these same objectives, the second of which at some point changed the word "Christian" to "spiritual," perhaps indicating a growing sensitivity to African cultural traditions.[49] Garvey's adoption of this goal has prompted debates among those who have tried to refute the leader's eligibility to be considered a black nationalist.[50] Others have made the same claim against Turner's nationalism, arguing that both leaders relied on racial and geographical commonality rather than cultural similarities.[51] There is no doubt that Garvey believed modern and Western civilization had much to offer Africans, as did Turner, but Garvey consistently argued that the African "race" had already proved, in the age of the ancient Egyptians, its ability to succeed, innovate, and even dominate other races.[52] Most black missionary supporters thought of African societies and religions, including Islam, as inferior and inadequate for salvation, yet they maintained a strong identification with Africans based on race and conditions of oppression under colonial rule.[53] Mission groups interpreted Psalms 68:31— "Princes shall come forth from Egypt. Ethiopia shall soon stretch forth her hand unto God."—as a sign that African civilization would rise again after Africans had embraced Christianity. This biblical passage was also the most often quoted piece of Scripture among Garveyite organizers from the highest to the most local levels. According to the official UNIA catechism, the verse had a political meaning: "That Negroes will set up their own government in Africa, with rulers of their own race."[54]

Important similarities between Garveyism and the philosophy emerging from black mission congresses included the primacy of racial consciousness and economic independence. The African mission movement, which operated primarily within autonomous state conventions during the years 1880 through 1894, was particularly strong in Mississippi. Later, after segregation became safely codified after the *Plessy v. Ferguson* decision, membership in all-black institutions like the church took on new meaning as a symbol of race loyalty.[55] Deteriorating racial conditions in 1895 and after brought black Baptists together, and the importance of racial unity became a theme among state missionary movements.[56] Racial consciousness in the South, according to Garvey, resulted from the poor treatment and nonrecognition of blacks by whites. Segregation laws and their enforcement helped solidify black denominations and shaped the identities of black people of all classes along racial lines. Cynicism toward white missionaries in the American Baptist Missionary Union caused the black Baptists' foreign missions convention to refuse white financial aid. Despite their dire need for resources, black Baptists eschewed any obligations that might hinder their economic independence.[57] This impulse to avoid dependence on white philanthropy also formed an essential tenet of Garveyism throughout its existence.

Turner's abiding interest in Africa and his missionary travels throughout West Africa and South Africa to organize the AME church there, along with the influence of the black Baptist missionary efforts primarily in Liberia and Nigeria, had important consequences for the thought of rural southerners before 1915.[58] Turner's four journeys through Africa attracted much attention in the *Christian Recorder*, where he published detailed and glowing accounts of his experiences. Missionary zeal and interest in the Fatherland increased as Turner's success there became publicized and discussed in rural communities. Local AME pastors, many of whom had been ordained by Turner, involved their congregations in the bishop's exciting and sacred mission of African redemption.[59] Baptist missionaries from the Baptist state conventions traveled to and from the African continent, reporting to their communities in the United States about the needs and opportunities in Liberia and elsewhere. The Baptist mission publications took the news even further, into southern communities where no missionaries lived.

These simultaneous activities involving the AME and Baptist denominations focused on mission work, but many other African Americans who felt destined for their African Motherland had purely economic motives in emigration and colonization.[60] They envisioned Africa, and especially Liberia, as a place where they could be independent. Martin Delaney, an early proponent of black nationalism, formed the Liberian Exodus Joint Stock Steamship Company. The company purchased the *Azor* and transported 206 black South Carolinian and Georgian emigrants from Charleston to Liberia in 1877 on its first and only voyage to Africa. A few of these black southerners reportedly became prosperous farmers.[61] The success of this first all-black venture no doubt paved the way for other ambitious black enterprises in the Charleston area and throughout the South. Six years later, Turner urged anyone to begin steamship transportation from the South's largest ports to Africa and guaranteed their ships would be filled to capacity with willing emigrants.[62] He made this statement four years before Garvey was born, but the commercial opportunities for steamship operations between the United States and Africa still held a powerful appeal when Garvey implemented the Black Star Line as the primary vehicle for black economic power in 1917.

Turner's suggestions also had a deep impact in Phillips County, Arkansas, from which emerged the Liberian Exodus Arkansas Colony (LEAC), which held its first convention after the cotton harvest in 1877. Its members chose Anthony L. Stanford, the former publications manager of the AME church, to serve as commissioner and travel to Liberia to acquire land and transportation for the hopeful emigrants. After Stanford and another commissioner traveled to Liberia in 1878, they reported that Liberia had much to offer and engaged the American Colonization Society for financial assistance. As plans progressed, local Klansmen became infuriated at the local blacks' plan to emigrate and beat and pistol-whipped several of them.[63] Some Mississippi blacks just across the river in Coahoma County experienced a similarly violent reaction. A black pastor had reported to the ACS that a group of white men had severely whipped three of the seventy-two men in his emigration group and made his congregation afraid to meet at his church.[64] The Phillips County LEAC group persisted, however, and eventually fifty-five blacks from Helena, the county seat, and forty-nine from surrounding towns and rural areas embarked for the East Coast. Their motivations mirrored those espoused by Turner: Christian duty to civilize and uplift the Fatherland and an urge to be self-sufficient in their natural home.[65]

Although ultimately successful in getting to the Fatherland, the LEAC group did not get to Liberia without incident. The "Arkansas Refugees," as they became known in the *New York Evening News*, verged on starvation, with no money or lodging, while they awaited their ships for Liberia in the northeastern winter. Many of their group had died en route, and the rest suffered in appalling squalor.[66] Finally, in May 1880, with the assistance of the ACS, they reached Liberia and settled in. The trials along the way did not deter other Arkansans from wanting to emigrate. In fact, 1880 marked the beginning of decades of interest in Africa. In his study of Back-to-Africa movements in the period between 1890 and 1910, Edwin Redkey consistently cites Arkansas as a state with the most intense interest in colonization, especially among farmers in the Delta.[67] More recently, historian Kenneth Barnes has left little doubt that this was the case in his assiduously researched book on the generations of Arkansans who emigrated to Liberia.[68] In 1895 apparently 3,000 blacks from Arkansas were willing to emigrate but had no money to cover their expenses. Perhaps hoping for the assistance from the ACS given to the LEAC, these Arkansans sent the organization an average of twenty-five requests per month for aid.[69]

A similar series of events occurred in Georgia under the auspices of Benjamin Gaston and the Congo Company. Gaston, a black Georgia minister, had moved to Liberia in 1866, then returned to the United States in the 1880s and became an agent for the United States and Congo Emigration Company. This venture, which sold stock certificates in the company mainly to blacks in Georgia, settled a colony in Liberia in 1894. A series of tragic scenes like those of the "Arkansas Refugees" in New York repeated themselves as nearly 500 farmers from rural hamlets in Georgia converged on Atlanta hoping to get from there to Savannah for the voyage to Africa.[70] After three years of litigation and controversy involving Gaston's financial irregularities, logistics were finally arranged, and a fraction of the original group actually embarked for Liberia. Bishop Turner visited the emigrants the next year and discovered that eleven of the forty-two emigrants had died. Yet again, however, the Congo Company did not dim the prospect of emigration to Africa for many. Apparently, interest surged in subsequent years as it had after the Phillips County, Arkansas, venture.[71]

It is curious to imagine the outcome if farmers from the South seeking land had been able to emigrate to Liberia to the same extent that they deserted the South for northern wage work. Although many negative reports circulated about conditions in the African colonies, a sense of mission and racial identity prevailed. The expense and risk of transportation to Liberia seem to have been the only things preventing a concurrent "Great Emigration." Thousands of blacks from Louisiana, Mississippi, Texas, and Tennessee seeking land and independence had settled for a shorter trek as part of the "Exodusters" who left the South for Kansas in 1879.[72] This movement to the prairie even sparked the imaginations of the Knighton family of southwest Georgia. In 1922, the same year they began reading Garvey's *Negro World*, they named their baby daughter "Kansas."[73] During the same era, many who wanted separation from whites had established all-black towns like Mound Bayou, Mississippi, in Bolivar County and Greenough, Georgia, in Mitchell County, both strongholds of Garveyism in the 1920s.

Although Booker T. Washington showed interest in the development of African agriculture and the promotion of racial uplift in Africa, he never advocated emigration. His twenty years of dominance as spokesman for self-reliance and hard work among African Americans ended with his death in

November of 1915. People all over the world mourned his passing. He had gained the respect and admiration of people of all races, even southern whites, and he had used his prestige as Tuskegee's founder and principal and as an adviser to Presidents Theodore Roosevelt and William H. Taft to wield as much political power as any African American. On an educational speaking tour of Mississippi, which included a stop in the Delta town of Mound Bayou and one trans–Mississippi River visit to the Agricultural College at Helena, in Phillips County, Arkansas, Washington expounded the virtues of rural life that he felt would help achieve the important goals of self-sufficiency, home and land ownership, and even education. He believed that urban settings had provided a backdrop for black crime and vice, which had led to negative stereotyping of the race.[74] On 10 October 1908, he spoke to over 6,000 individuals at Mound Bayou, which he had invested much time and energy into promoting.[75] The crowd wore hats labeled "Booker T. Washington Day," and Washington reveled in the pride of a town in which he could see his ideal of economic self-sufficiency in practice.[76]

At the time he toured the Mississippi Delta in 1908, his fame as a race leader had no equal. He used his power and notoriety to instill pride and optimism in rural black farmers by reciting encouraging statistics on land ownership and agricultural expertise and productivity while generally avoiding mention of racial violence and mob rule. He subtly challenged receptive whites by applauding their high-mindedness and courage for recognizing the importance of Negro education and by quietly disagreeing with Governor James K. Vardaman, Mississippi's most vocal and unapologetic opponent of black education.[77]

His 1895 Atlanta Exposition address, in which he seemed to acquiesce to segregation and disfranchisement, had catapulted his career in the same year that Frederick Douglass's death had left a gaping hole in the ranks of African American leadership. Though some protest had arisen from the black intelligentsia over the accommodationist tone of the speech, the almost universal approval of whites paved the way for Washington to have real personal influence in Republican politics, especially through recommending certain blacks for appointments. Black nationalists beyond U.S. borders applauded the so-called Atlanta Compromise speech, and Edward Wilmot Blyden even remarked, in a letter of praise, that the simile Washington used of "races being as separate as fingers on a hand working for mutual progress" was an old African adage.[78]

White philanthropists readily contributed to Tuskegee and the causes that Washington recommended, and southern blacks of all classes admired him above all other black men.[79] The year the Tuskegean died, soon-to-be devoted Garveyites Ed and Patsy Glass in Indian Bay, Arkansas (Monroe County), named their sixth son Booker T.; naming trends indicate thousands of other black rural families did the same.[80] In another act of reverence, the parents of Booker Simmons, later the energetic UNIA president of Duncan, Arkansas, chose their son's given name in 1895, just weeks after the Atlanta address.[81]

When the "Wizard of Tuskegee" died, the personal grief among some southern black farmers resembled that of a death in the family. No nationally recognized leader waited in the wings who seemed to understand their reality and embody their hopes. Washington's debt-ridden, undereducated, perse-cuted rural admirers could not picture an urban intellectual leading them "up from slavery." They looked for someone like Washington who emphasized the solidarity and separation of the black race and who believed that blacks could succeed economically through their own thrift and diligence. To them, politi-cal and social equality seemed distant and secondary goals.

Tuskegee Institute, founded in 1881, profoundly affected the lives of black farmers, particularly those in areas adjacent to the east-central Alabama school. Even those who did not own their own land could appreciate the dedi-cation and success of Tuskegee in promoting economic improvement for black people. After 1900, Farmers' Institutes for blacks emphasizing im-proved agricultural techniques grew out of an early program of conferences at Tuskegee that had offered assistance to local farmers. Southwest Georgia farmers, within easy reach of Tuskegee, could participate at varying levels in the practical and informal services offered at the Farmers' Institutes, from one-day courses to winter short courses to full-time study of scientific agricul-tural methods. The thousands who attended these conferences paid nothing but were told to spread what they learned like missionaries.[82] Tuskegee pro-fessors, most notably the institute's legendary agricultural specialist George Washington Carver, visited these rural institutions to teach and encourage better farming methods.[83]

Carver made his most politically charged public appearance in the midst of Garvey's most successful year. In 1922, the same year in which Congress debated the Dyer antilynching bill, Carver appeared before the U.S. House Ways and Means Committee to advocate for a protective tariff on imported peanuts to assist and encourage American peanut cultivation. The tenant farmers of southwest Georgia and even those in Arkansas and Mississippi could not choose to cultivate peanuts over cotton, the perennial cash crop, but they could see the logic in crop diversification, especially to a crop like peanuts with so many practical and dietary uses. Carver's extension work became a priority, and those in the immediate areas of Alabama and Georgia felt the greatest impact. He spoke at churches to illiterate farmers and wrote extensively for several newspapers like the *Negro Farmer*, the *Tuskegee Messenger*, and the *Tuskegee Student*, which circulated to varying degrees around the South.[84] Beginning in 1906, through Carver's initiative, the Jesup Wagon, a traveling school, visited farmers who could not leave home.[85]

In 1922 Mitchell County became a hotbed of Garveyism in southwest Georgia and also a mecca for black farmers wanting to improve their farming practices and to enhance the value of their property (if they owned any). The Negro Vocational Training School, which emphasized agriculture, opened with the contributions from the Julius Rosenwald Colored School Building Fund, the Smith-Hughes Fund for agricultural training, the city of Pelham, and the Mitchell County Board of Education.[86] These schools grew out of the Tuskegee legacy and provided a forum for farmers to organize. In 1924 an important "colored farmers conference" brought together 500 black farmers, only a fraction of the 10,000 in Mitchell County who showed support for the UNIA program in 1922.[87]

We do not know exactly when Garvey became aware of Booker T. Washington, but we know that Garvey read Washington's autobiography, *Up From Slavery*, while he lived in London between 1912 and 1914.[88] This literary classic, which has influenced generations of readers, apparently had a profound effect on the twenty-five-year-old Garvey. He began to see himself as the person who would lead blacks to nationhood.[89]

These important, intellectually stimulating years in London brought Garvey in close contact with Duse Mohammed Ali, editor of the *African Times and Orient Review*, an international newsletter from the African perspective. About the same time that Garvey arrived in London and began working at the publication's office, its editor provided positive coverage of Washington's International Conference of the Negro at Tuskegee. This event may have sparked Garvey's interest in Washington and prompted him to read the autobiography, which apparently set his life's course. Jamaicans at the conference had been encouraged to set up schools based on the Tuskegee model and to invite Washington to speak around the island as an adviser.[90] The conference's initiatives, combined with the virtues of self-help and economic independence found throughout Washington's book, served as models of popular strategy. The respect that Duse Mohammed Ali and African nationalists such as Edward Wilmot Blyden and Casely Hayford, founder of the National Congress of British West Africa, showed for Washington likely reinforced Garvey's attraction to these values and their applicability to blacks worldwide.[91]

Garvey wrote to Washington several times after founding the Universal Negro Improvement Association and African Communities League in Jamaica on 1 August 1914. He sent Tuskegee's principal the organization's circular appeal and asked to receive any Tuskegee publications in exchange for weekly issues of the incipient *Negro World.* The *Tuskegee Student,* the most likely journal sent to Garvey in such an exchange, featured Washington's transcribed Sunday evening talks.[92]

At this early stage, Garvey surely had no idea that he might assume Washington's role as leader of African Americans, especially in the South, which he had not yet visited. Yet his ideology and strategies clearly emerged from a conscious emulation of Washington's successful methods. Especially striking is how Garvey reproduced the format of Washington's meetings for Tuskegee students and faculty and followed them with exact transcriptions of his talks for his admirers in other parts of the country. Garvey not only set up local UNIA divisions for Sunday afternoon meetings, but he also printed verbatim his Liberty Hall addresses in the pages of the UNIA's organ, the *Negro World.* His international convention of the Negro Peoples of the World in 1920 had a much bolder agenda than Washington's 1912 conference, but with the end of World War I and deteriorating race relations in the United States, especially in the riot-torn year of 1919, conditions had drastically changed.

Washington possessed enormous control over the black press, which in turn enhanced his power among the members of his race. His influence and investment in assorted papers made opposition to the Tuskegee machine foolhardy, especially in the South. Garvey, too, recognized the press's potential for influencing thought. He made the production and editorial control of the *Negro World* his highest priority. In its pages he echoed Washington's emphasis on self-reliance, economic independence, and even social separatism.

Washington's cordial yet tepid response to Garvey's early solicitations puts the Jamaican's relative insignificance in 1914–15 in bold relief. In his efforts to raise money for the UNIA and African Communities League in Jamaica, Garvey planned a speaking tour in the United States. He had secured an invitation to visit Tuskegee and wrote back eagerly that he hoped to "do most of my public speaking in the South among the people of our race."[93] This plan indicated the UNIA leader's very early interest in and recognition of the importance of the southern region. Before Garvey made it to the United States, however, Washington died. The Jamaica UNIA held a memorial meeting in honor of Tuskegee's founder on 24 November 1915. Garvey recounted in detail the leader's rise from slavery to greatness: "Washington has raised the dignity and manhood of his race to midway, and it is now left to those with fine ideals who have felt this influence to lead the race on to the highest height in the adopted civilization of the age. He was the man for America."[94]

The Tuskegean's death opened a window of opportunity to all would-be race leaders. Others poised to take the mantle showed the proper respect for the deceased inventor of the Tuskegee machine, and then the void filled with competing heirs apparent. W. E. B. Du Bois, whom Garvey acknowledged as an influential voice on the international black scene, was nevertheless an uncompromising intellectual, committed to civil and political equality in America. Like Washington, Du Bois was willing to cooperate with white liberals and philanthropists to advance his objectives. But as Garvey soon discovered, Washington's goals of black economic independence and social separation still held wide appeal, especially in the South, while Du Bois, the NAACP, and the black socialists were more inclined toward cooperative efforts between the races. They had already set a new course for agitation, and now, in the absence of Washington's resistance, they could pursue it among the Tuskegean's former constituency. Leaders in the Du Bois camp emphasized the new strategy's merits and urged black people to abandon the so-called accommodationist, separatist model. In a five-year period between 1915 and 1920, the emerging "New Negro" rose fully from the ashes of the Tuskegee machine and the trenches of World War I; now, he would have to choose which program to promote with his newfound assertiveness.

When Garvey arrived in the United States for the first time, it was 24 March 1916. Instead of starting in the South as he had originally planned, he spoke in New York, Boston, Washington, Philadelphia, Chicago, Milwaukee, St. Louis, Detroit, Cleveland, Cincinnati, Indianapolis, and Louisville before ever speaking in the former Confederate states. His earliest appearances south of the Mason-Dixon Line took place in Nashville and then in Atlanta in March 1917. By 2 July 1918, the Universal Negro Improvement Association had been incorporated by the state of New York.[95] It had taken him less than two years to determine that race leadership actually might be within his grasp, and he judiciously reestablished his headquarters in Harlem. It would take him another two years to realize that much of America's urban black leadership did not accept him as the new spokesman of the race or agree with his tactics. Another year would elapse before Garvey became clearly conscious that the strongest and most loyal constituency for his personal leadership was to be found among southerners who had recently arrived in cities or remained in hard-to-reach rural areas.

The year immediately after the war brought new elements of strategy into play. Vocal protest about the mistreatment of black veterans and laborers and growing interest in Pan-African organization offered opportunities for publishers, editors, and orators to establish themselves with various black constituencies. Predominantly urban riots indicated a rising militancy among blacks in American cities. Some of Washington's rural supporters had only local leaders, usually their ministers. But they still looked for appropriate national leadership and, in the new, postwar context, even international leadership.

Garvey recognized an opportunity to succeed Washington in the Black Belt. His strategies squared with previous leaders of influence, although with important differences. He refused white ownership, investment, and philanthropy, which could attach strings to the fortunes of black business enterprise. Furthermore, the southern whites with whom he chose to negotiate in paving his way into the region were not the paternalistic and relatively moderate whites of Washington's liking, but the most notorious white supremacists of the day, especially the Klan's Edward Young Clarke. These risky associations scarred his reputation with most of black America's urban leadership. After Garvey's 1922 summit with Clarke in Atlanta, several prominent leaders in New York began the "Garvey Must Go" campaign. Months later, in a notorious letter to the attorney general condemning Garvey and seeking the government's aid in restraining him, Robert Abbott, Walter White, William Pickens, Robert Bagnall, Chandler Owen, and others wrote, "The UNIA is composed chiefly of the most primitive and ignorant West Indian and American Negroes. The so-called responsible element of the movement are largely ministers without churches, physicians without patients, lawyers without clients, and publishers without readers who are usually in search of 'easy money.' In short, this organization is composed in the main of Negro sharks and ignorant fanatics."[96] This statement offended Garvey and his devoted followers. To them it seemed their ideology was equated with insanity and ignorance as opposed to a conviction more in line with their circumstances.

Facing the opposition of many black leaders in the urban North and escalating scrutiny by the U.S. government, the movement was in trouble. Without the approval of outspoken race leaders who controlled opinion in most of the black papers of the day, and under an impending government crackdown on UNIA organization, fund-raising, and leadership, the Garvey movement in America was doomed. But until its founder finally shipped out for Jamaica on 2 December 1927, devotion to his leadership remained steadfast in the rural South.

Hundreds of letters and petitions from rural Arkansas, Mississippi, Louisiana, and Georgia acknowledging Garvey as "our only leader" or "the leader of our race" reached the files of the president, the attorney general, and the pardon attorney of the United States. A letter and signed petition arrived at the attorney general's office in June 1927 from Deeson, Mississippi, a tiny Bolivar County community just north of Mound Bayou:

> Your petitioners on behalf of the thousands of members of the universal negro improvement association in miss, do umbley request of his excellency, calvin coolidge, the release without deportation of the hon, marcus garvey, if he unknowingly transgresses against the laws of your grate country, his confinement has been long enough. . . . [T]he early release of the hon, marcus garvey will be an accomplished fact, thus causing god's eternal blessing on your country, and your petitioners in duty ever pray.[97]

Not only does this plea show that these UNIA members thought of the United States as "the white man's country" and not their own, but it also reveals the spiritual nature of their attachment to Garvey. Although some called Booker T. Washington the Black Moses for his role as a national guide of African Americans, he remained a secular leader whose power lay in his political influence with whites.[98] The local spokesmen for black communities in the South were ministers, and so were many of Garvey's most successful southern organizers. The UNIA leader must have listened carefully to their advice and adopted useful strategies to attract a significant rural and southern following.[99]

In 1926 75 percent of all black churches in America were in rural areas and had an average of ninety-one members. Urban black churches averaged only 220 members during this same period. Sixty-one percent of all black church members were Baptists, while nearly 20 percent were affiliated with the African Methodist Episcopal or African Methodist Episcopal Zion churches. Bishop George Alexander McGuire, the most influential UNIA chaplain general, developed the separate black African Orthodox Church during the UNIA's heyday, but in 1926 it had only 2,300 total members in thirteen congregations, all in urban areas outside the South.[100]

Garvey understood the influence of the black churches and their pastors in both the sacred and the secular realm, and as Randall Burkett has argued, Garvey fashioned the UNIA into a civil religion, replete with explanations of the roles that black people were to play in carrying out God's purposes. In articulating this purpose and promoting racial self-consciousness, Garvey called a black nation into being.[101] In this way, Garveyism supplemented the economic emphasis of the Tuskegee program and outmatched strictly secular groups like the NAACP and the black socialists. Garvey may have realized that if his movement had a sacred urgency, devotion to it naturally would be a lifelong commitment based on faith. This recognition of the primacy of the church as the spiritual and organizing center of the black community emerged again during the 1950s with the modern civil rights movement.[102]

The ardor for emigration and support for missionary work had deep roots along the banks of the Mississippi River in both Mississippi and especially Arkansas but also in Turner's home state of Georgia. Farmers seeking economic improvement through land ownership, devout Christians with strong racial identification with Africans and a desire to redeem them, and black nationalists with political ambitions for Africans to control Africa could all be found in the rural South before the arrival of Marcus Garvey. Booker T. Washington had taken leadership into the secular realm and applied the self-sufficiency and independence he advocated among farmers to the urban setting through the National Negro Business League. Washington had vast influence with ordinary African Americans because of his personal achievements, but possibly more so through his influence over black journalists. His stature as a strong and practical leader, combined with his censorship capabilities over much of the black press, allowed his challengers little space. His success provided a model for Garvey, whose appearance on the scene coincided with a serious leadership vacuum in the rural South with the deaths of Washington and Turner. The ideologies were in place awaiting a new leader with the right combination of charisma and vision to spread them through the ubiquitous print media. In the *Negro World* Garvey managed to reach out to this significant proportion of the African American population. Enough of his themes were familiar to attract a following of farmers, while his methods and strategies acknowledged the realities of the modern world, a world that began to break up the norms of rural life in the 1920s.

Even if the "Yarmouth" had gone down in that storm last January,
the Black Star Line would have been a success; because it would have
demonstrated the ability of the Negro to get together.
—William Henry Ferris, 21 April 1920

Marcus Garvey traveled, read, and listened prodigiously and possessed a remarkable learning curve for organization and politics. The strategies and ideas he learned from Booker T. Washington, Henry McNeal Turner, and others with a southern perspective provided a model of leadership but did not give him the ability to go into any community he wanted to organize the UNIA. In the South, especially, he began in urban areas. In cities the *Negro World* could circulate more readily, and his organizers could gather large crowds with less difficulty. Large urban churches or auditoriums frequently hosted speakers, and someone with the oratorical gifts of Garvey could pull a crowd any night of the week. The UNIA started in this way very quickly in several urban areas of the South in 1919 and 1920, and some of the difficult lessons learned there influenced the later, more carefully planned rhetoric and tactics that carried the Garvey message and program deep into the rural South. Examining this early period and the mistakes and problems the UNIA confronted south of the Mason-Dixon Line helps to explain some of Garvey's controversial tactics.

Two factors that made the South distinctive in the United States were segregation by custom and law and the high proportion of black population. The latter factor made the South the most attractive area in the country in which to organize blacks, while the former made it the most difficult to organize in the face of any white opposition. Segregation did not hinder race organization per se; it actually helped in a logistical sense. Separate black institutions, namely, black churches, fraternal orders, and lodges, provided ready forums for spreading the message. But the white supremacist disposition underpinning the Jim Crow system prohibited any assertiveness by organized blacks. Attempts to organize laborers of any race, especially in the same field or trade, were usually seen as a radical threat. The Red Scare at the federal level and the antilabor sentiment of the South during the interwar period exacerbated this tension. Thus, efforts to organize laboring blacks, even if only as a racially segregated group, presented a double threat to the status quo. Most UNIA promoters recognized early this extreme challenge to their plans. Some early participants, however, paid the price for failing to convince hostile whites or accommodationist blacks that the UNIA was neither an alien-dominated radical movement bent on overthrowing capitalism nor a civil rights organization committed to racial amalgamation.

Most urban southern UNIA divisions shared certain socioeconomic characteristics, and members of these groups tended to be workers and laborers in large industrialized towns, mainly along the Atlantic or Gulf Coasts. In eastern Virginia, New Orleans, Charleston, South Carolina, Mobile, Alabama, and Jacksonville, Florida, most Garveyites were longshoremen, shipbuilders, navy yard workers, or laborers. In Miami, Key West, and Tampa many were Bahamian and West Indian immigrants. In the interior urban areas UNIA activists worked in the tobacco industry of North Carolina or the lumber industry of Louisiana. Railroad workers, usually in the menial positions of locomotive firemen, were also affiliated with UNIA divisions throughout the Deep South.

These urban Garveyites of the South believed in race pride, but they were also deeply attracted to the internationalist and capitalist focus of the UNIA and Black Star Line (BSL). They lived in white-controlled, legally segregated cities and worked the same jobs as whites for lower wages. In cities where black enterprise within the segregated system had yielded wealth for black businessmen, Garveyites recognized how valuable independence from white control could be for their ability to control their own lives. Their hard labor had supported U.S. industries during wartime, and many workers understood the exploitative forces of world industrial capitalism for the first time. But in the years immediately after World War I they did not necessarily see capital as their exploiter as much as they did their better-paid white cohorts and white bosses.

Urban and industrial workers depended on white employers for their livelihoods. They needed jobs and had to accept wages far below those of white workers and too low to provide a decent existence for their families. They saw organization by race as a useful tool for leverage not only against capital but also within labor organizations. They liked the idea of working for and investing in black-owned enterprises, where they presumed they would receive better treatment and share in the profits of their labor. Blacks' participation in the war industries and on the battlefields had proved beyond doubt that they were the equals of whites, and like other blacks in America, they enthusiastically rejected the idea of black inferiority. However, the racial tension at home that followed the war abroad disillusioned black Americans. They had heard and digested Woodrow Wilson's rhetorical flourishes about the self-determination of nations and then turned to Garvey's vision of Africa as the home and birthright of the African.

The themes stressed by the nascent UNIA in its earliest organized segments of the black southern population foreshadowed the fundamental strands of ideology that carried the movement all over the region. Yet early mistakes in the South led to new strategies for Marcus Garvey and his organizers.

Organizing in Virginia

The busy port communities and towns around Hampton Roads, Virginia, hosted the earliest UNIA divisions south of the Mason-Dixon Line. Hampton Institute, the first and most important black industrial and agricultural school and Booker T. Washington's alma mater, resided on the long peninsula that protruded near the mouth of the Chesapeake Bay. Newport News had been created in the 1880s as a terminus for the Chesapeake and Ohio Railroad, to serve as the feeder for the coalfields of West Virginia to the massive expansion of steamship operations along the Atlantic seaboard. Accordingly, Newport News and the surrounding peninsular area became a hive of activity during and after World War I. During the war, Newport News also served as a primary port of embarkation for American soldiers and supplies going to Europe. In 1917 the population more than doubled in a few months from 24,000 to 60,000.

Workers, and especially black workers, from all over the South flocked to the area to fill important industrial support jobs. Many worked as longshoremen or labored in the U.S. Navy yards and on the railroads. Others worked in building trades spurred on by wartime expansion of the local community. Many blacks joined labor unions that were officially sanctioned and protected by the U.S. government and the National War Labor Board during wartime. After the war, Newport News became the primary port of debarkation. As soldiers returned and industrial work slowed, racial tensions rose in eastern Virginia. A special representative's report to the Camp Community Service Bureau warned of the potential for a race war because of conflicts between disgruntled black laborers and demobilized soldiers and local whites who were not willing to accept any inkling of social equality for blacks.[1]

In July 1919 Garvey spent fourteen days in Virginia, spearheading the organization of the divisions in Newport News and neighboring Portsmouth. Newport News received the sixth charter issued by the parent body of the UNIA, and the first shares of Black Star Line stock were sold at a mass meeting in the Dixie Theater.[2] These bustling centers of longshoremen, many of whom were recent arrivals from other parts of the South, took a keen interest in the formation of the Black Star Line as a natural outgrowth of their involvement in maritime trades. The impending sailing of the BSL's first ship, the SS *Frederick Douglass* (formerly the *Yarmouth*), set for 31 October 1919, brought excitement in the Chesapeake Bay area to a fever pitch. Estimates of UNIA membership for July through October 1919 for the Newport News branch alone ranged from 5,000 to 7,000. Garvey estimated that the Newport News division had 7,000 members while the New York division had only 7,500, making the former easily the second-largest branch. During these early months, contributions of up to $10,000 toward the BSL came from the Hampton Roads area.[3]

In 1910 blacks in Norfolk had formed the Transportation Workers' Association of Virginia, and during the war it joined the International Longshoremen's Association (ILA). Of the 9,000 members of the ILA in the Hampton Roads area, 6,000 were black. Because of these numbers, black union members dominated the organization, but the locals were always segregated. This was not only due to southern traditions of segregation, but also, as one investigator reported, because of a continuous preference for separation by the black longshoremen themselves.[4]

Some race consciousness and desire for separate organizations came not through custom or preference but through a process of struggle. Portsmouth, home to a major U.S. Navy yard, and its surrounding community were already deeply involved in labor organization when the UNIA arrived. Unequal access to jobs and unequal pay for blacks were sources of resentment among black workers there.[5] Through their local organizations some laborers belonged to the American Federation of Labor (AFL), though they were acutely frustrated with its discriminatory practices. A black-only labor organization, essentially for southern blacks, called the National Brotherhood Workers of America, founded in the District of Columbia in March 1919, had already established branches in the Hampton Roads area, as well as in other industrialized towns of the South. The Portsmouth members included caulkers, riveters, corkers, blacksmith helpers, and various unskilled laborers. This all-black organization helped to provide leverage with the AFL leadership, as the labor federation considered the demands of blacks for better representation in the group.[6] Laborers' negative experiences in class-conscious organizations demonstrated unceasing discrimination based on race and pointed them toward a specifically racial consciousness. In this sense, the black laborers of eastern Virginia were well prepared to receive the Garvey message of racial solidarity.

Garvey was delighted with the response of the Virginia UNIA supporters and returned for a mass meeting of the local division at the First Baptist Church of Newport News just before the end of October. He covered the crucial rallying points of the UNIA program—Africa for the Africans, freedom from dependence on whites, defense (by violence if necessary) of one's family and property, and lastly the importance of supporting Negro enterprises such as the BSL. He also sought further contributions to launch the maiden voyage of the BSL.[7] He felt enthusiastic about his return visit and reported to the *Negro World*, "the Negro of the South is a new and different man to what he was prior to the war. . . . The New Negro Manhood Movement is not confined to the North alone."[8]

The *Frederick Douglass* finally sailed in November 1919 and eventually reached the mouth of the Chesapeake to take on supplies at Norfolk but more importantly to provide inspiration for two of its important shareholding constituencies, the Newport News and Portsmouth local UNIA divisions. The enthusiasm generated by the steamship in the local black community compelled further interest in the activities of the UNIA and its leader. The psychological impact of seeing the nearly 1,500-ton steamship sailing through Hampton Roads, flying the red, black, and green flag of the black nationhood espoused by Garvey, probably cannot be overestimated.[9]

By February 1920, an African American agent of the U.S. Bureau of Investigation (the precursor to the FBI) had infiltrated the local division and reported that Garvey's African Legion, the paramilitary wing of the organization, had 200 men of the Newport News division drilling every Thursday night in the local Elks Hall.[10] The attention of federal authorities gives an indication of how Garvey was being viewed as a potentially dangerous agitator; local whites had also begun to notice the growing organization, and some formed objections to the movement as well. The Klan had started to create problems for UNIA organizers in the area by March 1920, and one New York visitor had been forced to leave town because of intimidation by the Invisible Empire's locals.[11] Even the *Newport News Star*, a black newspaper, had initiated a drumbeat of editorial criticism of the UNIA and BSL.[12] At the same time, Garvey and the UNIA received a mix of favorable publicity and criticism in P. B. Young's *Norfolk Journal and Guide*, a substantial African American paper that enjoyed contributions from the venerated editorialist T. Thomas Fortune. Historian Earl Lewis has argued that the Norfolk area suffered from class divisions between laborers who gravitated toward the UNIA and more prosperous elements who affiliated with other organizations, despite the fact that their ultimate goals remained very closely related.[13]

In early August 1920 the UNIA held its first annual convention in New York.

By all accounts, no spectacle before or since in Harlem matched the parade given in honor of the international gathering of UNIA delegates. The UNIA African Legions led the way in lockstep in their dark uniforms, followed by 200 Black Cross Nurses dressed all in white. Then the UNIA band preceded delegates with banners from twenty-five countries and numerous states as the procession made its way down Lenox Avenue. Enthusiastic cheers rang out as thousands of appreciative onlookers enjoyed the spectacle, the uniforms, the music, and the motorcade of 500 automobiles.[14] News of the parade and the discussions and speeches of the convention appeared throughout the black press. People far and wide read accounts of the stirring display of black unity and pride. As much as any event in Garvey's career, this day catapulted his movement into the wider public eye.

Only weeks before this momentous event, Garvey had returned to Virginia on an extensive speaking tour through the eastern part of the state, visiting Richmond, Petersburg, Suffolk, Franklin, Smithfield, Backwater, Oyster Point, Mundon Point, Tidewater, Newport News, and Norfolk over the course of two weeks in July.[15] The Norfolk division had grown and gained some prominence in early 1920. Local delegates' comments to the convention indicated that there the Garvey movement was flourishing despite some intermittent opposition. One Norfolk Garveyite reported that conditions for blacks in the city were regarded as relatively good compared with those in other parts of the South. Local whites had shown restraint in their criticism of blacks, and a local white paper had called the *Frederick Douglass*'s appearance at Hampton Roads "one of the grandest events that ever happened in the Negro race."[16]

An important lesson the UNIA organizers learned from this early experience in Virginia was that ministers had to approve the movement in places where they were powerful spokesmen for the community. Garvey spelled this out in a handbook for UNIA organizers: "When approaching ministers of the gospel, be always diplomatic enough to convince them of the Christian policy of the organization." He went on to explain that once the minister was on board, one could ask to raise money from his congregation and promise to give him a share of the collection for his church "if the preacher is won over and himself contributes."[17] Any problems Virginia organizers had faced, apparently, stemmed from vigorous objections by local black preachers. A vocal delegate from Norfolk was one of only a few local pastors who supported the movement in his community. It is unclear what their specific objections were, but references were made to the black community's having a choice between "two ways," one of which was the UNIA way.[18]

A delegate from Newport News complained to the UNIA convention in 1920 that one preacher had canceled a UNIA meeting at his church on short notice. The convention laughed upon hearing that the preacher's church had burned down the next day. Apparently, the sudden cancellation resulted from pressure brought to bear by other pastors who believed the UNIA was trying to "take all the money from the town." Another churchman complained about the UNIA to the mayor, who showed little interest in suppressing the movement there. This sort of tacit white approval was not so much an endorsement of the movement as an indication that it was not seen as important or threatening by whites in authority in some localities.[19]

The local Garveyites also complained bitterly about the double standards in education, employment, and restrictions on mingling with whites while "white people won't leave our girls alone." These specific complaints, especially those regarding the exploitation of black women, echoed again and again among southern Garveyites. The social independence they sought was directly related to this problem.[20]

The vast amount of money that Garvey was able to raise during the second half of 1919 and the first half of 1920 did not go unnoticed. His success and popularity generated lots of suspicion, and investigations and exposés followed. The Chicago-based *Defender*, the widest circulating black weekly in the nation, published a damaging report on 20 September 1919, which accused Garvey of falsely representing the Black Star Line as a legitimate, responsibly run shipping line.[21] The bad news devastated the Garveyites of the lower peninsula. Over a thousand people demanded an explanation of the facts from the local BSL stock salesperson, and the Portsmouth division of the UNIA dropped from a membership of 600 before the *Defender* article to 150 after.[22] On the heels of this report, the Bureau of Investigation stepped up its surveillance of the stock sales of the BSL, which turned out to be illegal because the corporation had not been licensed to sell stock in Virginia. As of 3 January 1921, Virginia officials were directed to deny a license to the BSL and to arrest Garvey if he returned to the state.[23] Captain E. L. Gaines, the UNIA minister of legions, one of Garvey's most active organizers in Virginia during 1921, reported that he faced continual harassment as he traveled through the state speaking to and organizing more communities for UNIA membership.[24]

The positive interest in the UNIA program, as well as the objections to and negative remarks about it from various community members in eastern Virginia, the earliest hotbed of southern Garveyism, are representative of the UNIA experience in many communities in the South. Southern black industrial workers were frustrated with job and wage discrimination based on their race. They recognized that organization along racial lines was crucial to providing the leverage they needed to improve their status and pay. Black ministers held alternative positions on the benefits of the UNIA and split communities by their divided leadership. Black families resented white men's exploiting black women and girls while enforcing a double standard where race intermingling was concerned. Yet above all other aspects of the UNIA platform, the Black Star Line and its promise for providing self-respect and better jobs and investment opportunities for blacks were essential to Garvey's early success in the Chesapeake region.[25] Later in the course of the Garvey movement, the BSL's failure would bring other aspects of the UNIA program to the forefront. These new emphases attracted constituencies with priorities not necessarily related to the modern world of stocks and investments but very much concerned with black economic and social autonomy.

Radicalism in Florida

While the Black Star Line electrified eastern Virginia's Garveyites, another distinctive segment of supporters formed in the farthest southern reaches of Florida. Although the peninsula's geography and demography make it unique in the region, its commitment to the Jim Crow system aligns it clearly with the southern states. And of all the states in the South, Florida had the largest documentable UNIA membership in the organization's twilight period from 1927 to 1928.[26] Early Floridian UNIA supporters were for the most part West Indian and, particularly, Bahamian. The large divisions in Miami and Key West hosted a vast majority of alien members and faced consistent resistance from native black and white Floridians. In his classic account of West Indian immigration to the United States in the early twentieth century, Ira DeA. Reid describes the multiple dilemmas of the black immigrant to the South.[27] The coastal Florida UNIA divisions had obvious ties to maritime interests, including the U.S. Navy, just as their laboring counterparts in Virginia did, but their activities created great fear among local whites and prompted close surveillance of Garveyites by federal authorities. The rhetoric of their meetings expressed deep-seated hostility toward American whites and the discriminatory practices of the U.S. government. Tension simmered consistently over the treatment of their leaders and organizations, putting local whites on constant alert for rioting.

Florida served as a gateway to the West Indies during the 1910s and 1920s, and immigration from the Bahamas, Cuba, Jamaica, and other Caribbean islands had increased as a result of the activities of the United Fruit Company. "Banana boats" brought steamship passengers to and from the West Indies in increasing numbers from 1904 into the 1920s. Most moved to New York, but a sizable expatriate community settled in South Florida, too. Black British citizens from the West Indies immigrated to the United States at a rate averaging from 3,000 to 7,000 a year during the 1910s.[28] Most of the black alien population of Florida had British citizenship, as did Garvey. Of the 10,000 blacks in Miami in 1920, 7,000 were West Indian. They resented the restrictions on their movement within the segregated southern society.[29] Part of their difficulty in adjusting to life in Florida's coastal cities stemmed from their unfamiliarity with the American racial system. Although caste considerations placed black West Indians in an inferior position in their home islands, their populations were not dominated by a majority of whites. In their new arrangement, they were in the minority and at the lowest level of society simultaneously, while also being aliens without the rights of citizenship. Some found southern whites to be rude and barbaric compared with the more formal and polite Europeans from the Caribbean islands.[30] The brutality of blacks' treatment in Florida shocked West Indian immigrants and quickly ended their expectations of a better life abroad. Conditions were largely intolerable for the Caribbean expatriates, and the UNIA provided a platform for their frustrations.[31] Others moved North or returned to their home islands.

As in other states in the South, the first evidence of UNIA presence in Florida came in the form of complaints to federal authorities over the content of the *Negro World*. Frank Burke, the assistant director of the Bureau of Investigation division in Jacksonville, received one such complaint in August 1919. A Cocoa, Florida, man had been distributing copies of the Garvey newspaper and "causing a great deal of unrest among the negroes [sic] in this section and particularly those [n]egroes who are trying to find some grievance against white people." Special Agent Treadway added to this independent complaint that sales of BSL stock were likely fraudulent and designed to fleece vulnerable local blacks.[32]

Nevertheless, by the end of 1920, the UNIA had a large, radical division in Miami. The English Wesleyan Church in Miami served as the host for the founding of the Miami division. The organizational meeting, composed of mainly West Indians, heard an address by a "fiery" Haitian-born medical doctor from West Palm Beach.[33] After the initial meeting, the branch began meeting each Sunday at Walker's Memorial AME Zion Church. The resident pastor, N. J. Conquest, had recently arrived from Los Angeles and was an ardent Garvey supporter. Percy Styles, a local businessman, served as regional organizer for South Florida. The Miami UNIA had 400 members by November 1920, 600 by March 1921, and 1,000 by July 1921.[34] Bureau of Investigation reports recorded the subjects covered at early meetings, which included many ideas not normally associated with Garveyism. Speakers here promoted equality and eventually supremacy of blacks and advocated intermarriage between races. The local division leased the Airdome building in the black section of town and posted a "UNIA MIAMI BRANCH" sign. The parent body suggested that each local division create its own "Liberty Hall," or UNIA meeting location, and the Miami group apparently had the resources to afford a nice gathering place, a film projector, and new benches. Successful gatherings each Sunday yielded an average of twenty-five dollars for *Negro World* newspapers, BSL stock, UNIA paraphernalia, and dues.[35]

A Bahamian UNIA member named James Nimmo, who was also a U.S. Army veteran of World War I, led regular drills for nearly 200 African Legion members in Miami on a regular basis. They wore the uniforms provided by headquarters in Harlem, which were navy blue with red stripes running down the leg sides. Although the men owned rifles, they usually drilled with wooden models of rifles; nevertheless, the police became hostile and broke them up frequently.[36]

These "armed" exercises drew constant covert attention from federal authorities. After Special Agent William Sausele witnessed the radicalism of the Miami Garveyites, upon returning to Jacksonville he felt compelled to canvass the black community there to determine the extent to which its members were armed. His calculations bore out his paranoid suspicions, with an estimate of 90 percent.[37] This discovery should not have surprised the agent, given that nearly 4,000 members of the Jacksonville Ku Klux Klan participated in a nighttime parade with robes, a burning cross, and banners reading "We were here Yesterday, We are here Forever" only six months before.[38] This display of white militancy had terrorized local blacks into arming themselves and banding together for self-defense in several divisions of the UNIA.[39]

West Indian and Bahamian blacks comprised the vast majority of the Key West UNIA division. Many worked at the U.S. Naval Station and resented their poor treatment by their employer. T. C. Glashen, a British Honduran, led the local group and provided some of its most incendiary rhetoric, promising to spill blood if necessary to achieve recognition of Negro rights.[40] Garvey spoke two nights to the Key West division in February 1921 while en route to the West Indies. His presence boosted the growth of the division from 300 to over 690. His speeches encouraged economic independence and promoted stock sales in the BSL. The community adhered to this message by operating a UNIA cooperative bakery and delivery wagon while investing heavily in the new steamship enterprise.[41]

By the summer of 1921, local whites, native blacks, and federal authorities had all attempted to eradicate the Garvey movement from South Florida. "Loyal [black] citizens," including one named George Washington, had written to U.S. attorney general Harry M. Daugherty complaining of the radical alien element that monopolized civil service jobs at the U.S. Naval Station in Key West while waving the UNIA flag, wearing UNIA lapel pins, and vowing loyalty only to the Negro nation envisioned by Garvey. Only a few American blacks, including a prominent local pastor, seemed willing to support the UNIA organization and its goals. The British consul's office reported that the Key West UNIA's purpose was to incite violence in order to gain rights. It was even rumored that when local African Americans refused to join the UNIA, they were even threatened with violence themselves.[42]

A few high-ranking officers in the Florida branches were leery of Garvey's financial practices, probably due to negative publicity in the *Chicago Defender* and the NAACP's *Crisis*. But the most effective resistance to the organization was from whites in the summer of 1921: Florida authorities arrested and deported UNIA Key West division president T. C. Glashen for inciting a riot.[43] The Reverend R. H. Higgs, a Bahamian UNIA organizer at Coconut Grove (near Miami), left South Florida for Nassau after a whipping administered by masked Klansmen. Marine patrols prevented further UNIA activity at Key West, and the remaining leadership in Miami became temporarily paralyzed. White citizens braced for a race war, and the Miami American Legion sent out patrols. Both white authorities and the black community armed themselves thoroughly and bought stores of ammunition.[44]

After a dormant period, these divisions, as well as many others in Florida, were revived, as fragmentary evidence from 1926–28 indicates. Kip Vought's discussion of the Miami UNIA elaborates possible local policy revisions after the tense and explosive early years. An important change was that meetings were held in the open, ending a veil of secrecy that had made the early divisions more suspect. Vought speculates that Garvey's meeting with the Klan in 1922, despite the furor it caused in some quarters, may have also eased tensions in South Florida.[45] But in 1920 and early 1921, the verdict was in on the radical brand of Garveyism voiced through Glashen and others. It would not be tolerated in the Jim Crow state of Florida.

One of the most revealing documents relating to the status of the UNIA in the South, and South Florida in particular, took the form of communication between G. Emonei Carter, a New Yorker who relocated to Miami in the early 1920s and became a UNIA organizer, and U.S. bureau agent Leon E. Howe. Apparently, Carter was carefully and diplomatically trying to persuade Howe that the southern UNIA members were not radical, and the West Indian element seen in Miami and Key West were aberrations. Southern delegates to the second annual UNIA convention in 1921 had emphasized their wish that only American Negroes be sent to organize divisions in the South. Further, Carter admitted that southern American blacks worried about the irregular finances of the organization. He made it clear that the presence of native-born southern blacks as delegates to the UNIA convention demonstrated southern members' prudence on behalf of their communities—not their unquestioning exuberance for the organization's fund-raising programs. Carter asserted his belief in Garvey's sincerity and support for the economic emphasis of the UNIA platform but conceded that friction over alien radicalism and trepidation about irregular finances were causing a rift.[46] Garvey and Howe pulled opposite meanings from the crisis described in this letter. Howe saw the imminent split between West Indians and Americans within the UNIA as the death knell of the organization, while Garvey recognized an urgent need to redirect the platform, organizers, and rhetoric in order to save the organization in the rich recruiting ground of the southern United States. Garvey and UNIA organizers thus moved to placate white objections and subdue the organization's most openly radical elements, particularly West Indians.

Soon other troubles with some black clergymen and hostile whites and government authorities would be compounded by the financial difficulties of the Black Star Line and Garvey's indictment on mail fraud. The shipping line's demise stemmed from several causes over a two-year period. The initial excitement over the *Frederick Douglass* disintegrated into loss, embarrassment, and scandal. The flagship and two other ships acquired by the BSL failed to succeed commercially and in some cases even to operate, and in May 1923 the government finally prosecuted Garvey for misrepresenting the condition of the company in a mailing.[47] The U.S. government and numerous Garvey critics provided impetus to the efforts to stop Garvey from promoting the already bankrupt and mismanaged business venture. During a lengthy investigation and trial, Garvey was in and out of jail, and after his final conviction he went to federal prison in Atlanta. Yet while the BSL enterprise fell apart and ultimately failed, the remainder of the UNIA program had enough substance and inspiring ideological underpinning to allow the movement to focus on other activities. These goals took precedence during the investigation and trial and Garvey's eventual incarceration on mail fraud charges. These other campaigns fueled the growing movement in yet unorganized areas, especially in the South. These alternative and secondary themes began to take precedence and attract new southern audiences. Garvey's emphasis on African redemption surged, while his definition of black separatism evolved and drew new attention and controversy.

Widening the Appeal in North Carolina

The displaced southern blacks living in new southern urban centers like Newport News and the West Indian immigrants in the growing towns of South Florida were similar in many respects to the Garveyites of booming urban areas outside of the South. New York's UNIA division hosted thousands of West Indian immigrants and migrants from the South. In fact, these were the constituents that many observers and critics of the Garvey movement came to associate with the core of the membership.[48] And indeed, in the early years of the organization, people in transition seemed to form the most accessible recruiting base for UNIA organizers.[49] But Garvey also recognized that his ideas resonated with southern blacks who lived in established but developing interior communities like Winston-Salem and Raleigh, North Carolina.

The Winston-Salem/Raleigh corridor of north-central North Carolina provided a strong UNIA base for the state. The heart of tobacco country and the home of the booming R. J. Reynolds Tobacco Company and its 10,000 employees formed a rich recruiting ground for disgruntled black laborers. In April 1919 a Department of Labor investigator had researched complaints by the AFL that Tobacco Workers' International Union members had faced dismissal by R. J. Reynolds for joining the local unions. After only two months, 600 black union members formed nearly a third of the total, proving that tobacco workers were organizing rapidly. The agent's report indicated that William Reynolds, the company president, had no apologies for his exploitative business practices, which had drawn government oversight. He boasted that labor organizations were powerless against his company because the government had no legal pretext on which to intervene.[50] Thus, labor in this section of the South faced formidable challenges in dealing with private employers. Black workers' prospects would have been especially grim.

A minister from Nash County, northeast of Raleigh, participated as a North Carolina delegate to the 1920 UNIA convention in New York, voicing strong complaints about whites' cruel and harsh domination over blacks in his area and blacks' "complete submission and subserviency."[51] Three months later the *Negro World* reported a case in Nash County: a prosperous black landowner's son had been imprisoned and faced frivolous charges of injuring a white woman in a car accident. The harsh treatment of the son of this independent farmer drew a swift reaction toward self-defense in the black community.

Many blacks in Spring Hope, a UNIA division town, were prepared to die resisting this affront to one of their leading men of color.[52]

These two examples illustrate the diversity in employment, resources, and conditions among blacks ranging from tobacco workers to independent land-owners. They also clearly reveal the limited options for recourse for blacks of various means. The UNIA philosophy addressed and relieved some of the stresses on the agricultural-industrial hybrid population of north-central North Carolina. Many of the black workers cultivated, primed, and cured the tobacco on farms surrounding Winston-Salem and Raleigh, while others pro-cessed the tobacco leaves and made them into cigarettes in factories. UNIA organizers quickly recognized that North Carolinians were receptive to the movement's emphasis on race pride and self-defense, as well as to its promo-tion of economic independence.

As in most other states in the South, 1921 was a big year for the UNIA in North Carolina. California minister and UNIA organizer E. L. Gaines spent several months speaking and organizing throughout the state, as did UNIA secretary general Reverend J. D. Brooks and North Carolina native and UNIA "Leader of American Negroes" Reverend J. W. H. Eason.[53] These three orga-nizers had remarkable success in gaining the almost universal support of all classes of North Carolina blacks. In no other southern state was urban and black middle-class participation as pronounced as in the Tar Heel State. Blacks there had read in the *Star of Zion*, the African Methodist Episcopal Zion (AMEZ) organ based in Charlotte, and in the white state daily, the *Charlotte Observer*, about the splendid UNIA conventions and Garvey's Black Star Line.

Brooks spoke to large and very curious crowds in Belhaven and Raleigh in January and February 1921, but the BSL was hardly mentioned. He focused instead on African redemption: "this is a white man's country," he explained, and it was now time that the black man had his own country in Africa. After-ward, two black physicians, a newspaper editor, a professor from Shaw Uni-versity, the ministers of the local ministers' union, and the Raleigh black school superintendent pledged themselves to the UNIA.[54] In nearby Wilson, state UNIA organizer E. W. Pearson rented the Globe Theater to show motion pictures of the 1920 UNIA international convention parade in Harlem and BSL ships at anchor to new division members and guests.[55] In 1922 E. L. Gaines, minister of the UNIA Legions, addressed a group of 700 black teachers in North Carolina who, after some debate, agreed that the UNIA program made the most sense as a strategy for racial uplift.[56]

The Winston-Salem division formed during the summer of 1921, and one of its early speakers drew loud applause with the statement that "the Negro wants no social equality, but human rights."[57] A speaker at a Raleigh division meeting at about the same time stated that the development of race pride came not "at once, but through a steady, conservative, accumulative program by which small means" were joined together into a whole.[58] These sentiments were reminiscent of the recently deceased founder of Tuskegee. The change in emphasis reflected in part previous advice from black leaders and lessons learned in South Florida and on the Virginia peninsula.

Some very early advice came to Garvey from Emmett J. Scott, personal adviser to Booker T. Washington until 1915 and secretary-treasurer of Tuskegee Institute. In 1918, in his capacity as special adviser to Secretary of War Newton Baker, Scott unwittingly assisted Garvey's organizational strategy by suggesting that the UNIA leader tone down his rhetoric. He told Garvey that the *Negro World* was promoting racial discord and that his editorials tended to "inspire unrest among members of the Negro race." Scott reported to Secretary Baker that Garvey had appreciated their detailed conversation and "thanked me most profusely for sending for him and pointing out to him the difficulties probably ahead of him and for the frank manner in which I talked to him and for the counsel offered him. He has promised to change the general policy of his publication."[59] Scott's account of this meeting sounds plausible because Garvey seemed always willing to learn from successful leaders, especially those who were influential and also familiar with American race relations. Garvey's astuteness at synthesizing advice and strategy aided his ability to lead such large numbers of American blacks despite his foreign origins. After meeting with Scott, however, Garvey did not hastily extinguish his incendiary rhetoric. It took him two years to complete the toning-down process, but clearly Scott's authoritative advice and wisdom had made an impression on Garvey's mind.

The essence of Garvey's dilemma was that to widen his reach into the South, his rhetoric had to be palatable to southern whites and also meaningful for southern blacks. Could he depend on southern blacks and his other supporters to understand a strategy that seemed to compromise his previously militant stance? The broad acceptance of Garveyism by both professional and laboring blacks in Belhaven, Raleigh, Winston-Salem, and surrounding communities indicated that American (instead of West Indian) organizers using moderate language might facilitate a wider degree of acceptance and therefore support for the Garvey movement in the South. The UNIA leadership was constantly formulating a program and organizational style with carefully modulated rhetoric in order to organize among black America's largest constituency, southerners.[60]

At the second annual UNIA convention in August 1921, clouds formed on the horizon for the North Carolina wing of the organization. Formal charges against J. D. Brooks for misappropriation of funds were presented to the convention. By late 1921 North Carolina had become a prime example of the graft and corruption problems that plagued the UNIA throughout its existence.[61] The UNIA administration recognized (and critics were quick to reveal) that many vulnerable supporters had been duped by scam artists and corrupt UNIA employees who yielded to the temptation of the huge potential for theft. The *Negro World* published reports that unscrupulous people had been collecting funds on behalf of the UNIA that were not reaching the parent body. Brooks was reportedly out of touch with headquarters, and suggestions indicated he had absconded with UNIA funds collected in the Tar Heel State.[62] Within two months he had been indicted for grand larceny.[63] By December the North Carolina secretary of state and insurance commissioner had checked into the UNIA's records and permitted the organization to operate in the state.[64] This was good news for the Garvey movement because North Carolina had proved an incredibly rich source of loyalty and support for Garvey's program.

The UNIA's Leader of American Negroes, the Reverend J. W. H. Eason, was dispatched immediately to reaffirm and galvanize the supporters who were left in Brooks's wake. Eason was an eloquent AMEZ minister and a native of North Carolina. Hubert Harrison, an early *Negro World* editor, considered Eason a "splendid orator," far more gifted than Garvey himself.[65] Although Eason's prestige and ego easily rivaled that of the UNIA's founder, he possessed the intimate understanding of southern race relations of which Garvey was quickly growing cognizant.[66] Garvey clearly valued Eason's abilities and needed his help, despite whatever competition might have arisen between the similarly gifted men.

In early 1922 Eason spoke four nights in Raleigh to 600 people and then in other locations around the state. In the midst of his rescue efforts to prevent the Brooks theft from discouraging members, it was revealed that Pearson, the state organizer for the UNIA, also had been suspected of stealing. An advertisement in the *Negro World* in bold letters warned "the Colored People of North Carolina" to be wary of yet other organizers who were not authorized by the UNIA parent body.[67]

One would imagine that between the mischief of Brooks and Pearson, North Carolina's blacks would have washed their hands of the UNIA, but the work of Eason and the return visits of the popular E. L. Gaines helped shore up the promising divisions. The Raleigh division thrived under its president, the Reverend W. M. Allen, who led the division through 1927. Eason drew in hundreds of new members, and Raleigh's pastor-president proclaimed his division the "stronghold of Garveyism in the state of North Carolina."[68] Division men drilled in the uniform of the African Legion, while a Black Cross Nurses auxiliary gave Raleigh's UNIA women an outlet for their desire to serve.[69]

The Case of James Walker Hood Eason

J. W. H. Eason thus played a critical role in spreading Garveyism into the South, becoming Garvey's greatest asset and also the greatest threat to his leadership. Evidence of Eason's prodigious organizational ability and his profound charisma appears in almost every issue of the *Negro World* during the time he served as "Leader of American Negroes" from August 1920 until Garvey spearheaded his impeachment in August 1922.[70]

Facts about Eason's early years are obscure, but he apparently was born in North Carolina in 1886, making him and Marcus Garvey the same age. His family farmed near the tiny village of Rich Square in Northampton County in northeastern North Carolina. Despite his humble origins, by his early twenties Eason lived in Salisbury and had graduated from the AMEZ church's Livingstone College and Hood Theological Seminary.[71] At both places he had eight to ten fellow students who came from states all around the Southeast, providing a network for later organizing. In 1910, as an undergraduate at Livingstone, he was already earning wages as a preacher, honing his oratorical gifts for his future as a UNIA organizer. His contacts while at Livingstone and Hood with Professor James E. K. Aggrey, a brilliant African scholar originally from Anamabu, Gold Coast, and well-known figure in the AMEZ denomination, no doubt piqued his interest in African mission work. Two of his classmates became AMEZ bishops and served in that capacity in Africa, providing more connections and relevance to his work for the UNIA.[72]

Eason served briefly as a pastor in Charlotte, but details of this experience are sketchy. W. I. Walls, editor of the *Star of Zion*, the AMEZ church organ published in that city, made negative remarks about Charlotte UNIA members and the dubious sincerity and leadership ability of the UNIA's national organizers.[73] This raises further questions about Eason's standing within his denomination. He moved to Philadelphia and soon after split an AMEZ congregation at Varick Memorial Church and founded People's Metropolitan AME Zion Church. Within months he joined Garvey and became the first chaplain general for the UNIA until August 1920. After he became the UNIA's Leader of American Negroes, his awe-inspiring division-building campaign began. At various stages of his nonstop organizing push, he based himself in New Orleans, Brunswick, Georgia, Charleston, South Carolina, and Washington, D.C.[74] If one examines the map of UNIA divisions in those regions closely and reads his reports to the *Negro World* between August 1920 and August 1922, it is obvious that Eason's travels profoundly influenced the spread of the UNIA in greater New Orleans, across southern Georgia, and in the South Carolina low country. His roots and education also drew him to his home state often, and his ministerial network enhanced the movement all across North Carolina.

Effective organizers like Eason developed pat speeches that worked well wherever they went in the South. Even though these speakers rehearsed and gave the same talk hundreds of times, they never forgot that the audiences were hearing their words for the first time. One of Eason's best talks, and certainly a model for future ones, appeared in the *Negro World* in July 1920. Its content provides clues to his message, which was eventually heard all over the South. He stressed the necessity of "vision" for accomplishment. He pleaded with and cajoled African Americans to do more than pray for improvement of the Negro situation: "It is time for Negroes to stop the old-time foolery, put their hands in their pockets, invest their money and get ready to go over home and while you are getting ready to go over home you better take means to protect yourself because the ghoulish mob is going to cower you tomorrow." He went on to describe his disillusionment with the Republican Party, which had "voted out all Negroes and swore that no Negro in the country would have a great big appointment. One Negro got so mad [about the Lily White movement in the Republican Party] . . . that he said 'from now on for me, God, Garvey, and a Gun!' " In conclusion, Eason rendered all credit for the growing awareness and vision of nationalist Negroes to Garvey: "there is one man who is absent and yet he is present, whose voice we cannot hear tonight yet he is speaking just the same. . . . Before we could speak he had to speak to us; before we could live he had to call us from the grave; before we could walk about he had to show us the princely stride of the black sons of Ethiopia . . . the leader of leaders, the champion of champions, a man of men . . . His Excellency, Marcus Garvey."[75]

This message resonated among the thousands of black southerners who heard Eason speak and who joined UNIA divisions between 1920 and 1922. It was so effective, in fact, that Garvey decided that Eason had become too popular (and untrustworthy) and convinced the 1922 convention delegates to expel him from the movement for treason and financial irregularities. So convincing was Eason to those he organized that the loyalty to Garvey that Eason had

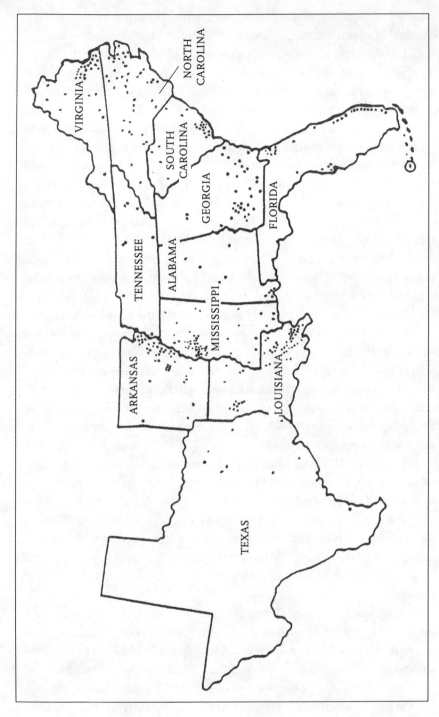

Map 1. *UNIA Divisions in the Former States of the Confederacy, 1920–1928*

promoted continued. When Eason then traveled around the eastern United States trying to organize an anti-Garvey movement, the Universal Negro Alliance, a few Garvey loyalists took it upon themselves to murder him.[76]

Eason was shot twice after a rally in New Orleans on 1 January 1923, and two local UNIA men and one from Detroit were implicated. None of them was convicted or punished for the crime, but Garvey and many of his followers experienced satisfaction at the demise of this "race traitor." A voluntary committee of women of the New Orleans UNIA, which endured harassment and surveillance in the wake of the killing, admonished New Orleans mayor Andrew McShane to provide some relief. The UNIA women denied any role of the local organization, its members, or Garvey in Eason's murder. Instead, they defended the UNIA, praised Jim Crow laws for protecting racial purity, and implied that Eason had it coming because he was a "handsome, intelligent, money-spending woman chaser."[77]

The acrimony between Garvey and Eason had escalated to a disturbing degree even as Eason promoted the UNIA and glorified its leader. The timing of the dispute is significant in that Garvey's Klan summit coincided with Eason and Garvey's irreconcilable rift. An intriguing and telling detail is that immediately following Eason's expulsion, he spoke to the NAACP's field secretary and later executive secretary Walter White, who was involved in the U.S. government's investigation of Garvey. Eason told White that he intended to destroy the Garvey movement and make Garvey resign, because "he [Eason] had control of the negroes [in the movement] and could make them do just as he wanted them to do."[78] If this were not enough incentive to bring radical Garvey loyalists out of the woodwork, the embittered Eason also agreed to testify against Garvey in the UNIA leader's upcoming mail fraud trial.[79]

Organizers like Eason could and did do prodigious work for the UNIA. But the *Negro World*, once it had agents and subscribers in the South, could shore up loyalty for Garvey and discredit Eason. The propaganda organ defended Garvey against Eason's countercharges and presented an unbalanced picture of Eason's alleged treachery. It is ironic that the spectacular powers of persuasion, which Eason had used to build up the UNIA in the remote corners of the South that Garvey never visited, worked so effectively that he could not undo the UNIA and undermine Garvey, and that the man and movement Eason had helped to create also caused his demise, when they turned on him.

The Negro State Fair at Raleigh

After Eason's impeachment and before his murder four months later, Garvey traveled specifically to Raleigh to speak at the North Carolina Negro State

Fair on 25 October 1922. Having been invited no doubt flattered Garvey, and the crowd's response to this important appearance would indicate how his rank-and-file southern constituency had reacted to his June meeting with Klan leadership and his recent dismissal of the popular North Carolina native Eason. Prominent black educator and businessman Berry O'Kelly considered Garvey an appropriate speaker for the Negro State Fair. A leader of great influence, a member of the North Carolina Interracial Commission, and with Booker T. Washington cofounder of the National Negro Business League, O'Kelly no doubt negotiated Garvey's appearance and collaborated to a certain extent on the content of his address. As president of the event, O'Kelly presided while Garvey berated the black audience in the tradition of generations of black ministers and leaders.[80]

To a mostly black audience of 500, Garvey excoriated African Americans for becoming lazy, "taking the customs of his former slave master," and doing nothing for themselves. Brock Barkley, the young white reporter who provided a detailed summary of Garvey's remarks, was astounded and slightly amused at the way the speaker " 'took the hide' off his hearers as they cheered almost his every word." Garvey accused the crowd of depending too much on whites and waiting for the Lord to determine their destiny. He explained that the UNIA favored racial equality but insisted that social equality was not the same thing: "I do not give a rap about that if a [white] man doesn't want to associate with me. I don't want to associate with him." What the UNIA wanted was a government for the Negro race because "both races cannot live together in peace and seek the same thing." He admonished his audience that white leaders had built the United States up from nothing in 200 years; blacks could do the same in Africa.[81] Garvey used the same device to encourage black self-reliance and economic development. In North Carolina he criticized his race for allegedly producing and organizing nothing, which to whites implied African Americans were inferior. To blacks, however, this implied they were capable of the same achievements as whites if they could organize.

Several northern-based black newspapers and journals caught wind of this speech and used it to criticize Garvey roundly, basically accusing him of playing into the hands of southern whites.[82] For Garvey to intimate that poor dependent blacks were responsible for their own circumstances excused the white employers and landowners who made sure that black laborers and tenant farmers could never get ahead. New York's black socialist journal, *The Messenger*, called Garvey a "Supreme Negro Jamaican Jackass" and "the southern white man's 'good nigger.' " Chandler Owen and A. Philip Randolph, its editors, even wrote that "a reliable source" suggested that Garvey had addressed the North Carolina audience as "niggers." Similarly, the *Baltimore Afro-American* allegedly reported that Garvey had thanked whites for lynching race consciousness into black southerners.[83] Pronouncements like this delighted white supremacists, who liked hearing a black leader doing their racist work for them. Indeed, the white *Greensboro Daily News* called it "quite the cleverest speech ever heard" at the Negro State Fair.[84] This unorthodox approach to his audience nevertheless allowed Garvey to openly discuss lynching, racial solidarity, and the possibility of black retaliation. As a result, the speech received an enthusiastic response from blacks at the Raleigh fairgrounds.

Although this speech by no means had the same impact or substance, the circumstances of this event mirror in some ways Booker T. Washington's 1895 Atlanta Cotton States Exposition address. In fact, Garvey's speech was geared to draw positive reactions from both local blacks and whites, as was the Tuskegee leader's so-called compromise address. In addition, the reactions to Garvey's address in the northern black press were critical, just as the reactions of William Monroe Trotter, John Hope, and other black leaders to Washington's "Atlanta Compromise" had been.

Aware that white reporters and law enforcement officials were present, on this special occasion Garvey had aimed the speech to a racially mixed audience in the heart of Dixie. The black members of the audience tolerated the criticism and presumably understood the UNIA leader's strategy. While eager to receive the UNIA leader's message of self-reliance, self-defense, and African redemption, Raleigh's black population understood the well-disguised message in Garvey's address in a way that whites did not. Robert T. Kerlin, a white professor at the University of Virginia, had already warned whites of the danger of this type of device: "We white people must give the colored people credit for more percipiency than we are wont to do. They have quite as good a faculty as we for reading between the lines, for taking the force of an innuendo, for perceiving the point of a bit of mild irony or gentle sarcasm. Vague and indirect pronouncements, perfectly harmless in appearance to us, are hand grenades to them. Editorial reticence they well understand to mean 'safety first' for the editor, a longer career of usefulness."[85]

Garveyism Flourishes in the Urban South

In May 1923, although the Raleigh division announced its goal to become the biggest and strongest UNIA division in North Carolina, of all fifty-eight divisions in the state the Winston-Salem division had the most prodigious history. Mrs. S. S. Womack served as the division's "lady president," while active organizers for the group ran the gamut from R. B. Jarrett, an ex-Union soldier, to Ren Oates, president of the Tobacco Workers' International Union. Oates provided a clue to the UNIA's order of importance among his associations while speaking at a May meeting in 1922, declaring that it was the "greatest force in organizing Negroes."[86] Winston-Salem's UNIA was so large that its weekly mass meetings had to be held in Symphony Hall. For its first several years it enjoyed the leadership of the Reverend J. A. Miller, a well-known Baptist minister who died in the spring of 1923.[87]

We begin to see two processes in motion as the UNIA becomes a vital organization, the *Negro World* gains readers, and Marcus Garvey becomes a revered figure among blacks in Virginia, Florida, and North Carolina. The organization's fundamental ideas have tremendous potential to attract a wide and diverse following in the South, from longshoremen to tobacco farmers to West Indian laborers to college professors to ministers. The negative and suspicious reaction of some black ministers and the hostile reaction of whites, particularly in Florida, to the most radical aspects of the UNIA forced a modification in strategy from the organizers at the top. Garvey and the UNIA organizers in the South faced this challenge successfully and managed to push further and further into the towns and rural areas of the region.

North Carolina turned out to be fraught with talented yet corrupt organizers like Brooks and Pearson. But both these men prior to their deceit showed Garvey a new way to reach a wider American audience. Similarly, the extremely influential and perhaps, in Garvey's mind, overly ambitious Eason took the message of African redemption and racial pride and separatism to the cities and towns of his home state. With a new line of rhetoric, new life was breathed into the UNIA.

The UNIA also had significantly large divisions and almost fanatical support in older coastal cities of the South like New Orleans, Charleston, and Mobile. Its base of supporters included industrial laborers tied to the shipping enterprises of these port cities. It also enjoyed some support from the substantial black middle class of these historic places. Garveyism also had strong appeal in the interior towns of Atlanta, Natchez, Mississippi, and Fort Smith, Arkansas. These places organized thriving divisions and brought together blacks of many backgrounds under the emphasis of African redemption, economic independence, and race pride. Garveyism was not just about the Black Star Line or emigration to Africa, as it has often been portrayed. It meant many things to many diverse communities. The common denominator in these southern places was the social organization dictated by segregation. The positive response to the UNIA indicated the extent to which its program meshed with existing community ideals and conditions.

Even with all of the UNIA's success in organizing the urban South, the richest potential source for new members was rural, agricultural areas. Five million of the 10 million blacks in America in 1920 lived in rural areas. Thirty-six percent of all African Americans worked as farmers, by far the largest single occupation for black people.[88] Some of the fundamental conditions of these rural and agricultural areas required further revision of the rhetoric and strategies of the movement. The greatest organizational challenge of Garvey and the UNIA was successfully to reach, stimulate, and organize black farmers scattered throughout the rural South.

3 Growth

The truth is that Garvey aroused the Negroes of Georgia as much as those of New York, except where the black preacher discouraged anything that threatened his income, or where white domination smothered every earthly hope.—E. Franklin Frazier, The Nation, 18 August 1926

In his first year of organizing in the United States, Garvey took a logical and practical approach in deciding how to expand the UNIA. The New York division took off, word spread to Philadelphia, and soon the *Negro World* and enthusiastic leaders and recruiters mobilized black activism throughout urban centers of black population. Always studying and estimating his options, Garvey undoubtedly noticed that in the North and West, most blacks lived in urban areas, particularly in large cities like New York, Chicago, Philadelphia, and Detroit. All four of these cities had fewer than 100,000 blacks in 1910 but experienced dramatic increases by 1920. Detroit grew from about 6,000 to 40,000 black residents in a decade, and New York grew from 92,000 to 152,000 in the same period.[1] Garvey and UNIA organizers staked out territory with these crucial variables in mind. They concentrated on areas where the UNIA and the idea of the Black Star Line gained the most rapid acceptance. Garvey's two earliest divisions emerged, not surprisingly, in the two most accessible cities, New York and Philadelphia, both brimming with black migrants from the South; however, within a year the UNIA organ had begun to circulate in the most remote farming communities of the Deep South.

Early in 1917, on an exploratory mission, Garvey spoke in Nashville, Tennessee, and at Big Bethel AME Church in Atlanta, Georgia.[2] These early forays into the heart of Dixie enhanced his understanding of the potential for organization and support among southern blacks. By the time the UNIA had taken hold in the more easily accessible urban areas of the North and South, the rural Black Belt became the next focus for organization. The most expansive growth areas for the UNIA emerged in very densely populated rural areas of the South in which blacks made up the majority and where cotton tenancy circumscribed the lives of much of the farming population.

It is also apparent that the skill and determination of individuals at the regional and local levels had much to do with where the UNIA sprouted successful divisions. Ultimately, the Garvey movement spread into the South due to the work of these local and national organizers and with the aid of expanding literacy and the UNIA's weekly organ, the *Negro World*. Examining chronological patterns of development for divisions within the eleven southern states helps to illuminate which of these influences had the greatest impact. In some cases a dynamic speaker from UNIA headquarters motivated a community to organize a division, while in other places a popular local minister's leadership held sway. In many instances an indigenous layman or woman took the initiative to begin a UNIA branch.

The UNIA appointed high commissioners for twelve sections of the United States, who were held responsible for organizing and supervising the work of divisions within their areas.[3] Some individual states had designated leaders who tended to work closely with the regional commissioners. Early on, as seen in the cases of Florida and Virginia, the variety of settings from which UNIA divisions arose, coupled with the differing styles of organizers, allowed for diverse forms and expressions of Garveyite sentiment throughout the region. But more important, over time the *Negro World* provided a remarkable consistency of themes and programs, while the UNIA constitution and the Declaration of the Rights of the Negro Peoples of the World, also referred to as the Negro Bill of Rights, adopted at the 1920 convention, provided guidelines and standardization to Garveyism from one UNIA division to the next.[4]

During its publication from August 1918 through 1933, the entire front page of the UNIA weekly organ normally featured Garvey's speeches and editorials.[5] This medium was the most vital instrument in the dispersal of Garvey's ideas and programs and in the growth of the UNIA in the South. The paper's content influenced a wide and diverse readership within the black communities of the African diaspora, while it also reflected attitudes and community values that differed according to local and regional conditions. Three thousand copies of the *Negro World*'s first issue appeared in the second half of 1918 and, after six months of publication, its circulation reached near 50,000.[6] In a sense, the UNIA organ provided both the spark that ignited the ideological inferno of Garveyism and the fuel that sustained it from week to week.

Among African Americans in the 1920s printed sources and especially newspapers provided the most effective method for the dissemination of information and ideas. The southern black press flourished at the local level in the late nineteenth and early twentieth centuries, generally as a recorder of church news and social activities. The black Baptist press, especially, had over forty serials in circulation, which included topics discussed at the denomination's annual conventions. Anticipating the women's page, a feature of the *Negro World*, some included a woman's column, which indicated at least an acknowledgment of women as important participants in the black community and even revealed hints of their ever-growing assertiveness.[7]

The most influential and widely distributed black interest periodicals in the United States during the late nineteenth century were the *Indianapolis Freeman*, the *New York Age*, and the AME *Christian Recorder*. Of remarkable notoriety, especially in the South, was the long-running newsletter of the American Colonization Society, the *African Repository*.[8] Black people acknowledged literacy as a critical component of education and advancement and frequently emphasized the need to make excellent African American newspapers available to children and others in every home.[9] More protest-oriented black journals emerged in the twentieth century, particularly in the wartime years, and they came in national editions. Robert Vann's *Pittsburgh Courier*, Robert Abbott's *Chicago Defender*, and the NAACP's *Crisis*, edited by W. E. B. Du Bois, documented much of the post–World War I agitation in which blacks participated at the national level.[10] The *Negro World* joined these other important papers as a vital source of information and news of the black world beyond local communities.[11]

It is no mystery why the UNIA leader put such emphasis on producing an interesting and unique propaganda organ. Garvey had learned the printing trade as a young teen in his native Jamaica and had cut his teeth as an organizer of the printers' union there. After starting several short-lived publications, he came to the United States knowing the profound potential of the printed word.[12] Most black southerners probably first heard of Garvey and Garveyism through the *Negro World*. Its originality helped it gain early attention wherever it was distributed, and it stood apart from the other race papers in its format. The *Negro World* placed Garvey's ideas on the front page, not in editorials in the back section after the news. It was clearly designed to serve as the mouthpiece of Garvey and the organ of the UNIA. Despite this distinct purpose, it enjoyed acceptance beyond UNIA membership. Letters to the editor often noted that readers cherished the paper even though they were not affiliated with the organization.

The *Defender*'s editorial bent promoted migration to the North and black involvement in politics. The paper and its influential editor, Robert Abbott, a native of coastal Georgia, achieved their greatest popularity in the years during and immediately after World War I. Abbott's paper reached more than 230,000 copies in 1915, and circulation peaked at 283,571 in 1920.[13] He maintained a keen interest in the fortunes of black southerners and included much pertinent information for his southern readers. He replicated the standard newspaper format, using the editorial page in the back to express his sentiments on issues of the day, including discrimination, politics, and racial violence.

Although never so widely distributed in the South as the *Defender*, the *Negro World* did reach into the region's hinterlands. The white justice of the peace in tiny Wabbaseka, Arkansas, R. J. Watkins, complained to the U.S. Bureau of Investigation of the radical content of the *Negro World* and the *Defender*, claiming "there is no danger immediate or otherwise from our old time darkey but from the present younger crowd." Watkins made these complaints through an Arkansas attorney in hopes that both papers could be legally suppressed. Watkins attached to the complaint a 22 February 1919 issue of the *Negro World*, which had likely been intercepted as it passed through the Wabbaseka postal system, where Watkins's daughter served as postmistress.[14]

Garvey's front page would have been hard to ignore, as it was often filled with bold headlines such as "The Negro Race Must Assert Its Manhood and Power" or "The Common People Ruling the World."[15] There were no attempts to make the authorship of Garvey's opinions ambiguous. Each reprinted speech, letter, or editorial bore Garvey's name so that readers would never confuse his words with someone else's.

The *Negro World* saved tantalizing news stories about lynchings and other race-related violence for the inside pages of the paper, while the *Defender* used shocking stories up front to boost its readership.[16] The difference in the formats indicated the varying functions and appeals of the two popular national black papers of the early 1920s. Garvey's was made to build and propel an ideological movement and thus contained the essential ideas on its cover. On its subsequent pages, it contained race-related news items, reports from divisions, and information about fund-raising, with occasional human interest stories toward the back. Contributors to various UNIA causes could see their names and town addresses on extensive lists printed in the paper along with the amounts they donated. Most of these contributions were nickels and dimes from people of meager means. At various stages of the movement, a woman's page edited by Amy Jacques Garvey, the leader's wife, and Spanish and French pages filled out the back section. During convention weeks, the *Negro World* provided detailed descriptions of the proceedings and transcripts of debates among convention delegates. By contrast, the *Defender* included more news, politics, sports, and social fare while emphasizing the better opportunities and jobs for blacks in the North.

Probably anyone who could read would have been interested in the contents of both papers. John Hope Franklin, the eminent African American historian, recalled people avidly reading the *Negro World* during his childhood in the all-black village of Rentiesville, Oklahoma.[17] And the news, as it does at any time, formed the basis for numerous conversations and debates. Newspapers were passed around in black households and communities, and subscription numbers usually represented as little as one-fourth of the actual readership. Conversations among coworkers, families, churchgoers, and social club members transmitted the news from the *Defender* and the *Negro World* to even larger audiences.[18] In small southern towns these papers were regarded as a lifeline to the wider world. Sometime shortly after the UNIA's first convention, Susie Wilder of Chunchula in southwest Alabama wrote the following to the *Negro World* editor: "Although it has been only a short time that we have been receiving your paper, it seems as one of the family. We look forward to its coming with as much joy as we do to one of us, and there is not much done until it is read through and through."[19]

Black Pullman porters and others in the Yazoo-Mississippi Delta circulated the *Negro World* and the *Defender* despite the opposition of whites. Greenville was a major distribution site, and hundreds of copies disappeared quickly and quietly when they reached the area by train. Personal accounts recalled that "Negroes grab the *Chicago Defender* like a hungry mule grabs fodder" and "even the sharecroppers are subscribers."[20] The editor of the white newspaper the *Natchez Mississippi Democrat* recognized the popularity of the UNIA and *Negro World* in the Deep South when he wrote, "[T]he work of such charlatans as Marcus Garvey among illiterate Negroes is building up a low prejudice against whites in all sections of the country. Ignorant Negroes of the South are now pouring thousands of dollars into Garvey's coffers every year, on the belief that he is going to establish a home and a government for them somewhere in Africa."[21] Both papers raised objections from some white members of local southern communities, however. The *Defender*, because of its wider circulation and because of its promotion of migration from the South, met the most regional opposition.[22] Nevertheless, both of these papers evidently enjoyed comprehensive circulation and discussion in almost every urban and rural southern black community.

A natural competition for readers and support emerged between Abbott and Garvey and eventually caused a rift between them. The Chicago-based editor joined critics of the Garvey movement and incurred the wrath of the UNIA leader. Disparaging stories and editorials about Garvey and the Black Star Line threatened to inhibit the UNIA's growth, and Garvey singled out

Abbott for legal action. Numerous issues of the *Negro World* devoted space to forceful criticism of Abbott and his supposedly insidious libel.[23]

One of Garvey's challenges in keeping the UNIA growing in the South, an area that provided a major constituency of the *Defender*, required him successfully to defend and vindicate himself in the pages of his own paper. Garvey often dramatized his persecution whenever he was questioned or opposed by an individual or group. His continued popularity in the South suggests that his self-characterization as the favorite target of those he called "race traitors," like Abbott, influenced a sizable number of southern supporters.[24] Even after several years of controversy in print, Mrs. J. W. Johnson of Albany, Georgia, presented her view to *Negro World* readers in the paper's "People's Forum." Although she was not a UNIA member, she loved Marcus Garvey and believed his paper should "be in every Negro home."[25] And despite the rivalry and eventual enmity of their editors, the *Defender* and the *Negro World* coexisted and prospered in the South, one encouraging migration and the other Garveyism. In the same way that the *Defender* spurred a significant number of southern blacks to move north, the *Negro World* provided a proportional number the will to remain in their homes in the Southland.

Editors of the *Negro World*

The larger-than-life persona and problems of Marcus Garvey exert a powerful pull on scholars examining the Garvey movement, creating a distraction from the impact its ideology had on participants and their communities. While the force of his charisma made the UNIA successful, the centrality of one man's fate also made the movement vulnerable. Yet the simple fact that Marcus Garvey could not possibly have created a movement with the scope of the UNIA without help is often overlooked. In fact, the hard work of organizing and publicizing the million-plus group in America was handled by hundreds of unselfish and determined people who adopted Garvey's breathtaking vision of black uplift. In addition, several of the most dedicated servants of the movement willingly gave all of the credit to its visionary leader, even though a number of them directly influenced the success of the UNIA's philosophy and direction.

It is extremely important in studying the UNIA in the South, an area where Garvey made few personal appearances and where local divisions were stripped of the pageantry of the larger divisions in urban areas outside the South, that we recognize its most critical organizers and propagandizers. For the southern region, the most important of these participants were the editors of the

Negro World. Because the paper was the only point of contact with the organization for numerous rural southern divisions, its editorial content must not be neglected here. Garvey, who had ample experience as a publisher and printer before the *Negro World* debuted in Harlem in 1918, delegated the editorship of the UNIA's organ at various times to extremely competent and loyal people such as William Henry Ferris and to his second wife, Amy Jacques Garvey. He also persuaded Hubert Harrison, a leading Harlem organizer, and two immensely qualified and respected journalists, John Edward Bruce and Timothy Thomas Fortune, to help define the editorial content of the paper during its most crucial years.

The *Negro World*'s first editor was W. A. Domingo, a Jamaican with whom Garvey had a close relationship but also specific conflicts over Domingo's radical editorial bent. The UNIA leader brought Domingo in front of the executive committee, charging the editor with expressing views inconsistent with UNIA goals in his *Negro World* editorials. By July 1919 Domingo had left the UNIA organ and affiliated with several socialist journals.[26] The *Negro World*'s next editor was not a West Indian radical, but an American. William Ferris was a scholar, minister, writer, and journalist and had all the credentials of the most elite and educated members of African American society. Ferris was forty-two years old when the UNIA was incorporated in New York. A native of New Haven, Connecticut, he held A.B. and M.A. degrees from Yale. He also received a master's degree from Harvard University and spent two additional years in Cambridge as a divinity student. He served his first pastorate at the Congregational church in Wilmington, North Carolina, between 1905 and 1910. His connections there no doubt contributed heavily to the UNIA's early organizational success in southeastern North Carolina. In 1910 he returned to the North to lead two AME Zion mission churches in Massachusetts.[27]

Ferris met Marcus Garvey in 1917 while working at Chicago's *Champion Magazine*. There he no doubt became familiar with many aspects of popular journalism as well as the editorial practices of the most popular black daily in America, the *Chicago Defender*. Ferris's other experience included serving as assistant to R. R. Wright Jr., editor of the Philadelphia-based AME publication, the *Christian Recorder*. This weekly had the longest continuous run of any black journal in America and a large southern readership. Ferris's tenure there came on the heels of the death of AME bishop Henry McNeal Turner, an immensely influential voice for black nationalism and emigrationism.[28]

Perhaps because Ferris spread himself thin, holding many different positions and living in so many regions of the United States, he is not as well known as his credentials warrant. But the extent of his travel around the

United States, and the close observation and study of African Americans he carried out while researching his book *The African Abroad; or, His Evolution in Western Civilization: Tracing His Development Under Caucasian Milieu* (1913), surely served him well in catering to a national and even international black audience as literary editor of the *Negro World*. And indeed his success at promoting the Garvey movement through the UNIA organ was his most noteworthy accomplishment.

In his scholarly writing Ferris reviewed the "deeds, achievements, and progress of the colored race in Africa, Europe, Hayti, the West Indies and America."[29] In his choice of subject matter he was thinking and studying in the same vein as his fellow members of the American Negro Academy and the Negro Society for Historical Research. The ancient Egyptians and the Empire of Songhay were recalled and recounted alongside famous men of African ancestry through the Middle Ages to the present. In several chapters he analyzed the inadequacy of the leadership of either Booker T. Washington or W. E. B. Du Bois and in another lamented the lack of motivation in members of his race, pleading with them to "stop whining and buckle down to hard work."[30] From Ferris's perspective, although delayed in their progress and leaderless when *The African Abroad* was published in 1913, black people's fortunes changed dramatically within five years. Ferris found the inspirational leader he had hoped for when he met Garvey.[31] In 1919 Garvey asked him to become literary editor of the *Negro World*, a position he held until September 1923.[32]

Because we have Ferris's book, we can learn his philosophy and opinions on many pertinent race-related questions and then look for them in the *Negro World* issues he edited. It is very obvious through such a comparison just how influential Ferris was over the UNIA organ's content. Much of Ferris's philosophy of history can be found in the early issues of the *Negro World*, and this ideology, which permeated editorials and guided the selection of news articles, came to represent "Garveyism." Randall K. Burkett has explained that Ferris's Social Darwinist belief system led him to praise the Anglo-Saxon race for its aggressive pursuit of economic and political power and even to encourage blacks to emulate whites in pursuing similar goals for the Negro race.[33] This racialist and civilizationist perspective, although thoroughly out of favor in today's thought, was influential and pervasive during the Progressive Era. Popular white authors of the period, such as Thomas Dixon Jr. in *The Clansman* (1905) and *The Leopard's Spots* (1902), promoted notions of inherent white chivalry and purity while demonizing black people as brutal and ruthless savages. Ferris used the same race-centered model to argue a completely different position: that Negroes as a race could contribute much to civilization by counteracting the materialistic and unchristian tendencies of other races through their "spiritual and emotional qualities which can soften human nature."[34] By way of explaining the brutality of whites, Ferris argued that it was only to be expected; since "the Caucasian races have had to struggle, strive and fight to get where they are, it is but natural that the strenuous rather than the natural aspects of human nature should be developed in them."[35]

In his late twenties and early thirties, Ferris lived in Florida and North Carolina and traveled all over the South and eastern seaboard states while researching *The African Abroad*.[36] In this 1913 publication Ferris weighed in harshly on his black brethren and lamented what he considered the emasculation that southern white society had imposed on black men. Without knowing it himself, Ferris foreshadowed controversial UNIA rhetoric and strategies for black and white relations in the South. At the same time he encouraged manliness and courage, he recommended caution and pragmatism:

> The main reason why the Negro is despised and looked down upon by his Anglo-Saxon neighbors is not because of his color and hair, his illiteracy and poverty, but because he and his ancestors so tamely and cowardly submitted to chattel slavery. As many degrees as the race rises in manliness and courage, just so many degrees will the thermometer of the Anglo-Saxon's respect, admiration and appreciation for the Negro rise. I do not mean that colored leaders should wave the bloody shirt and stir up race riots in the South. . . . It is advisable for the Southern Negro, who is in the lion's den, to move with caution, circumspection and discretion for the present and acquiesce in existing conditions.[37]

An emphasis on courage and self-defense appeared regularly in the *Negro World*, but so did advisories on the consequences of confronting the Anglo-Saxon race in "a white man's country." Editorials challenged black people to learn about their glorious African past and to see self-respect and racial pride as sacred mandates. Ferris promoted education and literacy as keystones of a revival of African greatness and enlightenment. The philosophies and strategies found in the UNIA organ became doctrine at the divisional level, especially in isolated rural areas. These tactics and ideology were not blindly adopted either. They made sense to those who joined the UNIA and who made contributions to its growth and success. And Ferris, although born and reared in the North, showed remarkable affinity for southerners who devoured the *Negro World* issues he carefully constructed for four years during the peak growth years of the UNIA.

Ferris relished his opportunity to play a key role in this great movement under an inspiring and charismatic leader with whom he shared so many ideals. Garvey benefited enormously from having someone so capable and trustworthy to promote these aspirations, enabling the UNIA leader to use his enormous speaking talent to expand the organization's membership and to sell stock in the Black Star Line. In doing so Garvey traveled extensively and had many demands on his time. Although his presence was felt through his front-page letters to the people and his transcribed Liberty Hall speeches, so much of the paper's appeal through the years was due to the planning and calculation of its editors. During Garvey's extended absence from the American scene during his trip through the West Indies in February–July 1921, a period during which the regular front-page missives from the leader disappeared, Ferris served Garvey's vision and supplemented it generously with great loyalty and enthusiasm.

Ferris kept his finger on the pulse of the growing UNIA as he traveled to divisions, mostly outside the South. As a highly credentialed man of the cloth himself, he promoted the idea that the clergy strongly supported the movement. He served as liaison to clergymen at their regional and national denominational conferences in order to get feedback on the UNIA's standing in local communities. Ferris knew that the clergy's strong endorsement was critical to the movement, especially in the South. He also understood the importance of keeping a strong connection with divisions out of the organization's easy reach. Ferris chose numerous southern divisional reports to appear on the page in each issue devoted to "News and Views of UNIA Divisions." Southern contributors felt an individual connection because they could read their names, hometowns, and contribution amounts on the "Contributors' Page." Ferris thus showed a keen consciousness of the craving rural southerners felt for inclusion in the worldwide movement.

Ferris played another important role in the UNIA by employing one of his editorial trademarks: taking on the critics of the UNIA and Garvey by reprinting their words and then offering a rebuttal. For instance, when W. I. Walls, editor of the *Star of Zion*, commented on the local contingent of UNIA adherents in Charlotte, North Carolina, and then warned that the leaders in New York had never been successful in other endeavors, Ferris replied directly that the "old leadership" was bankrupt and appointed by whites.[38] He also took aim at competing editors of the New York black press and especially Robert Abbott, the editor of the *Chicago Defender* and one of Garvey's most despised rivals. This was an interesting strategy, especially since it provides researchers with a sense of which attacks the UNIA felt it necessary to address. Aggression by

Abbott threatened Garvey's constituency because of the enormous influence of the national edition of the *Defender*. Criticism by Du Bois and the NAACP were especially loathsome because of the national influence of that group.[39] Any competitor for leadership faced Ferris's poison pen. This defense was accompanied by Garvey's wrath, a sometimes pathological response that came to include people within his own organization.

Through the mass medium of the *Negro World*, Ferris brought his ideas to people all over the African diaspora in a way his little-known opus, *The African Abroad*, never did. His consistent spiritual tone and biblical references had their special appeal to the *Negro World* readership, and his sterling educational and theological credentials made his words more credible to the Christian believers, especially in the South, who participated fervently in the Garvey movement.

Hubert Harrison, a socialist and longtime journalist originally from Saint Croix, Danish West Indies, served as *Negro World* associate editor for most of 1920 and contributing editor from early 1921 through March 1922. Harrison had been the leader of the Liberty League of Harlem, which he believed was the prototype of the UNIA, which Garvey created in its image. Harrison later claimed to have reshaped the editorial and structural content of the UNIA organ, which in turn gave it its wide popularity. Although Harrison believed that neither Garvey nor Ferris were very talented journalists, he did admire Garvey as a propagandist without peer.[40] Harrison's remarks about Garvey after the UNIA leader's incarceration are critical in the extreme, especially for someone who had worked for the *Negro World*, Garvey's most successful instrument. In accord with Amy Jacques Garvey's resistance to the allegedly unpolished prose and ideas contained in many of her husband's editorials and speeches, Harrison accused Marcus Garvey of adding "an intensive propaganda more shrewdly adapted to the cruder psychology of the less intelligent masses, the sensationalism, self-glorification, and African liberation—although he knew next to nothing of Africa."[41] These comments, found in Harrison's private writings, suggest the distaste that a number of influential Harlem-based journalists felt as Garvey's activities began to focus on broad organizational expansion, including the southern field.

There were a few older and familiar southern-born editorial voices to balance the scales of public opinion. In May 1920 one of black America's most famous journalists became a weekly columnist at the age of sixty-four for the *Negro World*. John Edward Bruce, better known as "Bruce Grit," wrote many of the UNIA organ's most interesting and controversial pieces until his death in 1924. Bruce had been born a slave in Maryland and had worked his way into journalism doing clerical jobs for the *New York Times* and filing correspondence for William Coppinger of the American Colonization Society in Washington, D.C.[42] It is possible that Bruce joined the UNIA organ as a result of Ferris's association with the Negro Society for Historical Research, an organization that Bruce and Arthur Schomburg founded in 1911 in order to disseminate African history and evidence of African contributions to civilization. But it is also known that Bruce saw leadership qualities in Garvey that he believed could fill the void that Ferris had also lamented. Bruce wrote to his friend T. Thomas Fortune, later the editor of the *Negro World* from 1923 to 1928, that Garvey had "caught the vision; that the people of color throughout the world believe in his leadership and want him to lead them. . . . The old leaders were not able or were too lazy or indifferent or both, to work out a plan for the redemption and regeneration of the Race, as attractive and practical from any angle in which it is viewed, as that of Marcus Garvey." Bruce trusted the much younger and less experienced Garvey and put much faith in him as leader.[43]

Bruce had the reputation as a militant and even radical since his earliest days in journalism. He had consistently espoused black solidarity and nationalism, and in an essay from as early as 1881 he promoted what would have appeared in 1922 to be pure Garveyism.[44] He produced much powerful writing on race issues during his career, and most of his work appeared as freelance essays and opinion pieces under the nom de plume "Bruce Grit." This not-so-subtle alias became a fixture on page two of the *Negro World*.[45] This personal identification of the author gave his views autonomy from Garvey; at the same time, these opinions and views became tacitly endorsed by the UNIA.

Bruce wrote often about lynching and racial violence, pointing out the hypocrisy of white men defending white women's virtue while violating black womanhood. For this reason Bruce had special appeal to the southern audience, and his column no doubt resonated with southern blacks who lived under a vigilante system and with the constant threat of rape. One of the most incendiary statements to ever appear in the *Negro World* came straight from Bruce Grit's column: he urged black men to lynch white men who raped black women.[46] Garvey gave Bruce tremendous editorial freedom, and at times Bruce rambled on about issues that irritated him, especially the internecine wars between black leaders and organizations. Bruce, the established and august journalist, gave voice to opinions that might have caused Garvey more problems if the UNIA leader had written them himself.

Marcus Garvey had no problem stirring controversy, however, and the largest one of all occurred in June 1922 when he met with the acting leader of the

Klan in Atlanta. William Seraile, Bruce's biographer, struggles to explain why Bruce never condemned Garvey for this act, which drew the almost universal ire of black leaders in America. It perplexes Seraile why Bruce, a man he obviously admires deeply, would find anything reasonable or excusable about Garvey's action.[47] In fact, Bruce Grit defended Garvey as he did during so many of the leader's previous crises and scandals. Was this a lapse in judgment on Bruce's part or a sign that he recognized what Garvey was trying to do—find common ground for the defense of black women—and supported it? After all, this issue was critical to the southern constituency of the UNIA.

The most important journalist to edit the UNIA's organ, T. Thomas Fortune, served during the most difficult years of the Garvey movement. He began his tenure in 1923 when Garvey was already in jail and remained with the *Negro World* until his death in 1928, a year after the UNIA leader had been deported to Jamaica. Fortune was born in northwest Florida before the Civil War and, like Garvey, showed an early interest in the printing trade.[48] He moved to the North as a young man, and in 1884 he published his first book, *Black and White: Land, Labor, and Politics in the South*. In this remarkable work he analyzed the problems confronted by blacks in the post-Reconstruction period and weighed in on popular proposed solutions. Henry McNeal Turner had opined during this era that God's purpose for slavery was ultimately to Africa's benefit, but Fortune's response was outrage: "The talk about black people being brought to this country to evangelize Africa is so much religious nonsense boiled down to sycophantic platitude."[49] He insisted that blacks demand their constitutional rights and seek assimilation into white society. But in the second phase of his long career, he made many accommodations to Booker T. Washington, who secured financing for many of the papers for which Fortune wrote, ensuring his livelihood while inspiring repudiation by the anti-Tuskegee intellectual elite.[50]

Fortune was the mouthpiece of the influential *New York Age*, a nationally popular black newspaper, during the peak years of his influence in the 1890s, and the impact of this man's forceful and unremitting editorials still has not been fully appreciated or attributed to him. But in his golden years he wrote for a number of papers, including the pro-Garvey *Norfolk Journal and Guide*, and he enjoyed editing the *Negro World*. He kept the *Negro World* strong and worked with Amy Jacques Garvey and his friend John E. Bruce to continue the paper's appeal to the most loyal and broadest constituency. Although Fortune's later years brought him financial and personal difficulties, it would be a mistake to view him as a desperate, washed-up journalist who needed money and work. It is important to remember that when he took over the *Negro World*, the UNIA did not have much to pay him. He respected Garvey's sincerity and believed in the fundamentals of UNIA ideology. In 1927 he wrote:

> [Garvey] is a man of unusual ability, strength of character and determina-
> tion of purpose, and strictly honest. He is a fanatic on the Redemption of
> Africa from white overlordship and exploitation. . . . He has constrained the
> Negro to think Negro, as the Jew thinks Jew, and that is a very great achieve-
> ment, something no other Negro ever did. . . . To redeem Africa, to unify
> Negro sentiment and cooperation, to teach the Negro to conserve his so-
> cial, civil and economic values, under Negro leadership and financed by
> Negroes—that is a worthwhile program.[51]

The issue of repatriation is clearly omitted from Fortune's summation of Garvey's program. The idea of blacks returning to Africa was something For-tune never agreed with. He had a long record of opposition to the American Colonization Society and was unwilling to accept any justification for slavery. He objected stringently to Edward Wilmot Blyden's American speaking tour on behalf of the American Colonization Society and emigration.[52] He did, however, adopt the more anticolonial version of "African redemption." He relished the idea of Pan-African cooperation and black rule in Africa. As early as 1896 he himself had advocated "the formation of an association of Africans and descendants of Africa from all parts of the world."[53]

Fortune's contributions to the *Negro World* are evident in the success of the paper and the continued growth of the UNIA during Garvey's imprisonment. Fortune was successful at maintaining a national audience for the *New York Age* (formerly the *Globe* and the *New York Freeman*) and even the *Negro World* because he never lost his familiarity with the southern scene. He continued an interest in the average black southerner even after relocating to the North because in the late nineteenth century he understood that a national black audience was by definition southern by birth. The rigorous propaganda cam-paign to obtain Garvey's release from prison took place in the pages of the *Negro World* for nearly two years while Fortune kept the newspaper interesting and inspiring for the readers. The UNIA organ published a glowing obituary of Fortune, the "Dean of Negro journalists" and the UNIA's "wise counsel and sage," on 9 June 1928.

The pattern of editorship mirrors the pattern of UNIA growth. W. A. Do-mingo and Hubert Harrison, both originally from the West Indies, had very early and important roles in shaping the paper's content. But in the years in which we see the greatest devotion to Garvey and the UNIA in the South, it was the southern elder statesmen of black journalism who set the tone.

The UNIA Makes Its Own News

Early in the Garvey movement's history, two special events covered closely in the *Negro World* propelled the growth of the UNIA membership and augmented the popularity of Marcus Garvey. First came the November 1919 launch of the *Frederick Douglass*, and second was the UNIA first annual international convention in August 1920. The money and enterprise involved in organizing the Black Star Line, coupled with the excitement generated by the ideas expressed in convention sessions and the enthusiasm shown at the massive parade spectacle, provided urgency and hope to blacks in the southern states who vicariously experienced a sense of pride and achievement in these events. African American southerners jumped on the massive UNIA bandwagon by the thousands in the twenty months following the Black Star Line's maiden voyage. The UNIA became the vehicle for their aspirations, and the *Negro World* became the voice of their latent agenda.

The Garvey movement spread like wildfire, and as many as 80 percent of its divisions and chapters in the South were organized during a two-year period between July 1919 and August 1921. Only a few issues of the *Negro World* from 1919 and 1920 are extant, but most of them from February 1921 forward have been preserved. The contents of the newspaper during this earlier period hold more specific clues for understanding Garveyism's appeal during its most electrifying period, yet later issues provide much information as to how the South was organized and how the movement was sustained. The UNIA organ published detailed reports of the activities of field workers in the South and elsewhere. This evidence enables us to discover which areas the parent body considered ripe for organization and what rhetoric and strategies seemed to be most effective in those places.

As the movement spread beyond Virginia, Florida, and North Carolina, coastal areas of the South tended to host some of Garvey's strongest constituencies. Many of the UNIA's coastal divisions counted longshoremen and other previously but unsatisfactorily organized laborers as members. The important ports at New Orleans, Mobile, and Charleston each hosted large and active units of the UNIA throughout the 1920s. Many of the discriminatory conditions experienced by black laborers in unions such as the International Longshoremen's Association encouraged participation in race-conscious organizations like the UNIA. Each of these coastal cities gave rise to multiple units of the Garvey organization because in a sense labor organization had paved the way for Garveyism.

The black communities around the port of New Orleans embraced Garveyism as widely and devotedly as those in any other section of the South. Eventually, the popularity, factionalism, and scandal surrounding its local activities would attract the federal surveillance that partially contributed to Garvey's downfall in the United States. But for a time, the UNIA leader derived some of his most fanatical support among the laborers along the Mississippi River between New Orleans and Baton Rouge.

The New Orleans division formed at S. V. Robertson's home on 12 October 1920 and unveiled its charter on 4 January 1921.[54] Soon after, a West Indian organizer named Adrian Johnson brought the initial Crescent City supporters together and rallied another 2,000 by the time Marcus Garvey had his first major speaking engagement there in July 1921.[55] Within a few months, downtown New Orleans had three divisions of the UNIA, plus additional locals in the uptown Carrollton district and outlying communities of Algiers, Westwego, Kenner, and Gretna. And the spread of Garveyism in Louisiana did not stop there. Intensively cultivated sugarcane communities in the river parishes, over twenty of them between New Orleans and Baton Rouge, formed UNIA branches that year thanks to national organizers like Johnson and local people such as Louisiana's two UNIA state commissioners. Thomas W. Anderson, the first of these state leaders, reportedly "tamed" the New Orleans division in 1921 and did some organizing upstate.[56] In August 1922 he reported that "opposition to the UNIA in Louisiana comes from not one single white man but Negroes, especially preachers."[57] His successor, S. V. Robertson, who later became high commissioner for Louisiana, traveled further and further to the north in Louisiana and Mississippi, becoming at the 1924 convention the record holder for "having brought more members into the ranks of the UNIA than any other commissioner."[58] John Garrett, supervising engineer for the Black Star Line, was originally from Plaquemine, Louisiana, near Baton Rouge. Although he was in New York, his mother and others from his hometown maintained a faithful and active division.[59]

As the divisions spread through the Mississippi Valley, so did the *Negro World*. The paper inspired readers all along the river and elsewhere, sustaining this new group of Garveyites between visits from parent body and regional officers. Records indicate the presence of fifty-five divisions by August 1922 and at least eighty divisions and chapters by 1926 in the state of Louisiana.[60]

The way in which UNIA divisions were clustered around New Orleans was replicated in the communities around Mobile Bay, where six of the only thirteen Alabama divisions were located. It is likely that Adrian Johnson helped to organize the Mobile area because he was the first UNIA executive council member to visit Louisiana, Alabama, Mississippi, and Texas.[61] Mobile served as a feeder for the coalfields around Birmingham and had quite a strong contingent of churches, leaders, and laborers involved in a united effort to strengthen the UNIA.[62] The International Longshoremen's Association had a strong following there, and conditions of rapid development and racial tension mirrored similar wartime events in Newport News. Mobile's longshoremen, almost all of whom were black, suffered abuse from police for years, especially during strikes.[63]

T. M. Campbell, one of two black men working as extension field agents, alerted the U.S. Department of Agriculture of possible problems with the "Back to Africa" movement in his Gulf states district. He explained in February 1923 that interest in the Garvey movement and returning to Africa had hindered the progress of black farmers the previous season and had caused the dissolution of community farmers' clubs.[64] Campbell, who was closely affiliated with Tuskegee, got the secretary of agriculture's staff interested enough in this question to ask the local extension office in Alabama to consider this problem. The administrators in Washington tried to consult Robert Russa Moton, Tuskegee's principal, on the question of "Back to Africa propaganda," but there is no evidence that they ever did. It is clear, however, that at some point later that year Garvey found it necessary to explain the UNIA's purposes to Secretary of Agriculture Henry Wallace directly. He wrote a long letter explaining his program, its benefits for farmers, and its compatibility with southern rural ideology. He enclosed a copy of his *Philosophy and Opinions* and his essay "Appeal to the Soul of White America."[65] It is not at all clear what Wallace made of all of this literature or what, if anything, he did to get black Alabama farmers reconnected to their community clubs. It is apparent, however, that Garvey valued his rural constituency and saw his ideology as applicable to an agrarian setting.

One might suppose that Garvey's affinity for the Tuskegee philosophy of economic independence and social separateness, as well as his colonization plans, might have had an especially receptive audience in Booker T. Washington's home state. There is no evidence of open hostility to the UNIA by any group in Alabama. Garvey received warm receptions from a black ministers' conference in Birmingham and from students and administrators at Tuskegee in November 1923. While his mail fraud trial was still pending and after the Klan meeting and Eason's murder, Garvey was welcomed at Tuskegee, where he offered a subdued address to the student body. Afterward, Garvey and his wife received a cordial reception and hospitality from Moton, after which the fund-raising tables were turned, and Garvey made a fifty-dollar donation to Tuskegee.[66]

The only plausible excuse for the UNIA's lack of divisional strength in Alabama may simply have been a lack of manpower and resources. New Orleans–based S. V. Robertson, eventually the high commissioner for Louisiana, Mississippi, and Alabama, forfeited the opportunity to have the type of success he had in the first two states by not giving Alabama enough attention. And although we know from T. M. Campbell that Garvey's movement caught the imaginations of a significant number of farmers in Alabama, we find very little evidence of specific organizational activities beyond the Mobile area.[67]

South Carolina delegates to the 1920 UNIA convention carried a banner in the 1920 Harlem parade, and as in other places excitement generated during the convention assisted the growth of UNIA divisions there. An early visit by the flagship of the Black Star Line probably had much to do with the growth of interest of the Charleston community in the UNIA. The *Frederick Douglass* made port in Charleston in August 1920 while the convention was going on in New York. Septima Clark, later the linchpin of the voter education and civil rights movement in South Carolina, recalled the pride and exuberance she felt as a child along with her Charleston community upon seeing the arrival of the Black Star Line's first ship.[68] Charleston had three divisions and two chapters located in various black districts in the city. These divisions remained consistently active throughout the 1920s, and a strong auxiliary of Black Cross Nurses carried out service projects for the local community. The *Negro World* frequently reported the activities of the Charleston divisions, and it is clear that there was nothing clandestine about their meetings or their convictions.[69] On 1 January 1922, the Charleston Garveyites held an Emancipation Day parade down Calhoun Street, which included red, black, and green UNIA flags.[70] The community reacted positively to the display, and reports indicated that resistance to the movement subsided after that day.[71] The main division held other parades, sponsored rallies and petitions, and proudly wore UNIA lapel pins in the streets of Charleston throughout the 1920s. The demographics of South Carolina's UNIA divisions suggest that interest and organization radiated out from that city, as it had from New Orleans and Mobile. All but four of South Carolina's twenty-five divisions were located in the low country, most of them being within fifty miles of Charleston. Jacob W. Slappey, the UNIA commissioner for South Carolina, claimed to have waged a strenuous fight in order to get the pastors of Charleston and other towns nearby to embrace Garveyism. In New York's Liberty Hall in October 1923, he relished telling the audience that no opposition to the UNIA existed anywhere in his state since his work had been completed. In a report to the *Negro World*, he suggested that the strength of the South Carolina UNIA had eased racial tensions and reduced lynching in the early 1920s.[72] Although this claim and its connection to the UNIA cannot be verified, it is true that lynching dropped off significantly in the 1920s compared with the three previous decades in the South.[73] Those who fought courageously for antilynching legislation in 1921–22 could have easily made similar claims.

Just as ambiguous as the weakness of the UNIA in Alabama is the reason that Texas had only twelve divisions. Other than the distinct possibility that Texas had geographical and logistical conditions that made it more complicated to organize, one plausible explanation for Texas's dearth of UNIA presence was the outward violence experienced by race organizers in the state. In August 1919 a white mob in Austin had assaulted John Shillady, the white national secretary for the NAACP, in broad daylight during a visit on behalf of the organization. Apparently, this event was countenanced by state authorities, and the governor issued statements in support of the mob.[74] If a white man could receive such treatment in the Texas capital, a black man's prospects in the countryside would have seemed particularly dim.

The NAACP had thirty-one branches in the state before Shillady's attack and the massive rejuvenation of the Ku Klux Klan in the early 1920s, but the NAACP shrank to only five active branches by 1923. The only locale in which both the UNIA and NAACP operated was Dallas. But there NAACP members grew fearful of meeting at all, and the national office promoted very discreet fund-raising rather than local agitation.[75]

The UNIA's commissioner to Texas, R. B. Moseley, endured a severe and frightening beating by eight white men while traveling and speaking in his home state. Moseley, a Dallas chef, reported the incident to Garvey in June 1922, right after it occurred. The man's stolid account indicated his dedication to his duties and his bravery and pragmatism in the face of white intimidation. He had spoken to four churches, including one with 500 attendees, in less than a week. His journey had included visiting with farmers and canvassing black neighborhoods in the small towns of Fry's Gap, Cushing, Jacksonville, and Rusk in northeast Texas. He pressed on even after having been ominously followed and threatened during twilight hours. Eventually, state authorities picked him up, placed him in jail, and fined him for vagrancy. On his way to the station to return home to Dallas by train, he was waylaid and severely beaten.[76] The Interdenominational Negro Alliance of Dallas's black pastors had publicly rejected local UNIA leaders' request for an endorsement of Garvey's upcoming visit to Dallas just days earlier.[77] On 19 June the UNIA leader came anyway during a sweep through the South, the same trip that culminated in his meeting with the Klan's acting imperial wizard in Atlanta. Clearly, the issues of pressure and violence toward the UNIA confronted Garvey on this particular southern journey and perhaps influenced this strategic misstep.

Another possible factor influencing negative perceptions of the UNIA in Texas may have been its similarity to a previous emigration movement. Memories may have lingered of Chief Alfred Sam's project, which involved Texans around the Galveston area as well as a few hundred black Oklahomans. A trader-nationalist from the Gold Coast, Sam had been active in recruiting emigrants for Africa and stockholders in his Akim Trading Company, preceding the Garvey movement in its plans and ideals by less than a decade. The British colonial government had tried to obtain the U.S. government's help in curbing Sam's activities, and as a result, the mission-oriented entrepreneur received much negative publicity and drew a U.S. government investigation for mail fraud. Local efforts attempted to discourage African Americans from partaking of Sam's offer to transport African American farmers and mechanics to land he owned in the Gold Coast. Nevertheless, emigrants eventually sailed on the SS *Liberia*, a ship Sam had purchased and outfitted with stockholder money, from Galveston in 1914.[78] Whether Texans associated the UNIA with Chief Sam's project or not, in the violent atmosphere of the Lone Star State, UNIA organizers essentially abandoned Texas in favor of more hospitable southern climes.

Tennessee's experience with the UNIA had mixed results. Although the state suffered from erratic leadership and the organization developed only twelve divisions, a few elements of Garveyism merit mention. Apparently, organizational efforts in Tennessee focused on the larger cities of Knoxville, Memphis, Nashville, and Chattanooga. Knoxville had endured the worst urban race riot in the former Confederacy during the United States's traumatic year of violence in 1919. Some local black citizens looked to organizations for help, and within one year Knoxville hosted two UNIA locals. T. C. Glashen, the incendiary and militant British Guianan banished from Key West, reappeared as the president of one Knoxville division and then as UNIA commissioner for Tennessee. By August 1923 he was creating controversy again, this time not with local citizens, but with the UNIA parent body. For undisclosed reasons he was removed from his leadership role.[79] The first southern city to hear Garvey in person in 1917, Nashville began reading the *Negro World* as early as December 1919 and eventually had two divisions, one of which prospered and enjoyed participation by professional blacks. It had a physician as its president, as well as its own "Liberty Hall" and ladies' division.[80] Although the Memphis division was chartered quite early according to its division number, the origins and activities of division number 195 remain obscure. One might suspect that

Memphis played a role as the metropolis from which Garveyism spread into the Delta, but there is no evidence to support this connection. The *Negro World*, usually the best source for information about local divisions, is curiously silent on UNIA activities in Memphis.

Chattanooga serves as a rare example outside of Texas and Florida where violent hostility from white officials affected UNIA activities. In August 1927 local authorities raided the Chattanooga Liberty Hall, precipitating a gun battle that elicited substantial news coverage and attention by the white press. Some reports claimed that outside agitation among Chattanooga black laborers had expanded the local UNIA to 700 members. The group had aroused suspicion by trying to purchase military uniforms and 200 high-power "repeating" rifles.[81] This rather late emergence of a UNIA stronghold raises interesting questions about the effect that white hostility had on making a local group seem more radical. We do not know if the Chattanooga group intended to use aggression or if they were simply arming themselves for self-defense in the rapidly deteriorating racial climate of the community in which they organized.

As we come to understand the growth and spread of the UNIA in the early states of Virginia, Florida, and North Carolina, in the weakly organized states of Alabama, Texas, and Tennessee, and in important coastal cities like Charleston, Mobile, and New Orleans and their peripheries, the diversity among southern Garveyites becomes clearer. Although the reasons for the UNIA's relatively small numbers of divisions in Alabama, Texas, and Tennessee remain obscure, its contrasting divisional strength in southwest Georgia and in the Delta region along both sides of the Mississippi River demand an explanation. An obvious similarity between these two areas is their overlap with the Black Belt. But more striking perhaps is the rural character of the UNIA divisions in both areas. As these remote districts of the southern landscape became saturated with sympathy for the UNIA, Garveyism achieved an even higher degree of popular appeal and diversity.

Georgia as a Case Study in Rural Organization
Georgia hosted a very early UNIA division, chartered even before the first convention, at the port of Brunswick. In 1920 this coastal town of 14,413 was half black and half white.[82] But its population had grown, and racial proportions had vacillated during the war years. During 1918, the U.S. Department of Labor had surveyed working conditions there and found that although the population before the war included a majority of blacks, an influx of almost exclusively white industrial laborers for shipbuilding had altered the balance to

the point that whites outnumbered blacks after the war. Puerto Rican laborers, who helped build and run the new Picric Acid Plant, formed the only foreign segment of the population, and almost all were deported by 1918. Whites monopolized skilled jobs, and 75 percent of all labor remained unorganized.[83]

Brunswick's deep channel provided one of the best natural harbors on the Atlantic Coast and made it more attractive than Savannah as a site for heavy industry in 1918. It also served as an important port of call for the Clyde Line, a passenger steamship company that stopped in coastal cities from Jacksonville to New York.[84] Brunswick became the primary embarkation city for blacks from rural areas in extreme south Georgia who were migrating to the Northeast. Many migrants never made it past Brunswick, sometimes for lack of funds or because they found work at the port.[85]

In early 1921 the Reverend J. W. H. Eason found conditions in Brunswick and south Georgia ripe for expanding the UNIA in the Deep South. After his rewarding ventures in North Carolina, Eason became adept at gauging the UNIA message to local conditions. In January 1921 he spoke in seventeen locations in and around Brunswick and took a cash order for over 500 copies of the *Negro World*.[86] UNIA secretary Prendergast accompanied Eason on this worthwhile journey, and by late March local people praised and recognized their work for inspiring and organizing new divisions throughout southern Georgia.

Freedom for Africa predominated Eason's addresses as he introduced south Georgia's black population to the UNIA in this first spin through the state. H. F. Parlan of Brunswick reported on Eason's successful visits to several large churches in the Brunswick area. Eason began with a series of lectures to 700 people at Payne's Chapel, the Brunswick division president's home church. Enthusiastic listeners from the Reverend B. W. Jones's AME congregation purchased two hundred dollars worth of Black Star Line stock. Arkansas native E. J. Rozzell, who was known in Brunswick for bringing in black strikebreakers for white longshoremen, opened his church, Mount Olive Baptist, for Eason to speak. And the Reverend S. C. Roberts of Shiloh Baptist also welcomed the North Carolina pastor into his church for a mass meeting of 1,000 black citizens of Brunswick.[87]

Baptist and AME ministers in the Brunswick community welcomed the Garvey message and seemed especially receptive to Eason, a fellow clergyman. He understood their lives and challenges in the South from personal experience and was able to calibrate the UNIA's platform and Garvey's vision to local conditions. Not just in Georgia, but all over the South, ministers and their churches formed a crucial part of the UNIA infrastructure. Although they were not exclusively in charge of organizing and leading local UNIA divisions, at least thirty-two ministers, extant record fragments show, headed southern divisions, while eight served as local secretaries in 1926 through 1927.[88] Many more provided access to their congregations, use of their facilities, and support to local lay organizers. The *Negro World* also provides evidence of abundant ministerial support for Garveyism in the Southland. Randall Burkett has shown that as many as 250 active Garveyite clergy assisted the UNIA from 1921 through 1923.[89]

A Brunswick preacher named F. W. Ware became the state organizer for Georgia in 1921 and escorted Eason and Prendergast into the interior to organize further. After Eason rushed to Washington, D.C., to attend to other business, Ware and Prendergast visited Baxley, sixty miles northwest along the railroad, to follow up on early support indicated there. Columbus L. Halton, a sixty-year-old laborer who had lost his farm in the 1910s, later became division president in Baxley. Halton had already proved his commitment to the movement by attending the Harlem convention in August 1920. He not only signed the original Negro Bill of Rights but also delivered a graphic report on harsh conditions in Georgia, which had been recorded in convention minutes.[90] In Baxley, Prendergast delivered an earnest explanation of the red, black, and green UNIA flag and the meaning of plans to build up Africa with the help of some willing African American pioneers. Ware followed with a humorous and light-hearted lecture, which apparently aroused much affection and support for the movement.[91]

Ware also organized a division at Waycross, sixty miles due west of Brunswick, which yielded 150 members and even a separate ladies' division. Soon after, Waycross formed a second UNIA branch, chapter #34, because of expanding interest and conflicting leadership in the town. At the tiny railroad stop of Gardi, which lay between Brunswick and Baxley, thirty-three people formed a UNIA division, again with Ware's help, in early 1921.[92]

Although the work of Eason, Prendergast, and Ware left a trail of new divisions behind, Georgia's UNIA divisions did not arise in any systematic way, according to their charter numbers. The most notable pattern emerges in the way the organization stayed almost exclusively in the extreme southern part of the state. The rural piedmont in the east-central part of the state did not show any trace of support for Garvey or the UNIA, whereas the coastal plain and especially the southwest section of the state became thoroughly immersed in the movement.[93]

Although it is possible to group divisions in this way, there was not much difference between a division organized in January and one organized in

August 1921. More important to note, however, are influences on their organization. One important factor is whether Eason or Ware or other organizers brought the UNIA and the Garvey movement to a community or whether locals who read the *Negro World* took the initiative to organize their own divisions. By March 1921, the central administration of the UNIA recognized that its field workers could not move fast enough to meet the ravenous demand for new divisions. The UNIA constitution stipulated very strict rules governing the formation, leadership, and membership of divisions. At least seven members, all Negro, needed to pay dues for a charter to be issued. Relatives were not allowed to monopolize leadership posts within a division. Assuming he would have the ability to know all local leaders, the regulations required that the president general vouch for division presidents before they assumed their posts. Each division required a chaplain, and stringent record keeping and reporting to the parent body were mandated.[94]

Not even the enterprising Garvey could have predicted the explosive growth of the movement in rural communities, where many willing participants could not reasonably meet the constitution's restrictions. At some point the UNIA executive council must have decided that some of the rural divisions would be exempt from the most inapplicable requirements. These exceptions paved the way for autonomous divisions to form with the *Negro World*, the UNIA constitution, and the Negro Bill of Rights as their only guides.

Another problem arose as Garvey wanted to affiliate willing members quickly but did not have enough trustworthy and dynamic organizers like Eason to go around. J. D. Brooks and E. W. Pearson in North Carolina had provided early examples of corruption's potential in such a contribution-driven and fast-growing organization. Sometime during early 1921, Garvey must have decided to risk further opportunities for graft and strike while the irons were hot, allowing divisions to form on their own. The *Negro World* began to run a large advertisement encouraging the formation of local branches in specific states in the United States: "Start a Branch: Seven or more colored persons should get together now and start a branch of the Universal Negro Improvement Association in the following states." The list of thirty-three states included every southern state except for Virginia. The geographic focus for expansion was obviously on the Midwest, West, and South, while obvious states omitted were all in the Northeast plus California, Ohio, and Michigan, where an infrastructure was already in place.[95] As late as September 1922, August Handy of Maringouin, Louisiana, wrote to the *Negro World* editor that he had organized 135 people in his community and was "only waiting for the [UNIA] state commissioner."[96] People in some areas who read the UNIA paper and supported its causes never formed divisions. After suggesting the *Negro World* should be read in every Negro home in the world, Mrs. L. M. Palmer from a tiny community in coastal McIntosh County, Georgia, wrote in 1924: "We have not any branch of the UNIA here at Crescent, but most everybody has the Garvey spirit."[97]

The *Negro World* began arriving in large quantities to subscribers and agents in all the new divisions, where in turn it sparked further interest in neighboring communities. J. C. Wilson, a drayman and local mason, became the executive secretary of the Brunswick division. He reported continued growth to over 600 members in the months after Eason's departure. The beachhead division declared a goal of 2,000 just for Brunswick alone.[98]

The UNIA Spreads to the Rural, Interior South

By the summer of 1921 the UNIA had taken hold in the rural counties around Albany in southwest Georgia's Black Belt. Fourteen of Georgia's thirty-four UNIA divisions lay within a forty-mile radius of Albany. The most remote and isolated farming communities in the state ended up with the highest concentrations of UNIA supporters in the whole region. Camilla and Pelham in Mitchell County, twenty miles south of Albany, benefited from a strong local organizer, who, along with C. A. Halton of Baxley, had attended the 1920 UNIA convention and signed the Negro Bill of Rights. The Reverend O. C. Kelly brought in the high commissioner, S. V. Robertson, to inspire his already enthusiastic divisions. Robertson's address, "Marcus Garvey the Dreamer," contained now-familiar phrases and revealing clues to the movement's challenges and direction in rural areas:

> The UNIA does not teach you to be disloyal to any government but it teaches you the Redemption of Africa, our Motherland, and to be loyal to your race. . . . "Dream on Mr. Garvey, until the Negro wakes up everywhere." No Negro wants social equality, but wants social rights. Organize and get together. God has sent us a man to teach us to unite. . . . The UNIA teaches you that the Negroes will never be anything until they possess strong power; not until then will we be respected. . . . The UNIA is church-like. . . . Dream on until every Negro can say "free at last, free at last."[99]

Two months later, local organizer Kelly again turned out the community for an appearance by J. W. H. Eason. Ten thousand blacks from in and around Mitchell County spilled into the intersection of what is now Love Street and Liberia Avenue in front of Pelham's Summerhill Baptist Church on the night of 10 May 1922. The Leader of American Negroes spoke on the principles of

Summerhill Baptist Church, host to the largest UNIA mass meeting
in southwest Georgia, remains an active part of the black community in
Pelham, Mitchell County, Georgia. It sits atop a knoll at the corner of
Love Street and Liberia Avenue. (Photograph by author)

the UNIA and Africa for the Africans.[100] The message remained strong in their minds for months. At the summer's end, the nearby Camilla division held a celebration on 31 August, the date for the international Negro holiday suggested in the Negro Bill of Rights, at Union Grove Baptist Church.[101]

Nearby in Worth County, the Coverdale and Shingler divisions had formed in January 1922, and Commissioner S. V. Robertson helped members of these divisions organize a new division five miles down the road at Sylvester, the county seat.[102] By the end of 1922, the residents of Worth County had established five UNIA divisions among the county's 12,000 blacks, making this section of southwest Georgia the heart of the Garvey movement in the state.

The isolation of Worth County, Georgia, and its cotton economy were comparable in many ways to most of the Arkansas and Yazoo-Mississippi Deltas, the most purely pro-Garvey region in the United States. The Flint River formed the county's northwestern border and had served as a major transportation route out of the cotton-rich counties of southwest Georgia into the Gulf of Mexico. In the counties of extreme south Georgia, there was more of a racial balance, as compared with the counties adjacent to the Mississippi River, whether in Mississippi or Arkansas, where blacks made up well over half of the population. The Mississippi side was serviced by the great railroads extending from Chicago to New Orleans via Memphis. The Arkansas side included counties like Phillips, which was as isolated as any community in the Southeast but was home to at least six UNIA divisions. And of course the river and railroads were the major transportation route for all of the goods residents of these areas produced. The *Negro World* was read and appreciated by people from these remote communities.

As charter numbers suggest, Mississippi and Arkansas aligned with the UNIA slightly later than the rest of the southern states. Although the Delta area lagged by about six to twelve months, the thoroughness of organization made up for any tardiness. Sources give only a few clues as to how this region, obviously so rich in Garveyite sentiment, became organized. The *Negro World* does not tell us who organized there in 1921 and 1922, but we know that the Leader of American Negroes who replaced Eason in August 1922 was William LeVan Sherrill, a native of Jefferson County, Arkansas, an important crossroads in the Delta. In September 1923 S. V. Robertson, the high commissioner, was reassigned to Mississippi and had actually come into the Delta area while visiting Merigold in Bolivar County.[103]

Since *Negro World* advertisements encouraged communities to form divisions on their own initiative beginning in March 1921, this may explain the appearance of nearly 100 Delta divisions.[104] In imagining this process, the accessibility of the *Negro World* was crucial. Local people had ties to migrants in New York, Chicago, Detroit, and Philadelphia, and kinship and friendship networks no doubt provided information and encouragement in both directions.[105] In the absence of regional and national organizers it fell to indigenous, organic intellectuals to promote the cause of Pan-Africanism.[106]

In the rural South of the 1920s news of a visiting speaker, especially a gifted orator like Eason or Robertson, could command enormous audiences. The audience's appreciation was demonstrated in contributions, as UNIA converts joined the organization or purchased Black Star Line stock or *Negro World* subscriptions in the heat of their enthusiasm. But how a local person absorbed the UNIA platform through the *Negro World*, recognized its familiar and attractive themes, became inspired by the scope of Garvey's vision, and then called together friends and neighbors, convincing them to contribute their meager income to an international cause, is remarkable.

The community member most likely to have been capable of promoting such a cause would have been a pastor. In rural counties around the South many churches were too small to have a resident churchman, and in extreme cases itinerant ministers visited as many as forty churches a season. Preachers, rather than trained pastors, often had little beyond a grammar school education and made their living working alongside their flocks in the fields during the week. These men often served as the intellectuals of their communities, providing secular as well as spiritual leadership. Pastors in rural areas tended to be older than urban pastors, and their messages were more otherworldly. Records show that the rural preachers who promoted Garveyism usually fit this composite. They enjoyed the support of local laymen who may have been precisely those who held the mid-week services that were common in rural churches with itinerant preachers.[107]

Any race organization's biggest challenge in the east Arkansas Delta was not finding sympathy for its objectives but sending its representatives there safely to organize. Despite the dangers, numerous UNIA divisions appeared within a fifty-mile radius of Elaine in Phillips County, the site of the most notorious rural race riot of the post–World War I period. The three days of violence, which killed hundreds of local black farmers in September 1919, had been precipitated by farmers joining together for legal action in collecting their overdue crop payments.[108]

One would not think any race organization could succeed in proximity to Elaine so soon after this calamity. Nevertheless, Phillips County and neighboring Monroe County hosted at least six UNIA divisions each, while Lee and St. Francis Counties to the north had three or more divisions each. Six of the UNIA's most active divisions in the state of Mississippi and twenty-six others were within this fifty-mile radius of Elaine also, although they were across the river.[109] The fifteen Arkansas UNIA divisions close to Elaine existed in communities that averaged 200 or fewer people. Holly Grove and Round Pond both had populations between 500 and 1,000, and each hosted two UNIA branches. Most of these were on the Missouri-Pacific Railroad or the Missouri–North Arkansas Railroad lines, which were both used mainly for transporting lumber and cotton to Helena at the river's edge in Phillips County or Memphis, seventy miles to the north. Despite the widening reach of the automobile after

World War I and its ability to make travelers more anonymous, only two division towns could be reached by paved road, and thus visitors would need a substantial incentive for attempting to visit and organize in the area.[110]

Marcus Garvey and the UNIA program became familiar to local residents beginning with the circulation of the *Negro World* in Arkansas in 1919.[111] The complaint from Wabbaseka proved that early issues of the *Negro World* had increased racial tension with some white locals. A black drugstore owner in Camden, Arkansas, became a regular distributor of the paper, and George McCrary of Fort Smith was recognized as one of the top forty-two agents worldwide for *Negro World* circulation.[112] By late summer of 1921 thirty-five of Arkansas's divisions were awaiting charters. There is no evidence, however, of a national or even regional or state organizer traveling through Arkansas before that time. We must conclude that local UNIA supporters heeded the *Negro World* advertisements encouraging local UNIA supporters to set up their own divisions.[113]

Adam D. Newson of Merigold, Mississippi, was a farmer and preacher with several churches in Bolivar County under his guidance. He became instrumental in leading the UNIA in Mississippi, representing its divisions at the conventions in Harlem and preparing the state for visits and speeches of the high commissioner. He even appeared at a regional gathering of Delta UNIA divisions at Pine City, Arkansas, indicating links between divisions across the Mississippi.[114] Marcus Garvey never visited the Arkansas or Mississippi Deltas or southwest Georgia, but his influence was deeply felt nevertheless.

Rural ministers who rode the circuit may have served as the UNIA's best organizers, putting the most dutiful members of their various congregations in charge of correspondence with the New York headquarters, money collection, and meetings. E. B. "Britt" McKinney, who later became the black vice president of the Southern Tenant Farmers Union in 1934, was a minister, farmer, and devoted Garveyite who supervised over thirty-six churches comprising 4,000 people in the Arkansas Delta.[115] He claimed to have spent the forty-four years between 1894 and 1938 organizing his people around his Delta home in Marked Tree, where he believed his influence among his congregants was paramount in their decisions to join or stay out of an organization.[116]

Meanwhile, ministers in the larger Delta towns resisted any protest organizations disturbing the peace. Two weeks after the Elaine massacre, a committee of ministers and leading black citizens of Blytheville, Arkansas, published a resolution in which they promised to "allow no one to establish any organization among them that might create trouble."[117] Mississippi County blacks ignored the counsel of these men and established UNIA divisions at Armorel,

Burton Spurr, Hickman, Gosnell, and Burdett, and two at Blytheville, a Delta community forty miles north of Memphis, which hosted some of the most faithful and dynamic of UNIA's Arkansas divisions.[118] Even in the organization's waning days after Garvey's deportation, these divisions maintained correspondence, reports, and dues to the central division. Tiny Burton Spurr, too small to have its own post office, had thirty-two members in 1927, and its division president George Fowler was a tenant farmer.[119]

Blytheville had a number of black citizens who preferred the ideology of Garvey to the advice of their own conservative ministers. Contributions to the "Marcus Garvey Defense Fund," reported during the UNIA leader's mail fraud trial, indicate heavier support for Garvey in Blytheville than in any other Delta location.[120] R. H. McDowell represented Blytheville at the UNIA's 1924 convention in Harlem and reported problems:

> The people, who were mostly farmers, were struggling with the organization in the face of the opposition of the preachers and others, among them some professional men. But the organization had had the sympathetic consideration of the town authorities so much so that when members of another Negro organization sought to prevent them meeting in the town, complaining that the aims and objects of the association were not satisfactory, the mayor not only gave them permission but recommended the work as being very good for the race.[121]

Other Blytheville blacks voiced support to the UNIA. Mollie Bynum hoped local youth would become UNIA members before they became trapped in exploitative jobs; J. L. Cooper felt strongly enough about the positive influence of the *Negro World* to send in a letter to the editors praising their work.[122] Readers from nearby Marianna and Brinkley commented on the important educational value of the paper for instilling race pride and informing people of African descent of their long and remarkable history.[123]

The ministers of Holly Grove, Arkansas, in Monroe County, a community of 977 persons, had different dispositions from their brethren in Blytheville.[124] The local UNIA division had eighty-three members in 1922 and drew from four different local congregations. Sizable collections for the "UNIA Convention Fund" were sent on behalf of the four congregations as a whole rather than as individual donations.[125] Tom Bobo, the division president, was a fifty-three-year-old tenant farmer with six children. Although a layman, he enjoyed the support of local ministers and had one of the strongest UNIA divisions in the state.

The Reverend J. W. H. Eason and S. V. Robertson represent the best of clergymen and laymen from the UNIA parent body, using their organizational skills and diplomacy in the most challenging racial environment in the United States. Local organizers like Adam D. Newson, E. B. McKinney, and Tom Bobo demonstrate the effectiveness of ministers and community activists at the local level. The occasional visits by eloquent speakers like Eason and Robertson supplied inspiration for rural people while also providing reassurance that the UNIA existed and functioned at a higher level, implementing the programs it represented. The week-to-week efforts of local people and the regularity of the *Negro World* sustained and informed the grassroots membership. Unlike their national and regional counterparts, local leaders in small communities worked without salaries or recognition. Individually, they played very small roles in the organization, but when we begin to recognize the vast numbers of small divisions and contributions from all over the South that underpinned the Garvey movement, their sum takes on new significance. A closer look at local, rural, and southern members of the UNIA who made up this vital component of the organization will provide a context for their activism.

The Black Belt was not, as many assumed, a movement toward fields of labor under more genial climatic conditions; it was primarily a huddling for self-protection,—a massing of the black population for mutual defence [sic] in order to secure the peace and tranquility necessary to economic advance.—W. E. B. Du Bois, The Souls of Black Folk, *1903*

The Garvey movement attracted a very diverse group of southern blacks from urban and rural locations, coastal and interior cities, and the upper and lower South. But the archetypal American Garveyite lived in a majority-black community, farmed cotton on someone else's land, and struggled to maintain a stable and safe family. Those UNIA supporters who left the countryside and farming behind for industrial labor and urban living carried their experiences and sensibilities beyond the Black Belt. What they understood about economic dependence, racism, and the threat of violence and sexual exploitation was experienced in a new context.

In the sense that Garveyites came from "the masses," it is fair to say, in the case of the South, that most Garveyites were members of the lowest economic class. Garveyites who had some property or the advantages of professional status were the exceptions. Because of laborers' meager financial resources, the economic directives of the UNIA held wide appeal. Garvey's articulated philosophy encouraged independence first and foremost. One scholar's characterization of the Garveyite as a petit bourgeois striver derived mainly from an examination of the popularity of the Black Star Line and does not apply to the typical southern UNIA member.[1] The popularity of Black Star Line stock indicated interest in promoting a black-owned and -operated enterprise; it was never seen or even promoted as a way for any individual to get rich but instead as a vehicle for uplifting the Negro race as a whole. Particularly in the South, UNIA sympathizers and members may have dreamed of prosperity, but realistically most hoped for a way to escape dependence on exploitative landlords, capitalists, foremen, and managers. Class interpretations of the movement disregard the racialist aspects of the program, including race consciousness, race pride, and African redemption, which had unambivalent support, especially from southerners.

In the South there were many ways to find oneself in the lowest economic class. Most rural blacks in the region were tenant farmers, sharecroppers, and, particularly in the Arkansas and Yazoo-Mississippi Deltas, agricultural wage laborers. Others were industrial workers with varying degrees of skill. In coastal towns they worked as longshoremen, handling cargoes and supporting massive steamship operations for terribly low wages. Also in port cities, railroad workers, shipbuilders, coal trimmers, and stevedores provided important services for meager pay. Rural southern industries that employed significant numbers of blacks included timber cutting and sawmilling, turpentine collection and processing, and railroad construction. These were difficult jobs that required an itinerant lifestyle for much of the year. People from all of these exploited occupations were attracted to the UNIA's program because of its message of economic independence. In all of these settings, blacks labored alongside whites, and discrimination in pay made black workers more race-conscious and thus receptive to the message of race pride. As we examine more specific segments of the population of the South, other elements of the program take on greater importance, depending on local conditions of race relations and leadership.

By the 1930s, sociologists studying the South had generally agreed with Howard W. Odum's model of the southeastern United States as a region containing many subregions. Odum's "southern regions" paradigm described how geographic, social, cultural, and other features influenced the ways in which each of these subregions developed particular characteristics. Charles S. Johnson's 1941 study of the socioeconomic indices of 1,104 southern counties classified these county units by degree of isolation and dominant crop or industry. The counties that fell together in Johnson's categories did not necessarily have contiguous geographic borders, but they did have strikingly similar cultural and social characteristics, particularly in their impact on the lives of African Americans. For example, counties devoted to cotton cultivation uniformly had black majorities, high rates of tenancy, and very low expenditure for black education as compared with white education.[2]

In this examination of the level at which black communities of the former Confederate states expressed their sympathy with the Garvey movement, isolation from commercial centers is considered important. The difference between urban and rural conditions in the South was the most obvious demographic factor to have a significant impact on the social and political life of black southerners. The job opportunities, the anonymity, the avenues for receiving information and news, and the choices of churches and social activities provided by urban settings allowed an urban laborer to broaden and control more aspects of his own life. The rural farmer or laborer had few choices. His most celebrated option, exercised in great numbers in the World War I era and consistently ever since, was the option to leave.

Rural areas portray a certain static quality that is sometimes misleading, however. There is a popular misconception that the outmigrants proved their militancy by leaving dependence, stasis, and isolation behind in favor of life and labor in the cities. The implication of this belief is that those who remained behind were submissive.[3] The popularity of Garveyism in the South, and especially in the rural areas, provides an alternative interpretation. It is certain that limitations arising from race relations and local leadership, both black and white, existed for poor black farmers and laborers. But that is not to say that they did not try to take a stand, adopt new attitudes, improve their lives, and expand their understanding of what it meant to be black and part of a larger race-based global identity. Rural southern Garveyites were not submissive and did engage in their own forms of activism and protest.

In the South, the disposition of white government, law enforcement, and community leadership under the Jim Crow system influenced the extent to which these aspirations and beliefs could be expressed. Despite our images to the contrary, there was variation in social relations between blacks and whites from one southern community to the next. Fitzhugh Brundage deals eloquently with this question in his pioneering study of violence and lynching in the New South.[4] In smaller places, a few people could determine how race relations played out. Often, the proportion of blacks to whites in a southern county helped to determine how friendly and accommodating one group would be toward the other. The local minister could set the tone for the black community, while in other cases the white sheriff might establish harsh or relatively few limits on the black citizens of an area. In a few places whites knew and cared little about the private activities of the segregated black community, while in others suspicion and surveillance were rampant and relentless.

These relations affected the public participation of black people as they organized UNIA divisions; read the *Negro World*; discussed separatism, economic independence, and African redemption; and invited guest speakers from outside the community to UNIA division meetings. How local whites interpreted the meaning of Garvey sentiment or whether they noticed it at all and whether they were willing to accept and tolerate it would have had an impact on the survival of the local division. In some cases, the opposition of a black minister would prohibit the spread of Garveyite ideas, while in others whites considered Garveyism dangerous or inappropriate for the local black community. All of these factors influenced local individuals and their ideologies. A person's race, job, freedom, choices, isolation, wealth, and status, as well as the community's population and its leadership, would all combine to determine the feasibility of activism.

It is compelling to observe the high concentration of UNIA divisions in notably rural sections of the interior in southwest Georgia and the Arkansas and Yazoo-Mississippi Deltas. Although the term "rural" often evokes an image of a widely dispersed population living in so-called isolation, in 1920 these areas reached their peak density for all of recorded history. Many of these substantial rural populations in the South contained particularly high proportions of black farmers. The U.S. Census Bureau defined rural areas as towns or unincorporated areas of fewer than 2,500 people.[5] In this study, specific southern counties are examined, most of which contain no towns of more than 2,500 people, but many of which contain numerous towns of just less than that number. So even though the population was fairly evenly spread out over each county under examination and these counties had large populations, they did not contain areas where the population was highly concentrated into dense urban settings with large-scale business and industry unrelated to cotton production. However, because cotton cultivation required intensive labor, these rural counties of the Black Belt contained large proportions of the total black population in 1920. These segments of the South offer abundant material for case studies in rural Garveyism.

Population statistics indicate that the rural South contained the bulk of African Americans in 1920, and for the most part, rural southern counties were the only political subdivisions in the United States with black majorities.[6] In almost all southern towns of over 10,000 people, whites held an overwhelming majority. Also in this period, the South as a whole was essentially rural by definition, with Florida and Louisiana being the only states that did not have populations that were at least two-thirds in the rural classification.[7] Therefore southern, rural farmers represented a plurality of African Americans in 1920. The number of African Americans born into that category (even if later they became urban) would have been even higher. The typical UNIA supporter in southwest Georgia or the Delta was also a farmer. So although a Garveyite from one of these areas might not represent the feelings of all of his fellow farmers and certainly not all black Americans, our understanding of his attraction to the movement brings us closer than we presently are to grasping the motivations and thought of this group.

More black people lived in Georgia by far than in any other state in both 1910 and 1920. This fact alone made it a logical place to begin organizing the exclusively Negro UNIA. The southwest quadrant of the state included the greatest number of majority-black counties. Arkansas contained half the number of blacks that Georgia did, but they were concentrated in counties in the Delta, most of which were over three-fourths black in population. The counties of the South with the highest density of rural black population in 1920 were along the eastern side of the Mississippi River in the state of Mississippi.[8]

The Black Belt counties of southwest Georgia held striking numbers of rural UNIA divisions. Worth and Mitchell Counties hosted the strongest contingents of Garveyites, and black citizens there took enough interest to subscribe to the *Negro World*, form local divisions of the UNIA, and contribute part of their often meager incomes to UNIA convention funds, defense of Garvey in the courts, programs to establish a UNIA colony in Liberia, and loans to Garvey's Black Cross Navigation and Trading Company. In 1923 through 1927 numerous petitions and collections circulated on behalf of justice and clemency for Garvey. Also in southwest Georgia, divisions formed in Webster, Baker, Colquitt, and Early Counties, while contributions and letters of support reached the UNIA and *Negro World* from Terrell, Randolph, Thomas, and Dougherty Counties.[9]

The population schedules of the 1920 census provide rich data on the individuals and communities that embraced and supported the Garvey movement. Cross-referencing of UNIA and census records enables us to develop a more personal view of rural Garveyites and allows us to speculate as to their attraction to the UNIA and its programs.

Three-quarters of southwest Georgia's most dedicated Garveyites worked as tenant farmers or wage farm laborers.[10] All but one of the nineteen leaders found in the census were either married or widowed. Their ages ranged from twenty-nine to sixty-nine years, with the average age being forty-two. These men had families, and almost all had wives, daughters, sisters, mothers, or aunts in their households. Few owned their homes or the land they worked, but most had learned to read and write and sent their children to school during the year. Most of southwest Georgia's Garveyites were tied to the land by debt or to the community because of family. Records indicate that most were at least second-generation Georgians. Some chose to stay in farming because it was the skill they knew best and because migration was risky and expensive. Despite the best efforts of labor recruiters and encouragement from the *Chicago Defender*, many southern farmers chose the life they knew and sought improvement of conditions at home.

The black farmers of the Arkansas Delta manifested support for the UNIA and Garvey to a great extent, as had those in southwest Georgia.[11] Phillips and Monroe Counties, which both were nearly 75 percent black, formed six or more

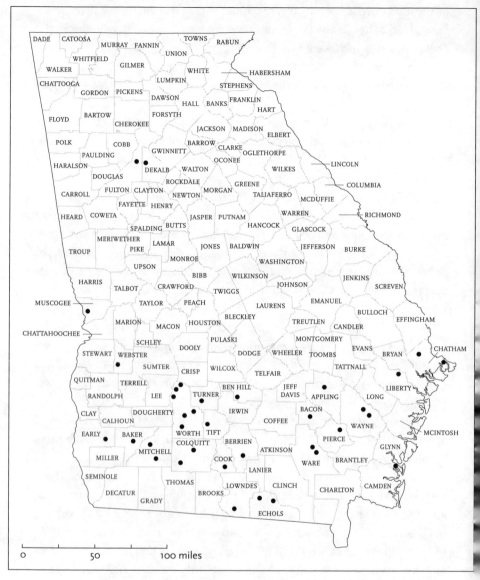

Map 2. UNIA Divisions in Georgia (by County)

UNIA divisions each. This area supported the UNIA with the same type of moral and financial support as did the Garveyites of southwest Georgia.

Phillips County divisions included Postelle, Lexa, Southland, Oneida, Barton, and Cypert. Monroe County had divisions at Duncan, Blackton, Pine City, and Indian Bay, and two at Holly Grove. Other Arkansas Delta counties showed a high density of Garvey sentiment through UNIA membership and support, particularly in the northwest corner of Mississippi County near Blytheville, which had at least seven UNIA divisions. All except one of the Arkansas Delta Garveyites found in the census farmed cotton and lived on farms. They appeared to be almost all married with children. The average age for male Arkansas UNIA supporters was forty-three, but as in Georgia, supporters were both young and old. All of the pro-Garvey households in the Arkansas Delta contained women, and about half of those held three or more females. Although this group tended to have large families, most of the children attended school, revealing an emphasis on education over employment and income. Eight of these men owned their own homes, and eight had home mortgages. In the area of home ownership, the Arkansas Delta Garveyites showed more outward signs of upward economic mobility than their Georgia counterparts. About half of these people had been born in other states, many in Mississippi and several in each of the other southern states. Many Arkansas blacks had migrated there in previous decades because the state had at one time enjoyed the reputation as a haven for upwardly mobile farmers who wanted land of their own.[12] Migratory tendencies may have seemed more natural to these Garveyites than to those in Georgia, yet the same types of debts, ties, and obligations may have kept them settled in the Delta.[13]

On the other side of the mighty river, Mississippi farmers from Bolivar, Tallahatchie, Sunflower, Coahoma, and Quitman Counties flocked to the movement. Although rural by definition, these Mississippi counties had extremely high population densities and were, like their Arkansas counterparts, overwhelmingly black by proportion. In Bolivar County 82.4 percent of the county was black in 1920, and there were 54.1 black persons per square mile. This county and Washington County just to its south contained by far the highest concentrations of black population in the southern Black Belt.[14] Bolivar County also held seventeen UNIA divisions, the most of any county in the United States.[15] In Bolivar, the all-black community of Mound Bayou supported two divisions, while the farmers around Merigold, a few miles to the south, created four of their own UNIA locals.

A sample of Yazoo-Mississippi Delta Garveyites reveals a greater diversity than among those of Georgia and Arkansas. Although most were married

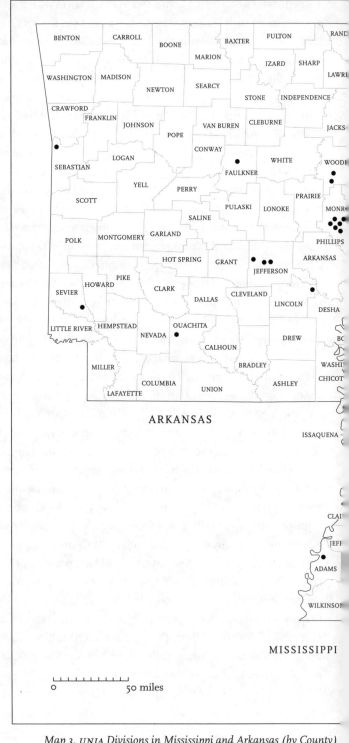

Map 3. *UNIA Divisions in Mississippi and Arkansas (by County)*

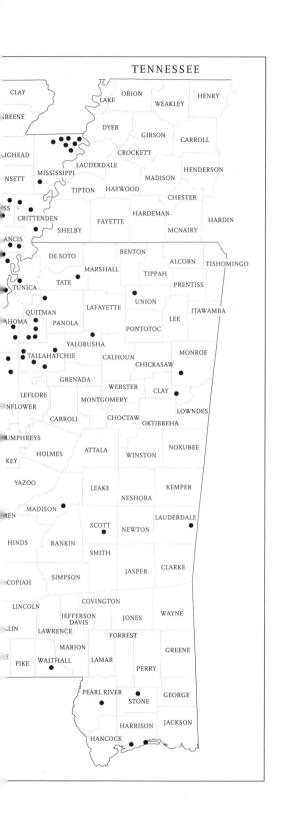

TENNESSEE

CLAY

GREENE

LAKE
OBION
WEAKLEY

HENRY

DYER
GIBSON
CARROLL

IGHEAD

CROCKETT

NSETT
MISSISSIPPI
LAUDERDALE

HENDERSON

TIPTON
HAYWOOD
MADISON

SS

CHESTER

CRITTENDEN
FAYETTE
HARDEMAN

HARDIN

ANCIS
SHELBY
MCNAIRY

BENTON

DE SOTO
ALCORN
TISHOMINGO

MARSHALL
TIPPAH

TUNICA
TATE
PRENTISS

LAFAYETTE
UNION

QUITMAN
LEE
ITAWAMBA

AHOMA
PANOLA
PONTOTOC

YALOBUSHA

TALLAHATCHIE
CALHOUN
MONROE

CHICKASAW

GRENADA
WEBSTER
CLAY

LEFLORE
MONTGOMERY

NFLOWER
LOWNDES

CARROLL
CHOCTAW
OKTIBBEHA

UMPHREYS

HOLMES
ATTALA
NOXUBEE

KEY
WINSTON

YAZOO

LEAKE
KEMPER

NESHOBA

MADISON

EN
LAUDERDALE

SCOTT

HINDS
RANKIN
NEWTON

SMITH

COPIAH
JASPER
CLARKE

SIMPSON

COVINGTON

LINCOLN

JEFFERSON
DAVIS
JONES
WAYNE

LIN
LAWRENCE
FORREST

MARION
GREENE

PIKE
WALTHALL
LAMAR

PERRY

PEARL RIVER
GEORGE

STONE

HARRISON
JACKSON

HANCOCK

farmers, they tended to be younger, averaging thirty-six years of age. A minister, a railroad laborer, and a woman restaurant worker led divisions in the Delta. More lived in towns than in Georgia or Arkansas, four out of thirteen, and only half had children. The men's wives worked more often than in the other two states, but like their counterparts, almost all were literate and all were native Mississippians. Several of the farmers involved with the UNIA in the Yazoo-Mississippi Delta used the title "Reverend" in their correspondence with the UNIA.

Adam D. Newson (often spelled Newsum or Newsome) was the most influential UNIA minister-farmer of Bolivar County. He pastored three churches in the county and faced down the initial opposition of Mound Bayou blacks, convincing the townspeople to support Garveyism.[16] The census paints a very different picture of Newson from the one in extant *Negro World* issues. From the 1920 census we envision simply a forty-four-year-old mulatto tenant farmer, living in a rented house on a farm with his wife, his twenty-year-old widowed niece and her two small children, and his three adolescent daughters. He lived in a house full of women and children, and his work supported them all. We do not see from the census that he was also a minister and "one of the greatest Negro pulpit orators."[17] We also learn from the *Negro World* that Newson had thoroughly organized the community around Merigold with the help of state commissioner S. V. Robertson during the summer of 1923. Robertson told the UNIA convention in Harlem, "I am glad we are all yet alive to see each others' face. It's no child's job, no fool's job, but a man's job to represent the UNIA in the States of Louisiana and Mississippi. The Negroes in those states are afraid to let the white man hear them say anything about racial uplift."[18]

A local convention that Newson and Robertson organized in Merigold in 1923 drew 1,500 attendees, including many local whites who were apparently impressed by the festivities and message, and the next year the Mississippi divisions sent Newson as their delegate for the UNIA's international convention in Harlem. At the major UNIA event, Newson received assurances that the national officers would devote more attention to his people in Mississippi, and he was photographed for the next issue of the *Negro World*.[19]

Newson convinced 137 people from his division in Merigold to donate money for the Marcus Garvey Defense Fund around the time of the UNIA leader's trial for mail fraud. Three hundred thirty people from Mound Bayou signed a petition for Marcus Garvey's release from prison and sent it to the pardon attorney in Washington.[20] Devoted Garveyites from neighboring Tallahatchie County joined their strong allies in Bolivar County in this cause. Seventy-two UNIA supporters from the tiny communities of Sumner, Swan

This photograph of Reverend Adam D. Newson, the UNIA's most important organizer in Bolivar County, Mississippi, in the heart of the Yazoo-Mississippi Delta, was featured in the Negro World during the UNIA's 1924 convention in Harlem. The caption read: "Rev. A. Newson of Cleveland, Miss., wishes to inform the Mississippi Divisions that he has safely arrived in New York City. He also wishes to thank the Parent Body of the U.N.I.A. for its kind hospitality shown to him here, as a member and delegation. He urges the members of the divisions to do all that they are able to do for the grand and noble cause for which the U.N.I.A. stands. Rev. Newson, while here as a delegate, has met many leaders of the cause who have promised to give the divisions of Mississippi more of their time in the future." (Negro World, 9 August 1924)

Lake, Macel, Mikoma, and Tutweiler contributed nickels and dimes to the leader's appeal fund.[21]

In southwest Georgia and the Arkansas and Yazoo-Mississippi Deltas, Garveyites almost exclusively made a living farming cotton, not very surprising considering the dominance of cotton cultivation in those areas. And of all Charles Johnson's categories, cotton counties tended to have more uniformity in social, economic, racial, and educational characteristics than counties dominated by other crops. Many of the indices provided in Johnson's county-by-county study help us understand the context of the rural communities in which Garveyism flourished. Most significantly in light of the black nationalism exhibited in the cotton belt, the bulk of the population in most cotton counties was composed of blacks.[22] Two of the most important studies of black organization, agency, and politics in the rural South have found pronounced and distinctive patterns of resistance in cotton-dominated areas of the South.[23] This fundamental similarity among cotton counties of the Black Belt begs the questions: Did rural Garveyites have a distinctive perspective on race based on their familiarity with a predominantly black society? Did living in a majority-black community make a separate black sphere seem more plausible and attractive?

In the case of the UNIA division towns of Mound Bayou and Renova in Bolivar County, blacks had already created all-black towns to demonstrate the worthiness of the race for self-government and ideally to live free of white domination.[24] Many black Arkansans and Mississippians migrated in the 1890s to Oklahoma, where the largest number of such all-black towns appeared, four of which hosted UNIA divisions.[25] In other parts of the Delta, perhaps the paradox of domination by the white minority seemed even more offensive than in most southern communities where blacks formed a minority. Brundage has shown that the very conditions that prevailed in southwest Georgia for blacks went hand in hand with relentless violence. He concludes, "The hardcore of southern counties where lynch mobs carried on their bloody work year after year was comprised of large black populations and had economies dependent on cotton cultivation."[26] Perhaps common sense suggested to these farmers that their true potential for power lay in self-defense by numbers and in their critical economic importance to agriculture. To older Garveyites who grew up while blacks in the South were effectively stripped of political power after Reconstruction, direct physical or economic strategies held more promise.

The increase in black majorities in rural areas and white migration to rural towns and cities disturbed North Carolinian Clarence Poe, the white editor of the *Progressive Farmer*, who stated in 1909: "The saving of the rural South to the white race is one of the most important problems now before the people of the Cotton Belt."[27] Poe's paper circulated throughout the South and had both white and black readers. His observations of demographic trends and their consequences are instructive: he lamented the increasing ownership of land by blacks in the first two decades of the twentieth century, the preference of white landowners for black over white labor, the increasing blackness of the rural population, and the disappearance of white rural society and the accompanying growth of miscegenation. He pleaded for reforms that would perpetuate what he called a "great rural civilization" in which whites dominated and the races were segregated.[28] Despite his popular newspaper and his strenuous campaign for rural segregation, most of what Poe feared and hoped to change occurred apace until the boll weevil, the war, and the Great Migration began to shift blacks to the North.

In the case of increased black landownership, this phenomenon was rarest in cotton counties. The vast majority of farm operators in cotton counties were tenant farmers, and the median of ownership by black farmers in cotton counties was only 13.6 percent, significantly lower than in other crop-type counties. Blacks living in cotton counties (although clearly not among Garveyite families) tended to have higher rates of illiteracy. This fact is not surprising considering a parallel disparity: per capita education expenditure for black children was consistently much lower than for white children in cotton counties than in other types of counties.[29] Recognizing the importance of education to racial advancement, most Garveyites in cotton counties were literate despite these bleak statistics, and many more made the sacrifices necessary to send their children to school.[30]

The human geography of the Garvey movement reveals at a glance the diversity of southern communities that formed UNIA divisions. As surveyed in chapters 2 and 3, most very early urban and coastal Garveyites were laborers. Some of the strongest American UNIA bases formed in areas experiencing an influx of either West Indian immigrants or Deep South migrants from rural to urban settings. A large proportion of these people in transition would have been younger and more educated black men and women, the group with the greatest degree of mobility for practical and economic reasons.[31] Yet, the UNIA took hold perhaps even more solidly in rural settings among settled black farmers. That is not to say that transience among tenant farmers was not common.[32] Rural settings had distinctive challenges for blacks in the 1920s. Even here, black farmers, sometimes with their families in tow, were often in transition, even if only to better soils, better housing, or better landlords. Changing conditions in southern agriculture from 1915 through the 1960s contributed to continuous movement within and from the southern region. However, most found that moving to another farming situation did not provide a vastly different set of conditions. Interestingly enough, the census indicates a high level of stability and a notable lack of mobility among UNIA local leaders and supporters. In Georgia and Mississippi, Garveyites tended to be second-generation natives to their states, although this does not mean that they had not moved within state boundaries. Unlike Georgia and even Mississippi, Arkansas was a relatively new territory for farming, and fewer black farmers' parents had been actually born west of the Mississippi River. Yet most Arkansas UNIA supporters had been in the state for over ten years, as indicated by the age and state nativity of their children.

The generational commitment within Garveyite families to a state and to farming is significant in this time of massive migration. Whether this is a reflection of their being "tied down" unwillingly or willingly is hard to say. Yet their attraction to Garveyism reveals an interest in forming strategies for local, as well as universal, improvement for blacks. While bringing out black pride, the Garvey movement also reflected a belief that problems specific to people of African ancestry required solutions at the local level *and* at the international level. Garveyites believed an independent black-ruled vanguard nation in Africa might provide relief of worldwide black oppression. Despairing of multiracial solutions after decades of disillusionment and intractable racial strife, these Garveyites found the UNIA's ambitious international programs more promising and logical. At the same time, local activities focused on more subtle intellectual adjustments promoting education, race consciousness, and racial pride, as well as the community's physical, mental, and material preparation for self-defense.

Volatile economic factors associated with cotton farming shaped the conditions of many rural southern Garveyites. The devastating boll weevil blight crossed the Mississippi River by 1915 and crept across the South, reaching southern Virginia by 1922. Fluctuations in the cotton market worldwide yielded high profits, mainly for landowners, in good years but reduced the credit-heavy system to ruin in off years. Tenant farmers often remarked that they could not tell much difference between good and bad years in terms of how they came out after settling with the landlord. The war years boosted demand and prices for cotton, but the steep decline in prices just after the war led many independent owners into tenant farming and sharecropping.[33] Although not necessarily the cause, these economic influences coincided with the explosive growth of Garveyism in the rural South.

From emancipation to 1920, blacks had begun to accumulate more land each decade. In the first years of the Garvey movement in the South, many hopeful tenants and sharecroppers faced disappointment as ownership opportunities became remote and even black owners were losing their land. In the years between 1920 and 1930, acreage in the South owned by blacks declined by nearly 25 percent.[34] The dependence of black tenant farmers on white landowners thus increased during the 1920s, and this reliance seemed more and more like a permanent condition.

In many counties of the South where large numbers of black tenants cultivated cotton, the Garvey movement gained considerable notice. These areas included the largest communities of nonurban blacks. In most cases, cotton counties had high population densities despite their classification as rural. The labor-intensive work of preparing the soil, planting, chopping, and harvesting cotton required many hands. Some independent, but more often tenant, farmers lived on the farms they worked with their families, surrounded by neighbors engaged in the same work. Small groups of family members or close neighbors might work together each day doing monotonous and backbreaking work for most of the daylight hours.

The only day during the busy cultivating, chopping, and picking seasons when farmers had time for any social interaction outside the family or immediate neighbors was on Sunday for church. In the slower months of winter other opportunities might involve a long day's travel to the nearest market town to get supplies on a Saturday. As a cotton farmer, one's two best opportunities for extended breaks were in January or February between the long fall picking season and the land breaking and planting of late winter. In July when the cotton was "laid by" after the arduous thinning and chopping (weeding) of the crop, there might be another opportunity for gathering, organizing, and forming new UNIA divisions.[35] Garvey and his local organizers understood these cyclical schedules and worked within them, just as the organizers of fairs and religious revivals did.

News from further afield came through the mail or newspapers and magazines. Unless a farm family had a subscription to such publications, opportunities to purchase newspapers would come weekly at best. This isolation and its implications provide an intriguing setting for the spread of Garveyism. Exactly how the UNIA's program became so infectious in these rural corners of the South lies in the association of the UNIA with church and the relevance of Garvey's philosophies to people's insulated lives. The UNIA organ brought a frank but welcome discussion of pertinent racial issues into their world.

Agents for the *Negro World* might have owned shops or small businesses in Helena or Albany. In 1920 both of these important market towns had predominantly white populations and were surrounded by majority-black counties of the Black Belt.[36] But it is interesting to note that neither of these important commercial centers near the heart of the UNIA's strength in Arkansas and Georgia, respectively, had a local UNIA division of its own. "King Cole, the Newsboy," who worked out of the New Albany Hotel, no doubt lost much business selling the *Negro World* as Garvey's U.S. fortunes waned. He even wrote to President Calvin Coolidge on Garvey's behalf, stating, "Our very dear friend has been taught enough—kindly consider his appeal."[37]

Typically in smaller places, agents were division members who distributed the papers to members at meetings. Those who could afford the paper passed it along after reading the weekly issues. Mrs. D. H. Lester of Brinkley, Arkansas, in Monroe County described how she read the *Negro World* to her friends every Sunday and how they especially appreciated its educational content. She praised Marcus Garvey and his focus on teaching blacks more about African history and for promoting race pride.[38] For those who could not read, just as the Bible was read aloud in many American homes, someone often read the paper out loud. When a former Louisiana slave and Garveyite died at age 116, his obituary explained his love of hearing the Garvey speeches read from the front page, as he had never learned to read.[39]

Reports to the *Negro World* from the rural South stressed the importance of the direct transmission of Garvey's messages. In cities and towns, featured speakers often became the focus of a division meeting with an interesting or inspiring speech. But in relatively isolated places that provided less social and political interaction, Garvey's front-page addresses took the spotlight, allowing his philosophy to come across to followers in its purest form. In these places where the UNIA leader never visited, his persona became that of a "Black Moses," at once Messianic and prophetic. His personal struggles and universal goals took on mythical proportions. The *Negro World* and the ministers who promoted Garveyism encouraged this sense of the leader's vision and persecution.

For divisions not blessed with an eloquent preacher or charismatic layman for their leader, anyone reading the leader's weekly address in the *Negro World* took the role of transmitter. Garvey and longtime editor William Ferris, in particular, incorporated the language of conjuration. "Redemption" as a synonym for liberation harkened back to David Walker, Robert Alexander Young, and Henry Highland Garnet, three black antislavery writers who began the black literary tradition of Ethiopianism. This style substituted biblical figures like Moses and Ezekiel for African American leaders and predicted the same patterns of captivity, persecution, and redemption.[40] These symbolic and familiar figures from the Bible provided a framework for understanding the UNIA program and its visionary goals, as well as for accepting the persecution of its leader, Marcus Garvey.

For people living in rural isolation, church had paramount importance as a place for social gatherings. Preaching and speaking provided inspiration and even entertainment to rural people. UNIA meetings normally took place at three o'clock on Sundays, thereby extending the Sabbath's potential for social and organizational opportunities. So often the church or gathering place from earlier in the day provided the facilities for secular meetings for the community. Often, laymen had to perform mid-week services if a church used the services of an itinerant preacher.[41] Activities held in churches on Sunday afternoons would not necessarily arouse the suspicions of local whites. The spiritual and secular activities often blended in such a way that they became entwined in the consciousness of participants. In rural areas, therefore, the Garvey movement had a particularly sacred flavor. In rural divisions, UNIA paraphernalia, such as the red, black, and green lapel pins given to each member, were likely seen on Sundays. Unlike the case of urban places such as Charleston and New Orleans, which provided a higher level of social interaction on a daily basis, these symbols of support took on additional significance in country churches.

The UNIA's constitution required each local division or chapter to appoint a chaplain.[42] And although in rural divisions this was not always possible, a number of divisional reports published in the *Negro World* indicated that black ministers played a role in organizing the UNIA in rural areas. For each active clergy organizer, there were others who provided to lay leaders their church buildings or access to their congregations. The spiritual character of UNIA meetings grew naturally out of these circumstances. With many division meetings being led by ministers or being held in churches, hymns and prayers became integral parts of UNIA gatherings, especially in rural areas. The UNIA had its own hymnbook, containing twenty hymns, many of them original compositions by UNIA musical director Arnold J. Ford.[43] A staple at rural southern division meetings was "From Greenland's Icy Mountains," a traditional missionary hymn, composed by an English divine and used widely by white missionary groups. The other commonly sung hymn was Ford's own "Universal Ethiopian Anthem":

> Ethiopia, thou land of our fathers, Thou land where the gods loved to be,
> As storm cloud at night sudden gathers, our armies come rushing to thee.
> We must in the fight be victorious, When swords are thrust outward to glean;
> For us will the Vict'ry be glorious, When led by the red, black and green
>
> Chorus
> Advance, advance to victory! Let Africa be free!
> Advance to meet the foe with the might of the red, the black, and the green.
> Ethiopia the tyrant's falling, Who smote thee upon thy knees;
> And thy children are lustily calling, From over the distant seas.
> Jehovah the Great One has heard us, Has noted our sighs and our tears,
> With his spirit of love He has stirred us, To be one through the coming years.
>
> Chorus
> O Jehovah thou God of the ages, Grant unto our sons that lead,
> The wisdom thou gav'st to thy sages, When Israel was sore in need.
> Thou voice thro' the dim past has spoken, Ethiopia shall stretch forth her hand,
> By thee shall all fetters be broken, And Heav'n bless our dear Motherland.[44]

UNIA divisions from all over the South sent brief descriptions of their meeting agendas to the editor of the *Negro World*. Although there was some variation between divisions, a typical report in the "News and Views of UNIA Divisions" section of the paper included the following information: the name of a church where the meeting took place, the name of a minister who presided, the prayers and hymns performed, a description of how Marcus Garvey's address from the first page of the *Negro World* was read, and the main topics covered in discussions among division members. If special guest speakers appeared, their addresses usually reiterated UNIA objectives, praised Marcus Garvey as the greatest of all race leaders, or sometimes reported to the group about Africa.

The content of these reports and the positions and ideas outlined in Garvey's front-page addresses provide clues as to what aspects of Garvey's philosophy inspired rural southerners. The familiar themes in Garveyism resonated so deeply with rural southerners that a number of them became devoted beyond question to the organization's founder and leader. Belle Beatty from Webster County saw Garvey as "a God sent man to lead his race back to their native homeland."[45] R. E. Knighton, a supporter from nearby Dawson, reported an intellectual awakening since learning about the UNIA: "I never had much to talk about but ever since I have been reading the *Negro World* I have something to talk about and never get tired of talking about that wonderful leader, Marcus Garvey."[46] An especially revealing headline in the *Negro World* during Marcus Garvey's trial exclaimed, "Greatest Negro Movement in the World Now on Trial." The inseparability of Garvey and the movement he led existed beyond the imagination of the *Negro World* editor. This immutable connection pervaded letters praising Garvey from rural southerners to the paper and to President Calvin Coolidge and the pardon attorney.[47] This general perception existed in a lesser form in the larger urban divisions in which the movement had other important leaders and pursued local aims. Garvey's permanent imprisonment after 1925 sapped the organization's resources and demonstrated the leader's centrality to the vitality of the UNIA in rural areas. The rank and file focused on attaining Garvey's release. When these efforts led not to his triumphant return but to his deportation in 1927, further organizational disarray disintegrated the UNIA's impetus.

Southwest Georgia provided fertile soil for cotton and evidently for Garveyism. Visits by UNIA parent body officials helped inspire local divisions to form and provided the authority for organization. State commissioner S. V. Robertson and Leader of American Negroes J. W. H. Eason played pivotal roles in the period between 1921 and 1922.[48] But the real organizational and potentially dangerous work came when local people sustained the movement between and after their visits. When the UNIA held its first convention, a Georgia delegate, the Reverend Oscar C. Kelly of Dawson, had recently lost his wife. After journeying to New York, the sixty-year-old minister poured himself into organizing UNIA divisions around the southwest section of the state. A second-generation Georgian, Kelly owned his own home along the Americus Road in Terrell County.[49] He served as a liaison to visitors like Robertson and Eason, ensuring large audiences when they arrived and providing inspiration and leadership in their absence. Kelly traveled as far south as Pelham, fifty miles away, to bring UNIA supporters together.[50]

The local leaders of and contributors to the UNIA in the rural counties of southwest Georgia had much in common with each other. Unlike Kelly, who was a full-time minister, they farmed for a living. Almost all of them had wives who stayed at home and children who attended school. Some owned their modest homes and small farms, but most lived in perpetual debt and dependence as tenant farmers. Almost all of these men were second-generation Georgians with obvious familial ties to their region.[51] Migration for these mostly middle-aged to older Garveyites was not an option. Their nuclear and extended families and often their debts and obligations kept them on the farm. Their daily social and economic problems required complicated and thoughtful solutions. Their political problems as a race would have to play out on the world stage.

Men dominated the Garvey movement's leadership, but as in other African American institutions women played important roles as organizers.[52] In particular, young women from small communities in Georgia took an active role in extending the reach of the movement. Anna Halton, wife of Columbus L. Halton of Baxley and a rural schoolteacher, took over leadership of the local division when her husband, a signer of the UNIA's Declaration of the Rights of the Negro Peoples of the World, died and after the first vice president was killed. Despite the hardships of becoming a widow at age thirty-six, Mrs. Halton and the division secretary, Miss Lassie Oxendine, kept the group together. Eason returned to reignite this division in May 1922.[53] The next year the female-led local UNIA division held a massive rally protesting Garvey's imprisonment and sent contributions to the Marcus Garvey Defense Fund and a petition of over 200 names to the Justice Department asking for justice in Garvey's case.[54]

Lizzie Jordan, a local family cook, and Mary Boyd of the neighboring Shingler division gave addresses to the first division meeting at Sylvester. These women headlined the meeting in which S. V. Robertson gave official sanction to the new Worth County branch.[55] Jordan was fifty years old and had a twenty-five-year-old daughter and two granddaughters. Her husband died in the

1920s, as did her daughter's, and although literate, she and all her female progeny remained in Sylvester until at least 1930.[56] Worth County UNIA divisions seemed especially ripe with eloquent and dynamic women. Coverdale, just over the line in Turner County, also hosted female speakers. Miss C. Burke, Mrs. C. L. Wimberly, and Mrs. L. M. Ousley led an enthusiastic meeting and reported a strong commitment to the UNIA in their community in April 1922.[57]

The UNIA women of Merigold, Mississippi, dominated the organization in Bolivar County.[58] They walked for miles from the surrounding countryside to the First Missionary Baptist Church, where they would change into the pristine white shoes that they wore only for marching in town as Black Cross Nurses. Dozens of them would provide a weekly spectacle for the townspeople every Sunday afternoon. Lee McCarty recalled sitting on the front porch of his home as a small boy watching the marchers in their solid white shoes, hosiery, skirts, blouses, and "nun or nurse" hoods, singing and displaying a tremendous sense of unity.[59]

In Waycross, Georgia, another south Georgia community, a twenty-three-year-old black schoolteacher named Nellie Anderson served as the secretary of the local UNIA ladies' division. She was single and boarded with an independent farmer and his wife and daughters at their farm. Nellie Anderson's parents were Georgia natives, although presumably they lived elsewhere. She showed her independence and her orientation toward community service through her teaching and assistance to the UNIA.[60]

Worth County is relatively remote and unknown today, but it was the focus of much black attention in the post–World War I period, from not just the UNIA but also its rival the NAACP. In an address to the 1919 NAACP national conference, H. A. Hunt of Fort Valley singled out Worth County as one of the worst counties in south Georgia for tenant farmers. He explained that landlords there frequently took a tenant's whole crop and called the account even. Hunt opined that "there would be difficulty lining up our people in the rural population" to correct these ills. At the same meeting, a Dublin minister described Worth County as an area notorious for whites' locking up and even lynching farmers who tried to leave the land.[61] Yet by 1926, Worth County was the most extensively UNIA-organized county in the state. Charity Grove, Sylvester, Shingler, Oakfield, and Powellton, all in Worth County, had active UNIA divisions. Garveyites, and especially outspoken women, in this hard-pressed section of southwest Georgia saw promise and meaning in the organization's ideology and lined up together behind it.

Although local leaders in the rural South tended to be farmers, grassroots support for the UNIA came from all quarters. At one extreme was twenty-four-year-old Lonnie James of Sumner, Worth County. When the census enumerator found him, he was laboring with forty-five other young black men on the Turner County prison road gang. As the men worked on the National Highway between Dakota and Worth (now Interstate 75), each was called aside for a quick interview. Although we do not know why James was there, many black men in this area ended up in peonage. When James got out of jail, despite his financial hardships, we know he respected Garvey enough to contribute to the Marcus Garvey Defense Fund two years later.[62]

Another UNIA man from the South ended up in the Missouri state penitentiary in Jefferson by 1930. For what crime he served time we do not know, but he had survived combat as a veteran of the Spanish-American War, the "Mexican Expedition" (presumably the occupation of Vera Cruz), and World War I. Frank M. Liston was also spared from being hanged by a mob in Hope City, Arkansas, in 1921. Seeing that he wore a red, black, and green UNIA button on his lapel, the vigilantes determined he could not be the criminal they were seeking and released him.[63]

A contributor who could much better afford to make donations was Jonas Odom of Baker County, Georgia. Jonas's biological father had been a white boy of fourteen who later, as a grown man, married a white woman and had a family, became the sheriff of Baker County, a state representative and senator, a charter founder and president of the Bank of Baker County, chairman of the Baker board of commissioners, and a very large landowner. Jonas's mother, Lucille, was a very young domestic servant who was black. The young girl was removed to Macon to bear the child, and Jonas's white aunt and two other white women reared the boy at an elegant home in Bibb County. At a young age he was returned to his mother, who had returned to Baker County and married a black man named Houston. Lucille Houston and her husband took the mulatto boy in but never changed his name. From the time he was a small boy, Jonas Odom lived in a manner typical of the condition of most blacks in the county. Apparently, he never owned shoes until the age of twelve. As an adult he did receive clandestine financial assistance from the white Odoms, and he became a plantation foreman and eventually a successful farm owner and grocer. Jonas's white first cousin, Robert Benton Odom, became a lawyer and helped Jonas with legal difficulties with a white businessman who had obtained goods and services from the black merchant without paying for them. As an older man of sixty, Jonas Odom was a generous contributor to the

UNIA and a Black Star Line stock owner; as his generosity came to Garvey's attention, he was offered the award of "1923 Captains in the Crusade of African Freedom."[64]

Odom's response to the UNIA's programs points to the appeal of Garveyism to a range of rural people. Jonas Odom had opportunities to prosper, get educated, buy land, and own a grocery and supply store, yet his color and illegitimacy prevented him from receiving the advantages of status that his birth father's white children enjoyed. All of his advantages and the legal assistance of his white cousin the attorney were not enough. Local realities dictated that he never forget his alleged inferior position. Thus, in Baker County, even the most privileged and elite of its black men favored Garvey's racial vision.

Unlike in Georgia where UNIA supporters came almost exclusively from rural areas, large towns in Arkansas like Pine Bluff and Fort Smith had large black middle-class segments and also thriving divisions of the UNIA.[65] For the most part, however, the small towns and communities of the Delta hosted the mass of UNIA supporters. The black population of Arkansas farmed in dense concentration all along the Mississippi, St. Francis, and White Rivers. This rich, flood-prone bottomland supported the most productive and valuable cotton crop in the United States in the early twentieth century. What had held virgin timber in the early nineteenth century became enormously profitable plantation land by the end of Reconstruction, intensively cultivated by tenant farmers for mostly absentee landlords. Tenancy among black farmers had reached up to 80 percent in most Delta counties by the time the *Negro World* reached the area.[66]

Despite their marginalization as individuals, black cotton farmers in the Delta formed a formidable and essential resource for the area's wealth. The U.S. Department of Commerce acknowledged that the "farming activities of the Negro are generally listed as an asset to the resources and wealth of the Nation."[67] Perhaps even more so than in Georgia, where some alternative crops were grown, the fortunes of the Delta plantation economy rose and fell with the price of cotton on the world market. Cotton farmers had a vivid and personal interest in world trade because it often determined the adequacy of their basic subsistence. The livelihoods of professional blacks did not rest on the fluctuations in the world markets. Although economic fluctuations were hard on the black community as a whole, including teachers, doctors, and especially businessmen, those with the most precarious existence were the landless farmers. Vulnerable to both economic and environmental caprices, they had to stay with their crops and their debts from year to year and hope for more gradual processes for improvement. Over the years they had learned to face hardship and most of all have patience. Garvey's visionary plans all involved great optimism, patience, and perseverance. The leader acknowledged that his solutions could not be achieved quickly. Farmers required these basic qualities to make a living and were able to call on these virtues in deciding to support the Garvey movement.

The UNIA enjoyed broad support among the blacks of Phillips County, one of Arkansas's most established Delta counties. Helena, the county seat, had served as an important stop along the river before the railroads began to handle the bulk of transportation of cotton and lumber from all parts of the Delta in the 1870s and 1880s.[68] Numerous Arkansas UNIA divisions formed west of Helena in the interior of Phillips County and into Monroe County even further to the west. A sample study of contributors and members from Phillips and Monroe Counties indicates that Arkansas Delta Garveyites were almost without exception tenant farmers who were married. They tended to be in their forties and fifties. Husbands and wives apparently attended meetings of the UNIA together at small places like Southland, Lexa, Oneida, Cypert, and Postelle. They contributed five, ten, or twenty-five cents each for Marcus Garvey's Defense Fund in 1923 and managed to pay ten-cent monthly installments for the death tax, which ensured each UNIA member a decent burial.[69]

The tiny Indian Bay community of twenty-nine people in the swamps of Monroe County, Arkansas, only fifteen miles from the scene of the massacre of African Americans at Elaine in 1919, maintained a strong UNIA division for at least four years, between 1922 and 1926. In fact, the division had sixty-four members, over twice the population of Indian Bay itself, indicating it drew support from the surrounding Montgomery district. Lambrook, only five miles from Indian Bay, was the site of much of the slaughter and the resting place of numerous black corpses produced by the Phillips County outrage.[70] Of the thirty-one UNIA members found in the 1920 census, all listed their occupation as "cotton farmer." All were black as opposed to mulatto, most were married with children, and all worked "on shares." Rank-and-file members' ages varied from twenty to seventy, about half were literate, and all were native to southern states, mostly Arkansas and Mississippi.[71]

Like Phillips County, Arkansas, Bolivar County, Mississippi, had rich black soil and produced some of the highest cotton yields per acre in the world. In 1933 Arthur F. Raper, the noted sociologist of the South in the period, devoted significant effort to studying the racial, economic, and social setting of "Imperial Bolivar." Some of his observations included the high proportion of Negro tenant labor, the low expenditure on Negro education, and relatively low church participation by blacks. Only 23 percent of Bolivar County blacks were church members in 1930, compared with a state average of 48 percent. County landowners valued the sheriff's work highly and paid him $40,000 a year, ten times more than Mississippi's governor.[72]

One anomalous feature of Bolivar was the existence of America's most famous all-black town, Mound Bayou. Its founder, Isaiah T. Montgomery, had been a slave and body servant to Confederate president Jefferson Davis, and after the war, Montgomery had accumulated property and money and bought the land near the Louisville, New Orleans, and Texas Railroad on which Mound Bayou was built in the late 1880s. Montgomery held the respect of both blacks and whites, and on his death in 1923, a prominent white man of Bolivar County eulogized him in terms that identify him as an ideological friend of local Garveyites. Walter Sillers of Rosedale described Montgomery as "a Moses," a visionary, and a purely Negro man whose "native genius" should have given pride to his race:

> He was the first to draw the color line in Mississippi; and he would sell the lands in the territory of Mound Bayou to none save the people of his own race, knowing it was best for every race to dwell unto itself. . . . [H]e demonstrated the fitness of his people, their capacity for self-government, their ability to establish and maintain a creditable civilization. . . . [H]e felt as I do about the future: that the hopes of his people can never be realized until the Negro is given a country of his own, freed from the weight of the dominant race.[73]

Montgomery apparently felt the need to seek recognition from and get along with local whites in authority in the surrounding county. In 1910, without objection, he watched as the white deputy sheriff of Merigold beat some local blacks with a whip. He also believed that whites respected the "better Negroes" and did not object to their controlling black criminals themselves.[74] These events suggest that one of Garvey's most controversial strategies had already been utilized by successful separatists who preceded him in Bolivar County. Montgomery's cooperation and perhaps accommodation to the white power structure of the county had not diminished his stature with local blacks.

In the southern part of Bolivar County, the Delta and Pine Land Company owned thousands of acres and employed thousands of black farmers to cultivate its cotton. So many worked there that the group of plantations even produced its own newspaper, *The Cotton Farmer*. The paper's decorative heading showed a black man behind a mule and plow furrowing a vast, flat field with overflowing baskets of cotton and corn around the edges. This paper originated in Scott, the central town of the eighteen company plantations, and was "published by the colored tenants of Delta and Pine Land Company." Its editor, Reverend Addison Wimbs, reported that the paper had readership all over the cotton belt and noted that even readers in Bocas de Toro, Panama, had shown an interest in subscribing. Wimbs reckoned that his fair coverage of Garvey and the movement gave his paper its wide acceptability. He recognized Garvey's popularity in Bocas, which had four UNIA divisions, and even though he objected to the Liberian colonization plan, he believed that Garvey should not be "crucified" by his critics and maintained in jail by the U.S. government.[75]

Racial violence, and particularly lynching, occurred most frequently in cotton counties. Charles S. Johnson's statistical analysis indicated that between 1900 and 1931, at least one lynching had occurred in over 60 percent of cotton counties but in only 30 percent of other crop-type counties.[76] For the three areas under examination here, not only did aspects of the cotton culture seem to promote the occasional lynching, but lynching and racial violence were carried to extremes. Some of the most heinous acts of racial violence on record occurred amid the volatile racial climate just after World War I.

In May 1918 eleven blacks in Brooks and Lowndes Counties in southwest Georgia, including a woman, were murdered by vigilantes over an eight-day period. Mary Turner, the wife of the black man who allegedly touched off the slaughter by killing a white man, had been hung by her feet and bisected. Her eight-month-old fetus fell from her abdomen and was crushed underfoot by her killers.[77] The UNIA and Negro World had these events in mind throughout the year. In August 1919 Garvey reminded a large audience in New York's Carnegie Hall of Mary Turner's fate: "In America, below the Mason and Dixon Line, what did they do to Mary Turner? Oh I will not repeat because it is common knowledge to the world."[78]

The black community around the section of Georgia where Mary Turner was murdered fell into turmoil. Extreme fear prevented many locals from even talking to blacks from out of town, and continuing anxiety caused over 500 blacks to leave the region before their newly planted crops matured. Many others left immediately after the 1918 harvest.[79] The 1918 lynchings put Brooks County way ahead of other southwest Georgia counties for the highest number of lynchings in the early part of the twentieth century. In second place, however, Worth County had five separate lynchings during the same period, between 1900 and 1931. Phillips County, Arkansas, had seven and Bolivar County, Mississippi, had eight lynchings, keeping these majority-black communities constantly interested in self-preservation.[80] These lawless events became familiar to readers of the black press around the country but lingered daily in the minds of blacks in the areas where the killings occurred.

Less than a month after Garvey recalled the Mary Turner lynching to a massive New York audience, the Phillips County riot also gained notoriety all over the country. This most catastrophic and best-known rural riot occurred in the tiny hamlet of Elaine, Arkansas, in late September and early October 1919.[81] The violence there arose from events surrounding the continuing exploitation of black farmers under the plantation system. In this case, share-croppers, whose cotton crop went to market in October 1918, had to wait until July 1919 for landowners and farm managers to settle their accounts. Not only was their wait ridiculously long, but accounts seldom if ever came out fairly, and never with any documentation.[82] That summer, rumors spread through-out Phillips County that blacks were organizing a union, stockpiling arms, and plotting the murder of at least twenty-four white planters near Elaine. On 30 September the deputy sheriff of Phillips County was allegedly shot by blacks guarding a meeting of the Progressive Farmers and Household Union of America in a church three miles from Elaine. In a separate incident within one day of the deputy's death, twenty-five to fifty sharecroppers in Phillips County had spoken to O. S. Bratton, the son of a white Little Rock lawyer, to begin a legal case by which they could fairly settle their accounts with the landowners who consistently exploited them. While he set about collecting statements in the village of Ratio, six armed white men interrupted and carried Bratton and two black farmers off to Elaine, where an inflamed mob had assembled. Over the next four days, local whites and the state militia randomly massacred an undetermined number of black Phillips County residents, somewhere be-tween the modest, white-reported estimate of twenty-five to the wide-ranging alternative reports of between 200 and 850.[83] Even whites from the Mis-sissippi side of the river crossed into Arkansas to join in the suppression of black assertiveness.[84] Five whites died in the fray, and for that, sixty-seven blacks went to jail for rioting, and twelve were sentenced to die by a mob-influenced jury that deliberated for under ten minutes.[85]

No doubt the violence in Phillips County made Delta blacks of all classes long for more peaceful race relations, but achieving this goal while improving their material conditions was another matter. The condemned men and the sixty-seven imprisoned rioters could have been any of the Delta sharecroppers. A white guest editor for the *Arkansas Gazette* reported that he did not see among the nearly 100 prisoners "what I could consider a bad [N]egro. They are all the peaceable working class type." Intending to soothe tensions in the white community, the writer argued that the unscrupulous black organizers of the

Progressive Farmers Union had hoodwinked the local farmers into launching the "insurrection."[86] Yet what this report said to African Americans was that whites had neither respect for their intelligence nor regard for their completely legitimate grievances. By describing the black effort for economic fairness and self-defense as a conscious, organized insurrection, the *Gazette* shifted blame for the violence to the black community. Arkansas whites became alarmed at the prospect of blacks' arming themselves. Obviously to the fearful and perhaps paranoid white minority of the Delta, blacks' enhancing their ability for self-defense was synonymous to stockpiling arms for aggression.

Such arbitrariness and misrepresentation provoked outrage among local blacks but apparently created a stronger impulse: a complete rejection of the possibility that whites could ever fairly administer justice or acknowledge that blacks deserved fair treatment in settling their annual farm accounts. Dependence on anything controlled by whites—politics, economics, or justice— would no longer be acceptable to people who had endured the failure of Reconstruction and its economic promises of "forty acres and a mule," betrayal by the national Republicans in protecting their political and civil rights, the race-baiting end of the Farmers' Alliance and the Populist movement, disfranchisement, the disillusionment of their patriotic notions after World War I, and now the slaughter of innocent farmers for attempting to achieve fair settlements for their annual crops. The independence from whites espoused by the UNIA made more sense in the wake of the Phillips County massacre than cooperation or legal solutions that had failed before. The UNIA built its strength in the immediate vicinity of Elaine on both sides of the river less than two years later and amid the rigorous appeal process underwritten by the national NAACP and pursued by a black Little Rock lawyer named Scipio Africanus Jones. The theme that gained even more pertinence after the Delta incident, a desire for self-defense, persisted in the form of Garveyism.

The tiny community of Pine City, Arkansas, in the southern part of Monroe County, less than five miles from Phillips County, provides a stark example of how Delta farmers reacted to the events surrounding the Elaine massacre. George W. Davis, a black man, served as the secretary of a Pine City Masonic lodge. He reportedly paid death benefits for 103 masons who were killed in the Elaine incident. In August 1923 Pine City hosted a three-day convention for the UNIA divisions in the surrounding areas of the Delta. Various members gave papers on such topics as "Why We Should Follow President Garvey" and "Negro, Get into the Movement," while assorted pastors led prayers and scripture readings. Choirs from Postelle, Pine City, and Mt. Pleasant provided music at various times, and members from Indian Bay contributed reports and addresses. Even the Reverend Adam Newson of Bolivar County, Mississippi, attended the Pine City regional UNIA convention and preached the closing sermon on the third day.[87]

Black, rural, southern farmers showed enormous strength during the 1920s by figuring out ways to struggle and survive economic hardships associated with tenancy and postwar racial tension. Some chose to migrate to the North or to cities of the South, some chose complete submission, but a significant number found hope in the UNIA and inspiration through the *Negro World*. Garvey and his organization adapted the rhetoric and strategies of the movement to their purposes, within unavoidable constraints. To most farmers and laborers, alignment with more radical organizations such as the NAACP or Industrial Workers of the World (IWW) did not seem practical and perhaps was not even desirable in this period.

Even though laissez-faire capitalism had reached its apex in the industrialized parts of the United States, and Garvey's appeals clearly rejected class-based internationalism, the UNIA's appeal was nationalistic and racial, not capitalistic. Black majorities in rural southern counties wanted to shed their dependence on whites, whom they were no longer willing to trust. Sexual exploitation, dependence, tenancy, poor educational opportunity, peonage, and racial violence were most pronounced for black people in cotton-dominated counties. Their legitimate cynicism toward whites did not attribute greed to human nature, but to competing races of people. Their implicit assumption was that a black community would treat fairly and justly all of its members.

In going forward with this belief, the Garvey movement also merged itself with traditional rural institutions, particularly the church. And although the church had always provided a forum for black activism, Garveyism became an extension of traditional religious ideology, as important to survival in secular life as salvation and redemption were for the afterlife.[88] Other modern organizations had not yet adopted black uplift as a sacred obligation. This unique and essential component of Garveyism made racial pride, self-defense, and African redemption sanctified causes. This hallowed attachment helped carry these principles through subsequent generations.

The typical UNIA advocate confronted these social, economic, and political realities in the rural South and struggled with a variety of ideas and strategies. Although the Garvey movement had a broad spectrum of popular support, stable communities of economically dependent cotton farmers (mostly with heavily female households) in majority-black counties of southwest Georgia, the Yazoo-Mississippi Delta, and the Arkansas Delta provided a crucible for essential Garveyism.

5 Appeal

We may not agree with Mr. Garvey; we may think his methods and ideals are wrong; but we must nevertheless recognize that there are thousands of simple, honest, black folk whose emotions have been profoundly stirred by his words and schemes. He represents an attitude of mind towards the world problem of race that we must study in his followers perhaps, rather than in himself.
—H. W. Peet, Southern Workman, *October 1928*

The Garvey movement was not a radical fringe organization despite some of the controversial tactics of its leader. The UNIA had broad popularity and was able to start divisions everywhere it was known in the South, beginning with the Virginia peninsula in 1919 and ending with the Delta of eastern Arkansas in late 1922. Its essential tenets had taken root very quickly, and its agenda gained wide acceptance because Garveyites believed in the program and the strategies of the organization and clung tenaciously to their faith in its leader throughout the UNIA's turbulent existence. As an organization, the southern wing of the UNIA survived for nearly a decade, but Garveyism as an ideology lingered much longer. Voices of individual Garveyites explain their attraction to Garvey's philosophy and the UNIA's platform, and through an exhaustive examination of their letters and comments we learn that rural southerners embraced self-defense and separatism as temporary remedies for their immediate, local troubles and African redemption as a more permanent, comprehensive solution to the problems affecting people of African descent all over the world. At the community level, rural southern Garveyites pursued strategies of self-defense and separation to protect their families from lynching and sexual exploitation in extreme cases and to uphold their dignity in everyday interactions with whites. In the long term, they sought to end dependence on whites for their economic survival and to recover Africa from the control of white imperialists. To the deeply religious, rural, southern Garveyites, redeeming Africa involved more than reclaiming and developing the continent's bountiful resources for their race; it also meant modernizing it and continuing the spiritual redemption begun by black Baptist and AME missionaries.[1] Some southern UNIA supporters even hoped to serve these purposes by relocating to the continent as part of Garvey's Liberian colonization plan.

Defending the Race at Home

The three literary sources that consistently connected isolated UNIA members to the UNIA program and philosophy were the UNIA constitution, the Declaration of Rights of the Negro Peoples of the World (also known as the Negro Bill of Rights), and editorials and addresses in the weekly *Negro World*. Rural southern supporters repeated words, phrases, and sentiments expressed in these documents almost verbatim in their letters, petitions, and reports. Garvey's philosophy and strategies gained influence in the rural South at the same time that urban elite race leaders began their united effort to stop the UNIA, indicating divergent opinions on the so-called extreme tactics of the movement.[2]

In August 1920, when the delegates to the first UNIA convention collected and compiled grievances and demands into the Negro Bill of Rights, the list pointedly addressed white abuses: "In certain parts of the United States of America our race is denied the right of public trial accorded to other races when accused of crime, but are lynched and burned by mobs, and such brutal and inhuman treatment is even practiced upon our women." Later it continued on this theme of violence: "We believe that the Negro should adopt every means to protect himself against the barbarous practices inflicted upon him because of color." "With the help of almighty God," the statement asserted, "we declare ourselves the sworn protectors of the honor and virtue of our women and children, and pledge our lives for their protection and defense everywhere, and under all circumstances from wrongs and outrages."[3]

This document represented the culmination of the reports to the convention from all corners of the black world and synthesized the responses adopted by the delegates who signed it; accordingly, these principles became the blueprint for future action. It is presumed that this document appeared prominently in the pages of *Negro World* issues that have been lost; scattered evidence suggests that it had circulated widely throughout the South. The echoes of these themes coming from southern supporters in subsequent years indicate not only a familiarity with the Negro Bill of Rights and the UNIA constitution (which each division member received upon joining), but also an understanding of the ideas and opinions expressed in the UNIA organ, the *Negro World*. We can assume that two of the Georgia signers of the document, C. L. Halton of Baxley and O. C. Kelly of Dawson, took copies home and used them in organizing the southern region of their state.[4]

The signed letters and names of donors from all over the rural South, which appeared in the *Negro World* from 1921 to 1927, reveal the loyalty and devotion to the UNIA and its leader throughout his most difficult financial and legal problems and amid searing criticism by almost every influential leader of color.[5] Focus on self-defense and protection of Negro women and girls continued as late as July 1927, just months before Garvey's deportation. (That month, the *Negro World* urged all local divisions to study the Negro Bill of Rights as part of their regional conventions that year.)[6] Southern organizer S. A. Haynes wrote a compelling feature in the UNIA paper emphasizing the point that rural communities of black farmers bore the brunt of most white outrages while bravely remaining in the region they loved in spite of the violence they faced: "If a Negro attempts to assert his manhood in defense of his home and family, he is killed outright as an example to others. He is kicked about, whipped, and mercilessly persecuted for the fun of it. Negro women are cruelly abused and insulted at will. . . . The life of a dog, a bird, a rabbit, even a wild duck is more secure in Dixie than that of a Negro woman."[7] This theme had reverberated for years in black periodicals, even those which on other issues mercilessly criticized Garvey and the UNIA. In an editorial to the Harlem-based *Messenger*, for example, a black reporter touring Florida remarked on the issue of sexual predators: "The white men here are the worst I ever saw about making bold advances to colored girls."[8]

After World War I, black leaders had hotly debated strategies for ending racial violence, most notably lynching. While the NAACP spearheaded federal legislation to punish lynchers and deter the lawlessness of mobs, Garveyites wanted to end lynching not by punishment after the fact, but by defending themselves before any violence occurred. The consensus on this issue among southern delegates to the first UNIA convention was that white law enforcement officers could never be expected to protect blacks in the South. A woman delegate from Jesup, Georgia, explained that in her home, "the lynching state," blacks were lynched by lawless men for the fun of it. "Force will respect force!" she claimed. Another delegate from South Carolina said, "In my section we have been preaching and praying and begging for protection for years, but lynching goes on just the same. The only thing to do if the law cannot protect a man's family and his home is for Negroes to organize to protect themselves." A Louisiana elder proudly displayed scars he had developed from taking on a mob of twelve white men who objected to his protecting a colored girl whom they apparently had kidnapped.[9] For self-defense to work, the delegates acknowledged, black people had to organize into race-conscious groups in their communities. The same type of leverage and recognition that black laborers hoped to gain through UNIA organization in the port cities of the South might also help well-armed and organized blacks in rural areas, especially in black-majority communities.

UNIA convention delegates, even during the more radical early years, rarely openly discussed self-defense in terms of guns, ammunition, strategy, or specific action. Recognizing the difficulty of organizing in the South, the UNIA held a secret session for southern delegates to the first annual UNIA convention. The Reverend J. W. H. Eason and the Reverend J. D. Brooks convened this clandestine session so that delegates who feared violence and retribution for their association with the Garvey movement could speak freely about the South's tempestuous conditions and discuss the possibility for assertive remedies.[10] It was no coincidence that UNIA locals were called "divisions," a blatantly military term; the UNIA's African Legions similarly formed an important symbolic component of the Garvey movement's appeal. UNIA recruiters and organizers showed films of the Legions marching in the convention parades in Harlem.[11] UNIA African Legions even reportedly drilled in Raleigh, Atlanta, Miami, and other fair-sized southern cities.[12]

Internationally, militarism was in style and served as a demonstration of national pride and strength. The military tradition in the South before World War I was that of the Confederate nation and the "southern" way of life it represented, although that would hardly have been an appropriate way for a southern African American to identify himself. The military dress of World War I or of Garvey's paramilitary wing offered more fitting opportunities to demonstrate national pride either as Americans or as Negroes. Some black World War I veterans returned to their homes in the South and continued to wear their U.S. Army uniforms. Ten died at the hands of angry whites resentful of their pride and self-assertion. In 1919 Georgia and Mississippi mobs lynched three black veterans in each state, while Arkansas came in a close second, murdering two.[13] It is doubtful that rural farming Garveyites established formal, uniformed division units of the African Legions. They had to be more secretive than their urban associates about displays of power because their numerical superiority in the Black Belt was a more literal threat to white supremacy.

In rural parts of the South, where protection and punishment mechanisms had not moved far beyond the domain of the plantation, black communities began to show a greater tendency toward self-policing. Where no reliable recourse through the developing legal system existed, whites and blacks sometimes took the law, self-protection, and retribution into their own hands, in what Stewart E. Tolnay and E. M. Beck have called popular justice.[14] Whether treated unfairly in a financial transaction such as a crop settlement or assaulted or raped by a white person, black community members were encouraged to defy abuse and humiliation by force if necessary.

The UNIA indicated its approval of this strategy by congratulating black individuals and vigilante groups in *Negro World* features and editorials. For example, the paper followed the story of Joe Pullen, a black tenant farmer from Drew, Mississippi, a Delta town with a UNIA division on its eastern edge. The forty-year-old Pullen had become irate when W. T. Sanders, the landowner whose land he farmed, tried to collect a debt that Pullen denied owing him. Pullen, already armed with a .32 caliber revolver, shot Sanders and fled to his mother's house nearby to collect more guns and ammunition for defense against what he knew would be an angry posse of local whites. The seven-hour battle ended in Pullen's death, but not until he had killed nine white men and injured nine others. The story of the sharecropper's tenacity made the news around the country, and the *Negro World*'s detailed account appeared on page two under the headline " 'Debt-Collecting' in Mississippi Takes Heavy Toll of Lives."[15] Three weeks later, the *Negro World* printed an editorial headlined, "Negro Tenant Farmer Shot to Kill and Should Have a Monument." Describing Pullen as "an industrious citizen," the article suggested that "Black men of the Pullen type should be encouraged and not exterminated."[16]

As early as November 1921, the *Negro World* made congratulatory remarks about black men who policed the behavior of white men. In Texarkana, Texas, only thirty miles from a cluster of UNIA divisions in the cotton counties of northwest Louisiana and other Garveyites in southwest Arkansas, an organization of black men calling themselves the Knight Owls caught a black woman and a white man together near a "colored baseball park." They whipped them both until their backs were severely lacerated and then forced the white man to leave town.[17] This incident raises many questions about what and whom exactly the Knight Owls were trying to punish. The fact that they punished the woman suggests that she, in the minds of the vigilantes, had willingly joined the white man or at least insufficiently resisted him. The fact that the attack on the white man apparently drew no reprisals from the white community indicates that he was considered unimportant to the community or that local whites tacitly approved of the punishment and disapproved of the "crime." But one thing we can surmise is that an organized group of black men was imitating the tactics of the Knights of the Ku Klux Klan by enforcing their standards on the black community. That the UNIA's paper reported this story with approval indicates the extent of the organization's fervor for racial solidarity and purity.

The Rural UNIA and the Politics of Protection

What are we to make of the Garveyite women who by all appearances tolerated the patriarchal editorial bent of the *Negro World* and looked to UNIA leadership for solutions to racial strife? We know so little about the inner lives of black farm women of this era. Historian Jacqueline Jones has skillfully described their world of home and work from slavery until the recent past. She interprets their feelings, attitudes, and aspirations using a remarkable combination of obscure and recalcitrant sources and literary and theoretical imagination. Few, if any, others have attempted the difficult task of reconstructing these ordinary women's lives. As Jones makes abundantly clear, for rural women of the 1920s we must rely heavily on census data, which tell us about their households. The census reveals that Garveyite women were at home "keeping house" or working on the "home farm," but they were not working as domestics or cooks in the homes of white landowners as many other black rural women were. For black farm women there are few oral histories and only scattered remnants of authentic voices from newspapers and other written sources.[18]

Facing this dearth of information, it is tempting to use urban working women's history to imagine rural women's struggles regarding sex, class, and race. But in many ways black farm women's conditions so resembled slavery that parallels between their circumstances and the perils in the lives of slave women may be more accurate.[19] For slave women allegiances to race superseded any gender or class solidarities they might have felt.[20] In the process of teaching slave children survival strategies, race consciousness was constantly reinforced and from a much earlier age—much more than were specific gender roles. The Garveyite women in the rural South as late as the 1920s still worried about their children's vulnerability and relied on their own ingenuity to deflect and avoid unwanted sexual advances, but they also welcomed the protection of black men when it was offered.

Of course romantic or consensual interracial sex sometimes occurred between black women and white men, and these instances complicated the issue of protection. When black men policed these particular relationships and prevented or punished them, they were no longer protecting individual women but instead their own notions of proper behavior for women as part of the black community and the black race. In the case of the UNIA women in rural areas, we have no authentic voices revealing either approval or disapproval of these gendered roles and expectations. But we do know that the *Negro World*, especially through editorials by John E. Bruce, lauded black men's efforts to protect, police, and punish. There is also, however, adequate evidence that women joined the UNIA in large numbers in rural communities and participated as organizers in significant numbers, suggesting perhaps a different set of priorities in the rural context.[21]

It is also possible that schisms existed among rural black women over issues of interracial sex and that these differences had little to do with one's social class. Jacqueline Jones makes an important observation that differentiates the situation of black and white sharecroppers' wives: for black people, "the preservation of family integrity served as a political statement to the white South."[22] Anything that black women (or black men for that matter) did to put their families first challenged whites in the community who wanted full access to blacks' obedience, labor, and bodies. Garveyites in places like Sylvester, Georgia, extended this prerogative to protecting the Negro community from white sexual predators and preserving the race against miscegenation. This idea was not original to the UNIA, and was perhaps more organic to southern communities than we realize. In Concord, North Carolina, in 1898, long before the UNIA's existence, similar squads of local black men regularly policed interracial liaisons and whipped offenders, both the white men and the black women.[23]

After emancipation, when black men's and women's bodies were not as easily controlled, lynching and rape became political and psychological methods of whites regaining dominance.[24] Garveyites resisted these efforts directly through individualized and community self-defense and, in extreme cases in which black women were punished for interracial liaisons, through violent patriarchal and misogynistic practices. An alternative way for black tenant farmers to make a political statement was through migration to cities and to the North. To many, the threat of racial violence, particularly lynching and rape, may have proved more intolerable than perpetual debt and poverty. And although economic factors clearly propelled many migrants, recent scholars grappling with the question of rape where it bears upon migration have concluded that sexual exploitation was so rampant that some black women perceived migration as the only viable remedy.[25] Whether moving to get away from victimization or fighting back to prevent it, southern Garveyites made their objections strong and clear.

Feminist scholar Hazel Carby suggests that our overabundant focus on the lynching of black men instead of the rape of black women as a central symbol of racial oppression needs correction, but the Garvey movement did not make this oversight.[26] The *Negro World* and the Negro Bill of Rights gave black women's exploitation broad coverage. This attention manifested itself in controversial ways: in the context of maintaining race purity; reserving black women for black men only; and asserting for black men patriarchal control over the black community—all things that white men were also trying to do overtly or as members of Klan-style vigilante organizations.

Because the reality of black women being raped and exploited by white men far exceeded the bona fide examples of black men committing rape against white women, we tend to be more sympathetic to black men's goal of protecting women of their race. In addition, because the law often did not offer an alternative to popular justice for black women the way it did for white women, it becomes easier to understand the impulse toward extralegal violence in protecting black women, especially in a rural context. There are, however, problems inherent in black women's accepting protection from black men and acknowledging the sincerity of their efforts. By accepting what Farah Griffin calls the promise of protection, black women set themselves up for further dependence, subordination, and even victimization.[27]

Black men asserted their masculinity through protecting their daughters and wives, but organized black women had also pushed the protection issue early on. The National Association of Colored Women (NACW) put the protection of women on the black uplift agenda, and urban social service organizations grew out of these efforts. The National Urban League and individual branches of the NACW spent considerable resources on shielding female migrants to the city from a life of what amounted to forced prostitution.[28] The black clergy, especially of the National Baptist Convention, and other leaders, including Garvey, recognized the way women cared about protection issues.[29]

In her interpretation of "What Does the Garvey Movement Mean for Negro Womanhood," Mrs. Lavinia D. M. Smith, a Cleveland, Ohio, schoolteacher and UNIA reporter explained, "Marcus Garvey has . . . removed our girls from the position of temptations and placed them among their own group. . . . [He] has said that the consorts of members of the Universal Negro Improvement Association must be of the Negro race. What does that portend? A more uniform Negro race in the future in respect to color, and not the old Negro race ranging from after dinner coffee to lemon meringue."[30] Two months later, the *Negro World*'s bold headline stated, "Negro Mothers Pure in Their Morals Should Refuse to Perpetuate the Abuses of Slavery by Living with White Men." Underneath, Garvey's letter to the people urged black women to choose "true Negro men," not those with ambiguous racial loyalties. He openly judged the idea of black women living with white men in a time of freedom to be morally unacceptable.[31]

Michele Mitchell situates this protection problem into the context of nationalism and black masculinity. She explains that many southern blacks saw emigration to Africa as the best solution to the racial double standard on women's sexuality, which created a drag on black manhood. Many subscribed to the idea that for people of African descent to have a positive "Racial Destiny" they needed ultimately to control the reproduction of the race's women. The best opportunity for this was in the promise of a black nation.[32] These objectives converged with the ideological framework of Garveyism, but to what extent the rural UNIA divisions became philosophical about racial destiny we can only guess. Specifically, there is little we can prove about how much black rural women, especially in this understudied agricultural context, were willing to accept a subordinate, protected position vis-à-vis black men in return for a modicum of protection from rape and exploitation by white men.[33]

The only example we have of the direct impact of the UNIA on antimiscegenation activity came in southwest Georgia. State commissioner S. V. Robertson organized a UNIA division in Sylvester, the county seat of Worth County, which held its first meeting on Sunday, 26 February 1922. Hymns, prayers, and female speakers preceded a speech by the UNIA organizer.[34] Exactly four weeks later, "indignation and resentment ran high among Negroes [in Sylvester] last Sunday when a group of them discovered a colored woman maintaining improper relations with a white man."[35] The group did not catch the frightened white man who fled the scene but punished the woman by administering a severe whipping. The report to the *Negro World* referred to a "certain lecture on race purity," which the men read to the woman before her punishment. Marcus Garvey's published lecture entitled "Purity of Race" read as follows:

> I believe in a pure black race just as how all self respecting whites believe in a pure white race, as far as that can be. I am conscious of the fact that slavery brought upon us the curse of many colors within the Negro race, but that is no reason why we ourselves should perpetuate the evil; hence instead of encouraging a wholesale bastardy in the race, we feel that we should now set out to create a race type and standard of our own which could not, in the future, be stigmatized by bastardy, but could be recognized and respected as the true race type anteceding even our own time.[36]

The white man, the black woman, and the local black men, presumably UNIA men, appeared in court to pay fines the next day, the severest of which went to the white man. He paid twenty dollars, while the woman paid fifteen and each vigilante paid five. This event parallels the Texarkana incident, but it is more revealing because we know that the Garvey movement had its strongest contingent in Georgia in Worth County. It is also interesting to note the leadership of local women as speakers and organizers in the county. At their first ever meeting, three community women served as speakers before the UNIA state commissioner gave his address.[37] We can see from the fines established by the white judge that the sexual liaison between the white man and black woman was considered more publicly reprehensible than the assault or vigilantism. The incident also reveals the type of white approval that might be gained for a movement espousing racial purity, even to the extent that blacks could assert themselves against the will of white men in some cases.

There must have been some response from readers because two weeks later the *Negro World* followed up on this report with a glowing editorial in support of the Sylvester men's actions. The column framed the praise in a diatribe against white men's hypocrisy in violating the sanctity of Negro women while lynching in defense of their own race's women.[38]

In a similar editorial in the *Negro World*, readers learned of a mysterious group of blacks in Birmingham, Alabama, who were held responsible for ax-murdering ten black women and killing or injuring their white male companions. In another attack on so-called white hypocrisy, the piece argued that these deaths were the unfortunate yet inevitable outcome of interracial liaisons: "The Ax-iomatic Association for the Protection of Negro Womanhood, in Birmingham, is a standing answer to the 100 per cent white lechers who associate with black women in the dark and repudiate their colored bastards in the light and who insist that white womanhood should be inviolate while actively engaged in the dirty business of corrupting black women."[39] There is no published female Garveyite editorial response agreeing or disagreeing with the report's implying that black men held black women accountable in all of these cases and that the coercion that white men had once used against black women of the South no longer applied. It went on to say that women should resist interracial relations as willfully as men should protect Negro womanhood.[40]

The most disturbing aspect of the Birmingham case is that the black women died violently in the "Ax-iomatic Association's" self-described assertion of Negro masculinity. This assertion of the right to self-defense of the race by protecting the chastity of black women or preventing miscegenation through violence became the salient and compelling feature of Garveyism on which the movement could take hold and have a purpose in local communities in the South. It was a strategy seen as beneficial to the goals of both races. Blacks wanted to prevent interracial liaisons, many of which took the form of rape, and whites wanted to perpetuate white supremacy by publicly disapproving of interracial relations—relationships that alternately suggested racial equality and interfered with the also-current white vogue for race purity.

The *Negro World* recognized and reported the complexity of the miscegenation issue and noted that it was a parental, as well as an interadult, problem. A case in April 1921 in the Mississippi Delta town of Lula in Coahoma County illustrated the opinions and power relations of blacks and whites in this rural area. A meeting of black parents expressed outrage at a black teenager's on-going romantic affair with a much older white man, saying that it demoralized her classmates, their children. The white man, obviously a man of influence, defended his lover to the black school superintendent. Later, when she was expelled from the school, a white mob whipped the school's principal and drove him out of town into Arkansas. He feared for his life and did not return to his own family and community.[41] The black community objected to her affair and could not punish the white man, but it did punish the black girl by putting her out of school. The white mob in Coahoma County was more offended by the black community's protecting its own children from exposure to the "immorality" of miscegenation against the will of a prominent white man than by the white man's participation in an interracial affair. What the *Negro World*'s front-page report from Mississippi suggests is that racial separa-tion was an assertive act on the part of black communities, a way to promote the dignity of the community, though not without consequences.

All of these incidents in the South revolved around black assertiveness and self-defense, things that were often met with white violence. Garvey's inclu-sion of self-defense in the UNIA philosophy required tremendous rhetorical and editorial subtlety and accompanying conciliatory action. He managed to fuse several of his objectives into a framework that the Klan, the most recog-nized organization for white supremacy, could appreciate. He simultaneously promoted race preservation, self-defense, and antimiscegenation as part of a package that more moderate southern whites might accept and the most hos-tile white racists might welcome. This combination of issues provided the wedge needed to give the UNIA an opportunity to continue unopposed in the South.

The Antilynching Bill

The UNIA's most important period of growth in southwest Georgia and in the Delta coincided with two widely publicized and deeply contentious issues. Both grew out of Garvey's attempts to pave the way for wider acceptance among the political and legal powers of the segregated South. One maneuver to this end was Garvey's sudden about-face to oppose the federal antilynching bill proposed in 1921 by Missouri representative Leonidas Dyer. Although at first the UNIA had supported the proposal, which aimed to make lynching a federal crime and thus allow federal prosecution of lynchers, Garvey re-thought the issue and achieved two goals with one stroke. He strongly denounced the bill, suggesting that it was simply an attempt by white Republicans to appease blacks, the same argument made by southern Democrats. Both Garvey and white southern leaders argued that the Republicans were insincere, but Garvey implied not only that Republicans had no intention of actually enforcing the law, but also that there was no way they could do so effectively over the heads of local white officials, whom the new law would punish as well for not *preventing* mob violence.[42]

By condemning the bill, Garvey courted the sympathy of white southerners for his organization, while at the same time he undermined the pet cause of the UNIA's rival, the NAACP. White southern leaders clearly associated the bill with the NAACP: Arkansas Democratic senator T. H. Caraway called the proposal "an instrumentality of a certain association situated in New York, whose officers are white" and who wanted the "federal government to invade the sovereign states" of the South.[43] The bill passed the House but was filibustered in the Senate by Caraway and other southern Democratic senators, who no doubt appreciated Garvey's outspoken opposition to the bill and reproach of the rival party.

Continuing UNIA growth in the South indicated that although this switch angered rival organizations who argued persuasively that a strong federal law would send an important message and perhaps save lives (regardless of what additional strategies might also be employed), the UNIA's official stance did not sour Garvey's ripest constituency for the UNIA, namely, blacks in the rural South. Much southern support for this tactic came through in the comments of southern delegates to the UNIA convention in August 1922 on the subject of "lynching and how to correct it." Participants in the discussion, many of whom had witnessed mob violence, agreed that force against force provided the best solution. For example, the wife of Georgia's UNIA commissioner, who had been among UNIA divisions all over southwest Georgia, argued that "lynching could be stopped if they would organize themselves, meet force by force, and pay more respect and attention to their own women, teaching how to defend themselves in time of trouble."[44] An Alabama lynching witness showed an understanding of Garvey's mixed messages while affirming the importance of organized force: "To do effective work in bringing about a remedy of the evils there [are] now existing [in the South] means the sending of men who have enough sense to know what to say and what not to say."[45] H. W. Kirby's observations of whites gave him confidence that UNIA organization and group resistance could be effective in preventing white mob violence: "When a lynching is contemplated [white people] organized nearly the entire community to get one black man. . . . If some means were devised whereby the various divisions in a certain radius could get in rapid communication with each other the moment any trouble was brooding [sic] and confront the lynchers with an organized force of blacks there would be no lynching."[46]

Kirby's suggestion of divisional minutemen addressed the circumstances of rural blacks. Such a plan might have proven highly effective in southwest Georgia or parts of the Mississippi and Arkansas Deltas, which were well over 50 percent black, had no major metropolitan cities within close range (as in the case of Elaine, Arkansas, when the state militia arrived in the remote Delta over a course of three days), and included high concentrations of UNIA divisions. Kirby's was the most concrete suggestion for a rural self-defense strategy from the convention that year. It became obvious that among Garveyites the hope of resorting to legal protection had been abandoned completely.

South Carolina's organizer, J. A. Slappey, who was also a Baptist preacher, similarly advocated self-defense, admitting that he had even forsaken prayer as a remedy: "I have come to the conclusion that those people who believe in prayer let them pray; but let us who believe in fighting fight like the devil. (Applause) My own father prayed, my mother prayed, all the good old people prayed, but what is the Negro's lot everywhere? If you allow the white man to do all the getting and you all the praying, you will soon go to the devil." Slappey went on to echo a persistent explanation given by Garvey that juxtaposed white hypocrites with the unapologetically chauvinistic Klan. "Organizations such as the Ku Klux Klan [are] Heaven-sent," he argued, "for they [help] the Negro to understand truly where he stood."[47]

Two months before the 1922 international convention, Garvey had visited the South, and in June, while in Atlanta, he had met with Edward Young Clarke, the imperial wizard of the Knights of the Ku Klux Klan. Upon howling protest by the black press and leaders of the NAACP, Garvey defended this action, stating that he had wanted to face the Klan's leader man to man and to clarify the UNIA's program. Clarke was no mysterious figure to southerners, black or white. His opinions had appeared in the *Atlanta Constitution* since the time of the Atlanta race riot of 1906. That year, he investigated and reported the opinions of Atlanta's prominent clergymen on the causes of the rioting. The future Klansman used extensive quotations to reveal that most Atlanta pastors condemned the lawlessness of the mobs, regardless of the alleged provocation. However, that did not prevent Clarke from emphasizing in his report's headline, "When raping (of white women) stops, riots will cease." Reverend A. C. Ward, the minister from Temple Baptist Church, was the only black pastor quoted. He urged a "national separation" of blacks and whites declaring, "It looks to me like the time has come when there must be a separation of the races."[48] Clarke's article in the South's leading newspaper makes clear his point of view, as well as his editorial skill and support for racial separatism.

When Garvey met with him years later, Clarke had not changed this view; and now he had a popular black supporter for this idea in a position of mass leadership. Garvey explained that he wanted the UNIA's goals to be perfectly clear to the Klan so that the two organizations could avoid conflict. In a lengthy address in the Harlem Liberty Hall, transcribed in the *Negro World* for all to read, Garvey described in detail his interview with Clarke:

"Mr. Clark[e], what is your attitude on white men raping black women?" And he said: "We are as much against that as any self-respecting Negro can be, and we are organized to see that the purity of the race, and especially the purity of the white race, is upheld, and because of that we would not desire to impose upon you that which we do not intend to accept from you." I asked him: "What would be your attitude if a white man was to go into a colored neighborhood and endeavor to take advantage of the womanhood of our race?" and he said his attitude would be against that white man. "Let me tell you this," he said further, "that I would be in sympathy with any Negro organization that would uphold the integrity of the Negro race even as the white organizations are endeavoring to uphold the integrity of the white race."

Garvey went on to explain to Clarke yet another incident in which black vigilantes had flogged seven white men in Louisiana for sleeping with black women. The local white judge, a Klansman, had let all the black men go, exhorting them to "do some more of that."[49]

Of the subjects they discussed, the only common ground Garvey and Clarke found was their mutual disdain for miscegenation.[50] Garvey became more strident about this issue over his career as a race leader, as it was a convenient issue on which to find support in the white community. The *Negro World* went so far as to print a letter from a white Waco, Texas, man who attacked W. E. B. Du Bois's defense of intermarriage of the races. The rant included the notion that separatism promoted peace and more intermixture led to more violence. He believed the logical outcome of continued miscegenation was a race war.[51] The Klan used defense of race purity as an excuse to terrorize and lynch blacks, even though white males tended to be responsible for most race-mixing. Moreover, in rural cotton counties in the early twentieth century, racial violence, lynching, and vigilantism ruled the day more than in areas dominated by other crops.[52] Perhaps conventional wisdom ran that if community policing worked for whites, why not for blacks? Perhaps Garvey's tactic was seen by rural southerners as a logical starting point in the development of a larger program for self-defense.

When Marcus Garvey met secretly with Klansman Clarke in Atlanta on 25 June 1922, he must have imagined himself an intrepid representative of black manhood. He knew that the white supremacist group had enjoyed seven years of phenomenal growth since its revival in 1915, and he also realized it tacitly approved and directly sponsored violence against African Americans in the South. He was well aware that the Klan had spread well beyond the rural South to American cities in concert with the movement of blacks in the Great Migration. In fact, the rise and fall of the "new Klan" mirrored precisely the growth and demise of the UNIA, with both organizations reaching their peak of membership and political power in 1922.[53]

Garvey had known of Clarke since November 1920 from a message the Klan organizer had sent to prospective Klan members in New York. In a speech at Harlem's Liberty Hall, Garvey acknowledged that the then imperial kleagle Clarke had set out to organize a New York Klan. Confident and defiant, the UNIA leader gleefully welcomed the Klan's organizational attempts, calling his own organization, the UNIA, "a sort of Ku Klux Klan": "I think I will [send] the challenge through the columns of the Negro World to the Ku Klux Klan of Virginia and Georgia to come to Harlem, the city of the New York Fifteenth. . . . They can pull their stuff in the South, but let them come North . . . and there will be [lit]tle left of the Ku Klux Klan."[54]

Nevertheless, by the summer of 1922 Garvey became willing to do what very few black intellectuals and even many UNIA leaders could countenance.[55] Although Clarke never made an official report of the summit from his perspective, we have Garvey's account of the two-hour meeting, which appeared in full in the *Negro World* on 15 July 1922. The firestorm of objection was well under way when Garvey rose to the podium in Liberty Hall in Harlem to explain himself. And in subsequent months and years it appears that UNIA divisions in Klan strongholds of the South abided this controversial tactic. It is very interesting to note that other Klansmen heavily criticized Clarke for meeting with Garvey. This partially explains why the acting imperial wizard later distanced himself from Garvey and the UNIA and clearly did not want to discuss the content of their meeting. Garvey was aware of the criticism Clarke endured, and he sent a telegram to the *Atlanta Constitution*, which appeared on 22 August 1922: "Please inform the people of your community that there is absolutely no connection between the Ku Klux Klan and the Universal Negro Improvement Association, of which I am president general. The attack upon

Edward Young Clarke is unjustified. Mr. Clarke and I have entered into no alliance, and any statement to the contrary is false and wicked."[56]

Within months after the summit with Garvey, Clarke was expelled from Klan leadership. Then, in February 1923, Clarke testified before the grand jury that indicted Garvey that the UNIA leader had made overtures to the Klan regarding the Black Star Line.[57] Does this mean Garvey asked the Klan for a cash donation like the ones the white group had bestowed on a black hospital in Raleigh and a black vocational school in Atlanta?[58] Or was this the only part of the discussion that Clarke was willing to reveal, making Garvey look like a charlatan—precisely what the federal prosecutor wanted to prove in the Black Star Line mail fraud case? If Clarke used Garvey to improve the Klan's public relations, as historian Judith Stein has argued, it certainly backfired on him.[59]

William Pickens, field secretary and later director of branches for the NAACP, had shown interest in and public sympathy for Garvey's program prior to the Klan summit. Of all black leaders and intellectuals of the day, Pickens served as the keenest and fairest observer of the Garvey movement. Because of this, many consulted his opinions of Garvey's leadership. Socialist leader Norman Thomas, while associate editor for *The Nation*, sought Pickens's opinions on the movement, as did debating teams from Howard University and other black college students from Winston-Salem, North Carolina.[60] The *Negro World* appreciated Pickens's endorsement and happily reprinted his mostly complimentary essays on Garveyism, one of which defended the UNIA's racialist tendencies: "Is [the UNIA] not like the Ku Klux Klan? Not if it pursues legally and morally right ends, and deals, where the interests of outsiders are concerned, openly and lawfully and not covertly and unlawfully. The only thing wrong about the Klan is its lawlessness, its secret judgements and executions, its assumption of the functions of the state, and the exercise of authority over the conduct of people who are not members. It is not illegal for associating together the members of only one race or one economic group."[61]

Pickens, the son of sharecroppers whom labor agents had enticed into debt slavery in the Arkansas Delta, had even considered joining the staff of the UNIA before going with the NAACP. He had a personal bond with rural black farmers as a child and later as a student at Talladega College. While living in the Alabama Black Belt, he was "impressed by the simplicity, and universal peaceableness of American black folk when they are left practically unto themselves."[62] He wrote a prominent essay for *The Nation* that accorded much more credit to the UNIA and Garvey than had Pickens's NAACP colleagues W. E. B. Du Bois and Walter White. But by 1922, after he heard about Garvey's meeting with Clarke, Pickens simultaneously joined the "Garvey Must Go" campaign and wrote a blistering letter to Garvey in July 1922: "The UNIA is not (or at least has not been heretofore regarded as) in a class with those criminal organizations, but I gather from your recent utterances that you are now endorsing the Ku Klux Klan or at least conceding the justice of its aim to crush and repress colored Americans. . . . You compare the aim of the Ku Klux Klan in America with your aims in Africa." Pickens harangued Garvey for not being logical and queried suggestively whether Garvey might be compromising his principles: "If you are trying to fool the Klan, you have employed a losing stratagem. . . . If it is ever to be possible for you to negotiate a worse transaction than the Black Star Line, if at a very great expense, this must be IT. You actually did get some boats that are safe when in a good harbor,—but in this KKK deal, you get absolutely nothing for the group, and for yourself, you only get a little freer hand—perhaps—to exploit the more ignorant parts of the group in the Klux-ridden section of the country."[63]

The venom of the letter reveals Pickens's utter frustration and disappointment. As field secretary for the NAACP, he understood only too well what race organizers were up against in the South. His earlier ambivalence about whether to work for the UNIA and NAACP demonstrated the complexity of tactical approaches for someone dedicated to racial uplift who also had a personal history of farming, dependence, and exploitation in the South. Ultimately, Garvey validated Pickens's decision to work for the NAACP by way of a great tactical blunder. Garvey's ill-advised meeting with the Klan not only gave more fuel to those who opposed him, to the point that even black leaders were willing to help the government convict him, but also alienated many supporters and sympathizers. After the summer of 1922, Garvey was compelled to consolidate his loyal organizers and followers and cut his losses. His strongest advocates turned out to be in the rural South. The voices from the 1924 convention were mostly in favor of careful consideration of the Klan's strength, and ultimately, William Sherrill, the Leader of American Negroes who replaced Eason, a man who had grown up in the Arkansas Delta, and the acting president general of the UNIA, made the following recommendation: "The Klan is no friend of the Negro and to say so would give the appearance of indorsement of the Klan's alleged lynching and burning of Negroes. . . . [T]he association should adopt a policy of neutral opportunism towards the Klan. They should be watchful and ready to take advantage of any opportunity that might present itself in the program of the Ku Klux Klan to assist the Negro in realizing his objective."[64] This attitude carried the day, and several resolutions to that effect were adopted by the convention delegates.

Much attention shone on the Klan and the problems of the South at the

WHAT WE BELIEVE

THE Universal Negro Improvement Association advocates the uniting and blending of all Negroes into one strong healthy race. It is against miscegenation and race suicide.

It believes that the Negro race is as good as any other, and therefore should be as proud of itself as others are.

It believes in the purity of the Negro race and the purity of the white race.

It is against rich blacks marrying poor whites.

It is against rich or poor whites taking advantage of Negro women.

It believes in the spiritual Fatherhood of God and the Brotherhod of Man.

It believes in the social and political physical separation of all people to the extent that they promote their own ideals and civilization, with the privilege of trading and doing business with each other. It believes in the promotion of a strong and powerful Negro nation.

It believes in the rights of all men.

UNIVERSAL NEGRO IMPROVEMENT ASSN.

MARCUS GARVEY, President-General

January 1, 1924.

The UNIA creed was published in the Negro World *beginning in 1924 as a way of clarifying the organization's platform. The headline, "What We Believe," was later adopted by the Nation of Islam and was found in its publications with its own creed below. (*Negro World, *1 January 1924)*

1924 convention. Entire sessions were devoted to discussions of strategies for organizing in the South, and a committee of five was appointed to work on the issues. In the same discussion, a delegate recommended a clarification of the UNIA's positions to make the organization more transparent to southern whites. The West Virginia member of the committee suggested using the *Negro World* as a tool for explicating the UNIA's principles.[65] Beginning in January 1924, the *Negro World* had begun to publish a bold, signed declaration in the paper headlined, "WHAT WE BELIEVE." This declaration appeared frequently in the UNIA organ.

Garvey's antimiscegenation stance did not diverge from his original vision for race solidarity. Although opposition to antilynching legislation and negotiation with the Klan became extreme tactics in his effort to establish a foothold in the South, antimiscegenation was interpreted by many as the logical extension of his separatist doctrine, and these positions meshed with the reality of local conditions for blacks in the rural South. Antimiscegenation laws existed in many southern states at this time. Arkansas senator T. H. Caraway and South Carolina senator Cole Blease had proposed federal legislation to make interracial marriages illegal in 1926.[66] Historian Charles Robinson's study of antimiscegenation laws in Arkansas has shown that in that state, people were prosecuted under these laws only when a white man *married* a black woman. This is indicative of the fact that to white men in power, race mixing was not so much a repugnant and unacceptable private practice, but the suggestion of racial equality, which marriage presumed, was.[67]

The difference between the segregation imposed by white men either in fact or by law in the Jim Crow South and the social separatism espoused by the UNIA hinged on demographics within the region. In the 1920s urban segregation in the former Confederacy had a different character from its rural counterpart. In southern cities, most of which contained clear white majorities, municipal segregation laws governed the use of public facilities and the racial composition of neighborhoods. In urban communities, over time and through legal means, interracial associations became less acceptable and more clearly prohibited, and, as historian Glenda Gilmore has so lucidly explained, segregation laws were designed to prevent white women from sharing space with black men, especially those who were strangers.[68]

By contrast, segregation purely by custom persisted in rural areas; and in majority-black areas like the Delta, biracial interaction in stores, commissaries, and gins and on roads was common, accepted, and economically necessary for both races. Also in rural communities, as more whites lost their land and slipped into tenancy in the 1920s, exceptions to segregation practices in sharecropper housing were typical.[69]

In every Black Belt county in the South, male-female ratios were fairly balanced. Under prevailing conditions of white supremacy, white men had access to women of both races, while the inverse certainly did not apply for black men. A statistic that compounded this disparity in Black Belt counties was that there were far more black women than white women in the workforce, particularly as domestic servants or farmers. Because in most of these situations they were under contract to or under the supervision of white men, they became more vulnerable to sexual exploitation. In this context, UNIA men and perhaps even women desired strictly enforced social separatism more than they opposed legally sanctioned segregation. To rural Garveyites, separation meant the ability to protect women and female children against unwanted interracial sexual relations with whites. When possible, tenant farmers in the Black Belt who supported the UNIA kept their wives at home. Moreover, the census reveals that UNIA households contained a high proportion of females. A constant worry was that white men might subject these women to sexual assault with impunity.[70] As one Garveyite explained, the most compelling cause for the massive black migration north was the black man's desire to have "his wife and daughters removed from the omnipresent [N]egro-chasing white man."[71] Yet clearly, most blacks remained in the South and had to contend with the prevalence of interracial sex and its consequences.

Through his opposition to the ill-fated antilynching bill, his notorious Klan summit, and his espousal of racial separatism, Garvey curried favor with the powerful elements in white southern society. Perhaps rural, southern Garveyites showed, through their continued support for Garvey's seemingly "conservative" turn, an understanding of the necessity of whites' tacit approval of the movement, at least temporarily, for its survival. After the South's blacks became organized, they hoped, local problems of interracial violence and abuse could be mitigated.

The Long-Term Solution: African Redemption

Garveyites in the rural South believed that in the long term the solution to universal Negro problems would come through African redemption. Letters to the UNIA paper reveal a deep commitment to this goal among southern Garveyites, and phrases contained in them came straight from the Negro Bill of Rights. UNIA claims regarding Africa headed that statement's agenda: "Invoking the aid of the just and almighty God, [we] do declare all men, women and children of our blood throughout the world free citizens, and do claim them as free citizens of Africa, the motherland of all Negroes." To this nationalistic proclamation was added, "We strongly condemn the cupidity of those nations of the world who, by open aggression, or secret schemes, have seized the territories and inexhaustible natural wealth of Africa, and we place on record our most solemn determination to reclaim the treasures and possession of the vast continent of our forefathers."[72]

Garvey's idea for the redemption of Africa had an appealing sound. It echoed a nineteenth-century black religious tradition, which appeared again and again in most letters appearing in the *Negro World*. The cause of freeing the Motherland fueled the Garvey movement and became the single most important focal point of UNIA activity.[73] Whereas the UNIA divisions in large urban areas sometimes developed local programs, business enterprises, and services, the smaller, rural divisions fervently hoped for a political solution and committed themselves to Garvey's primary goal of African redemption. He preached that the other races would not view blacks as anything other than slaves so long as blacks in Africa remained under the control of white colonizers and creditors. Tenant farmers and unskilled laborers in the South could readily identify with this perception.

The UNIA leadership never clearly articulated the connection between the redemption of Africa and establishment of a politically and financially independent, modern African nation. But it became increasingly obvious that Garvey hoped to attract the most capable and resourceful people of African ancestry to a UNIA colony in Liberia. The Liberian colonization plan would provide a proving ground for self-government and economic prosperity, and a refuge for disenchanted Negroes from white-dominated countries.

Garvey undoubtedly shared a romanticized image of Africa with many African Americans who, like the UNIA leader, had never been there. Garvey traveled widely in the West Indies, Central America, Britain, and the United States, meeting and observing many of his race along the way. Probably his closest African acquaintance was Duse Mohammed Ali, for whom he worked while a young man in London. He studied African history and made a point to meet and associate with many Africans, as well as to read about and hear speakers on African issues. He sent delegations to Liberia and chartered UNIA divisions in six African countries. The imperialist nations of Europe, as well as the government of Liberia, recognized that the cry of African redemption was not empty rhetoric. The *Negro World* was banned in many of Europe's African colonies, and the government of Liberia denied visas to foreign UNIA members in 1924.[74]

Based on his ambitious vision of redemption, the 1920 UNIA convention elected Garvey the provisional president of the continent. He explained his organization's ultimate goal: "It is the desire to locate the Negro in a position of prosperity and happiness in the future that the UNIA is making this great fight for the race's emancipation everywhere and the founding of a great African government."[75] He convinced his followers that other black organizations had mistakenly compromised with whites, hoping for the unattainable goal of the American Dream. "Others of our race are being subsidized to turn the attention of the world toward a different desire on the part of Negroes," he contended, "but let me tell you that we who make up this organization know no turning back, we have pledged ourselves even unto the last drop of our sacred blood that Africa must be free."[76]

In the post–World War I era, when political and social equality seemed unattainable to many blacks, especially in the rural South, Garvey's message attracted serious attention. UNIA supporters felt that a strong, independent government in Africa, with Garvey in charge, offered an opportunity for blacks to gain the respect of other races. Supporters from all along the Mississippi River voiced approval of the goal to redeem Africa. Queenie Sudduth of Sunflower, Mississippi, related her aspirations to the *Negro World* editor: "I am just anxious for the redemption of Africa and a government for our race."[77] Another letter, from Merigold, Mississippi, stated, "[W]e are still on the map, working for the uplift and redemption of our motherland Africa."[78] Ministers who led UNIA divisions reiterated the cause that had belonged to African American missions since the early nineteenth century, based on Psalms 68:31: "Princes shall come forth from Egypt. Ethiopia shall soon stretch forth her hand to God." For example, Reverend J. Paynes of the St. Rose, Louisiana, division presided over a meeting in which the members agreed "to work harder during the coming year in order that the day of African redemption be hastened."[79] One after another, letters repeated the words of Mollie Bynum of Blytheville, Arkansas: "I pray God for the redemption of Africa."[80]

As a man of action, Garvey proposed the first step toward freeing Africa and setting up a black government. Six African countries had UNIA divisions, including Liberia, where Garvey proposed to resettle willing black Americans beginning in the fall of 1924. Although he was never specific about the process, which Garvey himself admitted would be long and arduous, apparently Liberia was the chosen beachhead from which the colonized remains of Africa could be freed. Garvey formally launched the African colonization plan in February 1924, yet his plan to repatriate African Americans to Liberia had been in its preliminary stages since 1920.[81] Before the plan became formalized in 1924, Garvey had included a provision in the UNIA constitution for an African Redemption Fund. This fund requested voluntary five-dollar donations from each loyal member of the UNIA "to create a working capital for the organization and to advance the cause for the building up of Africa."[82] After the *Negro World* began to advertise the colonization campaign in 1924, Garvey began actively to solicit contributions. The leader designated the money for a purchase of 500 square miles of land along the Cavalla River (the southern border of Liberia), planning and construction costs, and transportation to the Liberian UNIA colony. These plans appeared in the *Negro World*, and some southern UNIA supporters became excited about the prospects of an African home. Their enthusiasm shows clearly in their frequent and generous donations to the cause. James Nunally of Marianna, Arkansas, for example, professed a great interest in reading the *Negro World*, even though he was not a UNIA member: "I enjoy reading those inspiring Liberty Hall addresses, especially the Honorable Marcus Garvey's. I feel that we need a home because we have been working for the other races and it is time to start working for ourselves."[83]

A female UNIA president in Florida understood the expense involved in the plan and urged her division to "build up the community and help materially in recovering the Motherland."[84] To many, reclaiming a small bit of Liberia and helping to build up the country's economic base provided a logical first step in a larger process. In defending Garvey against charges by the white editor of the Natchez, Mississippi, *Democrat* that Garvey was robbing illiterate blacks using the impossible promise of establishing "a home and government for them somewhere in Africa," the *Negro World* managing editor argued, "The Negroes who want to go to Africa under the auspices of the UNIA will know where they are going when they start, and what to expect when they get there. Liberia is on the map. It is a member of the League of Nations, and the United States is not, and it has a black President . . . and it speaks the English language and professes the Christian faith, and that is more than the average white Mississippian speaks fluently on the one hand, and practices consistently when he professes it, on the other."[85]

The repatriation plan seemed attractive and workable, and southern UNIA supporters wanted to help make it happen. Thus, when the UNIA requested that each division send in a contribution for the colonization project, the southern divisions responded conscientiously. Of the divisions in the former Confederate states, thirty-seven paid on the central office's first request. The colonization fund paid for engineering, medical, and agricultural experts to study the area set aside for colonization and preparation for the first five hundred African American emigrants, expected in the fall of 1924. Fifteen-dollar contributions came immediately from divisions in rural communities such as Pooler and Camilla, Georgia; Burton Spurr, Round Pond, Armorel, Howell, Indian Bay, Blackton, and Pine City, Arkansas; and Askew, Merigold, Symonds, Drew, and Sumner, Mississippi.[86]

Much of the financial support for Garvey's African plan came from UNIA members and supporters who had no desire to emigrate themselves. Money flowed freely into the African Redemption and Colonization Funds from the Delta, southwest Georgia, and other parts of the southern Black Belt. Most of these contributors hoped that the Liberian plan could aid Garvey's grand design to promote respect and material wealth for the Negro race, although other supporters expressed a personal desire for repatriation. Leonard Thomas of Portland, Arkansas, wrote that he wanted to move to the Motherland after reading the *Negro World* and would gladly put $1 million into the movement if he had it.[87] Miss Lee Knighton of Dawson, Georgia, thanked God for Marcus Garvey's having made her dream of living in Africa possible.[88] S. B. Smith of Elm City, North Carolina, informed the *Negro World*'s "People's Forum" of his joy over the African colonization project: "I am glad indeed of the light that has been turned on the Negro race by the Honorable Marcus Garvey. I long to trod the soil of our motherland Africa. May God help us to ever press on and on until we reach a better land and see a brighter day."[89]

These rural blacks, for various reasons, found moving to Africa a more attractive idea than remaining in the rural South or migrating to the northern cities. Garvey's Liberty Hall addresses, reprinted in the *Negro World*, stressed that oppression in the North existed in the form of ghetto life, discrimination, and violence. Some southern blacks could no longer view the North as a land of opportunity and freedom from racism. According to the UNIA leader, every white man harbored racist feelings whether he admitted them or not: "Prejudice of the white race against the black race is not so much because of color as of condition; because as a race, to them, we have accomplished nothing; we have built no nation, no government; because we are dependent on them for our economic and political existence."[90] Garvey consistently reminded African Americans that they formed only a minority of the population in the United States. He and national organizers such as Eason and Robertson rejected the notion that America was anything other than "the white man's country" and stressed that their racial destiny, political independence, and national affiliation lay in Africa.

Living in Liberia under a black, independent government appealed to the prospective emigrants despite what they may have heard or read about the harsh conditions encountered by missionaries and emigrants or the long history of conflict between the descendants of African American emigrants from the 1810s and 1820s and the Susu and Ghebo peoples of Liberia.[91] Many rural southerners wrote to the American Colonization Society asking for information on Liberia. Mission work in West Africa continued through the African Methodist Episcopal and black Baptist churches, as well as through white missionary societies from Europe and the United States. In the *State*, the leading paper in South Carolina, a fairly evenhanded description of life in Liberia appeared on 28 April 1924. A white missionary who had spent three years there described the relatively successful black republic and the cultural differences and separation of the Americo-Liberian elites who monopolized Liberian government positions and the indigenous Liberians. Reports like these would have encouraged Garveyites with the important work to be done on the continent.[92]

Some skepticism about the emigration plan existed, but committed Garveyites did their best to reverse it. Two native Africans spoke to the Berkley, Virginia, division about their land and the virtues of Garvey's plan, and afterward many former skeptics indicated their readiness "to embark for Africa."[93]

A lengthy address by an African American missionary with fourteen years' acquaintance with Liberia appeared in a 1923 issue of the *Negro World.* "'We hear in America that the Africans are savages and will eat you up. I want to tell you,' said Dr. Jones. 'If you want to go where folks eat you up, go South; they do worse than that—they will burn you up.'"[94] Perhaps this feeling also met with agreement and approval from southern black readers.

In a feature article on his "Eight Weeks in Dixie," Floyd J. Calvin, a writer for the *Messenger*, told readers that white mob violence had encouraged blacks to leave the South. He implied that Garvey had misdirected blacks toward an unsuitable escape. In Calvin's view, the UNIA misled "the most ignorant and uninformed . . . to blindly want to go to Africa—anywhere to get away from down there!"[95] Like Calvin, some UNIA members had difficulty thinking of Africa as their natural home. For other UNIA skeptics, their difficulties with the plan lay in its actual execution. The Blytheville, Arkansas, division sent J. B. Simmons to the 1924 UNIA convention to find out "some definite information concerning the ship that is expected to sail [for Liberia, carrying 500 African American emigrants] on September 1."[96] The *Negro World* ran ads for applications for those wanting to settle in the Liberian UNIA colony in late 1924 or early 1925, but not all supporters of the repatriation plan took their enthusiasm that far. A woman from Ross, Texas, stated, "How I long to be in my native home," but she gave no indication of actually taking steps to move to Africa.[97] Fannie Kaigler, a native of Berrien County in southwest Georgia, claimed that many would have gone, even those like herself who were not UNIA members, if Garvey had successfully implemented the plan, but as things turned out, he never got that far.[98] J. L. Dennis of Blue Springs, Mississippi, wrote the *Negro World* that she hoped to become a UNIA member and already subscribed to the paper; however, she wrote primarily to say that she might not ever reach Africa but wanted to encourage everyone who was going.[99]

Pressure from the French and British governments, which had the most to lose from "African redemption" by Africans, had much to do with the Liberian government's deteriorating relations with Garvey and the UNIA in 1924.[100] And much to Garvey's dismay, the first phase of African redemption received a fatal blow just days before he was to sign the land deal with the Liberian government. Firestone Rubber of Akron, Ohio, acquired the land instead of the UNIA. It turned out that the Liberian government owed huge debts to foreign creditors, including the United States, and Firestone offered Liberian president C. D. B. King more money for the land than Garvey could pay. Thus, under pressure from creditors, King reneged on his agreement with the UNIA and destroyed Garvey's expensive plans.[101] Then, as the Liberian government also denied visas to UNIA members and to Garvey, the plan dissolved. Garvey's failure to accomplish this popular but costly goal damaged morale in the UNIA administration but did not observably hurt Garvey's popularity or mission with rural southerners. His followers continued to send him money and supportive letters throughout the months after the Liberian debacle. But letters and money from well-wishers could not save the Garvey movement from its inevitable undoing. Administrative power struggles in the leading division in New York caused large numbers of Garveyites to split from the movement.

Garvey's trials and appeals had already sapped much of the organization's momentum and resources, and not long after the Liberian failure Garvey lost his legal appeal and went to federal prison in Atlanta, where he would spend his last year and ten months in the United States. At this point, the UNIA leader and his wife devoted themselves entirely to cultivating powerful friends and mobilizing public opinion in favor of Garvey's release.[102] Among blacks of the rural South, support shown for the cause of freeing the Motherland shifted to freeing "our leader." Throughout Garvey's final imprisonment between 5 February 1925 and 26 November 1927, unquestioning devotion to the organization's founder and leader and efforts toward his release became the focal point of the South's UNIA activity.

Followers had for years thought of Garvey as a prophet or divine leader. Jennie Jones from the small Delta town of Trenton, Tennessee, explained her belief that Garvey was the fulfillment of a fifty-year-old prophecy of her father's, which predicted the coming of a great race leader. She admired Garvey for his great strength "amidst obstacles, persecution, and divers difficulties." This old woman stressed above all her desire for African redemption.[103]

Others compared the leader's tribulations to those of biblical figures. The president of the Prichard, Alabama, division compared Garvey to the Messiah for his noble deeds.[104] In rural Virginia a UNIA guest speaker likened Garvey's rejection by many of the Negro race to Jesus' rejection by the Jews.[105] A devotee from Preston, Georgia, called Garvey the Moses of black people.[106] And in Louisiana Garvey was likened to Ezekiel, the biblical visionary who endured a lifetime of personal suffering while explaining the reasons for Israel's captivity.[107] Ezekiel had delivered God's message to the Israelites in their exile in Babylon at a time when they had given up all hope: "I will put my spirit in you, and you will live and return home to your own land."[108] In the same vein, the *Negro World* printed the text of John Fenner Jr.'s address to the Richmond, Virginia, division in May 1924. The featured speaker referred to Garvey's work as a religious mission that corresponded with the Scriptures.[109] A rural Georgia woman suggested a Garvey Day, "and on that day at a certain

Five hundred people from the Indian Bay, Monroe County, Arkansas, black community rallied and sent this petition for clemency for Marcus Garvey to President Calvin Coolidge in 1925. (Records of the U.S. Pardon Attorney, RG 204, box 1161, National Archives II, College Park, Md.)

hour every Negro should lay aside all business and kneel in fervent prayer to God in behalf of Mr. Marcus Garvey, that he may overcome his enemies and be able to put this program [African redemption] over."[110]

This type of tribute to Garvey appeared in every issue of the *Negro World*. Even after the leader's financial and legal troubles mounted, his southern followers continued to support and praise him. Jerry Haley of Natchez, Mississippi, wrote that he regretted the abuse that Garvey had taken but remained confident that the provisional president of Africa would prevail.[111] In Merigold, Mississippi, UNIA members were "not a bit bothered or discouraged by the imprisonment of our great leader, but [were] more determined than ever."[112]

Rural southern Garveyites showed greater devotion to Garvey's leadership than those in urban areas. Faithful followers did not waver in their supportive letters and contributions after Garvey was convicted of mail fraud. They believed he had not maliciously misled potential Black Star Line stock purchasers about the financial condition of the company. Even the white press, which normally ignored Garvey, noted blacks' resentment over Garvey's conviction. The *Atlanta Constitution* reported that the Associated Press had received scores of telegrams from "nearly every state" protesting the leader's conviction and pleading with the white press to "turn on the searchlight of justice . . . to reverse this frame-up."[113] Letters and contributions similarly poured into the central UNIA office. For example, Bernard Andrews of the Gulfport, Mississippi, division wrote the *Negro World* declaring his division's strength despite Garvey's conviction.[114]

Of all the funds the UNIA advertised in the *Negro World*, the leader's personal "Defense Fund" drew the most financial support from southern blacks. The paper listed the name and hometown of each donor, revealing the amount of each gift. Contributions to the Marcus Garvey Defense Fund came from as many towns with UNIA divisions as those without during 1923, the year of the leader's conviction.[115]

Hundreds of Western Union telegrams poured into the offices of the president of the United States, the attorney general, and the pardon attorney pleading for a pardon, clemency, or a pardon without deportation, depending on the status of Garvey's ongoing trial and incarceration. Some were personal and original, while others bore identical text and represented the wishes of hundreds who had gathered to rally for Garvey's freedom.[116] The words used in the latter group of telegrams, presumably dictated by the UNIA parent body, are useful in establishing the wide and ardent support for the leader in the South. More revealing, however, are the handwritten or typed testimonials expressing Garvey's importance to individual rural blacks in the South. From Tulot, Arkansas, a tiny Delta community in Poinsett County, which never had a UNIA division, James and Mittie Jones and Margarette Oliver wrote on 16 June 1927:

> Hon. Calvin Coolidge. President. Of the U.S. Washington. D.C. Sir; we the
> Negro Citizens of Tulot, Ark. & Juddhill. ARK. Pass the following Resolu-

tion whereas we Believe that Marcus Gavey [*sic*] has been Punished more severely than his offence warrants and where as the whole Negro race in america, and the world over, is in sympathy with this man, by whom the lesson of racial Consciousness and respect has been taught, which ultimately will produce a better type of world Citizenship be it resolved, that we the Citizens of this place Petition. Hon; Calvin Coolidge. President of the. U.S. To. Grant a pardon. To Marcus Garvey.[117]

Garvey's personal popularity among southern blacks who had never heard his voice, seen his face, or even joined the UNIA speaks volumes about the power of his ideas. Through news, editorials, and UNIA programs publicized in the *Negro World* and by dedication to the most applicable principles outlined in the UNIA constitution and the Negro Bill of Rights, rural southern Garveyites formulated their own ideology for coping with the challenges of their daily existence in their local communities and their own method of mitigating the larger issue of racial oppression. By borrowing the most salient components of Garvey's multifaceted philosophies and strategies, they formed a distinctive and enduring legacy of pride, independence, self-defense, self-determination, and sacred obligation to the African heritage.

Garveyites in the large urban divisions, mostly in the North, had access to rising leaders and alternative organizations once Garvey's fortunes waned. Many remained loyal, and UNIA divisions thrived in many places but with their own local agendas, less dependent on the leader's freedom or proximity. Southern divisions, especially in rural areas, seemed most affected by the UNIA leader's tribulations. His personal destiny, to them, represented the possibilities of his vision's fulfillment.

Garvey's legal and financial troubles, along with his denunciation by almost all rival black organizations after his Klan summit, have been well chronicled. Because these conditions led to his imprisonment and eventual deportation in 1927, the momentum of the UNIA and Garveyism in America ended shortly thereafter. It is interesting, however, to examine his evolving strategy and to suppose that the South had become his most important target for expansion. By 1922, Garvey had become acutely aware of the enormous potential of the southern-born black masses to mobilize on behalf of the UNIA, and he reverted to a strategy for organization that alienated many urban elite members and perhaps even some of the working-class support he held in the cities.[118] The numerical potential of the rural southern agriculturalists (or the many who came from grassroots origins), combined with their unwavering and sometimes unquestioning devotion to him and his program—one that incorporated so many of their ideals—may have been irresistible for Garvey. He found ways to mesh his race-first philosophy into a framework that could meet white approval. In doing so, through providing a basis for black self-defense—the protection of Negro womanhood—and by tapping into the spiritual consciousness of rural blacks by making African redemption a sacred mission as well as an issue of national identification, he had begun to organize the most populous segment of African Americans in the only areas where they formed the racial majorities in their communities. The UNIA thus provided a short-term and long-term vision for black power.

It may be that even though [Garvey] has been banished to Jamaica the seed planted here will yet spring up and bring forth fruit which will mean the deliverance of the black race—that cause which was so dear to his heart.—Ida B. Wells

Although the strategies and objectives of the UNIA appeared diametrically opposed to those of organizations that were seeking legal equality and American citizenship for black people, the UNIA's organizational success and popularity in the South helped rival groups by teaching them important lessons. In the 1920s Garvey's unmatched ability to organize rural and urban laborers demonstrated the potency of "assimilating his own program to the religious experience of the Negro." The UNIA also highlighted the priorities and sentiments of a great many black people who felt alienated from American ideals of equality and justice. In 1926, as E. Franklin Frazier compared the UNIA and NAACP, he also noted, "The National Association for the Advancement of Colored People, which has fought uncompromisingly for equality for the Negro, has never secured, except locally and occasionally, the support of the masses."[1] The dominance of the UNIA and Garvey in the 1920s convinced competing associations that they must organize at the grassroots level and take seriously the most basic needs and impulses of laboring blacks, many of whom had been reared in the rural South. Consequently, leaders of groups like the NAACP and the Southern Tenant Farmers Union (STFU) carefully culled what they found useful from what they perceived as the strictly unacceptable aspects of Garveyism.

Despite Garveyism's appeal, the majority of influential black editors and intellectuals who opposed Garvey ridiculed the idea of an exodus to Africa and the acceptance of the United States as a "white man's country." These rival leaders believed that Garvey's racialist rhetoric went too far and that his interest in class conflict stemmed only from the fact that most blacks were impoverished. And while many may have liked the idea of African redemption, few of his critics believed it could be achieved, especially through colonization or militarization.

Self-defense remained a popular strategy and was most often employed in rural areas, but it, too, was problematic. Urban leaders viewed it as extralegal and inconsistent—a step backward, not a way to make America live up to its creed. Preparation for self-protection also had proved its potential to precipitate violence, lynching, rioting, and massacres. Elite black leaders preferred a responsive application of law over dangerous and costly individual and group efforts toward self-policing—including popular justice within a separate black sphere. In addition, Garvey's antimiscegenation ideas stirred explosive intraracial controversy. Yet blacks who saw whites' antimiscegenation position as simply a way to institutionalize the second-class citizenship of blacks were less likely to be those whose wives and daughters were in greatest danger of being raped and exploited.

On the other hand, the UNIA's emphasis on economic independence already had many black adherents and beneficiaries, especially businessmen in the segregated South. Booker T. Washington paved the way on the principle of economic independence; then Garveyites perpetuated this ideal through their "New Negro" leader. Black economic self-reliance made perfect sense to the still-dependent tenant farmer and often precariously independent black landowner.[2] Development of race pride and organization seemed universally accepted as worthy strategies, but the issue of separatism and its close relationship to segregation made Garveyism especially difficult to reconcile with other organizations' class-conscious or biracial outlooks.

Since the UNIA had universal popularity, and there was substantial overlap of the Garvey movement and subsequent efforts for racial improvement, why is the UNIA viewed by many as outside of the mainstream? Perhaps it is because so much of what we have heard about the Garvey movement has been influenced by interpretations drawn from the descriptions, critiques, and opinions of the black intellectual elite of the 1920s and 1930s. Some of these social commentators were affiliated with strictly class-conscious (yet white-dominated) socialist groups, predominantly in the urban North, while most of the rest aligned themselves ideologically with integrationist and social equality organizations like the NAACP. Much of the black press from which we derive information about the Garvey movement perpetuated anti-Garvey sentiment and ignored or dismissed the loyalty to UNIA ideology of the less-represented voices of the black working class. Despite the ways they ridiculed and dismissed Garvey, black intellectuals were both keenly aware of and deeply troubled by Garvey's popularity.

The NAACP and the STFU represent historically significant groups that, over time, vied for the support and leadership of blacks in the South, including rural farmers. Both groups emphasized interracial cooperation, had whites as leaders and members, and learned a great deal by observing the methods and rapid spread of the UNIA. When the UNIA dissolved on the national scene with

Garvey's deportation, attentive organizations filled the vacuum. Before Garvey arrived in the United States, the NAACP had organized in many areas of the South. After 1920, however, the group suffered a sharp decline that lasted for most of the decade. The years of the NAACP's weakness in the South, which coincided precisely with the UNIA's and the Ku Klux Klan's rise, illustrate how many southern blacks recognized the limited possibilities for the improvement of racial conditions, especially via interracial cooperation, in this decade of transition. UNIA advocates instead adopted strategies that addressed the exigencies of the early 1920s and that acknowledged the hard and discouraging lessons of the past.

When Garvey's ability to lead effectively from abroad became tenuous, organizers for these other groups struggled to gain legitimacy as the spokesmen for race and class reform and leadership. And while neither group compromised its principles or distinctive agendas, both benefited from the groundwork laid by the Garvey movement in the southern countryside. White leadership and membership were clearly organizational liabilities in the long run. Over the course of five decades, the NAACP ultimately succeeded in many of its objectives. By getting an early start, persisting through difficult periods, adapting to changing conditions, and cooperating with other race improvement organizations, the NAACP outlasted the UNIA and other short-lived local, regional, and national organizations, many of which became its affiliates. The organization became more successful in organizing larger numbers as blacks took over leadership positions. On the other hand, the STFU, popular mainly in the Arkansas Delta and a few places in Mississippi between 1934 and 1939, failed because it depended too heavily on participation by blacks, who became disillusioned by their continued subordination within the biracial organization, and because it wedded itself to anachronistic socioeconomic conditions in the form of tenant labor in an era of mechanization. Yet for black, rural southerners, although the UNIA and the *Negro World* ceased to exist during the mid-1930s, the guiding principles of UNIA organization—the religious association and exclusive black leadership—became paramount. As many of the elder Garveyites died off, the doctrine of Garveyism—racial dignity, autonomy, and pride—was passed to their progeny.

Foremost among changes influencing black thought as a whole in the post–World War I era was steady urbanization. The Great Migration of African Americans began in earnest around 1910, became a widely recognized phenomenon by 1920, and was a bona fide social revolution by 1930. The number of counties that the Census Bureau qualified as "Black Belt" (that is, having a majority-black population) shrank steadily from 264 in 1910 to 191 by

1930. Most of this decline resulted from blacks moving to predominantly white urban areas of the North and South.[3] Bolivar County, Mississippi, Phillips and Monroe Counties, Arkansas, and Baker County, Georgia, all saw substantial decreases in the percentage of black population during this period, indicating significant movement away from these areas.[4] Blacks from the Delta generally moved to Chicago or other cities of the Midwest, while Georgia migrants usually ended up in the Northeast.[5] Although the migration and urbanization of blacks had a significant impact on the North, in 1930 73.8 percent of African Americans still lived in their native states, overwhelmingly in the South. Only 1,355,789 blacks lived in the North, and fewer than 100,000 of them, mainly West Indians, were foreign-born. It is also crucial to the significance of this study to recognize that in 1930 58.0 percent of those blacks living in the North had been born in the South.[6] Southern conditions provided the foundation for most African Americans' ideologies, regardless of where they ended up living. For black migrants, moving from the Black Belt to a city, whether North or South, usually meant living in a racial minority for the first time. One's vulnerability might have seemed less acute in cities because geographically separate black communities within urban areas could organize themselves more easily. But the option of self-defense through physical force and numbers was actually reduced because blacks were outnumbered by urban whites. The urban riots of 1919 in Washington, D.C., Chicago, Omaha, Indianapolis, and Knoxville provided dramatic demonstrations of the new fact of minority status. This urban reality dictated the need for different strategies for achieving racial progress and harmony.

The NAACP Strategy Falters

The year 1915 saw the deaths of Booker T. Washington and Henry McNeal Turner and also the formal reestablishment of the Ku Klux Klan for the first time since Reconstruction. In early 1916 race leaders from the NAACP and Tuskegee, along with James Weldon Johnson and several men closely tied to the Atlanta community, met at NAACP leader Joel Spingarn's estate near Amenia, New York. The diverse group ranged from militant to moderate in perspective and held a unified opinion on the "peculiar difficulties" of race leadership in the South.[7] Soon after, the NAACP released a statement of demands, which clearly distanced the organization from the Tuskegee philosophy that American white leadership had embraced so heartily. This list called for an end to lynching, peonage, and segregation; the establishment of equal school facilities; and the right to register and vote without interference.[8] This new statement of goals encompassed the gravest concerns of southern African

Americans and revealed a new strategy that focused on the South and its overwhelming needs.[9]

Other broad changes influencing strategy and tactics occurred during the post–World War I period. Industrialization had progressed rapidly, increasing the size and wealth of cities to an unprecedented degree. The war had provided an international perspective to the American consciousness while offering economic opportunities and an impetus for further urbanization. Print media in this era enjoyed their greatest influence for the last time before the onslaught of radio and film. Racial nationalists, socialists, and liberals competed for territory and constituencies, while the black press vied for the hearts and minds of many blacks who were the first in their families to be able to read. Even among the best educated at black colleges, debate teams pitted the strategies of the UNIA and NAACP against each other.[10]

Before the UNIA or the *Negro World* ever reached below the Mason-Dixon Line, the NAACP had gained a foothold in many southern cities that hosted a sizable black professional class. The focus on organization in the South came from the NAACP's Florida-born field secretary from 1916 to 1920, James Weldon Johnson. His first organizing tour resulted in thirteen new branches in southern cities from Richmond to Tampa. Most NAACP local leaders came from the ranks of teachers, businessmen, physicians, and clergymen, but their local activities promoted the welfare of all classes of black people.[11]

Like Garvey, Johnson recognized the South's importance in legitimizing an organization's claims to race leadership. Booker T. Washington's passing had left a void, and his absence opened an opportunity for not only new leadership but also a new strategy. Conditions on the American scene seemed to favor change, and the blacks who influenced NAACP policy, like Johnson and *Crisis* editor W. E. B. Du Bois, recognized an opportunity to win over the more prosperous and educated blacks of the urban South, and through them to assist in improving conditions for the mass of industrial laborers and farmers of rural areas. Johnson kept a close watch on the activities of Garvey and his movement, resulting in an NAACP "Garvey File," which included correspondence to and from people around the South who kept him informed of the UNIA's activities. The NAACP's Garvey records include about 300 files, some of which contain newspaper clippings on the Garvey movement from southern newspapers.[12]

Much of Johnson's early work centered on friends and acquaintances from the Atlanta area, where he had attended Atlanta University and later taught in the rural schools of Henry County, just south of Georgia's capital. Seventeen NAACP branches sprang up throughout Georgia from January 1917 through

June 1920 in response to aggressive organizing campaigns by NAACP field workers and local black professionals.[13] These local units had varying degrees of success with sustaining membership rolls, pursuing improvements in local conditions for their black communities, and even remaining active. The NAACP branches in Georgia had as much potential for success as any of those in the Deep South states because of the influence of Atlanta University and the African American business community. Because of these ties to the capital city, Georgia drew the most attention from the NAACP's central administration, as compared with other southern states.[14]

The desire for a "new strategy" preoccupied many black leaders and intellectuals. W. E. B. Du Bois published his most famous work, *The Souls of Black Folk* (1903), while serving as a professor at Atlanta University. His concern over the future of black leadership (his response to the Atlanta Exposition "compromise" address) is eloquently stated in the section entitled, "Of Mr. Booker T. Washington and Others." But also immensely interesting is Du Bois's detailed descriptions of black folk in the Black Belt of southwest Georgia. "[T]he Negro is still supreme in a Cotton Kingdom larger than that on which the Confederacy builded [*sic*] its hopes. So the Negro forms to-day one of the chief figures in a great world industry; and this, for its own sake, and in light of historic interest, makes the field-hands of the cotton kingdom worth studying. . . . And yet how little we really know of these millions,—of their daily lives and longings, of their homely joys and sorrows, of their real shortcomings and the meaning of their crimes!"[15] Garvey undoubtedly pondered this thought while reading this classic tome, taking to heart other issues raised by Du Bois (of later significance to the UNIA) such as how American slavery had perpetuated the "red stain of bastardy," the "defilement of Negro women," and the "obliteration of the Negro home."[16] After Du Bois relocated to New York and became editor of the *Crisis*, his observations and sociological analysis of rural African Americans continued to guide his vision for black advancement.

In addition to Du Bois's and Johnson's input, the NAACP's records show the organization's close familiarity with rural conditions, especially in Georgia, from an early period. Educator H. A. Hunt of Fort Valley and the Reverend G. W. Williams of Dublin gave lengthy reports on the rural conditions of labor to the NAACP's 1919 conference in Cleveland, Ohio. Although these men were not farmers, the important points they made showed a keen understanding of the problems black tenants faced in rural parts of southern Georgia. Williams described in detail how farmers found themselves in an inescapable cycle of debt and dependence. Violence and intimidation followed those who resisted unfair treatment; cotton was the only crop acceptable to the landowners,

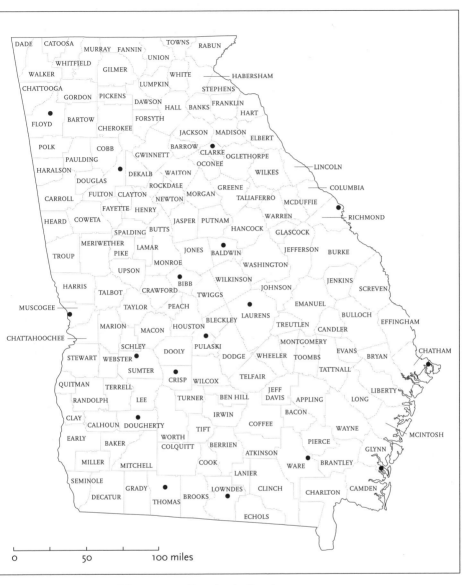

Map 4. NAACP Branches in Georgia, 1917–1930

so tenants could not diversify to protect themselves against volatile market prices. He included a vivid depiction of the murders of two different indebted tenants, who had been killed for trying to prevent the white landowners from having sex with their wives. Williams claimed that mistreatment and peonage of tenants' wives occurred often, "and the colored man has to take it or give his life for it." Worth County was among his leading six counties for abuses of the African American farmer. Hunt, the other speaker from Georgia, sounded much like Garvey at the state fair in Raleigh, blaming black people for part of their own misery and suggesting that conditions had improved mainly because of the leverage that migration had provided for those who remained on the farms. Despite the improvements, however, Hunt acknowledged the prevalence of peonage in Worth, Macon, and Dooly Counties of southwest Georgia in particular.[17]

The NAACP devoted significant energy and resources to collecting evidence on lynchings all over the South, and rural people sometimes wrote directly to the New York headquarters or to Du Bois at the *Crisis* to plead for assistance in harrowing situations of violence and intimidation. Only months before the UNIA arrived in southwest Georgia, the Joneses, a black farming family in Worth County, had suffered terribly at the hands of the landowner to whom they had contracted their labor. A. L. McDonald of Albany wrote to the secretary of the NAACP, John Shillady, about the assault and torture of Ben and Elnora Jones's twenty-year-old daughter Annie and the murders of three of their black neighbors. In a hasty trial, a local jury found the white landowner and his brother, Green and Elgie Whiddon, not guilty of murder. McDonald's letter to Shillady described the defendants as clearly reprehensible and guilty— a worthy case for the NAACP's consideration. The white men, frustrated at not being able to locate Ben Jones and his sons, had taken the black farmer's daughter Annie out of the home, chained her down in the barn, and beaten her with a three-ply rope and a pistol. They harassed the Joneses' younger children and forced Annie to plow the fields under guard; her mother hid in the swamp nearby to escape the same fate. Three black neighbors had become entangled in the dispute, and the Whiddon brothers had shot them dead.[18]

All of this violence came out of a disagreement over the terms of the Joneses' farming contract. Green Whiddon had become incensed that Ben Jones, who rented the house next door to his, had not performed any work for him while apparently farming for another landowner. The local newspaper reported a vastly different scenario in which the triple tragedy was the unfortunate outcome of labor poaching combined with a planned ambush of the white Whiddon brothers by three unscrupulous black men. The paper made no mention of the torture of Annie Jones or the torment of her mother and siblings as the black men's provocation.[19]

Even though key details from the NAACP document are missing from the local white paper's version, the basic outline of either story is plausible. Either the neighbors resorted to attacking the Whiddon brothers in Annie's defense, or the Whiddon brothers did not like the way the black men asserted themselves on her behalf. The black men had only knives and lost out in the struggle. They had no choice, really, because they knew the law in Worth County would not protect them against a large family of landowners like the Whiddons. After all, Ben Jones was no young troublemaker or shirker. He was fifty-eight years old, had eleven children, and his son Ben Jr. had registered for the draft in Worth County in 1917.[20] If the Joneses' neighbors did not take a stand against the abuse of women and children, what unhindered abuse might come next to the black community? In this case, certainly, the community recognized that their self-defense and protection efforts had failed, as the local jury quickly acquitted the Whiddon brothers of murder.

Legal action on behalf of the Jones family became the next option. By April the Jones family had found a way to get legal representation in Albany, twenty miles away, but needed financial assistance of up to $500. Their advocate told the NAACP, "The colored people are planning to take an active part in this case though we will have to work under cover, especially those that live in Worth County."[21] The local white newspaper printed an editorial warning black tenants and labor recruiters to beware: "Labor conditions in this section are bad enough and the farmers are having sufficient trouble in cultivating their land as it is. . . . It is no wonder they rise in their wrath. . . . Those folks should be taught a lesson and if they are not careful they will get it."[22] After two years the case had gone nowhere, and Worth County residents embraced the UNIA philosophy in droves.[23]

Blacks in Georgia knew about the NAACP not only because of the seventeen new branches but also because the *Crisis* circulated in the state among 1,924 regular subscribers, like Fannie Kaigler of southwest Georgia.[24] She was a young black woman in her early twenties who taught in a rural school in Tift County, ten miles east of Worth County, during and just after World War I. An avid reader, Kaigler recalled that some reports in the *Crisis* "would make your blood boil," but people wanted to know what was going on. One could not get the information one wanted in the local or even regional papers, and she suspected that many of the NAACP organ's most interesting reports were designed to promote conflict. "If [the races] got along it was all right and if [the races] didn't get along it was better," she recalled.[25] By contrast, the UNIA promoted separation as a basis for racial harmony. The *Negro World* reported racial conflict but devoted much more space to nationalist propaganda. The evidence suggests that white authorities perceived the *Chicago Defender* and the *Crisis* as more racially divisive than the *Negro World*. In 1919–20 numerous articles in the black press reported objections to and suppression of the *Defender* and the *Crisis* throughout the Deep South.[26]

Another opinion on the conflicting strategies of the UNIA and NAACP came from Perry Howard, Mississippi's most prominent black Republican stalwart. Howard had strained relations with NAACP leaders due to his perceived role in the defeat of the Dyer antilynching bill, yet he claimed neutrality in the struggles between the two organizations. Chandler Owen and A. Philip Randolph's *Messenger* called him "Pat's Perry" and an Uncle Tom for accommodating Mississippi senator Pat Harrison on defeating the Dyer bill and on other occasions.[27] Perry Howard became interested in the participation of many NAACP organizers in the "Garvey Must Go" campaign, which began in earnest after Garvey's meeting with the Klan leadership in June 1922. Howard wrote to William J. Burns, President Warren G. Harding's Bureau of Investigation director, to explain point by point the differences in the organizations and their tense rivalry. He called Garvey's vision "impossible" but harmless because it was apolitical, while the NAACP program was almost entirely politically oriented. The accusations of the NAACP toward Garvey's alleged "Ku Kluxism," he charged, were as relevant as a Methodist's "assailing the other fellow for being a Baptist." Howard even mentioned his close friendship with *Chicago Defender* editor Robert Abbott and stressed that the personal feud between Abbott and Garvey had much to do with Abbott's participation in defaming the UNIA leader. Of the notorious letter denouncing Garvey to the Justice Department signed by Abbott, as well as by William Pickens, Robert Bagnall, and Walter White of the NAACP (the letter that claimed, "Mr. Garvey only represents the views of ignorant West Indian and American Negroes"), Howard declared, "It reduces itself to a cannibalistic scheme of one rival getting rid of the other by annihilation or otherwise."[28] From the point of view of an African American in Mississippi, the NAACP-UNIA rivalry presumably seemed so counterproductive that black Mississippians must have felt only frustration at the organizations' quarrels. Black residents of any southern state would have welcomed any strategy for race uplift and even benefited from all of them if only intraracial and organizational competition could have been avoided.

Georgia seems to have been more accessible to the NAACP than Mississippi in a number of ways. The association formed its most successful local units in Georgia's largest urban areas. Branches developed in Atlanta, Albany, Savannah, Macon, Augusta, Athens, and Rome. Most of these towns had black newspapers that supported the aims and strategies of the NAACP, and most units managed to exist, albeit barely, through the 1920s.[29] They grew out of the combined efforts of then–field secretary James Weldon Johnson and state organizer and Atlanta University professor George A. Towns. Individual branch leaders came from the most successful members of the local black professional class.[30] That is not to say, however, that Towns and Johnson did not try to find support in smaller towns and rural counties. Towns reported having tested the waters in Sylvester, Worth County, but concluded that it was impossible to organize there because of white objections and threats.[31] Towns drew on these experiences, no doubt, in writing his first and perhaps only play, *The Sharecropper*. This work dramatized the exploitation and desperation of landless farmers and the personalized indignity of the relations between a sharecropping family and its landlord.[32]

Walter White, the Atlanta-born NAACP field secretary and later executive secretary, who courageously investigated the Mary Turner lynching and the ten associated deaths in southwest Georgia, made contacts in Valdosta, the closest town to the brutal events, which led to the establishment of a local NAACP branch in 1919. Cyrus G. Wiley became secretary of the branch for a year before moving to Savannah to assume the presidency of the State Industrial School for Negroes in Savannah. The branch became moribund after that time.[33]

The NAACP formed two other branches in large towns in southwest Georgia before the spring of 1919, both of which sent representatives to the NAACP conference in Cleveland that year. James Martin, a locomotive fireman, represented Albany, and Dr. M. L. Walton of Thomasville spoke for the Thomas County branch. The Thomasville Civic League, composed of 300 local blacks, had protested to the mayor about local "work or fight" laws under which women were being forced to work against their will. The mayor had compromised on the issue, and the victory became the group's inspiration to form an NAACP branch.[34] After their initial formation in 1919, both the Albany and Thomasville branches remained largely inactive until the 1930s.[35]

NAACP branches in the southernmost part of Georgia, precisely the areas where Garveyism flourished, fared poorly after their founding in 1918. Waycross began with thirty-one members, but within fifteen months the national office dropped the branch because it had neither paid dues nor sent reports. Brunswick began with seventy-five members in September 1918 but appears to have been barely active, as was Columbus, which had formed a branch the same month with 132 members.[36] Although we know little about these branches, their formation indicates that significant numbers sympathized with the organization's goals. Their dollar memberships went to cover expenses for lynching investigations and legal fees for poor victims of peonage.

The typical NAACP branch leader in Georgia, in sharp contrast to the rural-dwelling farmer of the UNIA, had urban, middle-class, and relatively non-dependent status. For example, two organizers of the Cordele branch were physicians. Dr. Henry Wilson lived in a black neighborhood on 16th Street, and Dr. W. S. Pace was the city's physician for the colored population.[37] In Americus, Miller A. Fountain, a Methodist minister, helped organize the local NAACP branch in 1919. Aiding him in organizing blacks in Sumter County was Samuel S. Humbert, superintendent of the Masonic Orphan's Home for Colored Children.[38]

The elite blacks who supported the NAACP in Atlanta eventually formed the state's most vital branch. However, it is interesting to note that the branch's success came only after its two young founders, Walter White and Harry Pace, convinced strong opponents from the local clergy to support the group and even become its leaders. They rallied over forty local pastors from the Baptist Ministers' Union, the African Methodist Union, and the Methodist Episcopal Union. The Reverend Adam Daniel Williams of Ebenezer Baptist Church had apparently opposed the organization strenuously until the appeals of White and Pace convinced him not only to support the Atlanta NAACP branch but also to become its president.[39]

Why the ministers needed convincing we do not know, just as we do not know the root of much opposition to Garvey and the UNIA by ministers in Blytheville, Arkansas, or in Norfolk, Virginia. The different ways in which some community leaders interpreted the organizations' strategies and objectives presumably caused some dissent. Amid continual confusion over their goals as organizations, both the UNIA and NAACP found themselves having to explain their motives to black and white groups in both rural and urban, northern and southern areas. The nuances of difference in individual organizers' interpretations and explanations made refinement of objectives a constant pursuit. Changing conditions and attitudes invariably added confusion to the ways various racial improvement groups were perceived by both blacks and whites.

The event that made southern whites, particularly in Georgia, aware of the NAACP was the organization's annual conference, which Atlanta hosted in 1920. The conference took place for the first time below the Mason-Dixon Line without incident, but the backlash began almost immediately. The Klan, which had its headquarters on Peachtree Street in Atlanta, voiced its opposition through its leader, William J. Simmons. The *Atlanta Constitution*, the South's largest circulating white newspaper, carried a front-page story and other coverage for several days running.[40] Hostility toward NAACP branches in Georgia began almost immediately. Thomasville branch president A. B. Johnson disbanded the local branch the day after the conference due to death threats against him. Even after dissolving the group, he lost his job as a mail carrier.[41] In August 1920, eight months after the Atlanta conference, the *Crisis* solicited the dues expected from each of the Georgia branches. By December, Albany, Columbus, Dublin, Hawkinsville, Macon, Savannah, Valdosta, and Waycross all risked revocation of their charters due to nonpayment and inactivity.[42]

Of those few chartered branches in other sections of the Deep South in the 1920s, many did absolutely nothing in terms of meeting, corresponding, or leading local protest activities after receiving their initial charters. The extremely dry period for the NAACP branches of the South lasted from 1919 to 1924. Almost every branch formed before that time was dormant during this period. Some reorganized in the late 1920s and most in the late 1930s, usually under new leaders who did not even know that their towns had previous charters and branches.[43] Even the Atlanta branch struggled to exist from 1924 to 1936, when A. T. Walden, Georgia's leading black civil rights attorney, served as branch president. Walden found himself in the odd position of speaking to lawyers for the Ku Klux Klan who had offices on the same downtown block as his own and operating an NAACP branch in a city whose mayor, Walter Sims, was a known Klan sympathizer.[44] And although this polite interaction between lawyers did not represent the typical encounters between the Klan rank and file and southern blacks, it did indicate that on some level, the Klan had to be acknowledged. If Walden's contact meant the Klan's acknowledgment of the NAACP, too, then all the better.

Additional problems that hindered the NAACP in the South, beyond the fact that its objectives met white resistance, economic reprisals, and sometimes violence, were the structural requirements of the organization for individual branches. The New York NAACP headquarters received considerable correspondence from rural places in Georgia, Arkansas, and even Mississippi. A significant problem that rural people encountered in forming a branch was that fifty paid memberships were required for an official charter. Even though the one-dollar yearly dues did not exceed the cost of UNIA membership ($1.20 per year, paid in ten-cent monthly installments), the NAACP was much more rigid about penalties for nonpayment. The NAACP's fifty-member requirement was simply impractical for people in rural communities. The seven-member charter requirement of the UNIA made logistics and, if necessary, secrecy much easier for rural African Americans. Whereas a small group could meet in someone's home or even out in the open, a group of fifty would need a larger space. The NAACP nevertheless encouraged local branches of fewer than fifty and eventually realized it must give preliminary authorization to incomplete branches that had insufficient numbers for a charter. In the NAACP's comprehensive records, however, these groups become invisible, usually until the 1940s and 1950s when many of them finally attained branch status.[45]

The rapid spread and success of the UNIA coincided precisely with the backlash against the NAACP in Georgia. The same trend occurred all over the South where the NAACP had experienced success in the immediate years after World War I. The new black field secretaries under Johnson, William Pickens and Robert Bagnall (both of whom participated in the "Garvey Must Go" campaign in 1922), developed a new strategy that sought to eliminate weak branches and support promising ones. As a result, the total number of branches shrank from 449 to 319 during the early 1920s. Most of these losses occurred in the southern states. The NAACP worked very hard to maintain the infrastructure in Georgia, however, and sent national representatives, including Bagnall, Pickens, Johnson, Walter White, W. E. B. Du Bois, and Addie Hunton, to resuscitate moribund branches. Though doing little, the Albany, Thomasville, and Americus branches in southwest Georgia were among those receiving special attention during the difficult years of the early 1920s.

The NAACP had very little success in organizing in the Yazoo-Mississippi Delta before 1920. Before the end of 1919, Vicksburg, just at the southernmost tip of the Delta, had an NAACP branch, as did the all-black town of Mound Bayou. Both collapsed almost immediately and failed to revive after several attempts. Overall, Mississippi provided the weakest NAACP toehold of any southern state in the interwar years.[46] Neil McMillen has attributed this dearth of organization to the twin ills of white coercion and black poverty. The Klan in Mississippi prevented the formation of NAACP branches as it had in many other rural and urban parts of the South.

We know how Garvey attempted to surmount the Klan problem, and this approach of "neutral opportunism" toward the Klan, despite continuing criticism, may have been the decisive factor in opening up the Magnolia State to the UNIA. The Klan, however, continued to suppress the NAACP, which did receive sporadic requests for help and information from blacks in the Delta. A speaker at the 1924 UNIA convention seemed to agree that the Klan could "stop *The Crisis* from going South, could break up every branch of the NAACP in the South, [and] could force them to move their headquarters from Fifth

Avenue."[47] Raising money or even collecting membership dues, as McMillen suggests, may have been a tremendous hardship in the Depression years for both the UNIA and NAACP, but Garvey did not find any difficulty raising money among Delta farmers in the preceding decade. The NAACP's program, no matter how well appreciated by Mississippi's black population, had no chance in an area in which it faced such violent and recalcitrant opposition.

Nevertheless, black Mississippians continued to be aware of the NAACP and its purposes even though the organization had little or no activity in the state. Some of the same issues critical to rural Garveyites appeared in letters to the NAACP during the years between the world wars. Blacks in Scott County complained of whites who sexually abused their women but despaired of being able to form an NAACP chapter. In addition, in reaction to the NAACP's attempts to organize in the state, the Mississippi legislature banned literature tending "to disturb relations between the races."[48] The *Defender* apparently managed to reach the Delta from Chicago through the ingenuity of black Pullman porters on the direct north-south lines, but the *Crisis* and *Negro World*, both originating in New York, had to come through the mail. The prevalence of the *Negro World* and the success of Bolivar County's *Cotton Farmer*, a paper relatively sympathetic to Garvey, demonstrate the white authorities' more accepting attitude toward the principles of the UNIA. In contrast, the NAACP would not change its propaganda to appease white objections because it could not do so without contradicting its own principles; as a result, its program was stifled in the Delta. The separatist ideology of Garveyism dovetailed just enough with segregationist fantasies of racial purity and second-class citizenship for blacks that the UNIA and white supremacists managed to inhabit the same black-majority districts of the Black Belt.

Because the uncompromising segregationist white political structure of Mississippi under leaders like James K. Vardaman and Theodore Bilbo effectively prevented the incursion of any organization advocating social equality, only avowedly nonpolitical or separatist organizations like the National Negro Business League and the UNIA could exist in the state. The only Delta towns that flirted with NAACP participation in the years after World War I, Vicksburg and Mound Bayou, quickly retreated and became host cities for divisions of the UNIA.[49] Between 1922 and 1928 the Yazoo-Mississippi Delta hosted over thirty-five units of Garvey's organization. Louisiana's Black Belt showed a very similar pattern, with only five weak urban branches of the NAACP at Shreveport, Alexandria, New Orleans, Baton Rouge, and Monroe, and two rural ones at St. Rose and Clarence.[50] In contrast, the UNIA had eighty divisions in Louisiana in the 1920s.

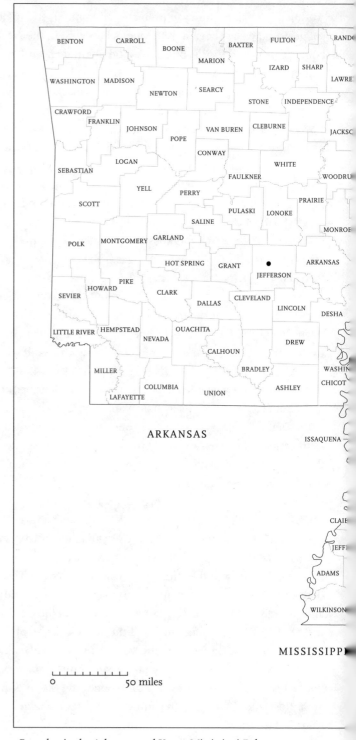

Map 5. NAACP *Branches in the Arkansas and Yazoo-Mississippi Deltas, 1919–1930*

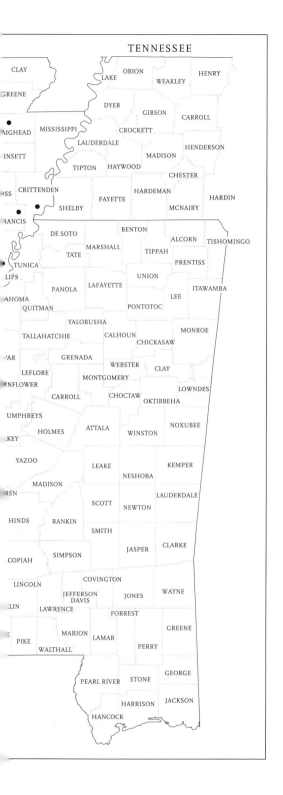

After the leader's deportation and the deaths of T. Thomas Fortune and John E. Bruce, we detect significantly less attention to the southern rural divisions of the UNIA in the *Negro World*. In order to get local reports published, the divisional news department stated a clear preference for typed reports.[51] This policy may have prevented many local rural divisions from getting publicity and thus from providing researchers with the evidence so plentiful for earlier years. By the 1930s, the paper's format had begun to resemble the *Defender* in many ways, devoting more attention to urban social matters and sports coverage and, reflecting the massive migration and urbanization of African Americans, "the latest news from your hometown."[52] Yet despite the growing urban focus of the *Negro World* and the removal of Garvey from the United States, small Mississippi divisions from the Delta kept themselves organized and sent regular reports to the UNIA into the early 1930s. The Sumner division in Tallahatchie County showed the greatest loyalty of all, under the leadership of Tom and Lula Sanders, its longtime president and secretary.[53] As late as March 1933, a man from Greenville, Mississippi, who could barely write, sent ten cents to New York for a copy of the *Negro World*.[54]

Although some UNIA loyalists appeared to hold out to the end, other organizers and contributors in Mississippi shifted their loyalty to the NAACP, which although weak locally remained viable nationally. An organizer in Vicksburg named V. L. Lewis organized for Garvey first and then for the NAACP. In East Drew, Mississippi, Reverend W. D. Norman was a UNIA secretary in the 1920s, but he affiliated with the NAACP in the neighboring community of Boyle (Bolivar County) by the late 1930s.[55] At the age of fifty-eight in 1920, while involved with the UNIA, Norman farmed as a tenant in Sunflower County and lived in a mortgaged home with his wife and daughter. By the time he reached seventy, his conditions had hardly changed, but the NAACP represented the most stable and best-organized national race organization.[56] Especially in the midst of the Great Depression, Norman's strategic outlook might have changed as well.

Across the river the UNIA and NAACP had similar experiences, though two NAACP branches formed among farmers in Arkansas near Memphis. Before anyone in the Arkansas Delta knew about the UNIA, a black farmer named Elizabeth Hall represented her small, all-black community of Edmondson at the 1919 NAACP conference at Cleveland, Ohio. She and a hundred others had formed a chapter in their small Delta community about ten miles from Tennessee's urban metropolis, but there is no further evidence of activity there.[57] Later that year, sharecroppers in Democrat, about five miles further into the Delta, started another branch of the association. The history of the Democrat chapter is extraordinary. The process of organizing and chartering the branch was arduous and dangerous. As problems emerged among local leaders in 1922, a near-Elaine situation seemed to be in the making. Local white postal employees tampered with the mail coming from the NAACP's New York head-quarters. The locals became very frustrated when they had not received word after they had applied for their charter; finally, the fraud was discovered, and the NAACP reported it to the postmaster general, demanding a federal inves-tigation. Local NAACP branch members ended up in jail, and police and land-owners harassed others.[58]

Only the Democrat and Edmondson branches sprang from Arkansas Delta farming communities before 1929. Another branch in Pine Bluff lasted lon-ger and was composed of mainly professionals and businessmen. In towns and cities of any size, the charter members of southern branches were physi-cians, dentists, businessmen, merchants, domestics, and other nonfarmers. In smaller, more rural places, however, farmers and laborers were well repre-sented on membership lists. Even so, the many Pine Bluff NAACP agricultural-ist members were more likely landowners than the typical UNIA sharecropper or tenant farmer. A short-lived unit in Jonesboro contrasted with the predomi-nantly rural Delta because it too was decidedly urban.[59]

Certainly 1919 was a watershed year for race relations in America and especially in the Delta because of the Elaine massacre, which began in late September. Life for black people on both sides of the river changed dramati-cally in light of this indiscriminate slaughter of blacks in Phillips County.[60] A letter by Ida B. Wells in the *Chicago Defender* a week after the mass murder brought wide publicity of these events to the attention of blacks all over the country. Many sent money to help in the legal defense of twelve blacks from Elaine who were sentenced to death for the murder of some local whites. One of the convicted men wrote to Wells thanking her for her letter and remarking that the help she had galvanized had preceded any such contributions from the local black community. Two weeks after the Elaine riots, a committee of ministers and leading black citizens of Blytheville, Arkansas, published a reso-lution in which they promised to "allow no one to establish any organization among them that might create trouble." Wells convinced the governor of Arkansas to investigate the fairness of the men's trial, a process that eventually led to an opportunity for a new trial and appeals.[61]

The notoriety of the Phillips County "riots" came from the black press's extensive coverage and the NAACP's active participation in the legal defense of the twelve convicted men. The decision was eventually referred to the U.S. Supreme Court, where in *Moore v. Dempsey* a state superior court decision was for the first time overturned based on the denial of due process assured by the Fourteenth Amendment. The NAACP's legal victory continues to have broad significance in defining the powers of the federal judiciary.[62]

The UNIA's prodigious growth in the Delta is especially noteworthy when it is contrasted with the anemia of the NAACP, the champion of the Phillips County sharecroppers imprisoned after the Elaine slaughter. The principal lawyers hired for the cases in Arkansas, former slave Scipio Africanus Jones and his white counterpart, ex-Confederate colonel George W. Murphy, both came from Little Rock and were able to remove themselves from the tense scene after the court proceedings.[63] As gratifying as it was to save those blacks accused of murder, it did not change the climate of race relations in the Delta for the better, nor did it boost NAACP affiliation.

In Arkansas as a whole, forty-six UNIA divisions and chapters developed by 1926, and all but five of these were in the eastern portion of the state.[64] The parent body of the UNIA chartered almost half of these divisions between 1921 and 1922. Almost without exception, both the officers and rank-and-file members of these UNIA divisions in the rural Delta were cotton sharecroppers, tenants, or day farm laborers, precisely the type of men saved from electrocution through the efforts of the NAACP. Between the time of the Elaine disaster, which ended in October 1919, and the Supreme Court decision that led to freedom for the Elaine prisoners in February 1923, the eastern Arkansas Delta became saturated with nationalist, separatist sentiment. The UNIA's ideological rival, the NAACP, began only the short-lived branch in Edmondson and the Democrat branch in St. Francis County, which incidentally also hosted at least four UNIA divisions.[65]

What forces caused some blacks to embrace the UNIA yet reject the very organization that had supported and organized the exhaustive litigation for the sharecroppers sentenced to die after the Phillips County riot? One can only surmise that while the larger black community felt relieved that the men won their freedom, it had different feelings about the most pragmatic approach to improving conditions for the race.[66]

Important studies by Fon Louise Gordon and M. Langley Biegert provide evidence of intraracial class conflict between the Arkansas black middle class and the east Arkansas sharecroppers in the early part of the twentieth century. The two groups' differing priorities, combined with their inability to coalesce in racial solidarity, set them on separate courses. Unlike in Georgia, where blacks who supported the NAACP kept the black farmer and laborer in mind, in Arkansas class divisions became more pronounced. According to Gordon, and consistent with the history of race organization in Arkansas, the black bourgeoisie was self-interested and self-preserving to the detriment of the agricultural workers, while the latter went their own way, continuously resisting, regrouping, and restrategizing without the benefit of support from the former.[67] Arkansas tenant farmers demonstrated great confidence in the UNIA, although not necessarily because of lack of faith or interest in the NAACP. Southland, which hosted a UNIA division in Phillips County, formed an NAACP branch in 1929. The Southland branch was composed of numerous farmers, and it also included local merchant Louis Martin, who contributed to both groups. Postelle, also a former UNIA town in Phillips County, reminded the *Crisis* of its county's violent heritage as it sent in the necessary fees and documents to earn an NAACP charter in 1939.[68]

In the Arkansas Delta, across the river in Mississippi, as well as in southwest Georgia, the UNIA enjoyed wide and relatively peaceful participation by farmers from 1921 through 1927. Preparing for self-defense locally and organizing for African redemption gave them hope, pride, and dignity. Garvey's encouragement through the *Negro World* inspired them to sustain their belief that people of African descent had a glorious past and, with proper race consciousness and organization, could have an equally bright future. But the UNIA in the rural South lost some of its most vital inspiration in the years after 1927. Its messianic leader no longer languished in the Atlanta federal penitentiary. Garvey was a free man living in Jamaica until 1935 and then in London until his death in 1940. Rallying in protest for his freedom no longer provided an urgent cause for organization.

The structure of the UNIA deteriorated while its official propaganda sheet and Garvey's mouthpiece transformed itself into a more typical urban black newspaper. Although Garvey had officially split with the leadership of the central division in New York in 1929, it continued publication of the *Negro World*. Without Garvey, New York's divisional leaders adopted an editorial policy less attentive to the rural southern constituency of the UNIA. This organizational split had a more divisive impact on the larger urban divisions than on Garvey's rural adherents. To farmers in the South, the movement *was* Marcus Garvey's leadership. Even so, his removal from the American scene reduced his ability to maintain any firm grip on leadership, even of his most loyal followers. In his absence, other organizations had better opportunities to organize among or at least claim to lead rural farmers in the South. By 1927, the year of Garvey's deportation, Robert Bagnall informed the NAACP board that he believed fear and trepidation had subsided in most areas of the South and that the NAACP's reputation was favorable and growing.[69] Its persistence had paid off, and the UNIA's weakening hold on the South cleared a path for the NAACP, the STFU, and other local improvement organizations.

UNIA Alternatives during the Depression

The Great Depression further damaged the South's agriculturally based economy among rural southern farmers of all races. Many landowners plowed under thousands of acres of planted cotton and eventually kicked sharecroppers and tenant farmers off their farms in response to incentives under the New Deal's Agricultural Adjustment Act (AAA). The federal government sought reduction in farm acreage under cultivation and subsidized landowners who complied in order to restore prices to acceptable levels. The first lands taken out of cultivation were the marginal areas often monopolized by black tenant farmers. Those tenant farmers and sharecroppers who remained on the land expected to receive part of the payments that the AAA program promised, but seldom did the landowners distribute the subsidies.[70]

The economic hardships for black farmers in the 1930s easily surpassed the difficulties that had led them to unite during the volatile 1920s. Forced abandonment of the land spurred the trend toward urbanization and broke the generational commitment to farming in many families. Economic priorities accentuated the differences among urban and rural-oriented black leaders and their strategies for racial improvement. To some, the New Deal seemed to provide a vehicle for government action on behalf of disadvantaged blacks, especially in labor unions, while to others it came to represent the promotion of elite blacks at the expense of the majority.[71] Certainly in the view of black farmers and the leaders interested in their welfare, Franklin D. Roosevelt's New Deal delivered as little to them as one might expect of programs administered by racist state governments or that required the political support of the southern segregationist stalwarts in the U.S. Senate.

In the 1930s the Garvey movement continued to have an active following in urban areas, especially in the northern metropolises of New York and Chicago, though under less direct authority of the UNIA founder, now in exile. Two organizations, both relatively new in the 1930s, drew numerous followers from the former Garvey movement. In New York, Father Divine and his Peace Mission Movement attracted thousands of former UNIA members, while in Chicago the Peace Movement of Ethiopia (PME), under former Garveyite Mittie Maud Lena Gordon, provided a new organization focusing on emigration to Africa.[72] Michael W. Fitzgerald has shown how the popularity of the PME's petition campaign on behalf of the Greater Liberia Bill of 1939 and the group's willingness to support Mississippi senator Theodore Bilbo's efforts to create an African state for the removal of African Americans reflected widespread discontent with New Deal liberal policies. The most pertinent part of Fitzgerald's analysis is the evidence that thousands of PME petition signatures in favor of the Greater Liberia Bill came from blacks in Mississippi. From his new home in London, Garvey supported the bill also and asked those still aligned with the UNIA to circulate more petitions and send them directly to Bilbo.[73]

We see no activity of this kind in Georgia, where the NAACP continued to revolve around the Atlanta branch, particularly in the 1930s, and maintained a strong interest and advocacy of blacks in rural parts of the state. The city became a refuge for the most ill treated and desperate victims of racial violence and peonage.[74] In 1933, however, Morris Davis of Cuthbert (Randolph County), in the heart of former Garvey territory in southwest Georgia, wrote to the *Negro World*, "I am writing you to ask you to let me be your agent in Cuthbert, Georgia for the Negro World. If I can be your agent, send me 20 copies in order to get me started. The Colored Peoples are thrilled to have the Negro World in Cuthbert so I am hoping to hear from you by return mail."[75] People in southwest Georgia still enjoyed reading the *Negro World*, which despite the UNIA split still published inspirational letters from Garvey on the front page.

Mississippi blacks, especially in the Delta, had few national or even regional resources due to the unrelenting hostility to any black organization that promoted integration or social equality. Subsequently, the UNIA persisted in places like Sumner in the heart of the Delta; few other groups found ways to crack the state's protective shield of white supremacy.[76] Merigold's Black Cross Nurses similarly continued their weekly marching, singing, and community service well into the 1930s.[77]

Thousands of the Arkansas Delta's black farmers, by contrast, joined the Southern Tenant Farmers Union after 1934. The STFU, founded in Tyronza, a small Arkansas Delta community, has become a celebrated example of southern, rural, and biracial activism from a very early period. This socialist-led organization sought to organize black and white landless farmers together in order to exert their economic power en masse and to protest New Deal policies that disproportionately harmed the most hard-pressed members of farming communities.[78]

Howard Kester, a white socialist who became deeply involved in the STFU, wrote a gripping account of the hardships of the Arkansas Delta sharecroppers and the successes of the union campaign prior to the STFU's demise. The organization's white cofounder and executive secretary, H. L. Mitchell, was active in labor movements well into the 1970s. He was rightfully proud of the STFU's accomplishments, and in some ways his seminal accounts have idealized aspects of the biracial group, which its black organizers saw differently.[79] These accounts of the organization gloss over racial divisions and the contentious disputes within the executive council in the summer and fall of 1938 between J. R. Butler, the STFU's white president, and E. B. "Britt" McKinney, an important black field organizer and vice president of the rural organization. Still a Garveyite well into the 1930s, McKinney became the STFU's vice president and one of the most significant factors in its success in recruiting black members into this biracial organization.

Historian Donald Grubbs has described how pragmatism enabled STFU organizers to get poor black and white farmers together in a union: "To reach and convince whites who would otherwise be antagonized, they used white organizers; to gain the confidence of Negroes fearful of being exploited, they used black organizers."[80] Between one-half and two-thirds of the STFU's 30,000 members were black. Most of the white tenant farmers were new to the tenant system, having been dispossessed more recently than the black farmers, who were more accustomed to the plantation tenancy of Arkansas. Blacks had greater solidarity and even higher rates of literacy than their white counterparts in the union.[81]

Black organizers like McKinney were crucial to the STFU because of their ability to draw in members. McKinney was a farmer but also an itinerant minister with over thirty-five congregations in the Delta. He and other clergymen used churches, hymns, and biblical analogies to promote the STFU. Many regarded the union as a religious organization, and its white organizers readily adopted this form and its rituals—some because this strategy proved very effective, and others, like Kester, because they were deeply religious themselves. John Handcox, a black sharecropper who organized for the union in St. Francis County, Arkansas, also wrote songs that were used regularly by the STFU to inspire and sustain its oppressed members.[82] For organizing black tenant farmers into a biracial group, black ministers paid a heavy price. McKinney's home was riddled with bullets, forcing him to send his wife and child to live in hiding in Memphis and later Holly Springs, Mississippi. Reverend A. B. Brookins was nearly lynched at the age of seventy. Reverend T. A. Allen was shot and dumped in the Coldwater River in northwest Mississippi for his role in organizing for the STFU.[83] Their bravery and sacrifice inspired their congregations to join the union.

E. B. "Britt" McKinney was an Arkansas farmer, an itinerant preacher, a committed Garveyite, and an organizer for the Southern Tenant Farmers Union. (Southern Tenant Farmers Union Papers, Southern Historical Collection, Wilson Library, University of North Carolina at Chapel Hill, Chapel Hill, N.C.)

Familiar themes of solidarity and organization pervaded the local meeting rhetoric.[84] The tactics recall exactly the Garveyite strategy for organizing the same areas over ten years earlier. The STFU had locals all around the Arkansas Delta in precisely the same communities in which the UNIA had divisions, and a similar overlap occurred on the Mississippi side of the river in Bolivar County.[85] The *Negro World* circulated in the Arkansas Delta well into 1933, when it ceased publication. The STFU formed in July 1934 and reached its peak in 1937. Whether the memberships of the UNIA and STFU overlapped is difficult to determine, but the involvement of a dedicated Garveyite like McKinney in both organizations strongly suggests a possibility of dual allegiance.

In many of the sources on the STFU, the black attitude in the organization has repeatedly been illustrated by a single statement from an elderly black farmer named Ike Shaw at the meeting at which the union was founded. Shaw, a member of the controversial farmer's union in Phillips County in

1919, survived the Elaine massacre and went on to be a strong voice for inter-racial solidarity for poor Delta farmers during the 1930s. H. L. Mitchell and Howard Kester both described Shaw's eloquence in convincing local leaders that despite the animosity between the races, black and white tenant farmers needed to join forces against their real foe, the landowner. Historian M. Lang-ley Biegert similarly uses Shaw as the central figure in her persuasive argu-ment about the "legacy of resistance" among black farmers in the Arkansas Delta.[86]

Britt McKinney, who disappeared from public life after the STFU began sending workers to industrial jobs during World War II, provides a different point of view from that of Shaw. Although McKinney worked tirelessly for the STFU in the 1930s, he did so with continuous suspicion that the white leaders used funds inappropriately and to the detriment of black dues-paying mem-bers. Mitchell and McKinney had a very good relationship; their correspon-dence reveals that whenever McKinney had doubts about the biracial STFU, he wrote to Mitchell for clarification. In a 1972 interview Mitchell stated, "E. B. McKinney became the best organizer we had, either white or black. He could organize both. He would attend the meetings and at one point he said there was just one white man that he would plow for, and that was H. L. Mitchell. He was more race conscious than anyone else. I don't really know, I have no knowledge that he actually was a Garveyite, but later some of them said he was."[87] Several documents contained in the STFU papers and other sources indicate that McKinney was in fact an active Garveyite in 1938.[88] He struggled for three years between his faith in Mitchell's sincerity and his passionate dislike for J. R. Butler, the white STFU president, and the white rank-and-file members, whom he never trusted. His Garveyite ideology comes through clearly in correspondence with a close black friend from his native Poinsett County. Wiley Harris, from Parkin, lived near the site of one of the most violent episodes in the STFU's history, and two years later he became McKin-ney's sounding board.

During this pivotal event in the STFU's history, McKinney's racial animosity flared up, making it hard for him to trust whites and especially white law enforcers. In January 1936 two Poinsett County deputies, supposedly the pro-tectors of both Harris's and McKinney's jurisdiction, had broken up a meeting of the union and severely injured several members. Word got out that a black man named Willie Hurst was willing to testify against the universally feared deputies Hood and Peacher. During a meeting of 450 sharecroppers the next night in Parkin, a group of planters and riding bosses used ax handles to crack the skulls of anyone they could reach, including women and children, threatening, "There's going to be another Elaine Massacre except this time we're going to kill whites as well as niggers."[89]

A few months later, McKinney complained to Mitchell about the way dues money was going to fund the administrative and travel activities of the head officers instead of directly helping the members. Mitchell vainly tried to explain the importance of maintaining an institutional presence and along those lines suggested that McKinney raise money in churches to help pay his way to the NAACP annual conference in January 1937.[90] The NAACP, under the leadership of executive secretary Walter White (who had also investigated in the Arkansas Delta after the Elaine massacre), had taken a keen interest in the STFU. Instead, McKinney evidently decided to raise money to get himself to the UNIA's conference to be held that year in Toronto. J. R. Butler immediately recommended McKinney's expulsion from the executive council, accusing the black organizer of trying to split the organization along racial lines. By raising money for himself and not for the STFU, Butler felt, McKinney was responsible for throwing the organization into dire financial straits.[91] In reaction to Butler's accusations, McKinney protested bitterly against the organization's white leadership in a series of letters to his friend Wiley Harris:

> It was my aim to have gone to Canada, to be there by the first of August, but the whole thing dependen [sic] upon what the people was able to do. Thousands of them were very anxious that I make the trip, but due to the financial condition of the country, it was impossible. . . . I am aware that the forces are working to stop us from trying to help ourselves, showing all sorts of scar [sic] crows, waving at us the Elaine Riot and the KKK. I am sure they know lots about both. For they are the very element who made up both. We have always been tools in the hands of those who have kept us down.[92]

McKinney indicated that "thousands" wanted him to attend the eighth international UNIA conference in Toronto in August 1938. He knew that to represent only blacks in an all-black forum was unacceptable to the white, class-conscious leadership of the STFU. Mitchell, Butler, and other white leaders bristled at the race consciousness consistently injected by McKinney, yet they could not eject him because he was too valuable as an organizer. The executive council went through a disciplinary process by which McKinney lost the title of vice president but maintained his post on the executive council. Next, he had to sign a document repudiating his separatism. McKinney submitted an appeal that contained a ten-point plan, including a vigorous plea for the improved treatment of blacks and a special recognition of Negro hardships within the organization. We do not know how each side of the dispute held to its commitments, because within a year the STFU had merged into other organizations, most of which became concerned with programs for industrial workers and migrants and, after the war, in organizing California farm workers.

McKinney's perspective on the STFU is instructive for understanding how at least one influential Garveyite in the Delta viewed his options in the 1930s. He remained deeply committed to UNIA principles of racial solidarity, distrust of whites, and the importance of organization. In letters to Wiley Harris, McKinney referred to the continuing lack of race pride displayed by black farmers, the "evils" of miscegenation, and the importance of racial solidarity.[93] He wanted the STFU to succeed, but he became disillusioned as white leaders and members failed to recognize the principles and goals important to him and his people. His feeling that the STFU leadership betrayed him may have trickled down to his thousands of black recruits in the Delta. In McKinney's eyes, not only did the STFU not help the people who provided over half of its membership and financial backing, but it also exploited them. Perhaps these perceived failures in a biracial, class-conscious organization reinforced the ideology of racial solidarity and separation that Garvey had so successfully promoted in the preceding decade. Black participation in the STFU, nevertheless, reveals that African American farmers in the Delta were open-minded to organizations that offered a way to help them improve their economic situations. In the end, however, it remains difficult to measure the degree of impact, both negative and positive, of the STFU's integrated efforts on behalf of Delta farmers. It is important to note, however, that the themes of justice, biracialism, and pacifism endorsed by ideologues of the STFU became staples of the modern civil rights movement. The organizational structure that reached the bulk of the people through their ministers, in their churches, and with their songs and adapted hymns came directly from the STFU and its much larger predecessor, the UNIA.

As the Great Depression gave way to the World War II era, another strong wave of urbanization pulled many more blacks north from rural areas of the Deep South. As time wore on, these disruptions to rural society made the once-attractive principles of rural Garveyism less pertinent. The black population was becoming increasingly urban, with blacks concentrated into cities and towns in which they did not form majorities as they had in Black Belt counties of the rural South. Arming for self-defense continued to appeal to residents of areas of near-majority black populations, including Garvey-influenced cities and towns in the South. For instance, Charleston, South Carolina, which consisted of nearly 60,000 people in 1930, was about half black.[94] A local black woman wrote in alarm to the city's police chief about the continuing influence of Garvey there in 1936:

> I can not sit idle by and see my people cause blood shed. . . . His [Marcus Garvey's] works are going on just the same. . . . Garvey has taught the people to buy up and lay by all the firearms they can *handle* and take care of so they have done that. They are *do* everything he says so I will tell you how you may know. They call their meeting place the UNIA. Then they have the NAACP fight for them in the court. They are raising the young people to do every mean thing they can become they say they are to [*sic*] young to go to Africa. I hope you will not ever let this is known. I want to tell this every-where and they have their firearms hid in their meeting places and in the lodge halls.[95]

This letter gives us a sense of the ways in which the UNIA and NAACP did not appear to be working at cross-purposes to southerners. It also reveals the possibility that younger blacks, though not rejecting self-defense, had begun to reject the African emigrationism of the previous generation. And although this report and conditions in Charleston did not represent all places, the en-durance of Garvey's principles continued in former UNIA strongholds and mingled with other strategies. In most white-dominated urban environments and increasingly white rural areas, cooperation with whites on some level seemed more important.

In the industrializing society so much in evidence after World War I, blacks who were once dependent on whites for land but at the same time essential to the productivity of southern agriculture became even less self-sufficient and powerful as members of a dispensable urban proletariat. Economic independence seemed less attainable in an urban, industrialized setting, but peonage was also less likely. Assimilation through education and upward mobility made social equality and meaningful citizenship in the United States seem more attainable to the black middle class, and their optimism and determination prevailed through organizations like the NAACP.

This tension over strategy and organization continued to challenge leaders of the rural and small town South during the height of the modern civil rights movement. Hubert Thomas, a Garveyite from Thomasville in south-west Georgia, joined with Frances Freeborn Pauley, a white organizer for the Southwest Georgia Council on Human Relations from 1962 to 1966. He and his father were what Pauley described as "black militants" who "hated white people." He worked intensively in Worth and Baker Counties to bring about change in the 1960s.[96] Similarly, Robert F. Williams of Monroe, North Carolina, who began his activist career as president of the local NAACP branch, proved willing to align with diverse groups of white liberals, socialists, communists, and black nationalists to achieve racial justice in America. He also subscribed to armed resistance and self-defense in the face of violence, a position that caused the national NAACP (but not his local followers) to rebuke him. Although Williams was born only in 1925, at his funeral his casket was draped with the red, black, and green flag of the UNIA.[97]

Black leaders like Thomas and Williams, however, pushed their organizations toward Garvey's ideal of black leadership for black people while they accepted white philanthropy and tolerated the cooperation of liberal whites. In the mid-1960s radical organizations like the Deacons for Defense in Louisiana and Mississippi defied the legalistic approach and advocated armed self-defense. Their local efforts in Klan strongholds forced the hand of the federal government in protecting black civil rights. As Lance Hill has shown, this strategy increased the appeal of nonviolent organizations like the Southern Christian Leadership Conference, the Student Nonviolent Coordinating Committee, and the NAACP and allowed them to operate more effectively in the South.[98]

Local, regional, and national movements on behalf of black advancement from the 1920s forward exhibited some of the core tenets of Garveyism, which perpetuated itself as a philosophy so central to black thought in the South that it is not even attributed to Garvey, the *Negro World*, and the UNIA.[99] General scholars of American history widely recognize the importance of Booker T. Washington as a man of his time and a leader of agrarian people in a period when the American South was a predominantly rural region. We have previously known nothing about Garvey's role in transitioning southern blacks from provincial to urban life, from Victorianism to modernism, and from the separatist ideals of Washington to the color-blind ones of Martin Luther King Jr. In Jamaica in 1965, King spoke at Garvey's shrine and acknowledged the UNIA leader's vast influence: "Marcus Garvey was the first man of color in the history of the United States to lead and develop a mass movement. . . . He was the first man on a mass scale and level to give millions of Negroes a sense of dignity and destiny, and make the Negro feel he is somebody."[100]

Most American historians continue to make the mistake of dismissing Garveyism as predominantly a back-to-Africa scheme rather than the seedbed of modern black ideology. But if we acknowledge that the UNIA and Garveyism were indeed strong influences in southern rural society, emerging in part from the existing ideologies of Washington, Turner, and others, we can begin to see Garvey and Garveyism not as an aberration or a short-lived cult of urban blacks, or even simply a watershed moment in the development of black nationalism, but as a core component of black thought bridging the Jim Crow era and the integrationist discourse of the modern civil rights movement. We can also more accurately view black nationalism as a deeply rooted ideology with an equally enduring legacy.

Epilogue

Legacy

The Garvey movement's direct intellectual legacy appears more discreetly in the integrationist tendencies of the modern civil rights movement than in the discourse of black nationalism, yet its influences are an important part of both. Activists at the local, state, regional, and national levels have had direct personal and community ties to the UNIA, while the core tenets of Garveyism, black pride and self-determination, weave through the fabric of black popular culture and thought. The roots of these ideas are harder to identify because throughout American history, separatist agendas originated with the people and were adopted by their spokesmen, not the other way around.

While black nationalism runs vigorously among ordinary and anonymous black people, from rural Georgia to Michigan and from New York to California, some of the twentieth century's most influential African Americans have acknowledged the formative influence of Garveyism. Elijah Muhammad, leader of the Nation of Islam during its greatest period of growth in the 1950s and 1960s, was a product of rural Georgia during the UNIA's heyday. Born Elijah Poole in Washington County, he spent his third through his twenty-first year (1900–1919) in Cordele, within a few miles of Worth County, the center of Garveyism in Georgia. His father, Willie Poole, was an itinerant minister, and Elijah often traveled with him as he offered the surrounding communities graphic sermons that included frightening portrayals of white people.[1] Elijah Poole moved to Macon, where he lived during the height of the Garvey movement. He married a Cordele woman named Clara, had two sons, and moved to Detroit during the period of Garvey's incarceration.[2] According to one of his biographers, Elijah Muhammad denied having been a UNIA member, but he acknowledged Garvey's strong influence.[3] Many of Muhammad's followers at the Nation of Islam's Temple No. 2 in Chicago in 1950 had a background similar to that of their leader, whom they called "the Messenger." They also had migrated to Chicago from the rural South and had endured life at the bottom rungs of society in both places.[4] Many were quick to believe that whites were evil and that blacks needed to exist separately from a polluted and decadent white society. The UNIA message framed the same notion more positively. In Garveyism, antimiscegenation and anti-assimilation beliefs and practices were demonstrations of love for one's own race. Under Elijah Muhammad and his predecessor, Wallace Fard Muhammad, pride in blackness seemed as much an abhorrence of whiteness as anything else.

Today, the Nation of Islam owns a large farm in Bronwood, Terrell County, Georgia. Louis Farrakhan, the Nation of Islam's current leader, repurchased 1,500 of nearly 5,000 acres that were formerly owned by Elijah Muhammad in the 1960s (then called the Temple Farms complex), which had been sold after his death in 1975. By coincidence, in the 1920s the UNIA's busiest organizer, O. C. Kelly, owned a farm within ten miles of the Nation of Islam's current Terrell County farm. Brother Al Muhammad, originally from Mississippi, is an adviser to the Muhammad Farms who acknowledges Garvey's movement as a crucial predecessor to the organization to which he has devoted his life.[5] Ridgely Muhammad, the farm's manager, has a Ph.D. from Michigan State University and M.A. and B.A. degrees from historically black North Carolina Agricultural and Technical University, a leading institution for students involved in the civil rights movement of the 1960s. Brother William Muhammad, who is over one hundred years old, sells vegetables grown on the farm locally, while the rest is trucked to the Nation of Islam's restaurants in Chicago and Detroit or is available for purchase by black families and small business owners at distribution centers.[6] Ridgely operates a website and edits *The Farmer*, which provides a network for black farmers who want to participate in race-conscious cooperatives. The distrust of whites and the U.S. government, similarly but less openly expressed in Garvey's heyday, is a theme of the newsletter.[7] Terrell County remains majority-black, yet the Nation of Islam seeks and receives little publicity there, similar to the habits of the UNIA divisions of the rural South in the 1920s.

Another direct descendant of the UNIA, the Nation of Islam, and their mutual commitment to racial pride and self-determination was Malcolm X. The iconic black nationalist and Muslim was a first-generation northerner, born to Earl and Louisa Little. Malcolm described his father as a "Georgia Negro," which seemed to imply great strength and a firsthand knowledge of the worst kind of racial oppression. Earl Little was born and reared in rural Taylor County in the southwestern quadrant of Georgia, then moved to Omaha and became an itinerant preacher and a UNIA division president. He encountered much harassment and intimidation by whites, and in time he moved to Wisconsin and later Michigan, all the way organizing UNIA divisions. Although the facts are disputed, Malcolm recounted that his father had been murdered by the Klan in Lansing in 1931.[8] Although Malcolm X's notoriety came during his association with the Nation of Islam, we must not neglect the formative influences of his childhood and the fact that his rhetoric was taking him in a new direction when he was killed in 1965. Malcolm X's bestselling autobiography, which paid tribute to his father's Garveyite ideology, piqued many a black youth's interest in the movement and led to the UNIA leader's popular "rediscovery" in the 1960s.[9]

The tenets of Garveyism flowed into intellectual as well as political realms. In rural Virginia in 1926, the UNIA purchased Smallwood-Corey Industrial Institute in Clarendon. The college survived for only three years under the new name Liberty University. The school's fortunes declined with those of the organization as a whole, but not before a group of young trainees learned how to organize in local black communities and were drilled in UNIA ideology. Liberty University's vice president, the Reverend John Gibbs St. Clair Drake, made an indelible mark.[10] Not only did he excel in community leadership, migrating with his rural Virginia flocks to Pittsburgh's steel jobs, but while in Suffolk, Virginia, a hotbed of Garveyism, he became the father of St. Clair Drake. Later in life the younger Drake, an eminent anthropologist and sociologist, launched African American studies at Stanford University and wrote several classic works, including *Black Metropolis* (1943) and *The Black Diaspora* (1972). At Stanford and elsewhere, the younger Drake mentored dozens of influential Pan-African thinkers.[11] One of his students was an influential ideologue of the Student Nonviolent Coordinating Committee (SNCC) named Bill Ware, who, along with other Atlanta members of SNCC's Vine City Project, advocated race consciousness, separatism, revolutionary struggle, and black leadership for the masses. Ware, who was born and reared in rural Mississippi, and Ivanhoe Donaldson, who recalled that his father had endorsed the tenets of Garveyism, shifted their faction of the civil rights organization away from interracial democracy and toward nationalism and resistance after 1966.[12]

Another example of SNCC's leaders' rifts over tactics occurred in the mid-1960s in Lowndes County, Alabama. Stokely Carmichael led a movement to empower black voters in this Black Belt county where they had the potential for political control at the county level. He was a native of Trinidad, born to a father who had openly revered Garvey. Carmichael had moved to Harlem at age eleven, but as a young man he found his true inspiration working among rural blacks of the Deep South. He came to articulate their agenda as a prominent black power advocate during the modern civil rights movement.[13] The

Black Panther Party of Lowndes County inspired the Black Panther Party for Self-Defense of Oakland, California, and many lesser-known local organizations for black community solidarity.[14]

SNCC's position paper on Black Power clearly expressed trepidation about allowing whites to participate in civil rights organizations because their mere presence undermined some black people's confidence and trust. This issue spawned irreconcilable rifts in SNCC and the freedom movement at large. In some cases, liberal whites were frozen out of the process, and in others, militant black leaders who thought like Britt McKinney of the Southern Tenant Farmers Union, Hubert Thomas of the Southwest Georgia Council on Human Relations, or Robert F. Williams of Monroe, North Carolina, made concessions. These black leaders found some whites to be sincere as individuals; moreover, they understood that white political leaders might have something practical to offer and could therefore be allowed a role in the black struggle. But at the same time, and in all of these contexts, self-defense and militant politics rather than nonviolent protest became increasingly useful tools for organization.[15]

In many urban areas the UNIA survives as an organization with an uninterrupted lineage.[16] In the fall of 2004, Mrs. Thelma Lewis died in Atlanta at age ninety-seven, and an African ceremony was held for this woman, also known as Queen Mother Nzinga Akua. Her son, Archbishop John H. Lewis III, of St. Augustine Imani African Orthodox Temple, called her the oldest living member of the Atlanta UNIA. Mrs. Lewis manifested certain traditional elements of the southern nationalist mindset. She had wanted to be a missionary to Africa and was devoted to her church and community. She was well known among folklorists for her knowledge of traditional hymns and Negro spirituals. Three of her five children became ministers, including Archbishop Lewis, who is also president of the Atlanta UNIA. For many years she had been at the center of the Atlanta UNIA division, which still holds annual Garvey Day celebrations at Mosely Park on Atlanta's West Side, an event that displays the popular black nationalism that has evolved over the last forty years.[17]

Although black popular culture has revived Garvey as an icon, most historians have not acknowledged the prevalence of grassroots Garveyism in almost every African American cultural, political, and intellectual movement since the 1930s. And even though every recent United States history textbook devotes a few paragraphs to the meteoric UNIA and the so-called Garvey "Back to Africa" movement of the urban North, the historical literature thus far ignores the UNIA in the South, reinforcing the perception that it was a short-lived, marginally influential, and obscure organization. Another barrier to recognizing the importance of the Garvey movement and its rural ideological origins is that it generally existed outside the purview of white and elite society. By recovering grassroots Garveyism from the fragments of the historical record, we can add a new dimension to our understanding of the enormous challenges and sometimes contradictory aspects of black organizational strategy.

Appendix A
UNIA Divisions in the Eleven States
of the Former Confederacy

The total number of UNIA divisions in the eleven states of the former Confederacy was 423. The following is a list of the divisions in each state. Division numbers are included in parentheses, if known. Division listings were taken from several sources. The two main ones are Robert A. Hill, ed., *The Marcus Garvey and Universal Negro Improvement Association Papers*, 7:986–96, and the index cards of divisions from the Universal Negro Improvement Association Records of the Central Division (New York), 1918–59, Schomburg Center for Research in Black Culture, New York Public Library, New York. Another listing appeared in the microfilmed part of that collection on reel 1, series A, box 2, section A16. I cross-referenced these sources, looked up the division names on maps from 1920 to 1930 (because some of these rural communities have disappeared), and eliminated ones that were listed under the wrong state or not found on the maps. Other divisions were added because they were specifically accounted for in *Negro World* issues from 1920 to 1933. I have also corrected the spelling when place-names were obviously transcribed incorrectly. Some towns had more than one division, and in many cases, these additional divisions were called chapters.

Alabama: Bessemer, Birmingham (660), Elba, Fairhope (816), Gadsden (759), Inverness (312), Mobile (744), Mobile (Northside), Neenah, Prichard (539), Ragland, Selma (807), Whistler.

Arkansas: Armorel (352), Barton, Blackton (702), Blythe (495), Blytheville (694), Brickeys (444), Burdett (809), Burton Spurr (412), Calexico (424), Clear Lake (642), Cotton Plant (515), Council (647), Crawfordsville (540), Cypert (602), Duncan (620), Earl (615), Forrest City, Fort Smith (687), Fry's Mill (Mississippi County), Good Hope (648), Gosnell (786), Green Brier (487), Hickman (437), Holly Grove (505), Holly Grove (chapter 70), Howell (576), Hughes (768), Indian Bay (656), Jefferson (749), Lake Hall (829), Lexa (698), Madison (760), Moten (447), New Home (Round Pond, 688), Oneida (663), Paraloma (Sevier County), Pine Bluff (689), Pine Bluff, Pine City (586), Postelle (Phillips County), Princedale, Round Pond (599), Simmsboro (806), South Bend (Lincoln County), Southland (Phillips County), Twist (591), Wynne (Cross County).

Florida: Boca Raton (366), Boynton (357), Campbell Hill (chapter 17A), Cent, Coconut Grove (175), Dania (333), Daytona, Deerfield (311), Del Ray (420), Denver (138), East Jacksonville (835), Fort Pierce (342), Hallandale (261), Jacksonville (286), Jacksonville (Hearns, chapter 73), Jensen (353), Key West (135), Lakeland (857), Leisburg (220), Merrill (398), Miami (136), North Jacksonville (chapter 40),

Odessa (573), Otter Creek (208), Palm Beach, Pleasant City, Pompano (264), St. Petersburg (456), South Jacksonville (467), Stuart (389), Tampa (90), Tavernier, Wabasee (381), West End (Jacksonville, chapter 16A), West Palm Beach (189), West Tampa (555).

Georgia: Adel, Alma (369), Atlanta (623), Baker County, Baxley (209), Brunswick (67), Camilla (232), Center Hill (Colquitt County), Charity Grove (Worth County, 590), Clyatville, Columbus, Coverdale (543), Damascus, Decatur, Fitzgerald (196), Gardi (388), Haylow (659), Howell, Jesup (392), Kimbrough (Webster County, 321), Limerick (778), Moultrie (376), Oakfield (567), Patterson (435), Pelham, Pooler (569), Powellton (Worth County, chapter 66), Ray City, Savannah, Shingler (458), Sylvester (605), TyTy (436), Warwick, Waycross (361), Waycross (chapter 34).

Louisiana: Algiers (327), Amite (779), Amite City (846), Arlington, Armistead (344), Bajou Goula (585), Baker (628), Baskin (811), Batchelor (783), Baton Rouge (489), Baton Rouge (chapter 39), Baton Rouge (Eaden Park, 762), Bayou Goula (551), Belle Chasse (654), Bermuda (330), Brusly (621), Carrolton (chapter 60), Clarence (604), Clouterville (504), College Grove (751), Comite River (chapter 84), Convent (751), Cypress Hall (579), Derry (578), Donalsonville (893), Donner (747), Dutch Bajou (Reserve, 815), Frenier (858), Funisburg (Lower Algiers, 527), Geismer (713), Gentilly (Lee Station, chapter 79), Gilbert, Good Hope (716), Gretna (520), Grosse Tete (636), Hymel, Industrial, Jesuit (542), Jordan Stream (618), Kenner (339), La Place (521), Lee Station, Livonia (649), Lockport (852), Luling (798), Luna (417), Lutcher (840), Marerro (765), Maringouin (588), Melrose (504), Modeste (671), Montz (288), Morganza (785), Natchez (575), Natchitoches (435), New Orleans (149), New Orleans (chapter 27), New Orleans (chapter 54), Oaknolia (652), Phoenix (401), Phoenix (chapter 9A), Plaquemine (482), Plaquemine (chapter 63), Powhaton, Robeline (235), Rosebud (chapter 94), St. Bernard (474), St. Mary (834), St. Rose (463), Scotlandville (550), South Baton Rouge (chapter 62), Taft (526), Trinity, Union (847), Ventress, Violet, Westwego (400), White Castle (459), Winnsboro (777), Zachary (577).

Mississippi: Aberdeen (831), Askew (440), Baltzer (793), Basic, Bethel, Beulah, Biloxi (369), Bobo, Bolivar, Canton (397), Clarksdale (824), Cleveland (679), East Cleveland (727), East Drew (722), East Merigold (chapter 86), East Mound Bayou (716), Elizabeth (chapter 96), Evansville (789), Forest (73), Greenville (682), Gulfport (414), Lambert (859), Liberty, Macel (609), Malvina, Marks (720), Mattson (799), Meridian (568), Merigold (606), Merigold (chapter 65), Mound Bayou (714), Mt. Calvary (882), Myrtle (307), Natchez (701), Pace (708), Poplarville (830), Renova (717), Shelby (770), Stillmore, Sumner (589), Symond (151), Turkey Creek (871), Tutwiler (724), Tylertown, Vance (724), Vance (784), Vicksburg (626), Water Valley (742), Waupun, Webb (643), West Boyle (735), West Cleveland (chapter 89), West Merigold (chapter 88), West Paine, West Point, Wiggins (896), Wyatt.

North Carolina: Acme, Asheville (252), Aulander (378), Bailey (562), Belhaven (218), Bellvedere, Bethel (657), Broadway (270), Charlotte (37), Columbia (147), Council (629), Duke (190), Durham, Elm City, Fairmont, Fayetteville (316), Gardners (510), Gaylord (517), Goldsboro (335), Goodwin (459), Greensboro (516), Hermondale (614), Jamesville (680), Kingston (757), Kinston (277), Lagrange, Lidling (325), Lillington, Mackeys (553), Magnolia, Matthews (535), Merry Hill (536), Morgantown (266), New Bern (219), Norwood, Pantego (210), Parmele (305), Pink Hill, Raleigh (228), Randleman (221), Ransomville (253), Red Springs (665), Ronake (Littleton, 324), St. Matthews (499), Salisbury (630), Sandford (773), Spencer (904), Spring Hope (324), Supply, Warrenton (168), Warsaw (396), Whittaker (637), Wilmington (297), Wilson (224), Windsor, Winston-Salem (79), Winston-Salem (399), Winston-Salem (chapter 92), Zebulon (394).

South Carolina: Anderson (572), Ashley Junction (chapter 25), Beaufort, Charleston (113), Charleston (886), Charleston (chapter 2), Cheraw (229), Church Parish (710), Coosaw Island, Dale (chapter 57), Georgetown (283), Green Pond (145), Lobeco (641), Lakeview (603), Marysville (chapter 44), Midland Park (Charleston, 471), Mt. Holly (559), Murray Hill (chapter 28), Pinopolis (596), Rock Hill (206), St. Andrews (519), Strawberry (616), Ten Mile Hill (chapter 29), Union Heights (289), Yemassee (207).

Tennessee: Alcoa (681), Chattanooga (595), Franklin, Henry County (364), Hyde Park (chapter 1A), Knoxville (584), Knoxville (chapter 81), Memphis (195), Nashville (199), New Market, Paris (264), South Nashville (chapter 16).

Texas: Acliff Heights (748), Cameron, Cushing, Dallas (191), Egypt (843), Elmo (610), Galveston, Glen Fawn (546), Hillsboro, Lemonville (845), Mill City (562), Waco (828), Whitney (319).

Virginia: Arringdale, Bacon's Castle (494), Bell's Mill (864), Berkley (chapter 67), Berkley Station (198), Capron (63), Danville (693), Dewitt (422), Ettricks (560), Fairfax (402), Franklin (25), Grafton (47), Green Bay, Grove (278), Hopewell (169), Kecoughtan City (chapter 45), Kenbridge, Lebanon, Meherrin (664), Munden (733), Munden (Berkley Division, 70), Munden (West), Newport News (6), Newport News (East End), Newport News (Jefferson Point, chapter 32), Norfolk (856), Norfolk (Oakwood, chapter 42), Norfolk (Campostella, 624), Norfolk (Tidewater, 43), Norfolk (West End, chapter 22), Oakwood Park (885), Oyster Point (173), Petersburg (854), Petersburg (174), Pocahontas (611), Portsmouth (11), Prospect (528), Rappahannock (234), Richmond (193), Roxbury, Royal (chapter 10A), Smithfield (170), Somerset (767), Suffolk (53), Titus Town (82), Virginia (99), Wallaceton, Warfield (153), Waverly (69), Tabbs (York County, 115), Zimi (176).

Appendix B
Numbers of Southern Members of
UNIA Divisions by State

The numbers of southern members of UNIA divisions were derived from a 1926–28 card file of UNIA divisions and chapters that was discovered with other fragments of UNIA Parent Body and Central Division records and papers in an abandoned apartment building in Harlem in 1970. The Schomburg Center for Research in Black Culture at the Harlem branch of the New York Public Library now holds this card file. It is the only part of those documents that has not been microfilmed. I have thoroughly examined each of these cards to determine membership numbers. This is the most complete evidence of UNIA divisions as a whole that is extant, although it dates from the twilight period of the American Garvey movement. The most pertinent information we derive from this collection is where divisions and chapters were located rather than actual membership numbers. Since most of the listed divisions received charters in 1921, these 1926–28 fragments reflect drastically reduced membership numbers. These numbers are an accounting of the most loyal and devoted of the UNIA's core, but they represent not even a fraction of the organization's size and popularity in its heyday.

Each card has a column for member numbers, which each division was to report after each meeting. These numbers reflect the actual number of members present at each meeting. The numbers fluctuated, and the numbers I used to add up state totals were for the largest local meeting attendance given for the two-year period between 1926 and 1928. Some divisions, although active, did not send in all the information the parent body requested, such as reports and member numbers. The card file contains records of the existence of these divisions, but no specific membership statistics for them. However, in order to form a division and receive a charter, a division had to have a minimum of seven charter members. For division cards with no member numbers recorded, I used seven as an estimate.

Alabama	287
Arkansas	395
Florida	4,974
Georgia	217
Louisiana	1,039
Mississippi	712
North Carolina	648
South Carolina	233
Tennessee	172
Texas	70
Virginia	776
TOTAL	9,523

Appendix C
Numbers of Sympathizers Involved in
Mass Meetings and Petitions for Garvey's
Release from Jail and Prison, 1923–1927

Hundreds of letters, telegrams, cablegrams, and petitions from Garvey supporters and UNIA divisions from all over the United States and the Caribbean can be found in the U.S. Pardon Attorney Records, Record Group 204: 42-793, boxes 1159–62, and the U.S. Department of Justice Records, Record Group 60: 198940, box 3053, at the National Archives II, College Park, Maryland. Most of these pleaded for the president or the attorney general to make a close examination of Garvey's case and to consider a recommendation for clemency. At various stages of Garvey's trial and imprisonment, Garvey's wife and other UNIA leaders urged his supporters to hold rallies and mass meetings and to pass resolutions and send petitions to the U.S. government to indicate the level of support for Garvey felt among black Americans. The numbers represented below were derived by counting petition signatures and adding numbers of people reportedly attending mass meetings, according to the letters and telegrams and enclosed petitions. The evidence of these mass meetings is one of our most graphic sources of information on the level of sympathy for Garvey and his movement among southern blacks.

Alabama	10,000
Arkansas	28,495
Florida	4,700
Georgia	6,000
Louisiana	57,576
Mississippi	16,898
South Carolina	5,200
Tennessee	100
Texas	5,250
Virginia	12,650
TOTAL	146,869

Appendix D
Phases of Organization of UNIA Divisions in the South by State

State	Phase 1	Phase 2	Phase 3	Phase 4	Unknown[a]
Alabama	0	1	6	0	6
Arkansas	0	2	35	0	7
Florida	1	19	10	1	5
Georgia	1	10	14	0	9
Louisiana	0	9	56	6	9
Mississippi	1	5	34	4	13
North Carolina	2	25	18	1	13
South Carolina	0	9	14	1	2
Tennessee	0	6	5	0	2
Texas	0	2	5	1	4
Virginia	10	13	18	2	11
TOTAL	15	101	215	16	81

Note: Division numbers give an indication of when individual divisions and chapters were organized and when charters were issued by the parent body. An examination of the numbers provides a sense of chronology for which states underwent thorough organization into divisions and at what stage in the UNIA's development each state experienced its greatest level of growth. Before 1 August 1920, the date of the first convention, the parent body issued 95 division charters, so any division number from 1 to 95 would have presumably been organized before that time. Division numbers 96 through 418 and chapters 1 through 19 were chartered between 1 August 1920 and 1 August 1921, the date of the second convention. Garvey reported that 422 more divisions had been organized and awaited charter numbers at the time of the August 1921 convention. This gives us three sequential phases for which dates are possible: phase 1 includes divisions 1 through 95, organized and chartered prior to 1 August 1920; phase 2 includes divisions 96 through 418 and chapters 1 through 19, chartered between 1 August 1920 and 1 August 1921; phase 3 includes divisions 419 through 841, organized before 1 August 1921 and chartered soon thereafter; and phase 4 includes all divisions with numbers above 841, which would have been organized and chartered after 1 August 1921. Chapters 20 and above fit into either phase 3 or 4, but in some cases it is impossible to determine which. See Hill, *Marcus Garvey and Universal Negro Improvement Association Papers*, 3:642.

[a] Records do not indicate charter numbers for these divisions.

Appendix E
Ministers as Southern UNIA Officers, 1926–1928

Name (Office)	Division/Chapter Location[a]
Rev. R. B. Gipson (P)	Birmingham, Ala.
Rev. J. A. Sweeney (S)	Birmingham, Ala.
Rev. M. C. McClinton (P)	Holly Grove, Ark. (chapter)
Rev. F. Folls (P)	Jefferson, Ark.
Rev. Archie Jackson (P)	Pine City, Ark.
Rev. E. C. Majority (P)	Twist, Ark.
Rev. R. I. Sims (P)	Jacksonville, Fla. (Hearns) (chapter 73)
Rev. T. L. Moran (P)	Leisburg, Fla.
Rev. J. E. Harris (S)	St. Petersburg, Fla.
Rev. C. H. Frazier (S)	West End, Fla. (Jacksonville) (chapter 16A)
Rev. S. L. Smith (P)	Gardi, Ga.
Rev. G. Lindsay (P)	Baton Rouge, La. (chapter 39)
Rev. Jas. Thomas (P)	Convent, La.
Rev. C. Sanders (P)	Jesuit Bend, La.
Rev. J. Taylor (P)	Lockport, La.
Rev. W. M. Bevene (P)	Luling, La.
Rev. E. D. Napolean (P)	Modesto, La.
Rev. G. W. Hudson (P)	New Orleans, La. (chapter)
Rev. John Miller (P)	Phoenix, La. (New Orleans)
Rev. J. H. Bailey (S)	Phoenix, La. (New Orleans)
Rev. R. E. Booker (P)	Clarksdale, Miss.
Rev. W. O. Norman (S)	East Drew, Miss. (Ruleville)
Rev. Jesse Bell (P)	Gulfport, Miss.
Rev. Dr. A. N. S. Brown (P)	Macel, Miss.
Rev. A. M. Newson (P)	Merigold, Miss. (division)
Rev. A. F. Teajean (P)	Merigold, Miss. (chapter)
Rev. J. P. Gayles (P)	Mound Bayou, Miss.
Rev. A. J. Polk (S)	Water Valley, Miss.
Rev. W. M. Reed (P)	West Merigold, Miss.
Rev. F. H. W. Boomer (P)	Pantego, N.C.
Rev. W. M. Allen (P)	Raleigh, N.C.
Rev. Thomas Plummer (P)	Warrenton, N.C.
Rev. J. C. Williams (S)	Warrenton, N.C.
Rev. M. D. W. Graham (S)	Whittaker, N.C.
Rev. M. Parker (P)	Yemassee, S.C.
Rev. J. R. Carethers (P)	South Nashville, Tenn.
Rev. M. A. Jones (P)	Franklin, Va.
Rev. E. Godfrey (P)	Newport News, Va. (Hampton)
Rev. Rufus Robinson (P)	Petersburg, Va.

Note: P = president; S = secretary.

[a]If the location of a division or chapter differs from the city in a person's address, the city follows the division, enclosed in parentheses.

Appendix F

Profiles of UNIA Members in Georgia, Arkansas, and Mississippi, 1922–1928, and NAACP Branch Leaders in Georgia (excluding Atlanta), 1917–1920

County	Division/Town/Branch	Office[a]	Name	Sex[b]	Age	Race[c]	Marital Status[d]	Residenc
Southwest Georgians Involved in the UNIA, 1922–1928								
Worth	Powellton	P	Isaiah G. Gates	M	39	B	M	F
Worth	Powellton	S	Willie Johnson	M	29	Mu	W	H
Worth	Oakfield (Pine Hill District)	P	James Evans	M	60	B	M	F
Worth	Oakfield	S	Albert Evans	M	35	B	M	F
Worth	Shingler	S	Lonzie Smith	M	30	B	M	F
Worth	Charity Grove (Warwick)	S '26 C '29	Richmond Britt	M	35	B	M	F
Worth	Warwick	C	Jasper N. Battle	M	57	Mu	M	F
Worth	Near TyTy (TyTy div.)	C	Henry Neal	M	35	B	M	F
Worth	Minton	C	Tom Tolbert	M	28	B	M	F
Turner	Turner Co. (Sumner div.)	C	Lonnie James	M	24	B	S	—
Worth	Sylvester	M/O	Lizzie Jordan	F	36	B	W	H
Terrell	Dawson (Pelham div.)	M/O	Oscar C. Kelley	M	60	Mu	W	H
Webster	Kimbrough	P	James E. Jackson	M	69	B	M	F
Webster	Kimbrough	S	Jim A. Hardwick	M	43	B	M	F
Turner	Coverdale	P	Murray K. Kellebrew	M	30	B	M	F
Colquitt	Moultrie	P	Porter Dublin	M	39	B	M	F
Baker	Baker Co. (Newton)	P	William H. Wright	M	53	B	M	F
Baker	Baker Co. (Newton)	S	Seaborn B. Presley	M	50	B	M	F
Baker	Newton	C	Jonas Odom	M	44	Mu	W	F
Terrell	Dawson	C	Lee Knighton	M	46	B	M	F
Arkansans Involved in the UNIA, 1922–1928								
Phillips	Lexa	S	Gent Willis	M	35	B	M	F
Phillips	Hornor Twp. (Lexa div.)	P	Albert Walker	M	52	B	M	F
Phillips	Marvel	C	Ed Newsom	M	48	Mu	M	F
Phillips	Southland	C	Louis Martin	M	45	B	M	F
Phillips	Southland	C	Walter Hampton	M	41	B	M	F
Phillips	Postelle	C	Levi Fields	M	58	B	M	F
Phillips	Oneida	C	Calvin Diggs	M	53	B	M	F
Phillips	Oneida	C	Estella Diggs	F	27	B	M	F

dence ʌsᶠ	Literate	State of Birth	Type of Work	Employmentᵍ	# of Children	# of Women in Household	Wife Working
	Y	LA	Farmer—general farm	OA	1	1	N
	Y	GA	Laborer—home farm (family)	W	—	—	N/A
	N	GA	Farmer—general farm	OA	3	1+	—
	N	GA	Farmer—general farm	W	6	3	—
	Y	GA	Farmer—general farm	OA	4	1+	—
	N	GA	Farmer—general farm	W	8	2	N
	Y	GA	Farmer—general farm	E	7	6	N
	Y	GA	Farmer—general farm	OA	0	2+	N
	N	GA	Farmer—general farm	OA	2	2	Y
	Y	GA	Prison laborer, roads	—	—	—	—
	Y	GA	Cook	W	4	4	N/A
	Y	GA	Minister	W	1	0	N/A
	N	GA	Laborer—general farm	OA	2	3	—
	Y	GA	Carpenter—home	W	4	2	—
	N	GA	Farmer—general farm	OA	2	2	—
	Y	GA	Farmer—general farm	OA	5	2	N
	Y	GA	Farmer—general farm	OA	8	5	—
	Y	GA	Farmer—general farm	OA	1	1	—
	Y	GA	Farmer/grocer	E	5	1	N/A
	Y	GA	Farmer	OA	4	3	N
	N	GA	Farmer	—	4	3	N
	Y	MS	Farmer	OA	0	1	Y
	Y	AR	Farmer	E	0	1	Y
	Y	TN	Farmer	OA	1	2	—
	N	AR	Farmer	OA	—	1	N
	Y	AL	Farmer	OA	2	2	—
	Y	NC	Farmer	W	0	2	N
	Y	MS	—	—	0	2	—

County	Division/Town/Branch	Office[a]	Name	Sex[b]	Age	Race[c]	Marital Status[d]	Residence
Phillips	Oneida	C	John H. McQueen	M	52	B	M	F
Phillips	Oneida	C	Mary McQueen	F	48	B	M	F
Phillips	Oneida (Indian Bay)	P	James Canon	M	47	B	M	F
Phillips	Marvel (Cypert)	P	Eugene Bridges	M	27	Mu	M	F
Monroe	Montgomery Twp. Indian Bay	M	Elbert Knowles	M	36	B	M	F
Monroe	Montgomery Twp. Indian Bay	M	Abe Collins	M	26	B	M	F
Monroe	Montgomery Twp. Indian Bay	M	James Hardeman	M	39	B	M	F
Monroe	Montgomery Twp. Indian Bay	M	Anna Ledbetter	F	20	B	M	F
Monroe	Montgomery Twp. Indian Bay	M	James Orange	M	46	B	M	F
Monroe	Montgomery Twp. Indian Bay	M	Will Gillium	M	49	B	M	F
Monroe	Montgomery Twp. Indian Bay	M	Ed Glass	M	46	B	M	F
Monroe	Montgomery Twp. Indian Bay	M	Patsy Glass	F	38	B	M	F
Monroe	Montgomery Twp. Indian Bay	M	Anna Dixon	F	36	B	M	F
Monroe	Montgomery Twp. Indian Bay	M	J. B. Suttles	M	35	B	M	F
Monroe	Montgomery Twp. Indian Bay	M	Daisy Suttles	F	28	B	M	F
Monroe	Montgomery Twp. Indian Bay	M	John Estes	M	47	B	M	F
Monroe	Montgomery Twp. Indian Bay	M	Cassie Estes	F	38	B	M	F
Monroe	Montgomery Twp. Indian Bay	M	Mattie Lee Estes	F	12	B	M	F
Monroe	Montgomery Twp. Indian Bay	M	William Foster	M	24	B	S	F
Monroe	Montgomery Twp. Indian Bay	M	Mary Glass	F	35	B	W	F
Monroe	Montgomery Twp. Indian Bay	M	J. V. Glass	M	48	B	M	F
Monroe	Montgomery Twp. Indian Bay	M	Ezianna Glass	F	45	B	M	F
Monroe	Montgomery Twp. Indian Bay	S '26 M '27	Earlie A. Foster	M	26	B	M	F

...dence ...us[f]	Literate	State of Birth	Type of Work	Employment[g]	# of Children	# of Women in Household	Wife Working
	Y	MS	Farmer	OA	—	1	N
	Y	MS	—	—	0	1	N
	Y	MS	Farmer	OA	4	—	N
	Y	—	Farmer—father's farm	OA	1	1	Y
	Y	MS	Farmer—cotton farm	OA	2	1	Y
	Y	AR	Farmer—cotton farm	OA	0	1	Y
	Y	AR	Farmer—cotton farm	OA	1	2	Y
	Y	AR	Farm laborer—home farm	W	2	2	Y
	Y	AR	Farmer—cotton farm	OA	0	1	Y
	Y	AR	Farmer—cotton farm	OA	2	3	Y
	Y	MS	Farmer—cotton farm	OA	8	2	Y
	Y	MS	Farm laborer—home farm	W	8	2	Y
	Y/N	AR	Farm laborer—home farm	W	1	2	Y
	Y	MS	Farmer—cotton farm	OA	0	1	Y
	Y	MS	Farm laborer—home farm	W	0	1	Y
	Y	MS	Farmer—cotton farm	OA	4	6	N
	Y	MS	None	—	4	6	N
	Y	MS	Farm laborer—home farm	W	0	6	N/A
	Y	MS	Farmer—cotton farm	OA	0	3	N/A
	Y	MS	Farmer—cotton farm	OA	3	3	N/A
	Y	MS	Farmer—cotton farm	OA	9	6	N
	N	MS	None	—	9	6	—
	Y	MS	Farmer—cotton farm	OA	2	1	N

County	Division/Town/Branch	Office[a]	Name	Sex[b]	Age	Race[c]	Marital Status[d]	Residence[e]
Monroe	Montgomery Twp. Indian Bay	M	Marvella Foster	F	22	B	M	F
Monroe	Montgomery Twp. Indian Bay	M	Sam Gillium	M	28	B	M	F
Monroe	Montgomery Twp. Indian Bay	S '26 M '27	James Boyce	M	44	B	M	F
Monroe	Montgomery Twp. Indian Bay	M	James Wilburn	M	55	B	M	F
Monroe	Montgomery Twp. Indian Bay	M	Etta Wilburn	F	32	B	M	F
Monroe	Montgomery Twp. Indian Bay	M	Will Wilburn	M	49	B	M	F
Monroe	Montgomery Twp. Indian Bay	M	Archie Bailey	M	24	B	S	F
Monroe	Montgomery Twp. Indian Bay	M	H. C. Wilburn	M	49	B	M	F
Monroe	Montgomery Twp. Indian Bay	M	Ellen Wilburn	F	45	B	M	F
Monroe	Duncan	P	Tom Bobo	M	51	Mu	M	F
Monroe	Montgomery District	C	J. C. Wilburn	M	49	B	M	F
Monroe	Raymond Twp.	C	Archie Jackson (Rev.)	M	30	B	M	F
Monroe	Montgomery Twp. Indian Bay	M	Will Urvin	M	45	B	M	F
Monroe	Montgomery Twp. Indian Bay	M	Thomas Sanford	M	36	B	M	F
Monroe	Montgomery Twp. Indian Bay	M	A. L. Jackson	M	52	B	M	F
Monroe	Montgomery Twp. Indian Bay	M	Walter Wells	M	36	B	M	F
Monroe	Montgomery Twp. Indian Bay	M	Allen Brown	M	56	B	M	F
Monroe	Montgomery Twp. Indian Bay	M	Nelson Wilburn	M	24	B	S	F
Monroe	Montgomery Twp. Indian Bay	M	Littris Jones	M	38	B	M	F
Monroe	Duncan	P	Booker Simmons	M	36	B	M	F
Poinsett	Little River Twp.	O	Britt E. McKinney	M	48	B	M	F
St. Francis	Griggs (Cotton Plant)	S	Fred Tolbert	M	40	B	M	F
Crittenden	Earle (Holly Grove)	P	Marcus McClinton (Rev.)	M	29	Mu	M	H

dence us[f]	Literate	State of Birth	Type of Work	Employment[g]	# of Children	# of Women in Household	Wife Working
	Y	AR	None	—	2	1	—
	Y	AR	Farmer—cotton farm	OA	3	4	Y
	Y	AR	Farmer—cotton farm	OA	7	5	Y
	Y/N	AR	Farmer—cotton farm	OA	4	5	Y
	N	AR	Farm laborer—home farm	W	4	5	Y
	Y	AR	Farmer—cotton farm	OA	6	4	Y
	N	AR	Sharecropper—home farm	OA	0	6	N/A
	Y	AR	Farmer—cotton farm	OA	5	4	Y
	Y	AL	Farm laborer—home farm	W	5	4	N/A
	Y	SC	Farmer	E	6	3	N
	Y	AR	Farmer—cotton farm	OA	5	3	Y
	Y	AR	Farmer	OA	3	1+	—
	Y	AR	Farmer—cotton farm	OA	1	2	Y
	Y	AR	Farmer—cotton farm	OA	2	3	Y
	Y	AR	Farmer—cotton farm	OA	0	2	Y
	Y	AR	Farmer—cotton farm	OA	2	2	Y
	Y	MS	Farmer—cotton farm	OA	6	5	N
	N	AR	Sharecropper—home farm (parents)	OA	—	3	N/A
	Y	AR	Farmer—cotton farm	OA	0	3	N
	Y	TN	Farmer—general farm	E	2	3	N
	Y	TN	Farmer	E	1	2	N
	—	MS	Farmer	E	2	2	Y
	Y	TN	Laborer—sawmill	W	3	3	Y

County	Division/ Town/Branch	Office[a]	Name	Sex[b]	Age	Race[c]	Marital Status[d]	Residence[e]
Mississippi	Scott Twp. (Burton Spurr)	P	George Fowler	M	46	B	M	F

Mississippians Involved in the UNIA, 1922–1928

County	Division/ Town/Branch	Office[a]	Name	Sex[b]	Age	Race[c]	Marital Status[d]	Residence[e]
Tallahatchie	Swan Lake (Beat 5 Twp.)	C/O	Aron W. Washington (Rev.)	M	24	B	M	H
Tallahatchie	Sumner (Beat 5 Twp.)	P '26	Tom Saunders	M	48	B	M	F
Tallahatchie	Webb (Beat 5 Twp.)	S '26	Henry Brown	M	33	B	M	F
Tallahatchie	Sumner (Beat 5 Twp.)	S '26	Tom Williams	M	30	B	M	F
Tallahatchie	Vance	S '26	Jeff (J. D.) Rayford	M	39	B	M	F
Tallahatchie	Vance	P '26	William Banks	M	48	B	M	H
Bolivar	Merigold div. Cleveland (Beat 4)	P '26	Adam Newsome (Newson) (Rev.)	M	44	Mu	M	F
Bolivar	Symond div. Cleveland (Beat 4)	P '26	Thomas White	M	32	Mu	M	F
Bolivar	Cleveland Chambers (Beat 4)	P '26	Susie Merrill	F	30	B	M	H
Bolivar	Merigold div. Cleveland (Beat 4)	P '26	Will Reed (Rev.)	M	40	B	S	H
Bolivar	Renova (Beat 2)	P '26	Weiseman Haywood	M	48	B	M	F
Cohoma	Baltzer (Beat 5)	P '26	Fred Swahn	M	24	B	M	F
Sunflower	Cleveland (Indianola)	P '26	Adam Hodge	M	32	B	M	F
Coahoma	Clarkesdale	S '26	W. D. Miles	M	44	B	M	H
Coahoma	Clarkesdale	P '26	R. E. Booker (Rev.)	M	—	B	M	H
Sunflower	Drew	S '26	W. O. Norman (Rev.)	M	58	B	M	F

NAACP Branch Leaders in Georgia (excluding Atlanta), 1917–1920

County	Division/ Town/Branch	Office[a]	Name	Sex[b]	Age	Race[c]	Marital Status[d]	Residence[e]
Baldwin	Milledgeville	P	Sam McComb	M	37	Mu	M	H
Baldwin	Milledgeville	O	William Wright	M	49	Mu	M	H
Bibb	Macon	P	Roland R. Hawes	M	42	Mu	M	H
Bibb	Macon	O	Emmett L. Wheaton	M	40	B	M	H
Crisp	Cordele	P	Herry J. Wilson	M	45	B	M	H
Dougherty	Albany	P	James Martin	M	37	B	M	H
Floyd	Rome	O	Mary D. Walton	F	56	B	M	H

idence us[f]	Literate	State of Birth	Type of Work	Employment[g]	# of Children	# of Women in Household	Wife Working
	Y	GA	Farmer	OA	4	4	N
	Y	MS	Minister	S	1	2	N
	Y	MS	Farmer—general farm	E	0	1	N
	Y	MS	Farmer—general farm	E	5	5	N
	Y	MS	Farm laborer—father's farm	W	0	1	Y
	Y	MS	Farmer	On halves	3	2	Y
	N	MS	Laborer—RR (lives in duplex)	W	1	2	N
	Y	MS	Farmer—general farm	OA	3	6	Y
	Y/N	MS	Farmer—general farm	OA	0	1	Y
	Y	MS	Restaurant	OA	0	N/A	N/A
	Y	MS	Farm laborer	W	0	0	N/A
	Y	MS	Farmer—cotton plantation	OA	3	1	N
	Y	MS	Farmer—general farm	OA	0	1	Y
	Y	MS	Laborer—odd jobs	W	0	1	Y
	Y	MS	Farm laborer	W	3	2	Y
	Y	MS	Sharecropper	OA	2	2	—
	N	MS	Farmer	OA	1	2	N
	Y	GA	Tailor	OA	3	3	N
	Y	GA	Barber	OA	1	2	N
	Y	GA	Dentist	OA	1	2	N
	Y	GA	Lawyer	OA	0	2	N
	Y	AL	Physician	OA	0	2	Y
	Y	SC	Locomotive fireman	W	0	1	Y
	Y	GA	None	—	6	3	N/A

County	Division/Town/Branch	Office[a]	Name	Sex[b]	Age	Race[c]	Marital Status[d]	Residence[e]
Laurens	Dublin	P	George W. Williams (Rev.)	M	48	B	M	H
Lowndes	Valdosta	P	Cyrus G. Wiley	M	38	B	M	H
Thomas	Thomasville	P	William J. Mosely (Dr.)	M	45	B	M	H
Richmond	Augusta	P	Alford W. Wimberly	M	58	Mu	M	H
Sumter	Americus	O	Miller A. Fountain (Rev.)	M	32	B	M	H
Sumter	Americus	P	Samuel S. Humbert	M	57	B	M	H

[a]C = contributor; M = member; O = organizer; P = president; S = secretary.
[b]F = female; M = male.
[c]B = black; Mu = mulatto.
[d]M = married; S = single; W = widowed.
[e]F = farm; H = house.
[f]F = free; M = mortgage; O = owner; R = renter.
[g]E = employer; OA = own account; S = salary; W = wages. A farmer whose employment type is "OA" is most likely a sharecropper if he rents his home and a tenant farmer (a slightly more secure, preferable, independent situation) if h owns or mortgages his home.

dence us[f]	Literate	State of Birth	Type of Work	Employment[g]	# of Children	# of Women in Household	Wife Working
	Y	FL	Minister	S	0	1	N
	Y	SC	School principal	S	0	2	N
	Y	GA	City physician	S	0	1	N
	Y	GA	Real estate	OA	0	1	N
	Y	GA	Minister	W	0	2	N
	Y	SC	Orphans' home superintendent	W	4	3	Y

Women Organizers in the UNIA in the South,
1922–1928

Name (Office)	Division/Chapter Location[a]
Annie McGrue (S)	Mobile, Ala.
Mrs. Rose Ellis (P)	Neenah, Ala. (Camden)
Mrs. Ola M. Martin (S)	Neenah, Ala. (Camden)
Miss Hattie Thomas[b] (S)	Prichard, Ala.
Henrietta Cobbs (S)	Blackton, Ark. (Holly Grove)
Miss Dora Gamlin[b] (S)	Calexico, Ark.
Vassie D. Gamlin (P)	Calexico, Ark.
Emma McCrary (S)	Ft. Smith, Ark.[c]
Ellen Lee (S)	Denver, Fla.
Amanda Johnson[b] (S)	South Jacksonville, Fla. (division 457)
Katie Clay (S)	Atlanta, Ga.
Tassie Onendial (S)	Baxley, Ga. (Atlanta)
Terrasee Varnadol (S)	Fitzgerald, Ga. (Atlanta)
Louise C. Smith (S)	Moultrie, Ga.
Mattie Jennings (S)	Amite, La. (779)
Mary Smith (S)	Amite City, La. (846)
Ms. Eliz. Edwards (S)	Carrolton, La. (chapter 100)[c]
Mrs. L. Brown (S)	Lutcher, La.
Mrs. Gertrude Hill (S)	New Orleans, La. (chapter)
Emily Handy (S)	Phoenix, La. (chapter)
Mattie Jenning (S)[d]	Trinity, La. (Amite)
Lorena Scott (S)	Biloxi, Miss.
Mrs. Ada Lindsey (S)	Greenville, Miss.
Miss A. B. Shinault (S)	Natchez, Miss.[c]
Ada Smith (S)	Shelby, Miss. (Merigold)
Daisy Hunt (S)	Asheville, N.C.
Lula Chester (S)	Bethel, N.C.
Virginia Sykes[b] (S)	Jamesville, N.C.
Mary Douglas (S)	Matthews, N.C.
Mrs. Queenie E. Powell (S)	Parmele, N.C.
Laura McCullough (S)	Ransomville, N.C.
Mrs. Emma Coneley (S)	Red Springs, N.C.
Minnie Warley (S)	Lake View, S.C.
Mayola Johnson (S)	Chattanooga, Tenn.[c]
Mrs. S. E. Nelson (S)	Knoxville, Tenn. (division)
Rosa Flack (S)	Knoxville, Tenn. (chapter)
Mrs. Willie Ducket (S)	Mill City, Tex. (Dallas)
Catherine Brown (S)	Campostella, Va. (Norfolk)

Virginia Banks (S)	East End, Va. (Newport News)
Maggie Lewis (S)	Grafton, Va.
Miss Blanch Roberts (S)	Grove, Va.
Eva Rowlett[b] (S)	Meherrin, Va.
Mrs. Bessie Smith[b] (S)	Oyster Point, Va.
Elvina Guy (S)	Prospect, Va. (Blackstone)
Mrs. Racilia W. S. Jones (S)	Royal, Va. (Richmond)
Geneva Jacksons[b] (S)	Somerset, Va.
Mrs. Malinda Clay (S)	Suffolk, Va.
Mrs. Nora Morris (S)	Tidewater, Va. (Norfolk)

Note: P = president; S = secretary.

[a] If the location of a division or chapter differs from the city in a person's address, the city follows the division, enclosed in parentheses.

[b] Woman has same last name as president, suggesting a team effort with the wife as scribe and subordinate.

[c] Very active division/chapter, as reflected in member numbers, correspondence to the *Negro World*, and contributions to various UNIA funds.

[d] This is likely the same person as "Mattie Jennings" of the Amite, Louisiana, division (779) above. She is listed twice because she was secretary of two different divisions, though she received mail for both at her home in Amite.

Notes

Abbreviations

ACS   American Colonization Society

GP   Robert A. Hill, ed., *The Marcus Garvey and Universal Negro
             Improvement Association Papers*, vols. 1–7 (Berkeley: University of
             California Press, 1983–90)

LC   Library of Congress, Manuscript Division, Washington, D.C.

NAACP   National Association for the Advancement of Colored People

NW   *Negro World*

RG   Record Group

STFU Papers *Southern Tenant Farmers Union Papers, 1934–1970* (microfilm;
             Glen Rock, N.J.: Microfilming Corporation of America, 1971)

UNIA   Universal Negro Improvement Association

UNIAR   Universal Negro Improvement Association, Records of the Central
             Division (New York), 1918–59, Schomburg Center for Research in
             Black Culture, New York Public Library, New York, N.Y.

Introduction

1. Sources do not exist for providing precise numbers of UNIA members. The seizures, losses, and abandonment of institutional records are recounted in *GP* 1:xcii–xciii. Urban divisions such as New York and Philadelphia clearly had thousands of members, while some rural communities may have only had the minimum requirement of seven, but fragmentary evidence suggests much larger numbers for even rural divisions. I have documented a paying membership of 9,523 for the eleven states of the former Confederacy in the twilight years of the Garvey movement, the only years for which membership records of any kind exist; see appendix B. However, to illustrate how low this figure must be, the Newport News, Virginia, division had 7,000 recorded members in 1920, Pelham, Georgia, held a UNIA rally of 10,000 people in 1922, and the tiny hamlet of Indian Bay, Arkansas, had 500 documented sympathizers in 1925. See appendix C. Since most of the listed divisions received charters in 1921, these 1926–28 fragments reflect drastically reduced membership numbers. These numbers are an accounting of the most loyal and devoted of the UNIA's core, but represent not even a fraction of its size in its heyday or even a small percentage of the sympathizers for the movement, who are so clearly revealed by hundreds of petitions to the U.S. Justice Department and the U.S. Pardon Attorney. Even so, it is the most complete record we have.
2. *GP* 1:xxxvii.
3. *NW*, 16 August 1924.

4. Although the term "Negro" has fallen out of formal use in favor of "African American" and "black," and although to many it has pejorative connotations, it must be recognized at the outset by the reader that this term obviously was embraced by the leaders and members of the Universal Negro Improvement Association. Garvey preferred the term "Negro" and insisted that it be capitalized to signify a proper name. This usage is so frequent in the literature that I have chosen to use it in places where Garvey and other UNIA supporters would have.

5. The way Garvey conveyed the concept of a Negro race as an essential category in opposition to the white race and the way he defined nation in terms of one's required loyalty to his or her African heritage, rather than to a government or place, fly in the face of contemporary analyses of those categories in cultural studies. Paul Gilroy has argued that racial categorization is anachronistic in the modern world, and that many black intellectuals in the United States, the West Indies, and Africa have layered, diaspora identities instead of this notion of the purely African or Negro racial identity that Garvey evoked so effectively. See Gilroy, *Black Atlantic*, 15–19; and Gilroy, *Against Race*. For numerous seminal essays on the question of race and identity in the African diaspora, see also Baker, Diawara, and Lindeborg, *Black British Cultural Studies*.

6. It is impossible to provide precise numbers of divisions in various regions. The only institutional records of the UNIA structure are the incomplete set of index cards containing the name (by location), charter number, and other data for UNIA divisions from 1926 to 1928. These cards are housed with the UNIAR. My division lists for the eleven states of the former Confederacy are based on extensive cross-referencing of these cards with information in the *Negro World*. I have relied on the lists in *GP* 7:986–1002 for the numbers of divisions in other regions of the United States and other countries. In checking the southern divisions I found that several locals had been filed under the wrong state or listed under two states, thus creating duplication. Some divisions of which I found other evidence were not listed at all. The UNIA's local units were called divisions. If another group in the same location wanted to charter a second unit, it was called a chapter.

7. The UNIA had eighty-four divisions in the West Indies (including twenty-nine in Trinidad, twenty-six in Cuba, and ten in Jamaica), and ninety in Central and South America (including thirty-nine in Panama and twenty-three in Costa Rica), eighteen in Africa, twenty-one in Canada, five in Great Britain, and one in Australia. *GP* 7:997–1000.

8. See "Dr. Eason Speaks," *NW*, 11 March 1922, 2, in which one of the UNIA's earliest organizers explains how Garvey pitched the philosophy to him before the organization became successful.

9. Amy Jacques Garvey, *Garvey and Garveyism*, 124–25.

10. James, *Holding Aloft the Banner of Ethiopia*, 2–5.

11. Hill, *Marcus Garvey*, 41.

12. The southern state (excluding Florida, which will be discussed in chapter 2) with the largest number of West Indian–born blacks in 1920 was Louisiana with 514. Of these, 505 lived in New Orleans. Virginia had 106, all of whom lived in coastal areas, especially around Hampton Roads. Georgia had the next-highest number with 49, all of whom lived in Savannah or coastal areas and in Atlanta. The other southern states had 25 or fewer West Indians in each, most of whom lived in coastal cities. There was absolutely no trace of West Indian–born blacks in either the Arkansas or Mississippi Delta or in southwest Georgia. Census data accessed at <http://www.ancestry.com>.

13. See Robert A. Hill's introductory essays, *GP* 1:lxxviii–lxxxv and 4:xxxii–xxxiii, for references to Garvey's changing rhetoric and activities.

14. Reid, *Negro Immigrant*, 89.

15. See appendix A. Although the division listings come from the incomplete set of file cards dated 1926–28, cross-referencing with data from the *Negro World* and other sources suggests that many of these divisions were organized in 1921. A portion of them had not maintained contact with the parent body through the 1926–28 period but remained on the books with active charters.

16. Reid, *Negro Immigrant*, 87–89, 221; James, *Holding Aloft the Banner of Ethiopia*; Dunn, *Black Miami*, 14–16, 124–27.

17. *GP* 1:lxxviii–lxxxiii.

18. See appendix D.

19. See reports of Andrew M. Battle to the Federal Bureau of Investigation, 20 July and 1 August 1922, *Marcus Garvey: FBI Investigation File*. (Files on this microfilm are not numbered but are in roughly chronological order.) On Garvey's relationship with Earnest Sevier Cox, cofounder of the Anglo-Saxon Clubs of America and author of numerous tracts against miscegenation, one of which he dedicated to Garvey, see Moten, "Racial Integrity or 'Race Suicide.'"

20. For a sampling of some of the best scholarship on Pan-Africanism and the African diaspora, see Lemelle and Kelley, *Imagining Home*.

21. Cronon, *Black Moses*.

22. Amy Jacques Garvey, *Garvey and Garveyism*, 139, 165.

23. Vincent, *Black Power and the Garvey Movement*, 20.

24. Clarke, *Marcus Garvey and the Vision of Africa*.

25. Martin, *Race First*, 16, 361–73.

26. *GP* 1:xci.

27. *Time*, 11 August 1924, 3–4; *Fayetteville Daily Democrat*, 3 September 1924, 2; *Morning News Review*, 15 August 1924, 2, and 4 September 1924, 2; *Atlanta Constitution*, 22 June 1923, 16; *Wichita Daily Times*, 1 October 1919, 11; *Wilmington Advocate*, 14 August 1920, 31.

28. *Savannah Tribune*, 14 September 1922.

29. Burkett, *Garveyism as a Religious Movement*; Burkett, *Black Redemption*.

30. Stein, *World of Marcus Garvey*.

31. Tolbert, *Universal Negro Improvement Association and Black Los Angeles*.

32. Before publication of his book-length study, Tolbert wrote a seminal article that turned the spotlight on the rank-and-file members of the UNIA and encouraged more local studies. See Tolbert, "Outpost Garveyism." Subsequent local studies include Gambrell [Rolinson], "Universal Negro Improvement Association in the Southern United States"; Rolinson, "UNIA in Georgia"; Bair, "Garveyism and Contested Political Terrain in 1920s Virginia"; Vought, "Racial Stirrings in Colored Town"; Close, "Black Southern Migration, Black Immigrants, Garveyism, and the Transformation of Black Hartford"; and Stephens, "Garveyism in Idlewild."

33. James, *Holding Aloft the Banner of Ethiopia*; Watkins-Owens, *Blood Relations*.

34. Earl Lewis, *In Their Own Interests*, 74–76.

35. Barbeau, *Unknown Soldiers*; John B. Kirby, *Black Americans in the Roosevelt Era*.

36. I have borrowed the very descriptive term "liberal integrationist framework" from a source that provides an authoritative and well-thought-out basis for breaking away from the traditional, intellectual paradigm through which scholars have continued to view questions of race: Hahn, *Nation Under Our Feet*, 6.

37. Two of the best volumes on the subject of the Great Migration are Harrison, *Black Exodus*; and Sernett, *Bound for the Promised Land*. For an indication of the vast literature on the Harlem Renaissance of the 1920s, see Margaret Perry, *Harlem Renaissance*. The classic work on black urbanization in this period is Osofsky, *Harlem*. Another recent demonstration of the abundance of scholarship on African American urban, rather than rural, life can be found in Higginbotham, Litwack, Hine, and Burkett, *Harvard Guide to African-American History*, 507–27.

38. Jack Temple Kirby, *Rural Worlds Lost*; Tolnay, *Bottom Rung*, 21.

39. The next two most common occupations were domestic/personal service, 28.6 percent, and manufacturing, 18.6 percent. U.S. Department of Commerce, Bureau of the Census, *Negroes in the United States*, 9, 287, 575. Population figures are rounded to the nearest 100,000.

40. Cohen, *At Freedom's Edge*; Daniel, *Shadow of Slavery*; Brundage, *Lynching in the New South*; Brundage, *Under Sentence of Death*; McMillen, *Dark Journey*; Tolnay and Beck, *Festival of Violence*.

41. There are notable exceptions and a growing literature on related subjects: see Hahn, *Nation Under Our Feet*; De Jong, *Different Day*; Woodruff, *American Congo*; Biegert, "Legacy of Resistance"; Hurt, *African American Life in the Rural South*; and Penningroth, *Claims of Kinfolk*.

42. Hahn, *Nation Under Our Feet*, 473.

43. Even these sources were precarious. Thompson, *Black Press in Mississippi*, documents the decrease in black newspapers during the 1920s and their primarily benign, church-related content.

44. After touring the United States for the first time in 1917, Garvey remarked in an early written statement, "The American Negro ought to compliment himself, as

well as the early prejudice of the South, for the racial progress made in fifty years, and for the discriminating attitude that has led the race up to the high mark of consciousness preserving it from extinction." *GP* 1:197.

45. See Garvey's discussion of African Fundamentalism in Hill, *Marcus Garvey: Life and Lessons*, 3–25.

46. Kipling, "White Man's Burden"; Dixon, *Clansman*, 216.

47. The UNIA constitution listed one of the organization's aims as spiritual redemption of Africans, the implication being to convert Africans from their indigenous religions to Western religious traditions, thereby redeeming their souls. See Davis and Sims, *Marcus Garvey*, 148. As early as 1914, when Garvey first organized the UNIA and African Communities League in Kingston, Jamaica, one of the stated objectives of the organization was "to assist in civilizing the backwards tribes of Africa" and "to promote a conscientious Christian worship among the native tribes of Africa." See *GP* 1:117.

48. *GP* 3:506.

49. See comments of Chandler Owen, coeditor of *The Messenger*, in *GP* 2:609; Johnson, *Growing Up in the Black Belt*, 243–44; Mays, *Born to Rebel*, 303.

50. See appendix C.

51. For a description of these women's protests, see James, *Holding Aloft the Banner of Ethiopia*, 138–40.

52. The term "micromobilizers" comes from the important sociological study of black women's leadership in the modern civil rights movement: Robnett, *How Long? How Long?* 13–15.

53. The UNIA parent body numbered local charters in the order in which they were issued, indicating a chronological order of organization. For further details, see appendix D.

54. Reid, *Negro Immigrant*, 85.

55. I found twenty "Sugar Bowl" UNIA division presidents or secretaries in the population schedules of the 1920 census. Many of these people lived in farming communities or on farms, but unlike their counterparts in southwest Georgia or the Delta, they were not typically farmers themselves.

56. De Jong, *Different Day*, 10–11.

57. Jahi Issa at Howard University has written a dissertation on the UNIA in Louisiana that is an important contribution to the study of a particularly unique brand of southern Garveyism. See Issa, "Universal Negro Improvement Association in Louisiana."

58. Carson, *In Struggle*.

59. Woodruff, *American Congo*.

60. For a general discussion of these transformations, see Kirby, *Black Americans in the Roosevelt Era*; and Sullivan, *Days of Hope*.

61. Robin D. G. Kelley, " 'Afric's Sons with Banner Red': African-American Communists and the Politics of Culture, 1919–1934," in *Imagining Home*, ed. Lemelle

and Kelley, 49; see also the introduction by Alex Lichtenstein in Kester, *Revolt among the Sharecroppers*.

62. Payne, *I've Got the Light of Freedom*; Dittmer, *Local People*; Curry, *Silver Rights*.

63. For an overview of Pan-Africanism and its shifting meanings and manifestations, see Lemelle and Kelley, *Imagining Home*, 1–8.

Chapter One

1. The preexisting traditions of black protest that preceded Garveyism have been studied in essays by two preeminent historians of African American history, August Meier and John Henrik Clarke. Neither, however, examined these assertions with the rural South specifically in mind. See Meier, "The Emergence of Negro Nationalism: A Study in Ideologies," in *Along the Color Line*, ed. Meier and Rudwick, 189–216; and Clarke, *Marcus Garvey and the Vision of Africa*.

2. *GP* 1:502. This phrasing is remarkably similar to the words of Sutton E. Griggs, a black historical novelist of the 1890s, in his *Imperium in Imperio*, 62.

3. *GP* 3:514, 2:111.

4. Beckert, "From Tuskegee to Togo," 498.

5. Harlan, "Booker T. Washington and the White Man's Burden," 442–44; extract from Booker T. Washington, *The Story of the Negro, 1909*, in Harlan, *Booker T. Washington Papers*, 1:411–12. For letters between Washington, the colonial societies, and agricultural experts from Tuskegee, see Harlan, *Booker T. Washington Papers*, 5:633–42; 6:26–27, 98–99, 110–11, 126–27, 142–43, 285–86, 417–18, 455–56, 480–81, 488–89, 494–95, 506–7; 7:425, 520–21; 8:127–28, 153–54, 288–89, 548–52; 9:231–33.

6. *Tuskegee Student*, 24 December 1910, 1, in Harlan, *Booker T. Washington Papers*, 10:512.

7. David Levering Lewis, *W. E. B. Du Bois*, 249–50.

8. Amy Jacques Garvey, *Philosophy and Opinions*, 56.

9. Oliver and Atmore, *Africa since 1800*, 122, 169.

10. For a discussion of how various groups of people with no land of their own to call a nation have adopted symbols, anthems, and rhetoric to create intellectual communities of nationalism, see Anderson, *Imagined Communities*.

11. Lynch, *Edward Wilmot Blyden*, 114–16.

12. Database search of 1920 U.S. Census Population Schedule, <http://www.ances try.com>.

13. Spence and Fleming, *History of Mitchell County*, 172–73.

14. Angell, *Bishop Henry McNeal Turner*, 134.

15. Quoted in ibid., 158.

16. Ibid., 175, 251. For documentation of the extensive emigrationist impulse in Arkansas, North Carolina, and Virginia, respectively, see Barnes, *Journey of Hope*; Clegg, *Price of Liberty*; and McGraw, "Richmond Free Blacks and African Colonization."

17. Angell, *Bishop Henry McNeal Turner*, 3–4.

18. Ibid., 47.

19. *Baltimore Afro-American*, [1917], Hampton University Newspaper Clipping File.

20. Angell and Pinn, *Social Protest Thought*, xviii.

21. Redkey, *Black Exodus*, 176–81.

22. *GP* 1:532–35; Rupert Lewis, *Marcus Garvey: Anti-Colonial Champion*, 25–28.

23. Rupert Lewis, *Marcus Garvey: Anti-Colonial Champion*, 26; Amy Jacques Garvey, *Garvey and Garveyism*, 7.

24. Redkey, *Black Exodus*, 30.

25. Ibid., 27–28; Turner quoted in Angell, *Bishop Henry McNeal Turner*, 137–38.

26. Staudenraus, *African Colonization Movement*.

27. Quoted in ibid., 198.

28. *Georgia Journal*, 16 May 1820, 2–3.

29. Bennett, "All Things to All People," 9; Egerton, "'Its Origin Is Not a Little Curious'"; *Georgia Journal*, 1 June 1819, 2–3; 22 June 1819, 3; 10 August 1819, 2; Gifford, "African Colonization Movement in Georgia"; Opper, "Mind of the White Participant in the African Colonization Movement"; *African Repository* 3 (February 1828): 369–70; McGraw, "Richmond Free Blacks and African Colonization"; Holder, "On Slavery," 339–40; Cohen, *At Freedom's Edge*.

30. Gifford, "African Colonization Movement in Georgia," 168.

31. Hahn, *Nation Under Our Feet*, 289–92; Formwalt, "Camilla Massacre of 1868."

32. Angell, *Bishop Henry McNeal Turner*, 133–40.

33. *American Colonization Society Records*, Incoming Correspondence 1819–1917, Domestic Letters, series 1A, container 284–95, reel 141. There are twelve microfilm reels for 1895–1917. From reel 141 alone I identified numerous letters of interest from southern farmers, including representatives from the southwest Georgia counties of Mitchell, Lowndes, and Clay; the Arkansas Delta counties of Mississippi, Woodruff, Jefferson, Monroe, Crittenden, and St. Francis; and the Yazoo-Mississippi Delta counties of Coahoma and Washington. For the specific letters mentioned in the text, see Kilgo to ACS, 23 January 1898, and application from Howell Station, Arkansas, 17 July 1892, both on reel 141. Kenneth Barnes and Steven Hahn have both mined the ACS correspondence files more thoroughly than I, and both of their recent books confirm very strong emigrationist sentiment among farmers in the cotton belt of the South. See Hahn, *Nation Under Our Feet*, 587 n. 70; and Barnes, *Journey of Hope*, 9.

34. Jackson to Addison, 17 July 1892, and Steele to Coppinger, 3 October 1892, both in *American Colonization Society Records*, series 1A, container 284, vol. 288, reel 141.

35. Lowe to ACS, 13 October 1892, and Ridgel to ACS, 4 December 1892, both in *American Colonization Society Records*, series 1A, container 284, vol. 288, reel 141.

36. Ridgel to Wilson, 1 June 1894, cited in Mitchell, "'Black Man's Burden,'" 86.

37. Nicholson to Coppinger, 2 May 1893, and Ellis to ACS, 1 August 1893, both in *American Colonization Society Records*, series 1A, container 284, vol. 288, reel 141.

38. Author interview (by phone) with Richard Perry, Brunswick, Ga., 6 April 1995.

39. Redkey, *Black Exodus*, 1, 5, 15.

40. Ibid., 32–37.

41. Quoted in Angell, *Bishop Henry McNeal Turner*, 264–65.

42. Ibid., 62.

43. Quoted in ibid., 228.

44. Ibid., 170–72.

45. Tony Martin, *Race First*, 347–48.

46. Redkey, *Black Exodus*, 293.

47. Sandy Martin, *Black Baptists and African Missions*, 38–39, 164, 189, 219.

48. *GP* 1:117.

49. Hill, *Marcus Garvey: Life and Lessons*, 209.

50. Walker, "Virtuoso Illusionist," 38.

51. Redkey, *Black Exodus*, 301.

52. There is a similar problem in placing Marcus Garvey in the spectrum of Pan-African thought. His affinity to Turner places him clearly in the early liberal-nationalist category, but his rhetoric also contains a clear anticolonial/resistance dimension that places him in later Afrocentric-nationalist historiography. Garveyism as nationalism or Pan-Africanism does not fit neatly or intuitively into critiques incorporating more recent dimensions of class and gender. For full explanations of these categorizations see Lemelle and Kelley, *Imagining Home*, 1–16.

53. Martin, *Black Baptists and African Missions*, 189–90.

54. Burkett, *Garveyism as a Religious Movement*, 34.

55. Angell, *Bishop Henry McNeal Turner*, 202.

56. Martin, *Black Baptists and African Missions*, 124–27, 164, 137–38.

57. Ibid., 221.

58. Of great significance to the understanding of how Turner and other African American missionaries paved the way for Garveyism and eventual independence of African nations is the fact that the precise areas of intense missionary activity coincide with the formation of UNIA divisions on the continent. UNIA divisions emerged in six African countries: Liberia (two), Gold Coast (now Ghana) (two), Sierra Leone (three), Nigeria (one), South Africa (eight), and Southwest Africa (now Namibia) (two). See Martin, *Race First*, 369–73; and Vinson, "Garvey Movement in South Africa."

59. Angell, *Bishop Henry McNeal Turner*, 225; Redkey, *Black Exodus*, 249.

60. "Fatherland" was used more often in the nineteenth century, especially by Turner, but Garvey almost always used "Motherland" to refer to Africa.

61. Angell, *Bishop Henry McNeal Turner*, 135; Redkey, *Black Exodus*, 22.

62. Redkey, *Black Exodus*, 39.

63. Patton, " 'Back-to-Africa' Movement in Arkansas," 167. Stanford had apparently left his AME position in disrepute for having allegedly embezzled funds. He

moved to Mississippi and later to Arkansas. See Angell, *Bishop Henry McNeal Turner*, 123.

64. Redkey, *Black Exodus*, 9.

65. Patton, " 'Back-to-Africa' Movement," 171–77.

66. Ibid., 174.

67. Redkey, *Black Exodus*, 171, 210–13, 220–24, 234.

68. Barnes, *Journey of Hope.*

69. Redkey, *Black Exodus*, 228.

70. *Atlanta Constitution*, 17–20 January 1891.

71. Redkey, *Black Exodus*, 150–69.

72. Painter, *Exodusters.*

73. *NW*, 21 June 1924, 14. The Knightons moved from Dawson, Georgia, in Terrell County in 1920 to Worth County, Georgia, in 1930. See U.S. Census, *Population Schedule*, Georgia, 1920 and 1930.

74. Hemmingway, "Booker T. Washington in Mississippi," 29–33.

75. August Meier, "Booker T. Washington and the Town of Mound Bayou," in *Along the Color Line*, ed. Meier and Rudwick, 217–37. See also Harlan, *Booker T. Washington*, 218.

76. Hemmingway, "Booker T. Washington in Mississippi," 36–37.

77. Ibid., 37.

78. Harlan, "Booker T. Washington and the White Man's Burden," 461.

79. Harlan, *Booker T. Washington.*

80. For family data on Booker T. Glass, see U.S. Census, *Population Schedule*, Monroe County, Arkansas, 1920. In the Social Security Death Index, 6,675 people were named Booker, and 2,199 of those were Booker T. In the 1920 census there were 1,200 Bookers and 305 Booker T.'s in the United States. Most of them were born in the period between 1900 and 1920 in the South, but many were born up into the 1950s. See <http://www.ancestry.com>. This gives an indication of the level of reverence for Washington among ordinary people.

81. For family data on Booker Simmons, see U.S. Census, *Population Schedule*, Monroe County, Arkansas, 1920. Another example is Booker T. Walker Sr. of McComb, Mississippi, born 6 August 1919. His son, Booker T. Walker Jr. of New Orleans, was interviewed by the author on 17 November 2001. He recalled the many other Booker T.'s he had met throughout his life and the common genesis of the name.

82. McMurray, *George Washington Carver*, 114–20.

83. Allen Jones, "Role of Tuskegee Institute in the Education of Black Farmers."

84. McMurray, *George Washington Carver*, 123–24.

85. Kramer, *George Washington Carver in His Own Words*, xvii.

86. Spence and Fleming, *History of Mitchell County*, 124.

87. *Savannah Tribune*, 20 November 1924; *NW*, 27 May 1922, 8.

88. Cronon, *Black Moses*, 16. Still in print, Washington's classic autobiography was first published in 1901.

89. See Harlan, *Booker T. Washington*, 280; Martin, *Race First*, 281.

90. *GP* 1:69 n. 1.

91. *GP* 1:25 n. 1; Harlan, *Booker T. Washington*, 274–76. Harlan, in "Booker T. Washington and the White Man's Burden," 461, makes the point that Washington and African nationalists imperfectly understood each other. Harlan believes that the segregation Washington accepted in his Atlanta Compromise was not equal to the separatism espoused by black nationalists. This became a serious problem for black integrationist leaders when Garvey introduced separatism into the segregated context of the United States.

92. *GP* 1:67 n. 3.

93. *GP* 1:116–17.

94. *GP* 1:166.

95. *GP* 1:186, 202, 246.

96. *Marcus Garvey: FBI Investigation File*, 15 January 1923. Files on this microfilm are not numbered but are in roughly chronological order.

97. U.S. Pardon Attorney Records, RG 204, box 1161, National Archives II, College Park, Md. (Quotation includes original errors in spelling and punctuation.)

98. Hemmingway, "Booker T. Washington in Mississippi," 42; Harlan, *Booker T. Washington*, 384.

99. Garvey's five-year plan for development of the UNIA and raising money included special instructions for places where the community had no "substantial" members such as educators, doctors, and lawyers. In these places, organizers were to specifically seek out ministers and convince them of the value of the UNIA program for the people and for strengthening their own congregations. See Hill, *Marcus Garvey: Life and Lessons*, 343–45.

100. U.S. Department of Commerce, Bureau of the Census, *Negroes in the United States*, 531–32; Burkett, *Black Redemption*, 157–80.

101. Burkett, *Garveyism as a Religious Movement*, 7.

102. For a discussion of this issue as it pertains to the modern civil rights movement, see Morris, *Origins of the Civil Rights Movement*.

Chapter Two

1. Grossman, *Black Workers in the Era of the Great Migration*, reel 22, 699–718; Marshall, *Labor in the South*, 26.

2. *GP* 2:119.

3. *GP* 1:504; 2:53, 57, 84.

4. Marshall, *Labor in the South*, 68.

5. *GP* 2:535.

6. *GP* 2:467.

7. *GP* 2:114–20.

8. *GP* 2:121.

9. Cronon, *Black Moses*, 53–55; Tony Martin, *Race First*, 156.

10. *GP* 2:202–3, 245.

11. *GP* 2:229.

12. *GP* 2:105.

13. Earl Lewis, *In Their Own Interests*, 72–76.

14. *GP* 2:492–93n; Cronon, *Black Moses*, 62–64.

15. *GP* 2:379.

16. *GP* 2:519.

17. Hill, *Marcus Garvey: Life and Lessons*, 344.

18. *GP* 2:518–19, 523.

19. *GP* 2:537.

20. Ibid.

21. *GP* 2:364–68.

22. *GP* 2:336.

23. *GP* 2:119–20.

24. *GP* 2:650, 3:163.

25. *NW*, 19 February 1921, 9.

26. See appendix B.

27. Reid, *Negro Immigrant*, 85–87, 221.

28. Palmer, *Pilgrims from the Sun*, 6–8.

29. *GP* 3:514.

30. Reid, *Negro Immigrant*, 193.

31. Palmer, *Pilgrims from the Sun*, 8; Vickerman, *Crosscurrents*, 40–41, 62, 92–93; Mohl, "Pattern of Race Relations in Miami," 342–43.

32. *GP* 1:479.

33. *GP* 3:91–92.

34. *GP* 3:247, 513–14.

35. *GP* 3:515.

36. Vought, "Racial Stirrings in Colored Town," 65–66; Dunn, *Black Miami in the Twentieth Century*.

37. *GP* 3:112, 247.

38. *NW*, 6 November 1920, 1.

39. There were at least five UNIA divisions and chapters in Jacksonville: #286 Jacksonville Division, #73 Jacksonville (Hearns) Chapter, #467 South Jacksonville Division, #16A West End (Jacksonville) Chapter, and #835 East Jacksonville Division. Division Card File, UNIAR.

40. *GP* 3:494–95.

41. *GP* 3:244–47, 494–95.

42. *GP* 3:375–76, 512–15.

43. T. C. Glashen apparently came back immediately to New York via Cuba. He represented Tennessee at the UNIA's 1921 convention, and at the 1922 conven-

tion he became the UNIA commissioner for the state of Tennessee. See *GP* 3:495, 786–89; and *NW*, 26 August 1922.

44. *GP* 3:512–15; *Miami Herald*, 2–3 July 1921.

45. Vought, "Racial Stirrings in Colored Town," 65.

46. *GP* 3:655–57.

47. Cronon, *Black Moses*, 112–18.

48. See remarks of Chandler Owen and A. Philip Randolph in *GP* 2:611; and Walker, "Virtuoso Illusionist," 35.

49. William Ferris, who organized UNIA branches in Connecticut, noted, after speaking at a church in Rockville, that "nearly every member of the church hails from South Carolina." *GP* 4:731; see also Close, "Black Southern Migration, Black Immigrants, Garveyism, and the Transformation of Black Hartford."

50. Grossman, *Black Workers in the Era of the Great Migration*, reel 1, 263–67.

51. *GP* 2:531.

52. *NW*, 6 November 1920, 10.

53. *GP* 2:650.

54. *NW*, 19 February 1921, 10.

55. *NW*, 3 September 1921, 11.

56. *GP* 4:829.

57. *NW*, 15 October 1921, 10.

58. *NW*, 2 July 1921, 9.

59. *GP* 1:322; Hill, *Marcus Garvey: Life and Lessons*, 423.

60. Robert A. Hill has explained the "retreat from radicalism" in the UNIA public rhetoric very clearly and logically. See *GP* 1:lxxviii–lxxxv. There is no doubt that Garvey's four-month difficulty in attaining a visa to reenter the United States in early 1921 was an important factor in the rhetorical modifications and apparent ideological shifts, which became pronounced after his readmission in June of that year. In North Carolina and other southern states, however, organizers had already begun to use different strategies based on the difficulties experienced in eastern Virginia and Florida and their familiarity with the southern racial status quo.

61. Corruption and fraud were ongoing problems, especially in the South, and the *Negro World* published numerous warnings to its readers in specific areas. For examples, see *NW*, 4 January, 15 July, and 7 December 1922, 21 April and 11 August 1923.

62. *NW*, 22 October 1921, 6.

63. *NW*, 21 January 1922, 10.

64. *NW*, 24 December 1921, 10.

65. Perry, *Hubert Harrison Reader*, 192–93.

66. *NW*, 9 October 1921, 1.

67. *NW*, 21 January 1922, 8.

68. *NW*, 12 May 1923, 9.

69. *NW*, 2 July 1921, 9.

70. *NW*, 2 September 1922, 3.

71. A thorough review of census data has revealed that Eason's family lived in Rich Square from at least 1880 to 1910. His father or grandfather was named Francis and was old enough to have been eleven years old in 1860. His mother or grandmother, Louisiana, was two years older. Eason was the only student of the eight at Livingstone described as mulatto rather than Negro, which indicates he must have been quite light-skinned. One wonders whether his obscure lineage may be an indication of his having had a white parent and/or having been adopted. These possibilities have great consequences given the racial ideology of Garveyism. See U.S. Census, *Population Schedules*, North Carolina, 1880 and 1910, <http://www.ancestry.com>.

72. Burkett, *Black Redemption*, 381–82; *NW*, 6 November 1920, 1.

73. *Star of Zion*, 8 September 1921, Hampton University Newspaper Clipping File, microfiche 469.

74. *NW*, 22 April 1922, 8.

75. *NW*, 2 July 1920.

76. Hill, *Marcus Garvey: Life and Lessons*, 381.

77. *New York Age*, 10 March 1923.

78. Report of James E. Amos, 23 August 1922, *Marcus Garvey: FBI Investigation File*.

79. Garvey scholars have provided a range of explications for the Eason affair. Judith Stein describes the Eason murder as political violence, which was endemic in the undisciplined and misdirected Garvey movement. Tony Martin states the facts of the case and is reluctant to speculate on Garvey's involvement, especially since nobody was ever convicted and punished by law. Randall Burkett's description of the Eason murder recognizes the very compelling circumstantial evidence implicating Garvey, while conceding that we will never know for certain if Garvey gave a direct order for the shooting. See Stein, *World of Marcus Garvey*, 171–85; Martin, *Race First*, 318–19; and Burkett, *Black Redemption*, 55–56.

80. *GP* 5:120 n. 3.

81. This article was enclosed with an unsigned letter to James Weldon Johnson of the NAACP and ended up in that organization's Garvey file. See *Papers of the NAACP, Part 11*, reel 35, file 899. See also *GP* 5:116–20. It is unclear which newspaper the article appeared in, although it was clearly a white state daily newspaper from North Carolina. The reporter was from Charlotte, and so it may have been the *Charlotte Observer*. U.S. Census, *Population Schedule*, North Carolina, 1930.

82. The speech and other controversial actions by the UNIA leader set off New York–based journalists on a relentless campaign to discredit Garvey. See *Messenger* 5 (January 1923): 561, 568–70; 5 (February 1923): 613; 5 (March 1923): 638; 5 (June 1923): 748; 5 (August 1923): 781; and 5 (October 1923): 835–36, 842. Also see the *Washington Post*, 5 February 1923, 1.

83. *Messenger* 5 (January 1923): 561.

84. *GP* 5:119 n. 1.

85. *Messenger* 5 (January 1923): 561; *Baltimore Afro-American*, 9 July 1920.

86. *NW*, 20 May 1922, 9.

87. *NW*, 11 October 1923, 7; *NW*, 5 May 1923, 8.

88. U.S. Department of Commerce, Bureau of the Census, *Negroes in the United States*, 9, 287, 575.

Chapter Three

1. U.S. Department of Commerce, Bureau of the Census, *Negroes in the United States*, 55.

2. *GP* 1:202.

3. UNIAR, reel 1, box 1, section A5, p. 55. The southern states I am examining were grouped as follows: District 3—Maryland, Virginia, Washington, D.C.; District 4—North Carolina, Tennessee, Kentucky; District 5—South Carolina, Georgia, Florida; District 8—Missouri, Kansas, Oklahoma, Arkansas; District 10—Alabama, Mississippi, Louisiana; and District 11—Texas, New Mexico, Arizona.

4. The text of the bill of rights was reproduced in the *Pittsburgh Courier* in 1930. See Hill, *Marcus Garvey: Life and Lessons*, 43–53.

5. Garvey disavowed editorials under his name in 1932. His control as managing editor became tenuous after a split in the organization in 1930. See Hill, *Marcus Garvey: Life and Lessons*, 414.

6. *GP* 1:382–83.

7. Higginbotham, *Righteous Discontent*, 76–77.

8. Hahn, *Nation Under Our Feet*, 326–27.

9. *Southwest Christian Advocate*, 26 June 1900.

10. Jordan, *Black Newspapers and America's War for Democracy*.

11. For the most part, the local and regional black newspapers that have survived from the late 1910s and 1920s ignored Garvey and his activities except where they involved scandals, his imprisonment, or his deportation and death. See Williams, "Newspapers Citations from the Tuskegee Archives," 16–37. Garvey's rivalry with leaders of the black elite and his alienation of many newspaper editors froze him out of most well-circulated black papers, except where unflattering news was possible. Notable examples of favorable coverage appear in the *Norfolk Journal and Guide* and the *Cotton Farmer* (Bolivar County, Mississippi).

12. Wolseley, *Black Press, U.S.A.*, 65–67.

13. Ibid., 54.

14. *GP* 1:386; U.S. Census, *Population Schedule*, Jefferson County, Arkansas, 1920.

15. *NW*, 22 February 1930, 1; *NW*, 1 March 1924, 1.

16. Jordan, *Black Newspapers and America's War for Democracy*, 32.

17. Cronon, *Black Moses*, xvii.

18. Julius Thompson, *Black Press in Mississippi*, 11.

19. *GP* 3:51.
20. Quoted in McMillen, *Dark Journey*, 174.
21. *NW*, 21 June 1924, 4.
22. Jordan, *Black Newspapers and America's War for Democracy*, 119–22; *GP* 1:386 n. 1.
23. Amy Jacques Garvey, *Philosophy and Opinions*, 240; Tony Martin, *Race First*, 316.
24. Garvey called people "race traitors" when they opposed him, suggesting that they would side with whites over blacks and thereby had abdicated their right to be leaders of blacks.
25. *NW*, 12 April 1924, 12.
26. Hill, *Marcus Garvey: Life and Lessons*, 378.
27. Burkett, *Black Redemption*, 65.
28. Ibid., 66–68.
29. Ferris, *African Abroad*, iii.
30. Ibid., 395.
31. *NW*, 2 December 1922, 2.
32. *GP* 5:xxxiv.
33. Burkett, *Black Redemption*, 65–70.
34. Quoted in ibid., 66.
35. *NW*, 6 November 1920, 2.
36. Burkett, *Black Redemption*, 65; Ferris, *African Abroad*, 301.
37. Ferris, *African Abroad*, 347.
38. *Star of Zion*, 8 September 1921; *NW*, 1 October 1921. These criticisms were aimed at J. W. H. Eason and William Ferris, both of whom had served as pastors in North Carolina before going north.
39. Issues of the *Crisis* that cover the UNIA or Garvey include the following dates: December 1920, January 1921, September 1922, January 1923, and May 1924.
40. Perry, *Hubert Harrison Reader*, 196–97.
41. Ibid., 197.
42. Perhaps it is more than an amazing coincidence that Bruce supplies this seemingly random connection between the leading proponent of black emigration to Liberia in the nineteenth century and the UNIA, an emigration-oriented group that appealed to much of the same southern constituency in the twentieth. We have much to learn by reading the very letters that Bruce would have filed from rural blacks all over the South who were desperate for information and assistance in emigrating to Liberia.
43. Thornbrough, *T. Thomas Fortune*, 358.
44. Seraile, *Bruce Grit*, 15.
45. Thornbrough, *T. Thomas Fortune*, 30.
46. Seraile, *Bruce Grit*, 189.
47. Ibid., 185.
48. Thornbrough, *T. Thomas Fortune*, 9.
49. Quoted in ibid., 73.

50. Ibid., ix–x, 175, 354.

51. Quoted in ibid., 361–62, from Fortune's periodical column "The Passing Show," in the *Norfolk Journal and Guide*, 13 December 1927.

52. Thornbrough, *T. Thomas Fortune*, 141–42.

53. Ibid., 144–45.

54. I believe this should have been S. V. Robertson, not H. V. Roberson as it was misprinted in the *Negro World*. There is a lot of activity reported by Sylvester Victor Robertson, and his name is regularly subjected to misspellings. *Negro World*, n.d. (ca. January 1921). This rare issue is held at University of California, Los Angeles, Center for African American Studies, Los Angeles, Calif.

55. *GP* 3:539–40.

56. *NW*, 25 February 1922, 8; *NW*, 4 March 1922, 9.

57. *GP* 4:792.

58. *NW*, 16 August 1924, 9.

59. *NW*, 29 March 1924, 3.

60. *GP* 4:729; Division Card File, UNIAR. A huge proportion of the UNIA divisions were between or near New Orleans and Baton Rouge right on the river, including eleven in or adjacent to New Orleans. Just south and east of New Orleans were eight more. Southwest of New Orleans were two divisions, and moving west and north along the river were twenty-seven UNIA divisions, including seven at Baton Rouge. Ten others were in the area immediately around Baton Rouge, and five others were within thirty to forty miles of Baton Rouge. Nine of Louisiana's UNIA divisions were in Natchitoches Parish in northwest Louisiana. Red River Parish, just north of Natchitoches, had one division at Armistead. There were four divisions in northeast Louisiana—three in Franklin Parish and one in Ouachita Parish at Luna. There was also a "Lemonville, Louisiana," division that was very active, though there was and is no such place in the state. The organizer's mailing address was Lauderdale, Louisiana, which is in the extreme southwest part of the state near Texas. There was, however, a place on the Texas-Louisiana border called Lemonville, which no longer exists. In the first three decades of the twentieth century, it was a short-lived sawmill town on the Texarkana and Fort Smith Railway. When local lumber was depleted, the town ceased to exist. Its largest estimated population was around 300. See "Lemonville, Texas," in the *Handbook of Texas Online*, <http://www.tsha.utexas.edu/handbook/online/articles/LL/htl10.html> (16 September 2004).Three unaccounted-for divisions in Louisiana include Arlington, Bermuda, and College Grove.

61. *GP* 3:539–43.

62. U.S. Pardon Attorney Records, RG 204, 42-793, box 1161, National Archives II, College Park, Md.

63. Nelson, "Organized Labor and the Struggle for Black Equality in Mobile," 965. Historian Robin D. G. Kelley has noted the relative weakness of Garveyism in

Alabama. Why the agricultural communities of this particular state might have eschewed Garveyism to the extent that they did is puzzling. Kelley's discussion of the Communist Party's success in organizing black workers in Alabama during the Depression years suggests a strong class consciousness among the state's black workers in a later decade, but this helps us little in understanding why Garveyism's "race first" ideology did not thrive there in the 1920s as it did in southwest Georgia. See Kelley, *Hammer and Hoe*, 8.

64. T. M. Campbell to L. N. Duncan, 9 February 1923, Office of Secretary of Agriculture, General Correspondence: Negroes, U.S. Secretary of Agriculture Records, RG 16, box 1, folder 1923, National Archives II, College Park, Md.

65. Letter to T. M. Campbell, 15 February 1923 (unsigned), and Marcus Garvey to Henry A. Wallace, 4 October 1923, both in ibid.

66. R. R. Moton to Marcus Garvey, 6 November 1923, in Williams, *Eight Negro Bibliographies*; *NW*, 24 November 1923, 2.

67. The history of divisions in the tiny villages of Inverness (Bullock County) and Neenah (Wilcox County), and the town of Selma (Dallas County), all in the central Alabama Black Belt, would be particularly interesting in light of events in the 1960s.

68. McFadden, "Septima P. Clark and the Struggle for Human Rights," 87.

69. For reports on the Charleston divisions and chapters see *NW*, 4 and 18 February, 4 and 11 March, 22 April, 9 July, and 5 August 1922; 20 January, 3 and 24 February, 17 March, 9 and 30 June, 25 August, 27 October 1923; 14 June 1924; and 18 May 1929. (Some of the above have several references per issue.)

70. *NW*, 4 February 1922, 10.

71. *NW*, 18 February 1922, 9.

72. *NW*, 27 October 1923, 3.

73. There are a number of sources for these statistics, none of which have identical or complete data for southern states and individual years, but all of which indicate a substantial drop in lynching after 1920. See <http://people.uncw.edu/hinese/HAL/HAL%20Web%20Page.htm> (26 May 2006) for lynching data from the Historic American Lynching Project (Project HAL) at the University of North Carolina at Wilmington; and Brundage, *Lynching in the New South*, 270–80.

74. Goings, *NAACP Comes of Age*, 10.

75. For more on the NAACP in Texas, see Reich, "Soldiers of Democracy," 1500–1504. See also Michael L. Gillette, "National Association for the Advancement of Colored People," *Handbook of Texas Online*, <http://www.tsha.utexas.edu/handbook/online/articles/NN/ven1.html> (26 May 2006).

76. *NW*, 3 June 1922; *GP* 4:649–50.

77. *Dallas Express*, 3 June 1922, Hampton University Newspaper Clipping File, microfiche 470.

78. *GP* 1:536–47.

79. *NW*, 11 August 1923, 7.

80. *GP* 2:169–70; *NW*, 29 October 1921, 11; *NW*, 11 February 1922, 10; *NW*, 4 March 1922, 8.

81. *GP* 6:578–83.

82. U.S. Department of Commerce, Bureau of the Census, *Fourteenth Census*, vol. 3: *Population Composition*, 201–27.

83. Grossman, *Black Workers in the Era of the Great Migration*, reel 22, 728–37, 746.

84. *Rand McNally Commercial Atlas*, 54th ed., 219.

85. Author interview (by phone) with Richard Perry, Brunswick, Ga., 6 April 1995; author interview with Fannie Kaigler of Tift, Berrien, and Glynn Counties, Ga., in Brunswick, Ga., 2 April 1995.

86. *NW*, 5 March 1921, 2.

87. *NW*, 16 April 1921, 8; author interview with Richard Perry.

88. See appendix E.

89. Burkett, *Black Redemption*, 9, 51.

90. Hill, *Marcus Garvey: Life and Lessons*, 53; *GP* 2:563. Cyril Crichlow and Isaac Newton Brathwaite were the stenographers for the thirty-one-day convention in 1920. They were paid $100 a day to record all of the proceedings. See Perry, *Hubert Harrison Reader*, 198. Halton's name was incorrectly recorded as "Holum," probably because the stenographer did not have the opportunity to check name spelling. U.S. Census, *Population Schedules*, Georgia, 1910, 1920.

91. *NW*, 16 April 1921, 8.

92. *NW*, 4 June 1921, 9; Division Card File, UNIAR.

93. This phenomenon will be examined in chapter 6. The influence of the black elite of Atlanta and its close ties with the surrounding piedmont region may explain how Garveyism never took hold there. According to division charter numbers, Georgia's divisions were organized in the following order prior to August 1921: Brunswick, Fitzgerald, Baxley, Camilla, Kimbrough (Webster County), Waycross, Alma, Moultrie, Gardi, and Jesup. The parent body issued the next wave of charters as follows: Patterson, TyTy, Shingler, Coverdale, Oakfield, Pooler, Charity Grove (Worth County), Sylvester, Atlanta, Haylow, Limerick. We do not know when the remaining nine divisions received charters. See also appendix D.

94. Davis and Sims, *Marcus Garvey*, 147–70.

95. *NW*, 5 March 1921, 6.

96. *NW*, 30 September 1922, 8.

97. *NW*, 15 March 1924, 12.

98. *NW*, 27 March 1921, 2.

99. For a complete text of this address, so reminiscent of Martin Luther King Jr.'s "I Have a Dream" speech, see *NW*, 4 March 1922, 10. S. V. Robertson was misidentified here as U. S. Robinson. Robertson served as UNIA commissioner for Georgia in 1922 before becoming high commissioner for Louisiana, Mississippi, and Alabama in 1923. See *NW*, 9 December 1922, 7.

100. *NW*, 27 May 1922, 8.

101. *NW*, 7 October 1922, 8; Hill, *Marcus Garvey: Life and Lessons*, 51.

102. *NW*, 18 March 1922, 8; *NW*, 15 April 1922, 9.

103. *NW*, 22 September 1923, 7.

104. These ads were still appearing every week as late as 24 June 1922. See *NW*, 24 June 1922, 10.

105. For a discussion of the historiographical trend that emphasizes community networks among migrants and their home communities, see Trotter, *Great Migration in Historical Perspective.*

106. Hoare and Smith, *Selections from the Prison Notebooks of Antonio Gramsci*, 6–10. Gramsci explains in the late 1920s that intellectuals who emerged from the peasantry tended to align with other social groups. He tentatively discusses the possibilities for African American intellectuals and is very perceptive in his analysis of what amounts to the mass leadership of a Garvey-style leader. See ibid., 21.

107. Mays and Nicholson, *Negro's Church*, 239–53.

108. Rogers, "Elaine Race Riots of 1919," 143–44; Cortner, *Mob Intent on Death*; Stockley, *Blood in Their Eyes*; Desmarais, "Military Intelligence Reports on Arkansas Riots."

109. Division Card File, UNIAR. The six most dynamic Mississippi UNIA divisions located within a fifty-mile radius of Elaine (Phillips County), Arkansas, included Clarksdale (Coahoma County), Merigold and East Mound Bayou (Bolivar County), Lambert (Quitman County), and Sumner and Vance (Tallahatchie County).

110. *Rand McNally Commercial Atlas*, 61st ed., 89–96; *Rand McNally Commercial Atlas*, 54th ed., 397.

111. E. J. Kerwin to the Chief, Bureau of Investigation (Pine Bluff, Ark.), *GP* 1:386.

112. *NW*, 9 December 1922, 5; *NW*, 31 December 1927, 3.

113. *NW*, 24 June 1922, 10.

114. *NW*, 6 October 1923, 7; *NW*, 9 August 1924, 11.

115. E. B. McKinney, the black vice president of the Southern Tenant Farmers Union in the mid-1930s, was a minister and a Garveyite. He was from Marked Tree, Crittenden County, in the heart of the east Arkansas Delta, and by 1930 he resided in Tyronza, Poinsett County. See E. B. McKinney–related correspondence in *STFU Papers*, April 1936–December 1938, particularly 29 July 1938, and 3, 11, 23 August 1938 (J. R. Butler to Norman Thomas), reel 2.

116. J. R. Butler to Norman Thomas, 23 August 1938, and E. B. McKinney to J. R. Butler, 31 August 1938, *STFU Papers*, reel 2.

117. *Arkansas Gazette*, 19 October 1919, 2.

118. Division Card File, UNIAR.

119. U.S. Census, *Population Schedule*, Arkansas, 1920.

120. *NW*, 1922–24. Contributions arrived weekly and were reported often, but for a

particularly notable example of support from Blytheville, Armorel, Cotton Plant, and Twist, Arkansas, see *NW*, 28 October 1922, 10. Reports show fifty-two donations from Blytheville alone.

121. *NW*, 16 August 1924, 2.
122. *NW*, 7 June 1924, 12; *NW*, 5 April 1924, 12.
123. *NW*, 23 February 1924, 12; *NW*, 17 May 1924, 12.
124. U.S. Census, *Population Schedule*, Arkansas, 1920; *Rand McNally Commercial Atlas*, 61st ed., 93.
125. *NW*, 25 March 1922, 2; *NW*, 22 April 1922, 2; *NW*, 5 August 1922, 12.

Chapter Four

1. Stein, *World of Marcus Garvey*, 144. I have found this class status to be true for all areas of the South, especially those rural areas under close examination. Earl Lewis has found the same general lower status to be true for Garveyites in the Norfolk area. See Lewis, *In Their Own Interests*, 74–75.
2. Odum, *Southern Regions of the United States*; see also Vance, *Human Geography of the South*. Most crucial to this study is Charles S. Johnson, *Statistical Atlas of Southern Counties*.
3. Neil McMillen has thoroughly analyzed and dispensed with this notion in his studies of the meaning of the Great Migration from Mississippi. See McMillen, "The Migration and Black Protest in Jim Crow Mississippi," in *Black Exodus*, ed. Harrison, 83–97.
4. Brundage, *Lynching in the New South*, 12–13. See also Schultz, *Rural Face of White Supremacy*.
5. U.S. Department of Commerce, Bureau of the Census, *Negroes in the United States*, 48.
6. Ibid., 9, 48, 287, 575.
7. Jack Temple Kirby, *Rural Worlds Lost*, 275.
8. U.S. Department of Commerce, Bureau of the Census, *Statistical Atlas of the United States*, 183, 202, 207, 209, 211.
9. See map 2, which shows the thirty-four locations of UNIA divisions in Georgia. There were dozens of other locations from which letters to the *Negro World* and contributions to UNIA funds originated.
10. For detailed data, refer to appendix F. For data on Georgia Garveyites from other parts of the state, see Rolinson, "UNIA in Georgia," 206.
11. See map 3, which shows UNIA division locations in Mississippi and Arkansas. At least 35 others in those states sent letters or contributions though they did not belong to chartered UNIA divisions.
12. Barnes, *Journey of Hope*, 35–39.
13. See appendix F.
14. U.S. Department of Commerce, Bureau of the Census, *Negroes in the United States*, 75.

15. These were in Beulah, Bolivar, West Boyle, Cleveland, East Cleveland, West Cleveland, Malvina, Merigold, Merigold (chapter), East Merigold, West Merigold, Mound Bayou, East Mound Bayou, Pace, Renova, Shelby, and Symond.

16. *GP* 5:745.

17. *NW*, 3 May 1924, 8.

18. *NW*, 16 August 1924, 9.

19. *NW*, 4 August 1923, 7; *NW*, 22 September 1923, 7; *NW*, 9 August 1924, 11.

20. U.S. Pardon Attorney Records, RG 204, box 1161, National Archives II, College Park, Md.

21. *NW*, 15, 22, 29 September 1923, 8.

22. Johnson, *Statistical Atlas of Southern Counties*, 4–6.

23. Genovese, *Roll, Jordan, Roll*; Hahn, *Nation Under Our Feet*.

24. Woodson, *Rural Negro*, 11; Wirt A. Williams, *History of Bolivar County, Mississippi*.

25. Oklahoma had dozens of all-black towns, and four of them, Bookertee, Porter, Red Bird, and Tullahassee, had a branch of the UNIA. See Woodson, *Rural Negro*, 11; Barnes, *Journey of Hope*, 178; and Tony Martin, *Race First*, 366.

26. Brundage, *Lynching in the New South*, 106.

27. *Progressive Farmer*, December 1909, Hampton University Newspaper Clipping File, microfiche 5.

28. Jack Temple Kirby, "Clarence Poe's Vision of a Segregated 'Great Rural Civilization.'"

29. Johnson, *Statistical Atlas of Southern Counties*, 17–26. Johnson uses the 1930 census for these statistics.

30. Although not included in the census data provided in appendix F, only a few of the Garveyites' children of school age had not attended school in the year between 1 January 1919 and 1 January 1920. Only a few were listed as illiterate.

31. Jacqueline Jones, *Labor of Love, Labor of Sorrow*, 156.

32. Kirby, *Rural Worlds Lost*, 277–78.

33. Ibid., 53, 276–78.

34. U.S. Department of Commerce, Bureau of the Census, *Negroes in the United States*, 596–97.

35. Daniel, *Breaking the Land*, 3.

36. In 1920 Helena, Arkansas, had a population that was only 50 percent black, while the surrounding Phillips County was 73.9 percent black. Albany, Georgia, was less than half black, while Dougherty County was 66 percent black. U.S. Department of Commerce, Bureau of the Census, *Negroes in the United States*, 56–57, 692, 705.

37. King Cole to Calvin Coolidge, 22 March 1927, U.S. Pardon Attorney Records, RG 204, box 1161, National Archives II, College Park, Md.

38. *NW*, 23 February 1924, 12.

39. *NW*, 19 July 1924, 9.

40. Smith, *Conjuring Culture*, 55–70.

41. Mays and Nicholson, *Negro's Church*, 241–53.

42. Burkett, *Black Redemption*, 10.

43. Kenneth J. King, "Some Notes on Arnold J. Ford," in *Black Apostles*, ed. Burkett and Newman, 49–52.

44. Burkett, *Garveyism as a Religious Movement*, 36, 77.

45. *NW*, 19 July 1924, 14.

46. *NW*, 21 June 1924, 14.

47. See especially *Negro World* issues between 1923 and 1924. For individual letters to the president and pardon attorney urging pardon and clemency for Garvey after his conviction, see U.S. Pardon Attorney Records, RG 204, boxes 1159–61, and U.S. Department of Justice Records, RG 60, box 3053, National Archives II, College Park, Md.

48. Robertson's commission expired in December 1922. Later he began intensive organization in Louisiana and Mississippi. Eason and Garvey developed a rift that became public at the 1922 convention. See *NW*, 2 September 1922, 2; and *NW*, 9 December 1922, 7.

49. U.S. Census, *Population Schedule*, Georgia, 1920; Hill, *Marcus Garvey: Life and Lessons*, 52.

50. *NW*, 4 March 1922, 10.

51. See appendix F for complete census data on southwest Georgia UNIA leaders, members, and contributors.

52. I identified two women who served as division president and forty-six women who served as secretary to their division in the southern states. Many divisions had separate ladies' divisions, which are only observable through *Negro World* reports and not through fragmentary division card records. See appendix G.

53. *NW*, 10 June 1922, 8.

54. *NW*, 4 August 1923, 7. The Baxley division remained in the UNIA card files through 1927, although we know little about its activities from that later time.

55. *NW*, 18 March 1922, 8.

56. U.S. Census, *Population Schedule*, Georgia, 1930; Census of Worth County, Georgia, 1920, <http://www.ancestry.com>.

57. *NW*, 15 April 1922, 9. The Ousleys continue to have a presence at their church, New Mount Pleasant Baptist Church, and have a male relative, a Vietnam casualty, buried at their Coverdale branch's cemetery.

58. *NW*, 3 May 1925, 8; *NW*, 22 September 1923, 7; *NW*, 4 August 1923, 7; "Defense Fund" contributions, *NW*, 11 November 1922, 10.

59. Author interview with Lee McCarty, Merigold, Miss., 19 February 2005; author interview (by phone) with Lee McCarty, 5 August 2005.

60. *NW*, 7 May 1921, 2; U.S. Census, *Population Schedule*, Georgia, 1920.

61. *Papers of the NAACP, Part 1*, reel 2, file 574.

62. U.S. Census, *Population Schedule*, Georgia, 1920.

63. U.S. Census, *Population Schedule*, Arkansas, 1930; *NW*, 18 June 1921, 1.

64. Author interview with David Carter, Jonas Odom's grandson, Toledo, Ohio, 14 June 1995, 3 March 1999, and 8 October 2003; Baker County Historical Society, *History of Baker County*, 224–25 (on Jonas's father, James Childs Odom, see p. 352). *NW*, 12 December 1921, 9, shows Odom's five-dollar donation to the African Redemption Fund; also see Odom-Carter Papers, Special Collections, Woodruff Library, Emory University, Atlanta, Ga. Ann Odom Bush, a distant white relative of Jonas Odom, acknowledged that there was a connection to the black Odoms through one of Jonas's sons, Joel (also known as Pince), but that her side of the family was not clear on or particularly interested in the specifics. Author interview with Ann Odom Bush, Newton, Ga., 8 October 2003.

65. For a thorough discussion of the black middle class in Arkansas, see Gordon, *Caste and Class*; see also Moneyhon, "Delta Towns," 219.

66. Holley, "Plantation Heritage."

67. U.S. Department of Commerce, Bureau of the Census, *Negroes in the United States*, xvi.

68. Moneyhon, "Delta Towns," 213–14.

69. *NW*, 15 September 1923, 8; *NW*, 22 September 1923, 8; *NW*, 29 September 1923, 8.

70. Woodruff, *American Congo*, 88.

71. See appendix F; U.S. Census, *Population Schedule*, Arkansas, 1920 (the mulatto designation was determined by the census enumerator, not the people within the household). Indian Bay, Arkansas (Monroe County), happens to be one division about which there is more evidence than others. Some of the UNIAR file cards include fragments of data on Indian Bay from 1922 to 1925. The information is written on the back of cards that were reused for another purpose.

72. Raper, *Tragedy of Lynching*, 94–106.

73. Williams, *History of Bolivar County*.

74. Crockett, *Black Towns*, 104.

75. *Cotton Farmer*, 5 February 1927; Kirby, *Rural Worlds Lost*, 54–55; Martin, *Race First*, 372.

76. Johnson, *Statistical Atlas of Southern Counties*, 37.

77. *Crisis*, September 1918, 221–23.

78. *GP* 1:501.

79. James Weldon Johnson, *Along This Way*, 334.

80. Johnson, *Statistical Atlas of Southern Counties*, 66, 113, 162.

81. Cortner, *Mob Intent on Death*, 1–2.

82. Rogers, "Elaine Race Riots of 1919," 143–44.

83. Woodruff, *American Congo*, 91.

84. McMillen, *Dark Journey*, 135.

85. The notoriety of the Phillips County riots comes from the extensive coverage and active participation by the NAACP in the legal defense of the convicted murderers. See Cortner, *Mob Intent on Death*, 1–2, 30–31, 39–40.

86. *Arkansas Gazette*, 12 October 1919, 1.

87. Biegert, "Legacy of Resistance," 98 n. 49; *NW*, 6 October 1923, 7.

88. Though not focusing on the South exclusively, Randall Burkett has explored Garveyism's role as a black civil religion in *Garveyism as a Religious Movement*.

Chapter Five

1. Sandy D. Martin, *Black Baptists and African Missions*, 189.

2. For examples, see *Messenger* 5 (March 1923): 638.

3. Hill, *Marcus Garvey: Life and Lessons*, 43, 46, 48.

4. Ibid., 52, 347.

5. The most striking examples of loyalty in the rural South occurred during Garvey's initial imprisonment in the summer of 1923. See the hundreds of donations to the Marcus Garvey Defense Fund recorded in the *Negro World* between June and September of that year. For individual letters to the president and pardon attorney urging pardon and clemency for Garvey after his conviction, see U.S. Pardon Attorney Records, RG 204, boxes 1159–61, and U.S. Department of Justice Records, RG 60, box 3053, National Archives II, College Park, Md.

6. *NW*, 16 July 1927, 3.

7. *NW*, 6 August 1927, 4.

8. *Messenger* 5 (February 1923): 616.

9. From the *New York World*, 18 August 1922, reprinted in *GP* 4:917–18.

10. Thanks to Dr. Janet Hudson of Winthrop College for finding this information and sharing it with me. See Governor Robert A. Cooper Papers, S535001, box 3, current situation folder, H.S.B. Reports, 4 December 1920, South Carolina Department of Archives and History, Columbia, S.C.

11. *NW*, 3 September 1921, 11.

12. Bernard West's interview with Arthur Idlett, Living Atlanta Collection, MSS 637, box 37, folder 13, Atlanta History Center, Atlanta, Ga.; *NW*, 2 July 1921, 9; Vought, "Racial Stirrings in Colored Town," 66–67.

13. Walter White, *Rope and Faggot*, 112; Hall, *Revolt against Chivalry*, 60–61.

14. Tolnay and Beck, *Festival of Violence*, 89–93.

15. *Fayetteville Daily Democrat*, 15 December 1923, 1; *Reno Evening Gazette*, 15 December 1923; *Wichita Daily Times*, 15 December 1923, 1; *NW*, 29 December 1923, 2. For a more detailed and slightly different account of the incident, see Woodruff, *American Congo*, 138–39. Fannie Lou Hamer recalled the lingering effect of this very drastic event in her hometown of Drew; see Lee, *For Freedom's Sake*, 16–17.

16. *NW*, 19 January 1924, 2.

17. *NW*, 26 November 1921, 7.

18. Jones, *Labor of Love, Labor of Sorrow*, 336–42. Amy Jacques Garvey's attitudes, as expressed through her writings in the *Negro World* and the "Women's Page" that she edited, indicate a more complicated relationship with the men of her race. Ula Taylor, her biographer, outlines the complexity of Jacques Garvey's politics and calls her ultimately a "community feminist." Jacques Garvey espoused and

promoted traditional gender roles of mother and helpmate, but she also wanted individual women to serve the community on an equal plane with men. Apparently she, like her husband, wanted there to be a place for every woman in the movement. For most black women, their circumstances limited their goals and options. Like Jacques Garvey, some black women who had moved to cities and gained some measure of higher education and class status began to seek more than just the race's right to protect their families and determine their sexuality and reproduction. Jacques Garvey tried to remain open to the views and sentiments of lesser-educated women in the movement, but she insisted that only well-written letters and editorials would be printed on the Women's Page of the *Negro World*. She urged less literary women to get help in writing opinion pieces, but this editorial policy eliminated letters that might have revealed the priorities and motives of rural women who may not have had anyone to help with their language and prose. See Taylor, *Veiled Garvey*, 69.

19. Jones, *Labor of Love, Labor of Sorrow*, 108–9. Jones's work remains the best we have on rural black working women. Hunter, *To 'Joy My Freedom*, is an example of the creative use of sources combined with theory and imagination to illuminate a world unknown and almost unknowable: the agency of domestic workers in Atlanta in resisting their own domination and control by white society. Darlene Clark Hine's seminal article, "Rape and the Inner Lives of Black Women," describes how in protecting themselves from their vulnerability in the workplace, black women often intentionally masked their true feelings and created a "cult of secrecy" while simultaneously creating an appearance of openness and disclosure. Ironically, this self-preservation strategy, particularly in black women's attempts to control their own sexuality and reproduction, has resulted in keeping their true feelings from being expressed in ways that historians would find useful.

20. For a brilliant exposition of this argument, see Deborah Gray White, *Ar'n't I a Woman?* Jacqueline Jones also asserts this "race first" position of rural, agricultural women in *Labor of Love, Labor of Sorrow*, 6.

21. See appendix G.

22. Jones, *Labor of Love, Labor of Sorrow*, 107.

23. *Raleigh Gazette*, 5 February 1898, cited in Gilmore, *Gender and Jim Crow*, 70–71.

24. Carby, " 'On the Threshold of the Women's Era,' " 268–70.

25. Hine, "Rape and the Inner Lives of Black Women," 912–13.

26. Carby, " 'On the Threshold of the Women's Era,' " 268–70.

27. Griffin, "Black Feminists and Du Bois."

28. "Protection of Women," unidentified clipping in Hampton University Newspaper Clipping File, microfiche 493.

29. S. Willie Layton, leader of the Women's Conference within the National Baptist Convention (NBC), was an exceptional voice on the issue of protection who showed concern for black women from all walks of life and all regions. Layton was raised in Memphis and Fort Smith, Arkansas, and became the most out-

spoken advocate of women's rights in the Baptist denomination in the early 1900s. Prior to the rise of Garveyism, she organized the Association for the Protection of Colored Women and spoke for non-elite, working black women in the executive board meetings of the Women's Conference. Concern for marginalized working women and their protection no doubt found its way to the male church leadership and dovetailed with the patriarchal, normative gender roles espoused within the NBC. Just as Amy Jacques Garvey pushed the envelope within the UNIA hierarchy, Layton also challenged the NBC, but to limited avail. See Higginbotham, *Righteous Discontent*, 157–58, 204–10.

30. *NW*, 20 August 1921, 5.

31. *NW*, 29 October 1921.

32. Mitchell, " 'Black Man's Burden' "; for a broader discussion of this issue, see Mitchell, "Adjusting the Race." In her most recent work, Mitchell also sees gender roles, especially motherhood and childbearing, as the defining purpose of women expected within the UNIA. As such, she concludes that Garveyism basically blamed miscegenation solely on black women and became an excuse for black men to punish and control black women. See Mitchell, *Righteous Propagation*, 224–39.

33. Even Evelyn Brooks Higginbotham's probing work, *Righteous Discontent*, which gives attention to the common people and their issues through Layton and others, deals mainly in the context of problems caused by urbanization and equates common people to domestic workers. See esp. 171–72, 212.

34. *NW*, 18 March 1922, 8.

35. *NW*, 1 April 1922, 2.

36. Amy Jacques Garvey, *Philosophy and Opinions*, 37.

37. *NW*, 18 March 1922, 8.

38. *NW*, 1 April 1922, 4.

39. *NW*, 15 December 1923, 4.

40. *NW*, 1 April 1922, 4.

41. *NW*, 23 April 1921, 1.

42. See *NW*, 12 January 1924, 3; *NW*, 27 October 1923, 1; *Worth County Local*, 3 February 1922, 1. For general studies of the antilynching campaigns, see Grant, *Anti-Lynching Movement*; and Zangrando, *NAACP Crusade against Lynching*.

43. U.S. Senate, *Congressional Record of the 67th Congress*, 3d sess., 20 November–4 December 1922, 406.

44. *NW*, 19 August 1922, 8.

45. Ibid.

46. Ibid.

47. *NW*, 27 October 1923, 3.

48. *Atlanta Constitution*, 24 September 1906.

49. *NW*, 15 July 1922, 12.

50. *GP* 4:707–14.

51. *NW*, 3 March 1923, 1.

52. Tolnay and Beck, *Festival of Violence*, 157–60.

53. Moseley, "Political Influence of the Ku Klux Klan in Georgia."

54. *GP* 3:82–83. The New York Fifteenth was a black regiment that served the U.S. Army in World War I.

55. For examples, see *Marcus Garvey: FBI Investigation File*. Letters are organized chronologically, and many letters and agent reports from July 1922 refer to UNIA leaders and New York division members who allegedly were upset over Garvey's Klan meeting (especially UNIA musical director Arnold J. Ford) and to some who intended to resign the movement because of it (namely, William H. Ferris).

56. *Atlanta Constitution*, 22 August 1922, 14.

57. *Atlanta Constitution*, 8 February 1923, 16.

58. Stein, *World of Marcus Garvey*, 158.

59. Ibid.

60. *Papers of the NAACP, Part 11*, reel 35 (hereinafter cited as NAACP Garvey File), 619–21, 628, 865–66.

61. *NW* clipping, n.d., NAACP Garvey File, 705.

62. Pickens, *Heir of Slaves*, 7, 22–30, 111–12.

63. William Pickens to Marcus Garvey, July 1922, NAACP Garvey File, 783–86.

64. *NW*, 16 August 1924, 3.

65. *GP* 5:684–87.

66. U.S. Congress, Records of the 69th Congress, RG 46, Judiciary Committee, box 133, National Archives, Washington, D.C.

67. Robinson, "Most Shamefully Common."

68. Gilmore, *Gender and Jim Crow*, 95–96.

69. Kirby, *Rural Worlds Lost*, 236–37.

70. See statistics of women in households in appendix F; and U.S. Department of Commerce, Bureau of the Census, *Negroes in the United States*, 17, 116.

71. *NW*, 19 May 1923, 3.

72. Hill, *Marcus Garvey: Life and Lessons*, 45–47.

73. See Drake, *Redemption of Africa and Black Religion*, for an explanation of the historical origins of the idea of African redemption and how it was a consistent theme in African American religion.

74. Martin, *Race First*, 128. By the summer of 1924, shipping companies were encouraged to deny passage to anyone affiliated with the UNIA.

75. Amy Jacques Garvey, *Philosophy and Opinions*, 66.

76. Ibid., 95.

77. *NW*, 24 May 1924, 12.

78. *NW*, 4 August 1923, 7.

79. *NW*, 19 January 1924, 7.

80. *NW*, 7 June 1924, 12.

81. Vincent, *Black Power and the Garvey Movement*, 178–85.

82. Davis and Sims, *Marcus Garvey*, 169–70.

83. *NW*, 17 May 1924, 12.

84. *NW*, 22 December 1923, 7.

85. *NW*, 21 June 1924, 4.

86. *NW*, 14 June 1924, 10.

87. *NW*, 19 July 1924, 14.

88. *NW*, 21 June 1924, 14.

89. *NW*, 5 July 1924, 14.

90. Amy Jacques Garvey, *Philosophy and Opinions*, 18.

91. Vincent, *Black Power and the Garvey Movement*, 178.

92. *State* (Columbia, S.C.), 28 April 1924.

93. *NW*, 12 July 1924, 9.

94. *NW*, 27 October 1923, 3.

95. *Messenger* 5 (January 1923): 577.

96. *NW*, 16 August 1924, 2.

97. *NW*, 2 August 1924, 16.

98. Author interview with Fannie Kaigler, Brunswick, Ga., 2 April 1995.

99. *NW*, 7 June 1924, 12.

100. Martin, *Race First*, 126–37.

101. Vincent, *Black Power and the Garvey Movement*, 183.

102. Taylor, *Veiled Garvey*, 56–62.

103. *NW*, 15 July 1922, 2.

104. *NW*, 12 January 1924, 9.

105. *NW*, 12 July 1924, 9.

106. *NW*, 19 July 1924, 14.

107. *NW*, 19 January 1924, 7.

108. Ezekiel 37:11–14.

109. *NW*, 31 May 1924, 8.

110. *NW*, 15 March 1924, 12.

111. *NW*, 7 June 1924, 12.

112. *NW*, 4 August 1923, 7.

113. *Atlanta Constitution*, 17 July 1923, 5.

114. *NW*, 28 July 1923, 9.

115. Rolinson, "Garvey Movement," 303.

116. U.S. Department of Justice Records, RG 60, box 3053; U.S. Pardon Attorney Records, RG 204, box 1159–61; both in National Archives II, College Park, Md.

117. Punctuation, capitalization, and spelling have been transcribed exactly from U.S. Pardon Attorney Records, RG 204, box 1161, National Archives II, College Park, Md.

118. UNIA music director Arnold J. Ford spoke a number of times to FBI secret agents in New York who were following Garvey's activities closely throughout 1922. In each of these conversations, Ford discussed Garvey's southern strategy,

which included plans to stockpile arms, march a black army south, and take over the states below the Mason-Dixon Line. Ford registered his personal disapproval of Garvey's Klan summit by describing it as Garvey's way of helping to drive southern blacks back to Africa. These two pronouncements were obviously contradictory, but one wonders if Ford were not revealing that Garvey had openly contemplated different clandestine southern strategies, of which northern members disapproved. Ford seemed loathe to defend against all the criticism that Garvey had taken, particularly from other race leaders in the North. *Marcus Garvey: FBI Investigation File*, 17 and 28 July 1922.

Chapter Six

1. Frazier, "Garvey," 147–48.
2. This tenet of Garveyism carried over from established organizations like Booker T. Washington's National Negro Business League.
3. U.S. Department of Commerce, Bureau of the Census, *Negroes in the United States*, 70.
4. Ibid., 74–76. For the years 1910, 1920, and 1930, Bolivar dropped from 87.4 to 82.4 to 74.0 percent Negro; Phillips dropped from 78.6 to 73.9 to 67.0 percent; Monroe dropped from 62.9 to 61.0 to 55.7 percent; and Baker dropped from 71.7 to 67.7 to 61.3 percent. The black percentage for Tallahatchie County, Mississippi, hovered consistently around 69.0 percent for the twenty-year period, while the populations of Worth and Mitchell Counties in Georgia remained fairly consistently around 50.0 percent for the same time frame.
5. Ibid., 17.
6. Ibid., 17, 48.
7. Levy, *James Weldon Johnson*, 180–82.
8. Ibid., 178.
9. Ross, *J. E. Spingarn and the Rise of the NAACP*, 23; James Weldon Johnson, *Along This Way*, 314.
10. *Papers of the NAACP, Part 11*, reel 35 (hereinafter cited as NAACP Garvey File), 865–66.
11. Eisenberg, "Only for the Bourgeois?" 112–13.
12. NAACP Garvey File, 596–872.
13. The seventeen branches organized in Georgia by 1920 were Albany, Americus, Athens, Atlanta, Augusta, Brunswick, Columbus, Cordele, Dublin, Hawkinsville, Macon, Milledgeville, Rome, Savannah, Thomasville, Valdosta, and Waycross. See *Crisis*, August 1920, 181.
14. I have gleaned this information from *Crisis*, minutes of the NAACP board meetings and business meetings, and from NAACP annual reports. Three works have been produced on the NAACP in selected states: Autry, "National Association for the Advancement of Colored People in Alabama"; Gavins, "NAACP in North Carolina during the Age of Segregation"; and Reich, "Soldiers of Democracy."

15. Du Bois, *Souls of Black Folk*, 302.

16. Ibid., 218.

17. *Papers of the NAACP, Part 1*, reel 8, files 574–79.

18. A. L. McDonald to John Shillady, 30 April 1920, *Papers of the NAACP, Part 12*, reel 9, files 798–99.

19. *Worth County Local*, 30 April 1920, 1; U.S. Census, *Population Schedule*, Worth County, Georgia, 1920.

20. Draft records for Worth County, Georgia, <http://www.ancestry.com>.

21. *Papers of the NAACP, Part 12*, reel 9, files 798–99.

22. *Worth County Local*, 30 April 1920, attached to McDonald letter in *Papers of the NAACP, Part 12*, reel 9, file 804.

23. *NW*, 1 April 1922, 2.

24. *Crisis*, January 1918, 146.

25. Author interview with Fannie Kaigler, Brunswick, Ga., 2 April 1995.

26. *The Freeman*, 1 November 1919 (reprint of editorial in the *Macon Telegraph* re-marking on comments in the *Cordele Dispatch*); *New York Age*, 8 May 1920; *Newport News Star*, 29 April 1920; *Chicago Defender*, 25 October 1919.

27. *Messenger* 5 (January 1923): 563.

28. Perry Howard to William Burns, 3 February 1923, *Marcus Garvey: FBI Investigation File*; *Messenger* 5 (February 1923): 613.

29. See references to black Georgia newspapers that used NAACP stories and printed press releases, including the *Rome Enterprise*, *Augusta Echo*, *Albany Supreme Circle News*, *Atlanta Independent*, *Savannah Tribune*, and *Savannah Journal*, in *NAACP Annual Report for 1923*, 32, and *NAACP Annual Report for 1924*, 52.

30. See appendix F.

31. Levy, *James Weldon Johnson*, 197–98.

32. George A. Towns, *The Sharecropper: A Play in One Act* (Fort Valley, Ga.: by the author, 1932). This work is found in the George A. Towns Papers, Trevor Arnett Negro Collection, Woodruff Library, Clark Atlanta University, Atlanta, Ga.

33. Walter White to John Shillady, 9 July 1918, *Papers of the NAACP, Part 12*, reel 9, file 695–96; *Crisis*, September 1921, 225.

34. *Crisis*, August 1918, 177; *Papers of the NAACP, Part 1*, reel 8, file 742–83.

35. Branch Files (Georgia), box 43, Albany folder, and box 46, Thomasville folder, series G, NAACP Papers, LC.

36. *Crisis*, December 1919, 73; *Papers of the NAACP, Part 1*, reel 13.

37. U.S. Census, *Population Schedule*, Georgia, 1920; *Crisis*, April 1920, 343.

38. U.S. Census, *Population Schedule*, Georgia, 1920; *Crisis*, May 1924, 28.

39. James Weldon Johnson to Harry Pace, 29 June 1918, and Pace to Johnson, 12 July 1918, *Papers of the NAACP, Part 12*, reel 9, files 697–99. Adam Daniel Williams would become the maternal grandfather of Martin Luther King Jr. See Rolinson, "Community and Leadership in the First Twenty Years of the Atlanta NAACP."

40. *Crisis*, May 1920, 39; *Crisis*, July 1920, 132; *Papers of the NAACP, Part 1*, reel 8, file

848; *Atlanta Constitution* 31 May 1920, 1 June 1920, 14 June 1920; *Savannah Tribune*, 5 June 1920, 1; James Weldon Johnson, *Along This Way*, 357; Ovington, *Walls Came Tumbling Down*, 178–79.

41. Dittmer, *Black Georgia*, 206–7.

42. *Crisis*, August and December 1920.

43. Branch Files (Georgia), boxes 43–46, series G, NAACP Papers, LC.

44. Moseley, "Political Influence of the Ku Klux Klan in Georgia," 242; *Papers of the NAACP, Part 1*, reel 8, files 199–202.

45. Branch Files (Arkansas, Georgia, Mississippi), boxes 11–13, 43–46, 105–6, series G, NAACP Papers, LC.

46. McMillen, *Dark Journey*, 314.

47. *NW*, 16 August 1924, 3.

48. Quoted in McMillen, *Dark Journey*, 315; see also Woodruff, "African-American Struggles for Citizenship," 43.

49. McMillen, *Dark Journey*, 314.

50. De Jong, *Different Day*, 67–68, 84.

51. For an example see *NW*, 9 August 1924, 11.

52. For an example see *NW*, 2 January 1932, 7.

53. See weekly reports from this division in *NW*, 12 and 26 December 1931, 3.

54. UNIAR, reel 1, 21 March 1933.

55. F. E. Pinson to NAACP, Vicksburg folder, and W. D. Norman to NAACP, Boyle folder, both in Branch Files (Mississippi), box 106, series G, NAACP Papers, LC; Rolinson, "Garvey Movement," 295.

56. U.S. Census, *Population Schedule*, Mississippi, 1920, 1930.

57. *Papers of the NAACP, Part 1*, reel 8, files 742–83.

58. Branch Files (Arkansas), boxes 11–13, Democrat folder, series G, NAACP Papers, LC.

59. *Papers of the NAACP, Part 1*, reel 8; Woodson, *Rural Negro*, 11; Woodruff, "African-American Struggles for Citizenship," 39.

60. Stockley, *Blood in Their Eyes*.

61. *Arkansas Gazette*, 19 October 1919, 2; Duster, *Crusade for Justice*, 397–401.

62. See Cortner, *Mob Intent on Death*, 1–2, 30–31, 39–40.

63. Ibid., 46–50.

64. The UNIA divisions in eastern Arkansas were in Armorel, Blackton, Blythe, Blytheville, Brickeys, Burdette (Blytheville), Burton Spurr, Calexico, Cotton Plant, Council, Crawfordsville, Cypert, Duncan, Earl, Fry's Mill, Gosnell, Hickman, Holly Grove (two), Howell, Hughes, Indian Bay, Jefferson, Lake Hall, Lexa, Madison, Moten, New Home (Round Pond), Oneida, Pine Bluff (two), Pine City, Postelle, Princedale, Round Pond, Simmsboro, South Bend, Southland, Twist, and Wynne. The five in other parts of the state were in Clear Lake, Fort Smith, Good Hope, Green Brier, and Paraloma. A division called Dos Canos could not be located in the *Rand McNally Commercial Atlas*, 61st ed., which was used to locate all

others. This list is a combination of the listings in Division Card File, UNIAR, a listing in *GP* 7:986–87, and places listed as having divisions in the *NW*, 1921–27.

65. The St. Francis County divisions of the UNIA were in Forrest City, New Home, Round Pond, and Hughes.

66. Black sentiment toward the NAACP after the Elaine litigation and *Moore v. Dempsey* may illustrate to a degree the intraracial conflict that Fon Louise Gordon has detected in her study of African Americans in Arkansas just prior to the 1920s. She describes the black middle class in Arkansas as exceptionally accommodationist in perspective during the period from 1895 to 1920 and acquiescent as they were stripped of political power. See Gordon, *Caste and Class*, 70–71. She argues that the mostly urban, economically independent or professional black middle class's acceptance of segregation made it much harder for the masses to get properly educated, save money, or improve their self-sufficiency within the plantation system. If she is correct, then, in Arkansas the NAACP's overt agitation for civil and political rights and equality went beyond the priorities of safety and comfort held by middle-class blacks. This description clearly opposes what I have found to be true of middle-class blacks of Georgia, with whom the NAACP had much success during its 1917–20 inception period.

In another study of blacks in Arkansas, in particular the Delta farmers' legacy of resistance, Melissa Langley Biegert helps us to understand why the tenant farmers and sharecroppers of east central Arkansas might have embraced Garveyism and rejected the elite-oriented NAACP. She traces the protest tradition of east Arkansas blacks from emancipation through the 1930s and shows that resistance had been a constant, though unrecorded, feature among the agricultural and rural segment of the black population. Much more is known about the activities of national organizations; those at the community level, although tedious and difficult to document, present a much less static picture of the dynamics of race relations than we tend to get through conventional studies. See Biegert, "Legacy of Resistance," 75–76. Although Biegert makes a powerful case for the existence of this legacy of resistance, she does so without acknowledging Garvey's supporters in the Delta.

67. Gordon, *Caste and Class*, 75–76.

68. Southland Charter, Lexa folder, and Postelle charter, Postelle folder, both in Branch Files (Arkansas), box 12, series G, NAACP Papers, LC.

69. Levy, *James Weldon Johnson*, 228; *Papers of the NAACP, Part 1*, reel 4, file 815.

70. Woofter, *Landlord and Tenant*, 66–68; Daniel, *Breaking the Land*, 239–44.

71. John B. Kirby, *Black Americans in the Roosevelt Era*, chaps. 6–8; Sitkoff, "The New Deal and Race Relations."

72. Watts, *God, Harlem U.S.A*; Fitzgerald, " 'We Have Found a Moses,' " 295.

73. Fitzgerald, " 'We Have Found a Moses,' " 302–5.

74. Rolinson, "Community and Leadership in the First Twenty Years of the Atlanta NAACP," 14.

75. Morris Davis to *Negro World* editor, 1933, UNIAR, reel 1.

76. See reports of the Sumner division in the *NW*, 12 and 23 December 1931.

77. Author interview with Lee McCarty, Merigold, Miss., 19 February 2005.

78. Venkataramani, "Norman Thomas, Arkansas Sharecroppers, and the Roosevelt Agricultural Policies."

79. Kester, *Revolt among the Sharecroppers*; Mitchell, "Founding and Early History of the Southern Tenant Farmers Union"; Mitchell, *Mean Things Happening in This Land*; Southern Tenant Farmers Union, *Oral History*.

80. Grubbs, *Cry from the Cotton*, 68.

81. Ibid.; Biegert, "Legacy of Resistance," 74.

82. Kester, *Revolt among the Sharecroppers*, 39.

83. Ibid., 83–85.

84. Grubbs, *Cry from the Cotton*, 65–69.

85. Listing of Arkansas and Mississippi locals, *STFU Papers*, reel 9 (pages on the microfilm are not numbered). Bolivar County STFU locals in 1938–39 included Shelby, Shaw, Scott, Rochdale, Stringtown, Cleveland, and Boyle. Arkansas STFU locals in towns that formerly held UNIA locals include at least the following: Blytheville, Council, Cotton Plant, Howell, and Round Pond. UNIA divisions and STFU locals existed all over the Arkansas Delta, and there is little doubt that black farmers in these areas knew about both organizations.

86. Kester, *Revolt among the Sharecroppers*, 56; Mitchell, "Founding and Early History of the Southern Tenant Farmers Union," 351–52; Biegert, "Legacy of Resistance."

87. Southern Tenant Farmers Union, *Oral History*, 1:17, 3:15–16, 4:25.

88. See J. R. Butler to Norman Thomas, 25 August 1938, *STFU Papers*, reel 8. See also *GP* 5:657–58 n. 5.

89. Grubbs, *Cry from the Cotton*, 91.

90. See correspondence between Mitchell and McKinney for April 1936 in *STFU Papers*, reel 2.

91. J. R. Butler to the STFU executive council, 18 July 1938, and J. R. Butler to Norman Thomas, 25 August 1938, *STFU Papers*, reel 2.

92. E. B. McKinney to Wiley Harris, 29 July 1938, *STFU Papers*, reel 2. For another very revealing letter concerning McKinney's racial perspectives on the STFU, see McKinney to Harris, 11 August 1938, *STFU Papers*, reel 2.

93. Ibid.

94. U.S. Department of Commerce, Bureau of the Census, *Negroes in the United States*, 64.

95. Mary Anis to Charleston chief of police, 20 March 1936, *Marcus Garvey: FBI Investigation File*.

96. Nasstrom, *Everybody's Grandmother and Nobody's Fool*, 97–99.

97. Tyson, *Radio Free Dixie*, 3.

98. Hill, *Deacons for Defense*, 259. The great proportion of NAACP branches in the South that now exist were chartered after 1945. Many branches that had brief

careers before the backlash of the 1920s were reestablished from the 1940s to the 1980s. Some states banned the organization altogether in the 1940s and 1950s (for example, Alabama), and the history of the NAACP's charters is even more complicated. See Autry, "National Association for the Advancement of Colored People in Alabama." Thanks to Lee Formwalt, who provided information on the NAACP charters in southwest Georgia from his contact with the NAACP national headquarters in 1995, with the assistance of Doris Edwards.

99. The best examples of scholarship on areas where the freedom struggle began in earnest in the rural areas I have studied here are Payne, *I've Got the Light of Freedom*; Dittmer, *Local People*; Carson, *In Struggle*; and Tuck, *Beyond Atlanta*.

100. Quoted in Burkett, *Garveyism as a Religious Movement*, xv.

Epilogue

1. There is much mystery surrounding the early years of Elijah Poole, and details of his origins are in dispute. Elijah Muhammad's own accounts, however, confirm these details. See Evanzz, *Messenger*, 21–23, 41–47. See also Clegg, *Original Man*, 8–13.

2. Muhammad, *Message to the Black Man in America*, 24–25.

3. Evanzz, *Messenger*, 529 n. 15.

4. Clegg, *Original Man*, 100.

5. Ibid., 253; *Atlanta Journal-Constitution*, 13 March 1995, C1; author interview with Alonzo Bryant (Brother Al Muhammad), Dawson, Ga., 15 May 2004.

6. Author interview with Alonzo Bryant; *Albany Herald*, 20 September 2002, B1; *Atlanta Journal-Constitution*, 19 March 1995.

7. For the website and *The Farmer* see <http://muhammadfarms.com> (25 January 2005).

8. Malcolm X and Haley, *Autobiography of Malcolm X*, 1–10; Bruce Perry, *Malcolm*, 2–14.

9. See St. Clair Drake's introduction to Burkett, *Garveyism as a Religious Movement*, xiv.

10. See Tony Martin, *Race First*, 36–37.

11. Salzman, Smith, and West, *Encyclopedia of African-American Culture and History*, 2:788.

12. Carson, *In Struggle*, 193–98, 201; Payne, *I've Got the Light of Freedom*, 234.

13. Hewitt, "Stokely Carmichael," 71–72, 78.

14. John Lewis, *Walking with the Wind*, 352–53.

15. For the text of the SNCC position paper "The Basis of Black Power" see <http://www3.iath.virginia.edu/sixties/HTML_docs/Resources/Primary/Manifestos/SNCC_black_power.html> (7 July 2006).

16. See the UNIA website at <http://www.UNIA-ACL.org> (9 June 2006).

17. *Atlanta Journal-Constitution*, 17 September 2004, D11.

Bibliography

PRIMARY SOURCES

Archival Sources

Hampton University Newspaper Clipping File (microfilm), Hampton University, Hampton, Va.

National Association for the Advancement of Colored People Papers, Series G, Branch Files (Arkansas, Georgia, Mississippi), Library of Congress, Manuscript Division, Washington, D.C.

Odom-Carter Papers, Special Collections, Woodruff Library, Emory University, Atlanta, Ga.

Southern Tenant Farmers Union Papers, Southern Historical Collection, Wilson Library, University of North Carolina at Chapel Hill, Chapel Hill, N.C.

George A. Towns Papers, Trevor Arnett Negro Collection, Woodruff Library, Clark Atlanta University, Atlanta, Ga.

Tuskegee Institute Clipping File (microfilm), Tuskegee University, Tuskegee, Ala.

Universal Negro Improvement Association, Records of the Central Division (New York), 1918–59, Schomburg Center for Research in Black Culture, New York Public Library, New York, N.Y.

U.S. Congress. Records of the 69th Congress, Record Group 46: 69A-J25, Judiciary Committee, box 133, National Archives, Washington, D.C.

U.S. Department of Justice Records, Record Group 60: 198940, box 3053, National Archives II, College Park, Md.

U.S. Pardon Attorney Records, Record Group 204: 42-793, boxes 1159–62, National Archives II, College Park, Md.

U.S. Secretary of Agriculture Records, Office of Secretary of Agriculture, General Correspondence: Negroes, box 1, folder 1923, National Archives II, College Park, Md.

Published Sources

Chafe, William H., Raymond Gavins, and Robert Korstad, et al., eds. *Remembering Jim Crow: African Americans Tell about Life in the Segregated South.* New York: New Press, 2001.

Dixon, Thomas, Jr. *The Clansman.* Garden City, N.Y.: Country Life Press, 1905.

——. *The Leopard's Spots: A Romance of the White Man's Burden, 1865–1900.* New York: Doubleday, Page and Company, 1902.

Du Bois, W. E. B. *The Souls of Black Folk.* Chicago: A. C. McClurg, 1903. Reprinted in *Three Negro Classics.* New York: Avon Books, 1965.

Duster, Alfreda M., ed. *Crusade for Justice: The Autobiography of Ida B. Wells.* Chicago: University of Chicago Press, 1970.

Ferris, William Henry. *The African Abroad*. New Haven, Conn.: Tuttle, Morehouse, and Taylor Press, 1913; reprint, New York: Johnson Reprint Corporation, n.d.

Fortune, T. Thomas. *Black and White: Land, Labor, and Politics in the South.* 1884; reprint, New York: Arno Press, 1968.

Frazier, E. Franklin. "Garvey: A Mass Leader." *The Nation*, 18 August 1926, 147–48.

Garvey, Amy Jacques. *Garvey and Garveyism*. Kingston, Jamaica: A. J. Garvey, 1963; reprint, New York: Collier Books, 1970.

——, ed. *Philosophy and Opinions of Marcus Garvey or Africa for the Africans*. 1923; London: Frank Cass, 1967.

Garvey, Marcus, ed. *The Black Man: A Monthly Magazine of Negro Thought and Opinion (The Blackman)*. 1933–39; Millwood, N.Y.: Kraus-Thompson Organization, Ltd., 1975.

Griggs, Sutton E. *Imperium in Imperio*. Cincinnati, Ohio, 1899.

Harlan, Louis R., ed. *The Booker T. Washington Papers*. Vols. 1–10. Urbana: University of Illinois Press, 1972–80.

Hill, Robert A., ed. *Marcus Garvey: Life and Lessons*. Berkeley: University of California Press, 1987.

——. *The Marcus Garvey and Universal Negro Improvement Association Papers*. Vols. 1–7. Berkeley: University of California Press, 1983–90.

Holder, Ray, ed. "On Slavery: Selected Letters of Parson Winans, 1820–1844." *Journal of Mississippi History* 46, no. 4 (1984): 323–54.

Jackson, Miles, ed. "Letters to a Friend: Correspondence from James Weldon Johnson to George A. Towns." *Phylon* 29 (1968): 182–98.

Johnson, Charles S. *Growing Up in the Black Belt: Negro Youth in the Rural South*. Washington, D.C.: American Council on Education, 1941; reprint, New York: Schocken Books, 1967.

——. *Shadow of the Plantation*. Chicago: University of Chicago Press, 1934.

——. *Statistical Atlas of Southern Counties: Listing and Analysis of Socio-Economic Indices of 1104 Southern Counties*. Chapel Hill: University of North Carolina Press, 1941.

Johnson, James Weldon. *Along This Way*. 1933; New York: Viking, 1968.

——. *Black Manhattan*. 1930; New York: Atheneum, 1968.

Kester, Howard. *Revolt among the Sharecroppers*. Edited with an introduction by Alex Lichtenstein. 1936; Knoxville: University of Tennessee Press, 1997.

Kipling, Rudyard. "The White Man's Burden: The United States and the Philippine Islands, 1899." In *Rudyard Kipling's Verse*. New York: Doubleday, 1929.

Lewis, John. *Walking with the Wind: A Memoir of the Movement*. New York: Simon and Schuster, 1998.

Malcolm X and Alex Haley. *The Autobiography of Malcolm X*. New York: Ballantine Books, 1964.

Mitchell, H. L. "The Founding and Early History of the Southern Tenant Farmers Union." *Arkansas Historical Quarterly* 32 (Winter 1973): 342–69.

——. *Mean Things Happening in This Land: The Life and Times of H. L. Mitchell, Co-Founder of the Southern Tenant Farmers Union*. Montclair, N.J.: Allanheld, Osmun, 1979.

——. *Roll the Union On*. Chicago: Charles H. Kerr Publishing Company, 1987.

Muhammad, Elijah. *Message to the Black Man in America*. Chicago: Muhammad Mosque No. 2, 1965.

NAACP Annual Reports for 1917–1940. New York: National Association for the Advancement of Colored People, 1919–41.

Ovington, Mary White. *The Walls Came Tumbling Down*. New York: Harcourt, Brace and Company, 1947.

Perry, Jeffrey B., ed. *A Hubert Harrison Reader*. Middletown, Conn.: Wesleyan University Press, 2001.

Pickens, William. "Africa for the Africans: The Garvey Movement." *The Nation*, 28 December 1921, 750–51.

——. *The Heir of Slaves: An Autobiography*. New York: Pilgrim Press, 1911.

——. *The New Negro: His Political, Civil, and Mental Status and Related Essays*. 1916; reprint, New York: Negro Universities Press, 1969.

Rand McNally Commercial Atlas. 52d ed. Chicago: Rand McNally and Company, 1921.

Rand McNally Commercial Atlas. 61st ed. New York: Rand McNally and Company, 1930.

Rand McNally Commercial Atlas of America. 54th ed. Chicago: Rand McNally and Company, 1923.

Smith-Irvin, Jeannette. *Footsoldiers of the Universal Negro Improvement Association: Their Own Words*. Trenton, N.J.: Africa World Press, 1989.

Southern Tenant Farmers Union. *Oral History of the Southern Tenant Farmers Union*. 4 parts. Montgomery, Ala.: Southern Rural Welfare Association, 1973.

U.S. Department of Commerce, Bureau of the Census. *Farm Tenancy in the United States*. Washington, D.C.: Government Printing Office, 1924.

——. *Fourteenth Census of the United States, 1920*. Vol. 3: *Population Composition and Characteristics of Population by State*. Washington, D.C.: Government Printing Office, 1921.

——. *Negroes in the United States, 1920–1932*. Washington, D.C.: Government Printing Office, 1935; reprint, New York: Kraus Reprint Company, 1965.

——. *Statistical Atlas of the United States*. Washington, D.C.: Government Printing Office, 1925.

U.S. Senate. *Congressional Record of the 67th Congress*, 3d session, 20 November–4 December 1922.

Washington, Booker T. *Up From Slavery*. 1901; New York: W. W. Norton, 1996.

White, Walter. *A Man Called White: The Autobiography of Walter White*. New York: Viking Press, 1948.

Williams, Daniel T., ed. "Newspaper Citations from the Tuskegee Archives: Marcus Garvey." In *Eight Negro Bibliographies*. New York: Kraus Reprint Company, 1970.

Work, Monroe, ed. *The Negro Yearbook, 1925–1926.* Tuskegee, Ala.: Negro Yearbook
Company, 1926.

Interviews

Bryant, Alonzo (Brother Al Muhammad). Dawson, Ga. Interview with author, 15 May
2004.

Bush, Ann Odom. Newton, Ga. Interview with author (by phone), 8 October 2003.

Carter, David. Toledo, Ohio. Interview with author (by phone), 13 March 1995,
14 June 1995, 16 March 1999.

Collins, Virginia. New Orleans, La. Interview in "Marcus Garvey: Look for Me in the
Whirlwind." *American Experience.* PBS. Stanley Nelson, director, 2001.

Crowe, Milburn. Mound Bayou, Miss. Interview with author, 4 April 2003.

Hymonds, Starlin. Holly Grove, Monroe County, Ark. Interview with author, 4 April
2003.

Idlett, Arthur. Atlanta, Ga. Interview with Bernard West, n.d. In the Living Atlanta
Collection, MSS 637, box 37, folder 13, Atlanta History Center, Atlanta, Ga.

James, Estelle. New Orleans, La. Interview in "Marcus Garvey: Look for Me in the
Whirlwind." *American Experience.* PBS. Stanley Nelson, director, 2001.

Kaigler, Fannie. Brunswick, Ga. Interview with author, 2 April 1995.

McCarty, Lee. Merigold, Miss. Interview with author, 19 February 2005, 5 August
2005 (by phone).

Perry, Richard. Brunswick, Ga. Interview with author (by phone), 6 April 1995.

Tillman, Reverend E. C. Atlanta, Ga. Interview with author, 5 March 1995.

Walker, Booker T., Jr. New Orleans, La. Interview with author, 17 November 2001.

West, Willie Lee and Beatrice. Pelham, Ga. Interview with author, 15 May 2004.

Williford, Gloria. Camilla, Ga. Interview with author, 15 May 2004.

Published Microfilm Collections

American Colonization Society Records. Washington, D.C.: Library of Congress
Photoduplication Service, 1971.

Grossman, James R., ed. *Black Workers in the Era of the Great Migration, 1916–1929.*
Frederick, Md.: University Publications of America, 1985.

Kornweibel, Theodore, Jr., ed. *Federal Surveillance of Afro-Americans, 1917–1925: The
First World War, the Red Scare, and the Garvey Movement.* Frederick, Md.:
University Publications of America, 1986.

Marcus Garvey: FBI Investigation File. Wilmington, Del.: Scholarly Resources, 1978.

*Papers of the NAACP, Part 1: Business Meetings, Board Minutes, Annual Conferences,
and Special Correspondence, 1913–1939.* Frederick, Md.: University Publications of
America, 1982.

Papers of the NAACP, Part 11: Special Subject Files, 1912–1939. Frederick, Md.:
University Publications of America, 1990.

Papers of the NAACP, Part 12: Selected Branch Files, 1913–1939, Series A: The South. Frederick, Md.: University Publications of America, 1982.

Peonage Files of the United States Department of Justice, 1901–1945. Frederick, Md.: University Publications of America, 1999.

Southern Tenant Farmers Union Papers, 1934–1970. Glen Rock, N.J.: Microfilming Corporation of America, 1971.

U.S. Department of Commerce, Bureau of the Census. *Population Schedules.* Georgia, Arkansas, and Mississippi, 1920 and 1930.

Periodicals

African Repository, 1828

Albany (Ga.) Herald, 2002

Arkansas Gazette (Little Rock, Ark.), 1915–30

Atlanta Constitution, 1891–1941

Atlanta Independent, 1916–30

Atlanta Journal-Constitution, 2004

Baltimore Afro-American, 1917–24

Charlotte (N.C.) Observer, 1917–25

Chicago Defender, 1915–30

Cotton Farmer (Scott, Bolivar County, Miss.), 1923–27

Crisis, 1915–34

Fayetteville (Ark.) Daily Democrat, 1924

The Freeman, 1919

Georgia Journal, 1818–23

The Messenger, 1923

Miami Herald, 1921

Morning News Review (Florence, S.C.), 1922, 1924

The Nation, 1919–30

Negro World, 1920–33

Newport News (Va.) Star, 1920

New York Age, 1905–6

Norfolk (Va.) Journal and Guide, 1921–26

Pelham (Ga.) Journal, 1921–26

Pittsburgh Courier, 1915–30

Reno (Nev.) Evening Gazette, 1923

Savannah (Ga.) Tribune, 1917–27

Southern Workman, 1928

Southwest Christian Advocate, 1900

Star of Zion (Charlotte, N.C.), 1921

The State (Columbia, S.C.), 1924

Time, 1924

Wichita Daily Times (Wichita Falls, Tex.), 1919

Wilmington (Del.) Advocate, 1920

Worth (Brunswick, Ga.), 1919–20

Worth County Local (Sylvester, Ga.), 1920–26

SECONDARY SOURCES

Anderson, Benedict. *Imagined Communities: Reflections on the Origin and Spread of Nationalism.* London: Verso, 1983.

Angell, Stephen Ward. *Bishop Henry McNeal Turner and African-American Religion in the South.* Knoxville: University of Tennessee Press, 1992.

Angell, Stephen Ward, and Anthony B. Pinn, eds. *Social Protest Thought in the African Methodist Episcopal Church, 1862–1939.* Knoxville: University of Tennessee Press, 2000.

Autry, Dorothy. "The National Association for the Advancement of Colored People in Alabama, 1913–1952." Ph.D. diss., University of Notre Dame, 1985.

Bair, Barbara. "Garveyism and Contested Political Terrain in 1920s Virginia." In *Afro-Virginian History and Culture*, edited by John Saillant, 227–49. New York: Garland, 1999.

———. "True Women, Real Men: Gender, Ideology, and Social Roles in the Garvey Movement." In *Gendered Domains: Rethinking Public and Private in Women's History*, edited by Dorothy O. Helly and Susan M. Reverby, 154–66. Ithaca, N.Y.: Cornell University Press, 1992.

Baker, Houston A., Jr., Manthia Diawara, and Ruth H. Lindeborg, eds. *Black British Cultural Studies: A Reader.* Chicago: University of Chicago Press, 1996.

Baker County Historical Society. *The History of Baker County, Georgia.* Roswell, Ga.: W. H. Wolfe Associates, 1991.

Barbeau, Arthur. *The Unknown Soldiers: Black American Troops in World War I.* Philadelphia: Temple University Press, 1974.

Barnes, Kenneth C. *Journey of Hope: The Back-to-Africa Movement in Arkansas in the Late 1800s.* Chapel Hill: University of North Carolina Press, 2004.

Barry, John M. *Rising Tide: The Great Mississippi Flood of 1927 and How It Changed America.* New York: Simon and Schuster, 1997.

Beckert, Sven. "From Tuskegee to Togo: The Problem of Freedom in the Empire of Cotton." *Journal of American History* 92 (September 2005): 498–526.

Bennett, Charles Raymond. "All Things to All People: The American Colonization Society in Kentucky, 1829–1860." Ph.D. diss., University of Kentucky, 1980.

Bethel, Elizabeth R. *Promiseland: A Century of Life in a Negro Community.* Philadelphia: Temple University Press, 1981.

Biegert, M. Langley. "Legacy of Resistance: Uncovering the History of Collective Action by Black Agricultural Workers in Central East Arkansas from the 1860s to the 1930s." *Journal of Social History* 32 (Fall 1998): 73–99.

Bolster, Paul Douglas. "Civil Rights Movements in Twentieth-Century Georgia."
    Ph.D. diss., University of Georgia, 1972.
Broderick, Francis, August Meier, and Elliott Rudwick, eds. *Black Protest Thought in
    the Twentieth Century*. 2d ed. New York: Bobbs-Merrill Company, 1971.
Brundage, W. Fitzhugh. *Lynching in the New South: Georgia and Virginia, 1880–1930.*
    Urbana: University of Illinois Press, 1993.
——, ed. *Under Sentence of Death: Lynching in the South.* Chapel Hill: University of
    North Carolina Press, 1997.
Burkett, Randall K. *Black Redemption: Churchmen Speak for the Garvey Movement.*
    Philadelphia: Temple University Press, 1978.
——. *Garveyism as a Religious Movement: The Institutionalization of a Black Civil
    Religion.* Metuchen, N.J.: Scarecrow Press, 1978.
Burkett, Randall K., and Richard Newman, eds. *Black Apostles: Afro-American Clergy
    Confront the Twentieth Century.* Boston: G. K. Hall and Company, 1978.
Carby, Hazel. " 'On the Threshold of the Women's Era': Lynching, Empire, and
    Sexuality in Black Feminist Theory." *Critical Inquiry* 12 (Autumn 1985): 262–77.
Carson, Clayborne. *In Struggle: SNCC and the Black Awakening of the 1960s.*
    Cambridge, Mass.: Harvard University Press, 1981.
Clarke, John Henrik. *Marcus Garvey and the Vision of Africa.* New York: Random
    House, 1974.
Clegg, Claude Andrew, III. *An Original Man: The Life and Times of Elijah Muhammad.*
    New York: St. Martin's Press, 1997.
——. *The Price of Liberty: African Americans and the Making of Liberia.* Chapel Hill:
    University of North Carolina Press, 2004.
Close, Stacey K. "Black Southern Migration, Black Immigrants, Garveyism, and the
    Transformation of Black Hartford, 1917–1922." *Griot* 22 (Spring 2003): 53–68.
Cobb, James C. *The Most Southern Place on Earth: The Mississippi Delta and the Roots of
    Regional Identity.* New York: Oxford University Press, 1992.
Cohen, William. *At Freedom's Edge: Black Mobility and the Southern White Quest for
    Racial Control, 1861–1915.* Baton Rouge: Louisiana State University Press, 1991.
Cortner, Richard C. *A Mob Intent on Death: The NAACP and the Arkansas Riot Cases.*
    Middletown, Conn.: Wesleyan University Press, 1988.
Crockett, Norman L. *The Black Towns.* Lawrence: Regents Press of Kansas, 1979.
Cronon, Edmund David. *Black Moses: The Story of Marcus Garvey and the Universal
    Negro Improvement Association.* Madison: University of Wisconsin Press, 1955.
Cruse, Harold. *The Crisis of the Negro Intellectual.* New York: William Morrow, 1967.
Curry, Constance. *Silver Rights.* New York: Harcourt, Brace and Company, 1995.
Daniel, Pete. *Breaking the Land: The Transformation of Cotton, Tobacco, and Rice
    Cultures since 1800.* Urbana: University of Illinois Press, 1985.
——. *The Shadow of Slavery: Peonage in the South, 1901–1969.* Urbana: University of
    Illinois Press, 1972.

Davis, Lenwood, and Janet Sims, eds. *Marcus Garvey: An Annotated Bibliography*. Westport, Conn.: Greenwood Press, 1980.

de Jong, Greta. *A Different Day: African American Struggles for Justice in Rural Louisiana, 1900–1970*. Chapel Hill: University of North Carolina Press, 2002.

Desmarais, Ralph H., ed. "The Military Intelligence Reports on Arkansas Riots: 1919–1920." *Arkansas Historical Quarterly* 33 (Summer 1974): 175–91.

Detweiler, Frederick G. *The Negro Press in the United States*. Chicago: University of Chicago Press, 1922.

Dittmer, John. *Black Georgia in the Progressive Era, 1900–1920*. Urbana: University of Illinois Press, 1977.

——. *Local People: The Struggle for Civil Rights in Mississippi*. Urbana: University of Illinois Press, 1994.

Drake, St. Clair. *The Redemption of Africa and Black Religion*. Chicago: Third World Press, 1970.

Drake, St. Clair, and Horace R. Cayton. *Black Metropolis: A Study of Negro Life in a Northern City*. Rev. and enl. ed. Chicago: University of Chicago Press, 1993.

Dunn, Marvin. *Black Miami in the Twentieth Century*. Gainesville: University Press of Florida, 1997.

Egerton, Douglas R. " 'Its Origin Is Not a Little Curious': A New Look at the American Colonization Society." *Journal of the Early Republic* 5 (Winter 1985): 463–80.

Eisenberg, Bernard. "Only for the Bourgeois? James Weldon Johnson and the NAACP, 1916–1930." *Phylon* 43, no. 2 (1982): 110–24.

Evanzz, Karl. *The Messenger: The Rise and Fall of Elijah Muhammad*. New York: Vintage Books, 1999.

Fannin, Mark. *Labor's Promised Land: Radical Visions of Gender, Race, and Religion in the South*. Knoxville: University of Tennessee Press, 2003.

Farajajé-Jones, Elias. *In Search of Zion: The Spiritual Significance of Africa in Black Religious Movements*. New York: P. Lang, 1991.

Fax, Elton. *Garvey: The Story of a Pioneer Black Nationalist*. New York: Dodd, Mead, 1972.

Felton, Ralph A. *Go Down, Moses: A Study of 21 Successful Negro Rural Pastors*. Madison, N.J.: Drew Theological Seminary, 1952.

Finley, Randy. "Black Arkansans and World War One." *Arkansas Historical Quarterly* 49 (Autumn 1990): 249–77.

Fitzgerald, Michael W. " 'We Have Found a Moses': Theodore Bilbo, Black Nationalism, and the Greater Liberia Bill of 1939." *Journal of Southern History* 63 (May 1997): 293–320.

Fleener, Nickieann. " 'Breaking Down Buyer Resistance': Marketing the 1935 *Pittsburgh Courier* to Mississippi Blacks." *Journalism History* 13 (1986): 78–85.

Formwalt, Lee. "The Camilla Massacre of 1868: Political Violence as Political Propaganda." *Georgia Historical Quarterly* 21 (Fall 1987): 399–426.

Gavins, Raymond. "The NAACP in North Carolina during the Age of Segregation." In *New Directions in Civil Rights Studies*, edited by Armstead Robinson and Patricia Sullivan, 105–25. Charlottesville: University Press of Virginia, 1991.

Genovese, Eugene D. *Roll, Jordan, Roll: The World the Slaves Made.* New York: Vintage Books, 1972.

Gifford, James M. "The African Colonization Movement in Georgia, 1817–1860." Ph.D. diss., University of Georgia, 1977.

Gilmore, Glenda Elizabeth. *Gender and Jim Crow: Women and the Politics of White Supremacy in North Carolina, 1896–1920.* Chapel Hill: University of North Carolina Press, 1996.

Gilroy, Paul. *Against Race: Imagining Political Culture beyond the Color Line.* Cambridge, Mass.: Belknap Press of Harvard University Press, 2000.

———. *The Black Atlantic: Modernity and Double Consciousness.* Cambridge, Mass.: Harvard University Press, 1993.

Goings, Kenneth W. *The NAACP Comes of Age: The Defeat of Judge John J. Parker.* Bloomington: Indiana University Press, 1990.

Gordon, Fon Louise. *Caste and Class: The Black Experience in Arkansas, 1880–1920.* Athens: University of Georgia Press, 1995.

Grant, Donald Lee. *The Anti-Lynching Movement, 1883–1932.* San Francisco: R & E Research Associates, 1975.

———. *The Way It Was in the South: The Black Experience in Georgia.* New York: Birch Lane Press, 1993.

Griffin, Farah Jasmine. "Black Feminists and Du Bois: Respectability, Protection, and Beyond." *Annals of the American Academy of Political and Social Science* 568 (March 2000): 28–40.

Grossman, James R. *Land of Hope: Chicago, Black Southerners, and the Great Migration.* Chicago: University of Chicago Press, 1989.

Grubbs, Donald H. *Cry from the Cotton: The Southern Tenant Farmers' Union and the New Deal.* Chapel Hill: University of North Carolina Press, 1971.

Grubbs, Lillie M. *History of Worth County, Georgia, for the First Eighty Years, 1854–1934.* Macon, Ga.: J. W. Burke and Company, 1934.

Guha, Ranajit, ed. *A Subaltern Studies Reader, 1986–1995.* Minneapolis: University of Minnesota Press, 1997.

Guha, Ranajit, and Gayatri Chakravorty Spivak, eds. *Selected Subaltern Studies.* New York: Oxford University Press, 1988.

Hahn, Steven. *A Nation Under Our Feet: Black Political Struggles in the Rural South from Slavery to the Great Migration.* Cambridge, Mass.: Belknap Press of Harvard University Press, 2003.

Hahn, Steven, and Jonathan Prude, eds. *The Countryside in the Age of Capitalist Transformation: Essays in the Social History of Rural America.* Chapel Hill: University of North Carolina Press, 1985.

Haley, Alex. *Roots: The Saga of an American Family.* Garden City, N.Y.: Doubleday, 1976.

Hall, Jacquelyn Dowd. *Revolt against Chivalry: Jessie Daniel Ames and the Women's Campaign against Lynching.* Rev. ed. New York: Columbia University Press, 1993.

Hamilton, Charles V. *The Black Preacher in America.* New York: William Morrow and Company, 1972.

The Handbook of Texas Online. <http:// www.tsha.utexas.edu/handbook/online/index.html>. 25 May 2006.

Harlan, Louis. "Booker T. Washington and the White Man's Burden." *American Historical Review* 71 (January 1966): 441–67.

——. *Booker T. Washington: The Wizard of Tuskegee, 1910–1915.* New York: Oxford University Press, 1983.

Harrison, Alferdteen, ed. *Black Exodus: The Great Migration from the American South.* Jackson : University Press of Mississippi, 1991.

Hemmingway, Theodore. "Booker T. Washington in Mississippi: October 1908." *Journal of Mississippi History* 46 (February 1984): 29–42.

Hewitt, Cynthia Lucas. "Stokely Carmichael: From Black Power to Pan-Africanism." *International Journal of Africana Studies* 10 (Fall/Winter 2004): 70–102.

Higginbotham, Evelyn Brooks. *Righteous Discontent: The Women's Movement in the Black Baptist Church, 1880–1920.* Cambridge, Mass.: Harvard University Press, 1993.

Higginbotham, Evelyn Brooks, Leon F. Litwack, Darlene Clark Hine, and Randall K. Burkett, eds. *The Harvard Guide to African-American History.* Cambridge, Mass: Harvard University Press, 2001.

Hill, Lance. *The Deacons for Defense: Armed Resistance and the Civil Rights Movement.* Chapel Hill: University of North Carolina Press, 2004.

Hine, Darlene Clark. "Rape and the Inner Lives of Black Women in the Middle West: Preliminary Thoughts on the Culture of Dissemblance." *Signs* 14 (Summer 1989): 912–20.

Hoare, Quintin, and Geoffrey Nowell Smith, eds. *Selections from the Prison Notebooks of Antonio Gramsci.* New York: International Publishers, 1971.

Holley, Donald. "The Plantation Heritage: Agriculture in the Arkansas Delta." In *Arkansas Delta: Land of Paradox,* edited by Jeannie Whayne and Willard B. Gatewood, 238–58. Fayetteville: University of Arkansas Press, 1993.

Hunter, Tera. *To 'Joy My Freedom: Southern Black Women's Lives and Labors after the Civil War.* Cambridge, Mass.: Harvard University Press, 1997.

Hurt, R. Douglas, ed. *African American Life in the Rural South, 1900–1950.* Columbia: University of Missouri Press, 2003.

Issa, Jahi. "The Universal Negro Improvement Association in Louisiana: Creating a Provisional Government in Exile." Ph.D. diss., Howard University, 2005.

Jackson, David H. "Charles Banks: Wizard of Mound Bayou." *Journal of Mississippi History* 62 (Winter 2000): 269–92.

James, Winston A. *Holding Aloft the Banner of Ethiopia: Caribbean Radicalism in Early Twentieth-Century America.* New York: Verso, 1998.

Jaynes, Gerald. *Branches without Roots: Genesis of the Black Working Class in the American South, 1862–1882.* New York: Oxford University Press, 1986.

Jones, Allen W. "The Role of Tuskegee Institute in the Education of Black Farmers." *Journal of Negro History* 60 (April 1975): 252–87.

Jones, Jacqueline. *Labor of Love, Labor of Sorrow: Black Women, Work, and the Family from Slavery to the Present.* New York: Vintage Books, 1986.

Jordan, William G. *Black Newspapers and America's War for Democracy, 1914–1920.* Chapel Hill: University of North Carolina Press, 2001.

Kelley, Robin D. G. *Hammer and Hoe: Alabama Communists during the Great Depression.* Chapel Hill: University of North Carolina Press, 1990.

Kellogg, Charles F. *NAACP: A History of the National Association for the Advancement of Colored People.* Vol. 1: *1909–1920.* Baltimore: Johns Hopkins University Press, 1967.

King, Kenneth J. "Some Notes on Arnold J. Ford and New World Black Attitudes to Ethiopia." In *Black Apostles: Afro-American Clergy Confront the Twentieth Century,* edited by Randall K. Burkett and Richard Newman, 49–52. Boston: G. K. Hall and Company, 1978.

Kirby, Jack Temple. "Clarence Poe's Vision of a Segregated 'Great Rural Civilization.'" *South Atlantic Quarterly* 68 (Winter 1969): 27–38.

———. *Rural Worlds Lost: The American South, 1920–1960.* Baton Rouge: Louisiana State University Press, 1987.

Kirby, John B. *Black Americans in the Roosevelt Era: Liberalism and Race.* Knoxville: University of Tennessee Press, 1980.

Kornweibel, Theodore. *Seeing Red: Federal Campaigns against Black Militancy, 1919–1925.* Bloomington: Indiana University Press, 1998.

Kramer, Gary R., ed. *George Washington Carver in His Own Words.* Columbia: University of Missouri Press, 1987.

Lee, Chana Kai. *For Freedom's Sake: The Life of Fannie Lou Hamer.* Urbana: University of Illinois Press, 1999.

Lee County Sesquicentennial Committee. *History of Lee County, Arkansas.* Dallas, Tex.: Curtis Media Corporation, 1987.

Lemelle, Sidney J., and Robin D. G. Kelley, eds. *Imagining Home: Class, Culture, and Nationalism in the African Diaspora.* New York: Verso, 1994.

Levine, Lawrence W. *Black Culture and Black Consciousness: Afro-American Folk Thought from Slavery to Freedom.* New York: Oxford University Press, 1977.

———. "Marcus Garvey and the Politics of Revitalization." In *Black Leaders of the Twentieth Century,* edited by John Hope Franklin and August Meier, 104–38. Urbana: University of Illinois Press, 1986.

Levy, Eugene. *James Weldon Johnson: Black Leader, Black Voice.* Chicago: University of Chicago Press, 1973.

Lewis, David Levering. *W. E. B. Du Bois: Biography of a Race, 1868–1919.* New York: Henry Holt and Company, 1993.

Lewis, Earl. *In Their Own Interests: Race, Class, and Power in Twentieth-Century Norfolk, Virginia.* Berkeley: University of California Press, 1991.

Lewis, Hylan. *Blackways of Kent.* New Haven, Conn.: College and University Press Publishers, 1955.

Lewis, Rupert. *Marcus Garvey: Anti-Colonial Champion.* Trenton, N.J.: Africa World Press, 1988.

———. *Marcus Garvey, His Work, and Impact.* Trenton, N.J.: African World Press, 1991.

Lewis, Todd Everett. "Race Relations in Arkansas, 1910–1929." Ph.D. diss., University of Arkansas, 1995.

Locke, Alain. *The New Negro.* 1925; New York: Atheneum, 1969.

Lynch, Hollis R. *Edward Wilmot Blyden: Pan-Negro Patriot, 1832–1912.* New York: Oxford University Press, 1967.

MacLean, Nancy. *Behind the Mask of Chivalry: The Making of the Second Ku Klux Klan.* New York: Oxford University Press, 1994.

Marshall, F. Ray. *Labor in the South.* Cambridge, Mass.: Harvard University Press, 1967.

Martin, Sandy D. *Black Baptists and African Missions: The Origins of a Movement, 1880–1915.* Macon, Ga.: Mercer University Press, 1989.

Martin, Tony, ed. *Global Garveyism.* Dover, Mass.: Majority Press, forthcoming.

———. *Marcus Garvey, Hero: A First Biography.* Dover, Mass.: Majority Press, 1983.

———. *Race First: The Ideological and Organizational Struggles of Marcus Garvey and the Universal Negro Improvement Association.* Westport, Conn.: Greenwood Press, 1976.

Matthews, John M. "Black Newspapermen and the Black Community in Georgia, 1890–1930." *Georgia Historical Quarterly* 68 (Fall 1984): 356–81.

———. "Studies in Race Relations in Georgia, 1890–1930." Ph.D. diss., Duke University, 1970.

Mays, Benjamin E. *Born to Rebel: An Autobiography.* New York: Charles Scribner's Sons, 1971.

Mays, Benjamin Elijah, and Joseph William Nicholson. *The Negro's Church.* Madison: State Historical Society of Wisconsin Library, 1933; reprint, Salem, N.H.: Ayer Company Publishers, 1988.

McFadden, Grace Jordan. "Septima P. Clark and the Struggle for Human Rights." In *Women in the Civil Rights Movement: Trailblazers and Torchbearers, 1941–1965,* edited by Vicki L. Crawford and Jacqueline A. Rouse, 85–97. Indianapolis: Indiana University Press, 1993.

McGraw, Marie Tyler. "Richmond Free Blacks and African Colonization, 1816–1832." *Journal of American Studies* 21, no. 2 (1987): 207–24.

McMillen, Neil R. *Dark Journey: Black Mississippians in the Age of Jim Crow.* Urbana: University of Illinois Press, 1989.

McMurray, Linda O. *George Washington Carver: Scientist and Symbol.* New York: Oxford University Press, 1981.

Meier, August. *Negro Thought in America, 1880–1915: Racial Ideologies in the Age of Booker T. Washington*. Ann Arbor: University of Michigan Press, 1963.

Meier, August, and Elliott Rudwick, eds. *Along the Color Line: Explorations in the Black Experience*. Urbana: University of Illinois Press, 1976.

Mitchell, Michele. "Adjusting the Race: Gender, Sexuality, and the Question of African-American Destiny, 1887–1930." Ph.D. diss., Northwestern University, 1998.

——." 'The Black Man's Burden': African Americans, Imperialism, and Notions of Racial Manhood, 1890–1910." *International Review of Social History* 44, suppl. (1999): 77–99.

——. *Righteous Propagation: African Americans and the Politics of Racial Destiny after Reconstruction*. Chapel Hill: University of North Carolina Press, 2004.

Mohl, Raymond A. "The Pattern of Race Relations in Miami since the 1920's." In *African-American Heritage of Florida*, edited by David R. Colburn and Jane L. Landers, 326–65. Tallahassee: University Press of Florida, 2000.

Moneyhon, Carl H. *Arkansas and the New South, 1974–1929*. Fayetteville: University of Arkansas Press, 1997.

——. "Delta Towns: Their Rise and Decline." In *Arkansas Delta: Land of Paradox*, edited by Jeannie Whayne and Willard B. Gatewood, 208–37. Fayetteville: University of Arkansas Press, 1993.

Morris, Aldon D. *The Origins of the Civil Rights Movement: Black Communities Organizing for Change*. New York: Free Press, 1984.

Moseley, Clement C. "The Political Influence of the Ku Klux Klan in Georgia, 1915–1925." *Georgia Historical Quarterly* 57 (Summer 1973): 235–55.

Moses, Wilson Jeremiah. *The Golden Age of Black Nationalism, 1850–1925*. New York: Oxford University Press, 1978.

Moten, Derryn E. "Racial Integrity or 'Race Suicide': Virginia's Eugenic Movement, W. E. B. Du Bois, and the Work of Walter A. Plecker." *Negro History Bulletin* 62 (April–September 1999): 6–17.

Nasstrom, Kathryn L. *Everybody's Grandmother and Nobody's Fool: Frances Freeborn Pauley and the Struggle for Social Justice*. Ithaca, N.Y.: Cornell University Press, 2000.

Nelson, Bruce. "Organized Labor and the Struggle for Black Equality in Mobile during World War II." *Journal of American History* 80 (December 1993): 952–88.

Odum, Howard W. *Southern Regions of the United States*. Chapel Hill: University of North Carolina Press, 1936.

Oliver, Roland, and Anthony Atmore. *Africa since 1800*. 3d ed. Cambridge, U.K.: Cambridge University Press, 1982.

Opper, Peter Kent. "The Mind of the White Participant in the African Colonization Movement, 1816–1840." Ph.D. diss., University of North Carolina, 1972.

Osofsky, Gilbert. *Harlem: The Making of a Ghetto, Negro New York, 1890–1930*. 2d ed. New York: Harper Torchbooks, 1971.

Painter, Nell Irvin. *Exodusters: Black Migration to Kansas after Reconstruction*. New York: Knopf, 1976.

Palmer, Ransford W. *Pilgrims from the Sun: West Indian Migration to America*. New York: Twayne Publishers, 1995.

Patton, Adell, Jr. "The 'Back-to-Africa' Movement in Arkansas." *Arkansas Historical Quarterly* 51 (Summer 1992): 164–77.

Payne, Charles M. *I've Got the Light of Freedom: The Organizing Tradition and the Mississippi Freedom Struggle*. Berkeley: University of California Press, 1995.

Penningroth, Dylan C. *The Claims of Kinfolk: African American Property and Community in the Nineteenth-Century South*. Chapel Hill: University of North Carolina Press, 2003.

Perry, Bruce. *Malcolm: The Life of a Man Who Changed Black America*. Barrytown, N.Y.: Station Hill Press, 1991.

Perry, Margaret, ed. *The Harlem Renaissance: An Annotated Bibliography and Commentary*. New York: Garland, 1982.

Raper, Arthur F. *The Tragedy of Lynching*. Chapel Hill: University of North Carolina Press, 1933.

Raper, Arthur F., and Ira DeA. Reid. *Sharecroppers All*. Chapel Hill: University of North Carolina Press, 1941.

Record, Wilson. *Race and Radicalism*. Ithaca, N.Y.: Cornell University Press, 1964.

Redkey, Edwin S. *Black Exodus: Black Nationalist and Back-to-Africa Movements, 1890–1910*. New Haven, Conn.: Yale University Press, 1969.

Reich, Steven. "Soldiers of Democracy: Black Texans and the Fight for Citizenship, 1917–1921." *Journal of American History* 82 (March 1996): 1478–1504.

Reid, Ira DeA. *The Negro Immigrant: His Background, Characteristics, and Social Adjustment, 1899–1937*. New York: Columbia University Press, 1939; reprint, New York: AMS Press, 1968.

Robinson, Charles F. "Most Shamefully Common: Arkansas and Miscegenation." *Arkansas Historical Quarterly* 60 (Fall 2001): 265–83.

Robnett, Belinda. *How Long? How Long? African-American Women in the Struggle for Civil Rights*. New York: Oxford University Press, 1997.

Rogers, O. A., Jr. "The Elaine Race Riots of 1919." *Arkansas Historical Quarterly* 19 (Summer 1960): 142–50.

Rolinson, Mary Gambrell. "Community and Leadership in the First Twenty Years of the Atlanta NAACP, 1917–1937." *Atlanta History* 42 (Fall 1998): 5–21.

——. "The Garvey Movement in the Rural South, 1920–1927." Ph.D. diss., Georgia State University, 2002.

——. "The UNIA in Georgia: Southern Strongholds of Garveyism." In *Georgia in Black and White: Explorations in the Race Relations of a Southern State, 1865–1950*, edited by John C. Inscoe, 202–24. Athens: University of Georgia Press, 1994.

—— [as Mary Latimer Gambrell]. "The Universal Negro Improvement Association in the Southern United States: Strongholds of Garveyism." M.A. thesis, University of Georgia, 1989.

Rosengarten, Theodore. *All God's Dangers: The Life of Nate Shaw.* New York: Knopf, 1975.

Ross, B. Joyce. *J. E. Spingarn and the Rise of the NAACP, 1911–1939.* New York: Atheneum, 1972.

Salzman, Jack, David Lionel Smith, and Cornel West, eds. *Encyclopedia of African-American Culture and History.* 5 vols. New York: Macmillan, 1996.

Schultz, Mark R. *The Rural Face of White Supremacy: Beyond Jim Crow.* Urbana: University of Illinois Press, 2004.

Seraile, William. *Bruce Grit: The Black Nationalist Writings of John Edward Bruce.* Knoxville: University of Tennessee Press, 2003.

Sernett, Milton C. *Bound for the Promised Land: African American Religion and the Great Migration.* Durham, N.C.: Duke University Press, 1997.

Sitkoff, Harvard. "The New Deal and Race Relations." In *Fifty Years Later: The New Deal Evaluated,* edited by Harvard Sitkoff, 93–111. New York: Alfred A. Knopf, 1985.

Smith, Theophus H. *Conjuring Culture: Biblical Formations of Black America.* New York: Oxford University Press, 1994.

Spence, Margaret, and Anna M. Fleming. *History of Mitchell County, 1857–1976.* Camilla, Ga.: Camilla Enterprise, 1976.

Staudenraus, P. J. *The African Colonization Movement, 1816–1865.* New York: Columbia University Press, 1961.

Stein, Judith. *The World of Marcus Garvey: Race and Class in Modern Society.* Baton Rouge: Louisiana State University Press, 1986.

Stephens, Ronald J. "Garveyism in Idlewild, 1927 to 1936." *Journal of Black Studies* 34 (March 2004): 462–88.

Stockley, Grif. *Blood in Their Eyes: The Elaine Race Massacres of 1919.* Fayetteville: University of Arkansas Press, 2001.

Stuckey, Sterling. *The Ideological Origins of Black Nationalism.* Boston: Beacon Press, 1972.

Suggs, Henry Lewis. "Black Strategy and Ideology in the Segregation Era: P. B. Young and the *Norfolk Journal and Guide,* 1910–1954." *Virginia Magazine of History and Biography* 91 (1983): 161–90.

——, ed. *The Black Press in the South, 1865–1979.* Westport, Conn.: Greenwood Press, 1983.

Sullivan, Patricia. *Days of Hope: Race and Democracy in the New Deal Era.* Chapel Hill: University of North Carolina Press, 1996.

Taylor, Ula Yvette. *The Veiled Garvey: The Life and Times of Amy Jacques Garvey.* Chapel Hill: University of North Carolina Press, 2002.

Thompson, Julius. *The Black Press in Mississippi, 1865–1985.* Gainesville: University Press of Florida, 1993.

Thompson, Robert F., III. "The Strange Case of Paul D. Peacher, Twentieth-Century Slaveholder." *Arkansas Historical Quarterly* 52, no. 4 (1993): 426–51.

Thornbrough, Emma Lou. *T. Thomas Fortune: Militant Journalist.* Chicago: University of Chicago Press, 1972.

Tolbert, Emory J. "Outpost Garveyism and the UNIA Rank and File." *Journal of Black Studies* 5 (March 1975): 242–51.

——. *The Universal Negro Improvement Association and Black Los Angeles: Ideology and Community in the American Garvey Movement.* Los Angeles: UCLA Center for Afro-American Studies, 1980.

Tolnay, Stewart E. *The Bottom Rung: African American Life on Southern Farms.* Urbana: University of Illinois Press, 1999.

Tolnay, Stewart E., and E. M. Beck. *A Festival of Violence: An Analysis of Southern Lynchings, 1882–1930.* Urbana: University of Illinois Press, 1995.

Trotter, Joe William, Jr., ed. *The Great Migration in Historical Perspective: New Dimensions of Race, Class, and Gender.* Bloomington: Indiana University Press, 1991.

Tuck, Stephen G. N. *Beyond Atlanta: The Struggle for Racial Equality in Georgia, 1940–1980.* Athens: University of Georgia Press, 2001.

Tyson, Timothy B. *Radio Free Dixie: Robert F. Williams and the Roots of Black Power* Chapel Hill: University of North Carolina Press, 1999.

Vance, Rupert B. *Human Factors in Cotton Culture: A Study in the Social Geography of the American South.* Chapel Hill: University of North Carolina Press, 1929.

——. *Human Geography of the South: A Study in Regional Resources and Human Adequacy.* Chapel Hill: University of North Carolina Press, 1932.

Venkataramani, M. S. "Norman Thomas, Arkansas Sharecroppers, and the Roosevelt Agricultural Policies, 1933–1937." *Arkansas Historical Quarterly* 24 (Spring 1965): 3–28.

Vickerman, Milton. *Crosscurrents: West Indian Immigrants and Race.* New York: Oxford University Press, 1999.

Vincent, Theodore. *Black Power and the Garvey Movement.* Berkeley, Calif.: Ramparts Press, 1971.

——. "The Garveyite Parents of Malcolm X." *Black Scholar* 20 (March/April 1989): 10–13.

Vinson, Robert. "In the Time of the Americans: Garveyism in Segregationist South Africa, 1920–1940." Ph.D. diss., Howard University, 2000.

Vought, Kip. "Racial Stirrings in Colored Town: The UNIA in Miami in the 1920s." *Tequesta* 60 (2000): 56–73.

Walker, Clarence E. "The Virtuoso Illusionist: Marcus Garvey." In *Deromanticizing Black History: Critical Essays and Reappraisals.* Knoxville: University of Tennessee Press, 1991.

Watkins-Owens, Irma. *Blood Relations: Caribbean Immigrants in the Harlem Community, 1900–1930.* Bloomington: Indiana University Press, 1996.

Watts, Jill. *God, Harlem U.S.A.: The Father Divine Story*. Berkeley: University of California Press, 1992.

Whayne, Jeannie M. *A New Plantation South: Land, Labor, and Federal Favor in Twentieth-Century Arkansas*. Charlottesville: University Press of Virginia, 1996.

White, Deborah Gray. *Ar'n't I a Woman? Female Slaves in the Plantation South*. New York: W. W. Norton, 1985.

White, Walter. *Rope and Faggot: The Biography of Judge Lynch*. New York: Alfred A. Knopf, 1929; reprint, New York: Arno Press, 1969.

Williams, Johnny Eric. "African American Religion and Activism: The African American Politicization of Religion in Arkansas." Ph.D. diss., Brandeis University, 1995.

Williams, Wirt A., ed. *History of Bolivar County, Mississippi*. Jackson, Miss: Hederman Brothers, 1948; reprint, Spartanburg, S.C.: Reprint Company, 1976.

Wilmore, Gayraud S. *Black Religion and Black Radicalism*. 3d ed. Maryknoll, N.Y.: Orbis Books, 1998.

Wolseley, Roland E. *The Black Press, U.S.A.* 2d ed. Ames: Iowa State University Press, 1990.

Woodruff, Nan Elizabeth. "African-American Struggles for Citizenship in the Arkansas and Mississippi Deltas in the Age of Jim Crow." *Radical History Review* 55 (Winter 1993): 33–51.

——. *American Congo: The African American Freedom Struggle in the Delta*. Cambridge, Mass.: Harvard University Press, 2003.

Woodson, Carter G. *The Rural Negro*. Washington, D.C.: Association for the Study of Negro Life and History, 1930; reprint, New York: Russell and Russell, 1969.

Woofter, T. J., Jr. *Landlord and Tenant on the Cotton Plantation*. Washington, D.C.: Works Progress Administration, 1936; reprint, New York: Negro Universities Press, 1969.

——. *Negro Migration: Changes in Rural Organization and Population of the Cotton Belt*. New York: W. D. Gray, 1920.

Woolfolk, Margaret Elizabeth. *A History of Crittenden County, Arkansas*. Greenville, S.C.: Southern Historical Press, 1991.

Zangrando, Robert L. *The NAACP Crusade against Lynching, 1909–1950*. Philadelphia: Temple University Press, 1980.

Index

Abbott, Robert, 45, 74–77, 81–82, 170

Africa: UNIA members in, 2, 4, 218 (n. 7); and European imperialism, 3, 16, 17, 25, 26, 131, 150, 151; political independence in, 3, 26, 131; history of, 16, 117; as blacks' natural and rightful home, 17; and Turner, 25, 29, 30–35, 37–38, 39; and Washington, 25–26, 27; Eason on, 93, 97; UNIA divisions in, 152, 224 (n. 58). *See also* African redemption

African American Christian missionaries: and African redemption, 3, 17, 24, 30–31, 35–36, 37, 47, 131, 152; Garvey's strategy compared to, 25, 28; reports from Africa, 154, 155

African American leaders: Du Bois on, 8, 166; legitimacy of, 24, 163, 165; views of Garvey, 25, 44; and rural blacks, 28, 163; and Washington's influence, 40–41, 43–44, 47; and biblical comparisons, 118; debates on lynching, 133; and integrationism, 226 (n. 91). *See also* Urban elite blacks

African American protest: Garveyism within tradition of, 7, 9, 17, 24, 222 (n. 1); leadership of, 8; and urban protests, 45; and black press, 74; and southern Garveyites, 105

African-born people of color, 27

African Communities League, 1, 36, 43

African diaspora: and UNIA, 1, 2; Garveyism's place in, 9; role of *New World* in, 15; achievements of blacks in, 16; and independent Africa, 26; and Ferris, 82; and layered identities, 218 (n. 5)

African Legions, 2, 52, 53, 57, 61, 64, 134

African Methodist Episcopal (AME) church: and Turner, 24, 28, 29, 30, 31, 35; and Blyden, 27; and emigration, 33–34; and African redemption, 37, 131; membership of, 46; and support of UNIA, 93; and mission work in Africa, 154

African Methodist Episcopal Zion church, 46, 56, 61

African Methodist Union, 172

African Orthodox church, 46

African redemption: and black government of Africa, 2, 26, 68, 151–52, 154; and African American Christian missionaries, 3, 17, 24, 30–31, 35–36, 37, 47, 131, 152; Garvey's message of, 15, 25, 27, 60; and Judeo-Christian traditions, 17, 221 (n. 47); biblical reference to, 36, 152; and Brooks, 61; and Eason, 70, 154; Bruce on, 85; Prendergast on, 94; and Robertson, 96, 154; and southern Garveyites, 103, 115, 150, 151–52, 153, 156, 160, 181; and Garveyism as civil religion, 130; as comprehensive solution, 131, 150–60; fund for, 152–53; feasibility of, 161; historical context of, 243 (n. 73)

African Repository, 32, 33, 74

African Times and Orient Review, 42

Aggrey, James E. K., 64

Agricultural Adjustment Administration, 22, 182

Akim Trading Company, 91

Alabama, 88–89, 92, 232–33 (n. 63), 233 (n. 67). *See also* Mobile, Alabama

Albany, Georgia, 21, 22, 96, 117, 237 (n. 36)

Ali, Duse Mohammed, 42, 151

Brimberry, John, 27
Brookins, A. B., 184
Brooks, J. D., 61, 63, 70, 95, 134
Bruce, John Edward, 78, 82–84, 136,
    178, 231 (n. 42)
Brundage, Fitzhugh, 105
Brunswick, Georgia, 92–93, 96, 114,
    171
Bryant, Alonzo (Brother Al Muham-
    mad), 193
Burke, C., 122
Burke, Frank, 56
Burkett, Randall K., 11–12, 46, 79, 94,
    229 (n. 79), 240 (n. 88)
Burns, William J., 170
Bush, Ann Odom, 239 (n. 64)
Butler, J. R., 184, 186, 187
Bynum, Mollie, 101, 152

Calvin, Floyd J., 155
Camilla, Georgia, 32, 97
Campbell, T. M., 88, 89
Camp Community Service Bureau, 50
Capitalism, 2, 9, 12, 49, 130
Caraway, T. H., 142, 148–49
Carby, Hazel, 137
Carmichael, Stokely, 194
Carter, C. Emonei, 58–59
Carver, George Washington, 41–42
Champion Magazine, 78
Charleston, South Carolina, 13, 49, 70,
    86, 87, 89, 92, 118, 188–89
Charlotte Observer, 61
Chattanooga, Tennessee, 92
Chicago, Illinois, 72, 164, 182
Chicago Defender, 15, 54, 74–78, 81–82,
    107, 170, 175, 178, 179
Christian Recorder, 27, 28, 29, 33, 34, 37,
    74, 78
Civil rights movement: ideological roots
    of, 13, 188, 191, 192; and rural blacks,
    23; role of black church in, 47, 188;

and tension over strategy, 189, 194–
    95
Clark, Septima, 89
Clarke, Edward Young, 45, 143–46
Clarke, John Henrik, 10, 222 (n. 1)
Class-based organization, 22, 51, 162,
    180. *See also* Southern Tenant Farmers
    Union
Coahoma County, Mississippi, 38
Collins, Virginia, 24
Communism, 9, 23
Compromise of 1820, 32
Congo Company, 39
Conquest, N. J., 56
Coolidge, Calvin, 7, 117, 119, 158–59
Cooper, J. L., 101
Coppinger, William, 33–34, 83
Cotton agricultural system: and south-
    ern Garveyites, 15, 19, 98, 104, 113–14,
    116–17, 124; and UNIA divisions, 20;
    and black landownership, 114, 116;
    and boll weevil blight, 116; and lynch-
    ing, 127–28, 144; and white land-
    owners, 166; and Great Depression,
    182
Cotton Farmer, The, 126–27, 175
Cox, Earnest Sevier, 35, 219 (n. 19)
Crichlow, Cyril, 234 (n. 90)
Crisis, 74, 165, 166, 168–70, 173, 175, 181,
    245 (n. 14)
Cronon, Edmund David, 9, 10
Cuffe, Paul, 31

Dallas, Texas, 90
Daugherty, Harry M., 58
Davis, George W., 129
Davis, J. Arthur, 25
Davis, Jefferson, 126
Davis, Morris, 183
Deacons for Defense, 190
Declaration of the Rights of the Negro
    Peoples of the World, 73, 121, 132

Delaney, Martin, 37
Delta and Pine Land Company, 126–27
Democratic Party, 142
Dennis, J. L., 155
Detroit, Michigan, 72
Divine, Father, 182
Dixon, Thomas, Jr., 79
Domingo, W. A., 78, 85
Donaldson, Ivanhoe, 194
Dougherty County, Georgia, 22, 107
Douglass, Frederick, 34, 40
Drake, John Gibbs St. Clair, 194
Drake, St. Clair, 194
Du Bois, W. E. B.: on African American leaders, 8, 166; and Africa, 26; and urban context, 28; and race relations, 44; and *Crisis*, 74; Ferris on, 79; criticism of Garvey, 82, 146; on Black Belt, 103, 166; and interracial marriage, 144; and NAACP policy, 165, 166, 174; and lynching, 168
Dyer, Leonidas, 141
Dyer antilynching bill, 41, 141–43, 148, 150, 170

Eason, J. W. H.: and UNIA organizing, 61, 63–65, 70, 101–2; charisma of, 64; family background of, 64, 229 (n. 71); relationship with Garvey, 65, 67, 68, 70, 229 (n. 79), 238 (n. 48); murder of, 67, 88; and African redemption, 70, 154; and Georgia, 93, 94, 95, 96–97, 120, 121; and self-defense, 134; criticism of, 231 (n. 38)
Economic independence: and Garveyism, 2, 10, 12, 15, 37, 88; and Black Star Line, 2, 12, 38, 52; and Washington, 10, 40, 41, 43, 44, 47, 162, 245 (n. 2); and black nationalism, 16, 25, 37; and southern Garveyism, 17, 25, 49, 52, 61, 70; historical context of, 24, 36; and Garvey's speeches, 57, 68; and

southern Garveyites, 103, 104, 131, 162; and industrialization, 189
Education: and literacy, 15, 73, 74, 107, 112, 114, 115, 117, 184; and Washington, 40; double standard in, 54, 104, 114–15, 125, 130; and Ferris, 80; of southern Garveyites, 107, 109, 116, 125, 237 (n. 30); and NAACP strategy, 164; and assimilation, 189
Elaine, Arkansas, 99, 100, 125, 128, 129, 143, 179–80, 186, 187, 248 (n. 66)
Ellis, A. E., 34
Emigration to Africa: historical context of, 10, 24, 25, 26, 28, 29, 30–35, 37–39; and Garveyism, 17; and Fortune, 85; and Sam's project, 91; and African redemption, 131, 153–54; and racial double standard on women's sexuality, 138; opposition to, 161, 189; and Peace Movement of Ethiopia, 182. *See also* African redemption
Ethiopia, 26, 36, 152
Ethiopianism, 118
European imperialism, 3, 16, 17, 25, 26, 131, 150, 151
Exodusters, 39

Farmer, The, 193
Farmers' Alliance, 129
Farmers' Institutes, 41
Farrakhan, Louis, 193
Fenner, John, Jr., 156
Ferris, William H., 15, 48, 78–82, 83, 118, 228 (n. 49), 231 (n. 38), 243 (n. 55)
Firestone Rubber, 155
Fitzgerald, Michael W., 182–83
Florida: and UNIA members, 6, 49, 55; and UNIA organizing, 19, 55–60, 62, 70, 73, 92, 228 (n. 60). *See also specific cities*
Ford, Arnold J., 119, 244–45 (n. 118)
Formwalt, Lee, 250 (n. 98)

Fort Smith, Arkansas, 70, 124

Fortune, T. Thomas, 15, 52, 78, 83, 84–85, 178

Fountain, Miller A., 172

Fourteenth Amendment, 180

Fowler, George, 101

France, 3, 17, 155

Franklin, John Hope, 76

Frazier, E. Franklin, 72, 161

Frazier, Paul, 27

Frederick Douglass, 51, 52, 53, 59, 86, 89

Gaines, E. L., 54, 61, 63

Gardi, Georgia, 94

Garnet, Henry Highland, 118

Garrett, John, 87

Garrison, William Lloyd, 31

Garvey, Marcus: family background of, 1; deportation of, 1, 7–8, 84, 101, 120, 133, 159, 162–63, 178, 181; position within UNIA, 2; charismatic leadership of, 3, 70; summit with Ku Klux Klan, 5, 11, 12, 45, 58, 67, 68, 83–84, 88, 90, 143–47, 150, 159, 170, 174, 243 (n. 55), 245 (n. 118); rhetoric of, 5–6, 7, 11, 15, 30, 48, 59, 62, 228 (n. 60); financial and legal problems of, 7, 11, 77, 159; press bias against, 8; historiography of, 9, 190; weekly addresses of, 10, 24; Turner compared to, 10, 25, 28, 30–36, 47, 48, 224 (n. 52); iconic status of, 11; desire for mass leadership, 18–19; visits to New Orleans, 20; Washington's influence on, 28, 42–44, 48; conciliation of whites, 35; U.S. speaking tours of, 44, 53; imprisonment of, 46, 85, 120, 121, 127, 156–58, 159, 181, 240 (n. 5); organizational skills of, 48; and Black Star Line stock controversy, 54; mail fraud indictment and trial of, 59, 67, 88, 101, 112, 120, 146, 156, 158; printing experience of,

74, 78; and Abbott, 76–77, 81–82, 170; Harrison on, 82; and Bruce, 83–84; and Fortune, 85; defense fund of, 107, 112–13, 121, 123, 125, 156, 158, 240 (n. 5); and biblical comparisons, 118, 156–57; and Dyer antilynching bill, 141–42; and Du Bois, 166; popular rediscovery of, 194

Garveyism: and black thought, 1, 3, 7, 28, 190–91, 192; influence of, 1, 7; goals of, 2, 5–6; evolution of, 3, 16; ideology of, 4–5, 8, 9, 15–19, 34, 37, 45, 73, 77, 79, 131, 163, 186, 190–91, 192, 194, 196, 218 (n. 8); within tradition of African American protest, 7, 9, 17, 24, 222 (n. 1); popularity of, 7, 17–18, 20, 131, 161, 162; and socialism, 9, 17, 46, 68, 162; dynamics of, 13; whites' attitudes toward, 105, 150, 175. *See also* Southern Garveyism

Gaston, Benjamin, 39

Georgia: Robertson in, 20, 96, 97, 120, 121, 234 (n. 99); UNIA and NAACP success in compared, 22; Turner in, 28, 31; and colonization of Liberia, 32; and emigration, 39, 47; rural organization in, 92–96, 106; UNIA divisions in, 94–95, 96, 234 (n. 93); black population of, 106–7; southern Garveyites in, 115; and lynching, 134; and NAACP strategy, 165–66, 168–74, 183, 245 (n. 13), 248 (n. 66). *See also* Southwest Georgia; *and specific cities and counties*

German Colonial Society, 25

Gilmore, Glenda, 149

Gilroy, Paul, 218 (n. 5)

Glashen, T. C., 57, 58, 91, 227–28 (n. 43)

Glass, Booker T., 41, 225 (n. 80)

Glass, Ed, 41

Glass, Patsy, 41

Gold Coast (Ghana), 224 (n. 58)

Gordon, Fon Louise, 180–81, 248 (n. 66)

Gordon, Mittie Maud Lena, 182

Gramsci, Antonio, 235 (n. 106)

Great Britain, 3, 17, 155, 218 (n. 7)

Great Depression, 22, 182–91

Greater Liberia Bill of 1939, 183

Great Migration, 14, 24–25, 39, 98, 105, 114, 137, 145, 149–50, 163

Greenough, Georgia, 39

Greensboro Daily News, 69

Griffin, Farah, 138

Griggs, Sutton E., 222 (n. 2)

Grubbs, Donald, 184

Hahn, Steven, 14, 220 (n. 36), 223 (n. 33)

Haiti, 26

Haley, Alex, 27

Haley, Jerry, 157–58

Hall, Elizabeth, 178

Halton, Anna, 121

Halton, Columbus L., 94, 96, 121, 132

Hamer, Fannie Lou, 240 (n. 15)

Hampton Institute, 50

Hampton Roads, Virginia, 50, 51

Handcox, John, 184

Handy, August, 95

Harding, Warren G., 170

Harlan, Louis R., 226 (n. 91)

Harlem Renaissance, 14

Harris, Wiley, 186, 187, 188

Harrison, Hubert, 15, 63, 78, 82, 85

Harrison, Pat, 170

Hayford, Casely, 42

Haynes, S. A., 133

Helena, Arkansas, 117, 125, 237 (n. 36)

Higginbotham, Evelyn Brooks, 242 (n. 33)

Higgs, R. H., 58

Hill, Lance, 190

Hill, Robert A., 7, 11, 228 (n. 60)

Hine, Darlene Clark, 241 (n. 19)

Holly Grove, Arkansas, 101

Hood Theological Seminary, 64

Hope, John, 28, 69

Houston, Lucille, 123

Howard, Perry, 170

Howe, Leon E., 58–59

Howell, Arkansas, 33

Hudson, Janet, 240 (n. 10)

Humbert, Samuel S., 172

Hunt, H. A., 122, 166, 168

Hunter, Tera, 241 (n. 19)

Hunton, Addie, 174

Hurst, Willie, 186

Imagined communities, 26, 222 (n. 10)

Indianapolis, Indiana, 164

Indianapolis Freeman, 74

Industrialization, 165, 189

Industrial laborers: and UNIA organizing, 13, 49, 52–53, 60, 61, 70, 86, 88; and Black Star Line, 20–21, 51; as southern Garveyites, 49, 87, 92, 104, 115, 161; and NAACP strategy, 165; and STFU, 188

Industrial Workers of the World (IWW), 130

Interdenominational Negro Alliance of Dallas, 90

International Conference of the Negro, 42

International Longshoremen's Association (ILA), 51, 86, 88

Islam, 36

Issa, Jahi, 221 (n. 57)

Italy, 26

Jackson, J. J., 33

Jacksonville, Florida, 49, 57, 227 (n. 39)

Jacques Garvey, Amy: and Garvey's writing, 4, 82; and Cronon, 9; on Garvey's life, 10; on Love, 30; and *Negro World,* 75, 78, 240–41 (n. 18); and Fortune,

Liberian Exodus Joint Stock Steamship
Company, 37
Liberty League of Harlem, 82
Liberty University, 194
Liston, Frank M., 123
Literacy, 15, 73, 74, 107, 112, 114, 115, 117,
184
Little, Earl, 193–94
Little, Louisa, 193
Livingstone College, 64
Los Angeles, California, 12
Lott Carey Foreign Mission Convention,
36
Louisiana: UNIA divisions in, 20–21,
87, 175, 221 (n. 57), 232 (n. 60); and
Great Migration, 39; UNIA organizing
in, 49; and NAACP strategy, 175; West
Indian immigrants in, 219 (n. 12);
rural communities in, 221 (n. 55). *See
also* New Orleans, Louisiana
Love, Joseph Robert, 30
Lowe, G. W., 33
Lumber industry, 21, 49, 104
Lynch, Hollis, 27
Lynching: and rural blacks, 14; *Negro
World* articles on, 19, 127; and Turner,
35; Dyer antilynching bill, 41, 141–43,
148, 150, 170; and Garvey's speeches,
69; and Bruce, 83; prevalence of, 89–
90, 114, 127, 233 (n. 73); studies of,
105, 127; in Worth County, 122, 127;
and self-defense, 127, 131, 132, 133,
142–43; African American leaders'
debates on, 133; and NAACP strategy,
133, 164, 168, 172; of black veterans,
134; and white dominance, 137

Malcolm X, 193–94
Martin, James, 171
Martin, Louis, 181
Martin, Tony, 10, 229 (n. 79)
Mays, Benjamin E., 18

McCarty, Lee, 122
McCrary, George, 100
McDonald, A. L., 168
McDowell, R. H., 101
McGuire, George Alexander, 46
McKinney, E. B. "Britt," 100, 102, 184,
185, 186–88, 195, 235 (n. 115)
McMillen, Neil, 174, 175
McNeil, Diane, 27
McShane, Andrew, 67
Meier, August, 222 (n. 1)
Memphis, Tennessee, 91–92
Merigold, Mississippi, 100, 109, 112,
122, 126, 158, 183
Messenger, The, 68–69, 133, 155, 170
Methodist Episcopal Union, 172
Miami, Florida, 49, 55, 56–57, 58, 59
Miller, J. A., 70
Miscegenation, 114, 137, 139–41, 144,
148–49, 162, 188, 193, 242 (n. 32)
Mississippi: and African mission move-
ment, 36; and emigration, 38, 47; and
Great Migration, 39; and UNIA
organizing, 98; UNIA divisions in,
100, 109, 174, 178, 181, 235 (n. 109);
black population of, 109; southern
Garveyites in, 115; and lynching, 134;
and self-defense, 143; and STFU, 163;
and NAACP, 170, 174–75, 178; and
Peace Movement of Ethiopia, 183. *See
also* Yazoo-Mississippi Delta; *and spe-
cific cities and counties*
Mississippi County, Arkansas, 109
Mitchell, H. L., 184, 186, 187
Mitchell, Michele, 138–39, 242 (n. 32)
Mitchell County, Georgia, 20, 27, 39, 42,
96–97, 107, 245 (n. 4)
Mixed-race African Americans, 3, 21
Mobile, Alabama, 49, 70, 86, 87–88, 89,
92
Monroe County, Arkansas, 20, 33, 99,
107, 109, 125, 164, 239 (n. 71), 245 (n. 4)

Montgomery, Isaiah T., 126
Moore v. Dempsey (1923), 179–80, 248
　(n. 66)
Moseley, R. B., 90
Moton, Robert Russa, 88
Mound Bayou, Mississippi, 21, 39, 40,
　109, 112, 113–14, 126, 174, 175
Muhammad, Brother Al, 193
Muhammad, Brother William, 193
Muhammad, Elijah, 192–93, 250
　(n. 1)
Muhammad, Ridgely, 193
Muhammad, Wallace Fard, 193
Murphy, George W., 180

Nash County, North Carolina, 60
Nashville, Tennessee, 72, 91
Natchez, Mississippi, 70
Natchez Mississippi Democrat, 76
Nation, The, 146
National Association for the Advance-
　ment of Colored People (NAACP):
　and Garvey's principles, 8, 46; South
　as ideological battleground for, 19,
　162–65; UNIA's success compared to,
　22–23, 161, 163, 174; and race rela-
　tions, 44; newspaper of, 74; criticism
　of Garvey, 82, 143, 170, 174; violence
　toward, 90; and Worth County, 122,
　168–69, 171; and Phillips County
　massacre, 129, 179–80, 239 (n. 85); as
　radical organization, 130; and lynch-
　ing, 133, 164, 168, 172; and Dyer anti-
　lynching bill, 142; and Pickens, 146–
　47; integrationist strategy of, 162;
　strategy of, 164–66, 168–75, 178–82,
　190, 249–50 (n. 98); "Garvey file" of,
　165; and UNIA's conflicting strategies,
　169–70, 172, 173–75, 178, 180–82;
　and STFU, 187
National Association of Colored Women
　(NACW), 138

National Baptist Convention (NBC), 36,
　138, 241–42 (n. 29)
National Brotherhood Workers of Amer-
　ica, 51
National Congress of British West
　Africa, 42
National Negro Business League, 47, 68,
　175, 245 (n. 2)
National Urban League, 138
National War Labor Board, 50
Nation of Islam, 23, 192–93, 194
"Negro": Garvey's preference for term,
　218 (n. 4)
Negro Bill of Rights, 73, 94, 95, 96, 121,
　132, 137, 150, 159
Negro Farmer, 42
Negro Peoples of the World, 43
Negro Society for Historical Research,
　79, 83
Negro Vocational Training School, 42
Negro World: circulation of, 1, 17, 48, 57,
　70, 73, 75, 87, 100, 117, 175, 185; role
　of, 3, 11, 15, 19, 43, 47, 62, 74, 75–76,
　101, 148, 183; in rural areas, 7, 15,
　98–100, 107, 117–18, 124, 130, 178;
　empirical data in, 9–10, 11; informa-
　tion on UNIA divisions in, 10, 18, 22,
　81, 86, 89, 92, 119–20, 178, 218 (n. 6);
　and tenets of Garveyism, 16–19; and
　Garvey's speeches, 24, 29, 73, 74, 75,
　117–18, 120, 132, 181, 230 (n. 5); distin-
　guishing UNIA program in, 25; and
　black clergy, 30, 118; complaints over
　content of, 56, 62; and self-defense,
　60, 135, 136; and graft and corruption
　reports, 63; and Eason, 64, 65, 67; and
　UNIA growth, 72, 73, 95–96, 98–99;
　and consistency of themes and pro-
　grams, 73; women's page of, 74, 75,
　241 (n. 18); editors of, 77–85; on
　Newsom, 112; and Negro Bill of
　Rights, 133; and black women's exploi-

tation, 137; and racial purity, 139; and
miscegenation, 140–41; and Garvey's
meeting with Clarke, 144, 145; and
African redemption, 150, 151–55; trib-
utes to Garvey in, 157–58; and racial
conflict, 169, 170; change in content
of, 181; and Garvey's letters, 183
New Deal, 13, 22, 182, 183
New Negro, 26, 44, 162
New Negro Manhood Movement, 52
New Orleans, Louisiana, 6, 13, 20–21,
70, 86–87, 92, 118, 232 (n. 60)
Newport News, Virginia, 13, 50–51, 52,
53–54, 60, 88
Newport News Star, 52
Newson, Adam D., 100, 102, 112, 130
New York, New York: and UNIA mem-
bers, 6, 60, 217 (n. 1); UNIA conven-
tion in, 52–53, 60; UNIA division in,
72, 156, 181, 182; and NAACP strategy,
173
New York Age, 74, 84, 85
New York Evening News, 38
Nicholson, Sarah, 33–34
Nimmo, James, 57
Norfolk, Virginia, 13, 51, 52–53, 172
Norfolk Journal and Guide, 52, 84
Norman, W. D., 178
North Carolina, 19, 20, 49, 60–62, 63,
70, 78, 92, 93, 228 (n. 60). *See also
specific cities*
North Carolina Interracial Commission,
68
Nunally, James, 152

Oates, Ren, 70
Odom, Jonas, 123–24, 239 (n. 64)
Odom, Robert Benton, 123
Odum, Howard W., 104
O'Kelly, Berry, 68
Oklahoma, 114, 237 (n. 25)
Oliver, Margaret, 158–59

Omaha, Nebraska, 164
Ousley, Mrs. L. M., 122
Owen, Chandler, 17, 45, 68, 170
Oxendine, Lassie, 121

Pace, Harry, 172
Pace, W. S., 172
Palmer, Mrs. L. M., 96
Pan-Africanism, 22, 23, 26, 45, 85, 98,
194, 224 (n. 52)
Parlan, H. F., 93
Patriarchy, 9, 18, 135–36, 137, 138
Pauley, Frances Freeborn, 189–90
Paynes, J., 152
Peace Mission Movement, 182
Peace Movement of Ethiopia (PME),
182–84
Pearson, E. W., 61, 63, 70, 95
Peet, H. W., 131
Peonage: of rural blacks, 14, 28, 123, 130,
183; and NAACP strategy, 164, 168,
172; and industrialization, 189
Philadelphia, Pennsylvania, 6, 72, 217
(n. 1)
Phillips County, Arkansas: UNIA divi-
sions in, 20, 98, 99, 107, 109, 125,
129, 181; massacre of rural blacks in,
21, 99, 100, 125, 128, 129, 179, 180,
186, 187, 239 (n. 85), 248 (n. 66); and
emigration, 38, 39; Washington in,
40; lynching in, 127; black population
of, 164, 245 (n. 4); and NAACP strat-
egy, 181; and STFU, 185–86
Pickens, William, 1, 45, 146–47, 170, 174
Pine Bluff, Arkansas, 124, 179
Pine City, Arkansas, 100, 129–30
Pittsburgh, Pennsylvania, 6
Pittsburgh Courier, 74
Plessy v. Ferguson (1896), 36
Poe, Clarence, 114
Poinsett County, Arkansas, 186–87
Poole, Clara, 192

Poole, Elijah, 192–93, 250 (n. 1)
Poole, Willie, 192
Populism, 129
Portsmouth, Virginia, 50, 51, 52
Powell, John, 35
Pragmatism, 24, 184
Prendergast (UNIA secretary), 93, 94
Progressive Farmer, 114
Progressive Farmers and Household
    Union of America, 128, 129
Pulaski County, Arkansas, 27
Pullen, Joe, 135

Race consciousness: and investments, 2;
    development of, 2–3, 46, 220–21
    (n. 44); and Garveyism, 16; legacy of,
    23, 194; historical context of, 36–37;
    and labor unions, 51; and Garvey's
    speeches, 69; and southern Garvey-
    ites, 103, 116, 181; and black women,
    136; of McKinney, 186–87
Race pride: popular appeal in rural com-
    munities, 13; Garvey's message of, 15,
    18, 25; and southern Garveyism, 17,
    70; legacy of, 23, 192; historical con-
    text of, 24, 28–29, 30; and southern
    Garveyites, 49, 61, 62, 103, 104, 115,
    116, 117, 163; and Ferris, 80; and *Negro
    World,* 101; and Garveyism as civil reli-
    gion, 130; universal acceptance of,
    162; and Nation of Islam, 193
Race relations: and integrationist tri-
    umph, 19; in Louisiana, 21; in Geor-
    gia, 22; and New Deal, 22; dynamics
    of, 22, 62, 129, 228 (n. 60); and race
    pride, 25; and ACS, 31; in post–World
    War I era, 43; and Du Bois, 44; in Vir-
    ginia, 50; in Florida, 56; and Eason,
    63; and Ferris, 80; and southern Gar-
    veyites, 89–90, 105; and *Negro World,*
    100; diversity of, 105; and Montgom-
    ery, 126; and Phillips County mas-

sacre, 179, 180. *See also* Racial separa-
    tism; Segregation
Race traitors, 77, 231 (n. 24)
Racial identity, 16, 218 (n. 5)
Racial purity: Garvey's promotion of, 3,
    138, 139; and social independence, 16;
    and Turner, 35; and sexual exploita-
    tion of black women, 137, 138, 139;
    and whites, 140, 144, 175; and Clarke,
    144
Racial separatism: Garvey's promotion
    of, 3, 7, 15, 60, 68, 150, 169–70, 226
    (n. 91); of black activists in South, 9;
    and black thought, 10, 192; popular
    appeal in rural communities, 13, 18,
    129; and all-black towns, 21, 39; and
    Black Power movement, 23; and
    Washington, 43, 44, 226 (n. 91); and
    black unions, 51; and Montgomery,
    126; as temporary remedy, 131; and
    southern Garveyites, 131, 180; and
    community dignity, 141; Ward on,
    143–44; and protection of black
    women, 149; segregation compared
    to, 149, 162, 175; and McKinney, 187;
    legacy of, 194
Railroad industry, 49, 104
Raleigh, North Carolina, 60, 61, 62, 63–
    64, 67–68, 69
Randolph, A. Philip, 11, 68, 170
Ransom, Reverdy, 29
Raper, Arthur F., 125
Reconstruction, 32, 129, 164
Redeemers, 32
Redkey, Edwin, 34, 38
Red Scare, 48
Reid, Ira DeA., 55
Renova, Mississippi, 113–14
Republican Party, 65, 129, 142, 170
Reynolds, William, 60
Ridgel, A. L., 33
R. J. Reynolds Tobacco Company, 60

Roberts, S. C., 93

Robertson, S. V.: as founder of New Orleans UNIA division, 20, 87, 232 (n. 54); and Georgia, 20, 96, 97, 120, 121, 234 (n. 99); and Alabama, 89; and African redemption, 96, 154; and Mississippi, 98; and UNIA organizing, 101–2; and racial purity, 139

Robinson, Charles, 149

Roosevelt, Franklin D., 22, 182

Roosevelt, Theodore, 40

Rozzell, E. J., 34, 93

Rural blacks: and Garveyism, 2, 13, 15–16, 24, 35; and intellectualism, 9; population of, 14; and black thought, 14, 25; and outside information sources, 15; women's participation in southern UNIA divisions, 18; and SNCC, 21; and NAACP, 22–23, 165; and African American leaders, 28, 163; and ACS, 32, 33, 223 (n. 33); and emigration, 34, 39, 47; and African American Christian missionaries, 37; and Washington, 40–41, 190; and Carver, 41–42; as tobacco workers, 60–61; as landowners, 60–61, 114, 116, 162; and UNIA organizing, 71; and Great Depression, 182; and urbanization, 188; and Carmichael, 194. *See also* Tenant farmers

Rural communities: and UNIA members, 3, 6, 13, 217 (n. 1); UNIA divisions in, 6, 13, 19, 72, 92–102, 106; Washington on, 40; black churches in, 46; norms of, 47; and UNIA organizing, 70, 71; isolation from commercial centers, 104; and self-defense, 133, 134, 137, 161; segregation in, 149; and NAACP strategy, 173–74; in Louisiana, 221 (n. 55)

Rural southern origins of African Americans, 4, 7, 12, 14, 85, 164

St. Francis County, Arkansas, 99

Sam, Chief Alfred, 91

Sanders, Lula, 178

Sanders, Tom, 178

Sanders, W. T., 135

Sausele, William, 57

Schomburg, Arthur, 83

Scott, Emmett J., 62

Segregation: and race consciousness, 36–37; and organization of blacks, 48, 70; and southern Garveyites, 49; of labor unions, 51; and West Indian immigrants, 56; racial separatism compared to, 149, 162, 175; and NAACP strategy, 164; and Washington, 226 (n. 91); intraracial conflict over, 248 (n. 66)

Self-defense: and Garveyism, 9, 16, 130; and southern Garveyism, 17, 52; historical context of, 24, 35; and white militancy, 57; in North Carolina, 60–61; and Ferris, 80; in Chattanooga, 92; and Black Belt, 103, 188–89; and southern Garveyites, 116, 131, 134, 144, 181; and lynching, 127, 131, 132, 133, 142–43; and Phillips County massacre, 129; and Negro Bill of Rights, 132, 133; and protection of black women, 140, 160; and Garvey's rhetoric, 141, 189; problems with, 161–62, 164; and NAACP strategy, 169, 190; and civil rights movement, 195

Self-determination, 2, 3, 8, 14, 23, 192

Self-sufficiency, 2, 30, 38, 39, 43, 47, 68, 189. *See also* Economic independence

Seraile, William, 84

Share Cropper's Union, 23

Shaw, Ike, 185–86

Sherrill, William LeVan, 98, 147

Shillady, John, 90, 168

Sierra Leone, 29, 31, 224 (n. 58)

Sillers, Walter, 126

Simmons, Booker, 41

Simmons, J. B., 155

Simmons, William J., 173

Sims, Walter, 173

Slappey, Jacob W., 89–90, 143

Slaves and slavery, 31, 32, 84, 166

Smallwood-Corey Industrial Institute, 194

Smith, Lavinia D. M., 138

Smith, S. B., 153

Smith-Hughes Fund, 42

Social Darwinism, 79

Social independence, 16, 43, 44, 88

Socialism: and Garveyism, 9, 17, 46, 68, 162; and rural blacks, 23; and STFU, 23, 183; and race relations, 44; and Domingo, 78; constituency of, 165

South Carolina, 89–90. *See also* Charleston, South Carolina

Southern Christian Leadership Conference, 190

Southern Garveyism: and rural blacks, 2, 13; solidarity within, 6; and Garvey's rhetoric, 6, 55, 59, 62, 71, 228 (n. 60); historiography of, 8–13, 195–96; and UNIA as black civil religion, 12, 46, 130, 240 (n. 88); ideology of, 13–14, 17; community-building processes of, 14; growth in 1920s, 19; popularity of, 20, 54, 161; historical context of, 24–28; and Garvey's strategy adjustments, 25–26, 29, 44–45, 50, 70, 130, 132, 159, 163, 245–46 (n. 118); radical element of, 58, 59, 70; and Harrison, 82

Southern Garveyites: and cotton agricultural system, 15, 19, 98, 104, 113–14, 116–17, 124; motivations of, 19; composite profile of, 21–22; industrial laborers as, 49, 87, 92, 104, 115, 161; socioeconomic characteristics of, 49, 103, 104, 236 (n. 1); in urban areas, 49–50, 60; and complaints of double

standard, 54, 55; and defense of black women, 54, 55, 84; radicalism of, 57, 58, 59; and Garvey's rhetoric, 62; and Ferris, 80, 81; diversity of, 92, 103, 109, 112, 115; tenant farmers as, 103, 104, 106, 107, 109, 115, 116–17, 121, 122, 123, 124–27, 130, 179, 180, 181, 248 (n. 66); and African redemption, 103, 115, 150, 151–52, 153, 156, 160, 181; education of, 107, 109, 116, 125, 237 (n. 30); and black women's role, 136; and Dyer antilynching bill, 142; and Garvey's summit with Ku Klux Klan, 145, 147, 150; and Garvey's defense fund, 156, 158; and Garvey's popularity, 159

Southern Tenant Farmers Union (STFU): biracial organization of, 21, 162–63, 183, 184, 186, 187, 188; and socialism, 23, 183; and McKinney, 100, 184, 185, 186, 187–88, 195, 235 (n. 115); and Garveyism, 161, 185; and Arkansas Delta, 163, 183–86; founding of, 182, 183–84; merges into other organizations, 188

Southern UNIA divisions: growth of, 3–4, 86, 141, 142; in rural communities, 6, 13, 19, 72, 92–102, 106; loyalty of, 10, 132–33, 156–60, 240 (n. 5); records of, 10, 218 (n. 6), 219 (n. 15); and black churches, 12; women's participation in, 18; publicized activities of, 19; organization of, 48; in urban areas, 48–72 passim, 115; rhetoric at meetings, 55, 61–62; and UNIA conventions, 59, 60, 61, 63, 86, 89, 94, 100, 107, 112, 120–21; leaders of, 77–78; and Garvey's defense fund, 158; numbering of local charters, 221 (n. 53)

Southwest Georgia: UNIA divisions in, 6, 20, 22, 92, 94, 97, 106, 107, 120–21, 181; and SNCC, 21; and Washington, 41; Arkansas Delta compared to, 98, 115; black population of, 106–7, 130; tenant farmers in, 107, 113, 121, 181; local UNIA leaders in, 120–21, 183; lynching in, 127–28; and Dyer antilynching bill, 141; and self-defense, 142–43; and African redemption, 153, 155; Du Bois on, 166; and NAACP strategy, 168, 171–72, 174

Southwest Georgia Council on Human Relations, 189

Spingarn, Joel, 164

Stanford, Anthony L., 38

Star of Zion, 61, 64, 81

State Industrial School for Negroes, 171

Steele, Theodore, 33

Stein, Judith, 12, 146, 229 (n. 79)

Student Nonviolent Coordinating Committee (SNCC), 21, 190, 194–95

Styles, Percy, 56

Sudduth, Queenie, 151–52

Taft, William H., 40

Talented tenth, 8

Tampa, Florida, 49

Tanner, Benjamin, 34

Taylor, Ula, 240–41 (n. 18)

Tenant farmers: historiography of, 8; economic circumstances of, 14, 116, 124–25, 130; and Agricultural Adjustment Administration, 22; and peanut cultivation, 41; and Garvey's speeches, 68; and UNIA organizing, 72, 101, 117; as southern Garveyites, 103, 104, 106, 107, 109, 115, 116–17, 121, 122, 123, 124–27, 130, 179, 180, 181, 248 (n. 66); and cotton agricultural system, 114, 166, 168; and landlords of Worth County, 122; and lynching, 128; and self-defense, 135; and racial separatism, 149; and African redemption, 150; and economic independence,

162; and NAACP strategy, 166, 248 (n. 66); Towns on, 171; and Garvey's leadership, 181; and Great Depression, 182. *See also* Southern Tenant Farmers Union

Tennessee, 39, 91–92

Texas, 39, 90–91, 92

Thomas, Hubert, 189–90, 195

Thomas, Leonard, 153

Thomas, Norman, 146

Thomasville Civic League, 171

Tobacco industry, 49, 60

Tobacco Workers' International Union, 60, 70

Tolbert, Emory, 12, 220 (n. 32)

Tolnay, Stewart E., 14, 134

Towns, George A., 171

Transportation Workers' Association of Virginia, 51

Trotter, William Monroe, 69

Turner, Henry McNeal: Garvey compared to, 10, 25, 28, 30–36, 47, 48, 224 (n. 52); and self-defense, 24, 35; and emigration, 25, 29, 30–35, 37–38, 39; and ACS, 27, 32; death of, 27, 164; influence of, 28, 78, 191; and race pride, 28–29, 30; rhetorical style of, 30; on purpose of slavery, 84

Turner, Mary, 127, 128, 171

Tuskegee Institute, 25–26, 40–43, 46, 62, 88, 164

Tuskegee Messenger, 42

Tuskegee Student, 42, 43

United Fruit Company, 55

United States and Congo Emigration Company, 39

Universal Negro Alliance, 67

Universal Negro Improvement Association (UNIA): Garvey's promotion of, 1; number of members of, 1, 4, 217 (n. 1); founding of, 1, 43, 44; and political organization, 2; goals of, 2–3, 9, 52, 77; legacy of, 3, 22, 192–96; geographical distribution of divisions, 3–4, 218 (nn. 6, 7); influence of, 4; documents of, 9, 11, 18; ideological precursors of, 10; as black civil religion, 12, 46, 130, 240 (n. 88); and redemption of Africans, 17, 221 (n. 47); South as ideological battleground for, 19; structure in South, 19; in urban South, 19, 48–72 passim; NAACP success compared to, 22–23, 161, 163, 174; historical context of, 25; and emigration, 34; and African redemption, 36; urban elite black opposition to, 45, 132; organizational obstacles of, 48–49; finances of, 59; ideology of, 59; graft and corruption problems in, 63, 95, 228 (n. 61); and Eason's murder, 67; constitution of, 73, 95, 119, 132, 152, 159; and race relations, 80; and militarism, 134; split over Liberian failure, 155–56; as outside mainstream, 162; dissolution of, 162–63, 181; and NAACP's conflicting strategies, 169–70, 172, 173–75, 178, 180–82. See also Garveyism; Southern UNIA divisions

Universal Negro Improvement Association (UNIA) conventions: and public notoriety of movement, 52–53; and southern UNIA divisions, 59, 60, 61, 63, 86, 89, 94, 100, 107, 112, 120–21; and Negro Bill of Rights, 73, 94, 96, 132; and Negro World, 75; and UNIA growth, 86, 89; and self-defense, 133–34, 142–43; and Ku Klux Klan, 147–48; and African redemption, 151, 155; and NAACP strategy, 174–75; records of, 234 (n. 90); and Garvey's relationship with Eason, 238 (n. 48)

Urban areas: UNIA members in, 6–7, 12, 13, 72, 159, 182, 195; and black thought, 13, 24–25; and print media, 15; and women's participation in UNIA divisions, 18; in Louisiana, 20, 21; and NAACP popularity, 22–23, 165, 170–71, 175; and African American leaders, 28; and Washington, 40, 47; and African American protests, 45; black churches in, 46; southern UNIA divisions in, 48–72 passim, 115; opportunities in, 104–5; and protection of black women, 138; segregation in, 149; and African redemption, 150; and self-defense, 161–62, 164; and industrialization, 165; and Negro World, 178; proportion of black population in, 188, 189

Urban elite blacks: and Garvey's racial segregationist rhetoric, 7; Garvey's alienation of, 18, 25, 44, 45; opposition to UNIA, 45, 132; interpretations of Garveyism, 162; on self-defense, 162; and NAACP strategy, 172; and Great Depression, 182; in Georgia, 234 (n. 93)

Urbanization: studies of, 14; and black thought, 163; and Negro World, 178; and Great Depression, 182; and World War II, 188

U.S. Bureau of Investigation, 52, 54, 56–59, 75, 170

U.S. Department of Agriculture, 88

U.S. Department of Commerce, 124

U.S. Department of Justice, 22, 121, 158, 170

U.S. Department of Labor, 60, 92

U.S. government: hostility toward Garveyism, 5; and Garvey, 7, 10, 35, 45, 52, 87; and petitions supporting Garvey, 18, 45–46, 158; discriminatory practices of, 55; and Great Depression, 182; and Nation of Islam, 193

U.S. Navy, 55

141; and sexual exploitation of black women, 149; and Black Belt, 175; in Mississippi, 183

White tenant farmers, 184

Wilder, Susie, 76

Wiley, Cyrus G., 171

Williams, Adam Daniel, 172, 246 (n. 39)

Williams, G. W., 166, 168

Williams, Henry Sylvester, 26

Williams, Robert F., 190, 195

Wilson, Henry, 172

Wilson, J. C., 96

Wilson, Woodrow, 50

Wimberly, Mrs. C. L., 122

Wimbs, Addison, 127

Winston-Salem, North Carolina, 13, 60, 61–62, 69–70

Womack, Mrs. S. S., 69

Women: as micromobilizers, 18, 221 (n. 52)

World War I, 1, 2, 13, 49–50, 127, 130, 134

World War II, 13, 188

Worth County, Georgia, 20, 97–98, 107, 121–22, 127, 139, 168–69, 171, 190, 245 (n. 4)

Wright, R. R., Jr., 78

Yazoo-Mississippi Delta: UNIA divisions in, 6, 20, 22, 92, 106, 109, 175, 178, 181, 183; and SNCC, 21; and African-born people of color, 27; and emigration, 33–34; and *Negro World*, 76; southwest Georgia compared to, 98; southern Garveyites in, 109, 112, 130; and African redemption, 153; and NAACP strategy, 174–75

Young, P. B., 52

Young, Robert Alexander, 118